Writing MS-DOS Device Drivers

Writing MS-DOS Device Drivers

Robert Lai/The Waite Group, Inc.

Addison-Wesley Publishing Company, Inc.

Reading, Massachusetts   Menlo Park, California   New York
Don Mills, Ontario   Wokingham, England   Amsterdam   Bonn
Sydney   Singapore   Tokyo   Madrid   Bogotá
Santiago   San Juan

Many of the designations used by manufacturers and sellers to distinguish their products are claimed as trademarks. Where those designations appear in this book and Addison-Wesley was aware of a trademark claim, the designations have been printed in capital letters (i.e., MS-DOS, PC-DOS, IBM MASM, Microsoft's MASM, Intel, Compaq, Victor, IBM, Microsoft, Data Base Decisions, Periscope, ATT, HP, Tandy, DEC, Rainbow).

Library of Congress Cataloging-in-Publication Data
Lai, Robert.
   Writing MS-DOS device drivers.
   Includes index.
   1. MS-DOS (Computer operating system)   I.Waite
Group.   II. Title.
QA76.76.063L35 1987   005.4'3   87-14650
ISBN 0-201-13185-4

The Waite Group Developmental Editors: Mitchell Waite and James Stockford
Technical reviewer: Kevin Jaeger
Illustrated by Carol Benioff
Cover design by Doliber Skeffington Design
Text design by Diana Davis and Kim Straitiff, adapted by Total Concept Associates.
Composition by Graphic Typesetting Service, Los Angeles, CA

ABCDEFGHIJ-HA-8987
First printing, September, 1987

To Ada Lee Lai

Acknowledgments

The author is very grateful for the suggestions, comments, help, and encouragement from Mitchell Waite, Jim Stockford, and Kevin Jaeger; and to my wife, Ada, for her support.

Robert S. Lai

The Waite group would like to thank Kevin Jaeger for his early developmental and technical reviews and Carol Benioff for her excellent illustrations.

The Waite Group

Contents

Preface

This book provides you with a useful, informative guide to designing and building your own custom MS-DOS device drivers. The first chapters explain working examples of device drivers, beginning with a very simple skeleton driver, followed by increasingly complex drivers. The last two chapters provide a complete kit of techniques for advanced design and debugging.

This book is the result of years of work. Back in 1982 I bought one of the first MS-DOS microcomputers. There was not much information on how the BIOS or DOS worked, even less on how to make the best use of the microcomputer's hardware and peripherals. As I learned about my own MS-DOS machine, I discovered that my programs were not always able to run on other MS-DOS computers or on the IBM PCs. I began looking for solutions to the problem of writing a single version of a software application that would run on any MS-DOS–or PC-DOS–based microcomputer.

I found that the best general solution is to use device drivers to take the machine-dependent features out of the application program and move them into DOS in the form of an installable device driver. These relatively small device drivers can be tailored to each machine, and the larger application programs can then be written as a single standardized version for all MS-DOS and PC-DOS microcomputers.

I welcome suggestions, criticisms, and comments regarding the material presented in this book. If you want to avoid the effort of typing in all of the examples, you may order a disk of all the programs in this book; send me your request with a check for ten dollars.

Robert S. Lai
P.O. Box 337
Moss Beach, CA 94038

Chapter 1

Introduction

- About This Book
- What You Will Need to Use This Book
- Conventions Used in This Book
- How to Use This Book
- Overview of the Chapters

Welcome to the universe of device drivers. Device drivers are the core of how MS-DOS controls the devices on your PC. If device drivers did not exist, every program you execute would require you to customize your program to the PC you are currently using. Device driver programs provide a standard interface between MS-DOS and the PC by following a uniform set of programming rules. These rules are common to both MS-DOS and PC-DOS for the IBM PC and IBM-PC–compatibles. In this book, *DOS* refers to both MS-DOS and PC-DOS, and *PC* refers to both the IBM PC and compatibles.

Most people understand that DOS is used to run application programs such as utilities, databases, word processors, and spreadsheets. DOS provides built-in "services" to store data, plot graphs, access the disk, and control external hardware. Fewer people understand that DOS has its own built-in device drivers to control hardware.

Standard DOS is set up to manage and control a set of standard PC devices, including the keyboard, screen, disks, and serial and parallel adapters. Standard device drivers are normally part of the operating system's device management and are not visible to the user. Prior to version 2.0, DOS did not provide a uniform manner for accessing external hardware. Instead, each device added to the PC required custom changes to DOS as well as changes to programs using the new device. As a result, providing support for new devices was difficult; it was not clear what DOS had to do compared to what the program had to do.

Beginning with version 2.0, DOS began allowing user-installable device drivers. These user device drivers complement those provided in DOS and allow a wider range of device support.

Device drivers must be written to the rules and regulations that Microsoft has specified in order for them to be installed in DOS. These rules provide a uniform interface to DOS, which allows DOS to treat a new device in the same way as existing ones. These rules specify a special format for the device driver program. Such a program must begin with a table that defines to DOS the attributes and type of device controlled. There is a provision within this table that tells DOS how to control (or call) the device driver. Lastly, the device driver program must contain code to process the standard commands that DOS expects of a device driver. These rules are not clearly defined in the *DOS Technical Reference* manual.

Installable device drivers give you the ability to add a new hardware device to the PC and use standard DOS services to access the device. Without installable device drivers, you would have to change your programs for each new device you wish to use. Newer versions of DOS would require you to modify your custom programs to suit the changes in the new DOS. The lack of driver standards would require each program to be different from others; no two programs would access new devices in the same way.

Although many users take for granted the ease of using the PC to read and write data, the steps taken to get a piece of data from the keyboard and then write that data to a disk file represent a long and complex process involving the software driver. It is hard to understand, because most users know so little about it. However, it is not so complex that it cannot be broken down into pieces to make it easier to understand the steps involved. That task is precisely what the early parts of this book are intended to accomplish.

About This Book

This book will teach you how to write your own device driver to interface to any hardware device in your system. We will explore the various parts of DOS device drivers by developing and coding several examples. In addition, we will examine what device drivers do, how they interface to DOS, and how they interact with various devices. Writing device drivers for new devices will be discussed, as well as writing replacements for the standard DOS device drivers.

Writing device drivers is one of the most challenging aspects of programming for the PC. Mastering this seemingly complex topic can be a rewarding experience. As a by-product of learning the secrets of device drivers, you will get a fairly thorough course in DOS system calls and internals, and a refresher course in assembly language. This is because understanding drivers requires using most of the services built into the BIOS.

With the knowledge of how device drivers work, you can begin to modify the device drivers in this book. You can change RAM disk device drivers to suit your needs and write new device drivers to control hardware in your PC. The possibilities are unlimited.

This Book's Intended Readers

This book has been written for many audiences. It will enable anyone who has a basic understanding of DOS and the PC to learn more about how DOS is able to manage the myriad of devices available for use on PCs. For those people who use PCs in their jobs, this book provides a valuable tool, enabling them to expand the capabilities of their PCs by adding more powerful devices. With this book, they can create the software to control these devices without requiring the use of outside professional help.

Educators will also find this book useful. Teachers of computer courses will find many books on DOS and the PC but few that deal with the topic of device drivers in more than a cursory manner. This book is intended to fill that gap.

All of these people have something in common: they have some understanding of assembly language programming for the PC. In addition, a basic knowledge of DOS and BIOS services is required.

Readers should be able to follow a simple 8086/8088 assembly language program. If necessary, readers should purchase one of the numerous books available that introduce the basic concepts of 8086/8088 assembly language programming. One such book is *Assembly Language Primer for the IBM PC and XT* by Robert Lafore (New York: Plume/Waite, New American Library, 1984). For readers who have some experience in PC assembly language programming, appendix A provides a refresher course on the 8086/8088 CPU, memory structure and segmentation techniques, the I/O structure, and the register structure. Readers who are not already acquainted with these aspects of the 8086/8088 architecture should take time now to read appendix A.

In addition, readers will find it useful to have some knowledge of the interrupts and function calls provided by DOS. The *Dos Technical Reference Manual*, published by IBM, is a good source of information on DOS interrupts and function calls. Another book is *Programmer's Reference Manual for IBM Personal Computers* by Steven Armbrust and Ted Forgeron (Illinois: Dow Jones-Irwin, 1986).

Readers should also have some familiarity with the BIOS code that resides in ROM. All that readers need is a basic knowledge of the BIOS functions and how they are used. For IBM systems, the hardware *Technical Reference Manual* for each system documents the BIOS calls. Suppliers of non-IBM systems usually publish similar reference manuals.

Finally, because this book focuses on device drivers, readers should be familiar with each device attached to their PC. This should include a general understanding of the type of device (keyboard, printer, disk drive, etc.) and its function (input, output, both).

What You Will Need to Use This Book

The first thing you will need to use this book is a lot of curiosity about device drivers and DOS: what they are, what they do, what their various parts are, and how to write one. We will attempt to encourage and satisfy this curiosity as we present the various topics in this book.

To best utilize this book, you should be sure that certain hardware and software requirements are fulfilled. The hardware and software requirements of this book are listed below:

- IBM PC, XT, AT or compatible (clone) personal computer

- MS-DOS or PC-DOS operating system, version 2.0 or higher

- Microsoft or IBM's MASM (8086/8088/80286 Macro Assembler)

- LINK (this is the MASM Linker that resolves the address information that is contained in the object output from MASM)

- EXE2BIN (this converts the Linker output into a form required by DOS for device drivers)

- Text editor or word processor (this is used to input the source text of the device driver)

The key requirement is that your computer system be based on the Intel 8086/8088/80286/80386 CPU chips and that the operating system be a variation of MS-DOS, version 2.00 or higher.

Although systems based on the Intel 80286/80386 CPU chips, such as the IBM PC AT, may also be used, we will base our code on the 8086/8088 member of this family without considering the enhanced capabilities of the 80286/80386 systems. All references to your PC system will assume that it uses 8086/8088 chips, but the techniques will apply to all 80286/80386 systems as well. To use the examples, your operating system must be an equivalent of MS-DOS or PC-DOS, version 2.0 or higher (because MS-DOS and PC-DOS are functionally equivalent, subsequent references to these operating systems will appear simply as references to *DOS*). We will occasionally make reference to DOS version 3.00. In particular, we will devote material to the special device driver requirements for DOS version 3.20. This version of DOS expands the role of device drivers by providing more capability for the device driver in the areas of physical control, networking, and device sharing.

Throughout this book, we will present examples of actual code for you to copy, study, and use. Because the code provided is written in 8086/8088 assembly language, you will require three major DOS utilities: MASM, LINK, and EXE2BIN.

LINK and EXE2BIN are standard utilities that are generally provided with DOS. You should be able to find them on the diskettes that comprise the copy of DOS provided by the supplier of your PC system. These utilities assist you in building device drivers.

MASM is the Microsoft Macro Assembler for MS-DOS/PC-DOS systems. This product is offered from two sources, IBM and Microsoft. For the purposes of this book, the IBM and Microsoft Macro Assemblers are identical, and we will not distinguish one from the other. If you use a different assembler, be sure that the features used in the examples are available or at least convertible to equivalent features on the assembler you use.

In addition to the three DOS utilities discussed above, you will need some kind of text editor or word processor so that you can create ASCII text files of the examples. The EDLIN program that is supplied with DOS is adequate for entering some of the short examples. Because of the limited capabilities of EDLIN, however, we recommend that you use one of the many flexible and powerful word processors available on the market today.

Why This Book Was Written

In the years since 1981, when the IBM PC was introduced, an incredible number of programs have been written for the PC. This has been matched by the amount of information available in magazines, periodicals, and books. However, the information on how DOS works with programs and devices has been either too complex or incomplete. Finding the necessary information on device drivers involved an unsatisfying process of, combing through articles and books, looking for clues on how they work.

This book was written to satisfy the need for one source of information about writing and understanding device drivers. The information contained in this book will appeal to the casual PC user who has questions about the inner workings of DOS. The professional PC user will find information about why device drivers are needed and why they are built the way they are. For the serious PC programmer, the book provides information about how DOS services interact with the device driver and the device. The book's primary goal is to provide the framework for writing device drivers; the theory behind such programs is also discussed. On the practical side, this book contains several working device drivers that can be used by most PCs.

Conventions Used in This Book

This book follows the conventions that are assumed by the many users of PCs. Numbers used in this book are in hexadecimal form if they have a suffix of *h,* otherwise they are in decimal form. *DOS* refers to both PC-DOS and MS-DOS unless otherwise indicated. *Disk* refers to both hard and floppy disks. *Diskettes* refers to the type of disks that are removable. A *routine* is a set of lines of code that perform a function and have no particular format. A *procedure* is the set of code lines that have a defined format and are invoked by a *call*.

How to Use This Book

This book presents material on device drivers in a progressive fashion; the book is intended to be read from beginning to end. The beginning of this book is introductory in nature; basic concepts are presented to assure that the reader will not be lost in later chapters. Subsequent chapters present working device drivers. With each chapter, more information is presented about various types of device drivers. In the last chapters, we present an overall guide to building device drivers from scratch, as well as tips and techniques in debugging such programs.

This book is also intended to be a reference document. Many of the figures, listings, and tables contain information that is important to programmers who wish to write their own device drivers. In this respect, chapter 9 ("Building A Complete Full Function Device Driver") and chapter 10 ("Tips and Techniques") are particularly useful.

Overview of the Chapters

Chapter 2 is a quick overview of the material needed to understand the role of device drivers within the framework of the PC environment. We will see how devices are programmed, what the various parts of DOS are, and how device drivers fit into the whole picture. The rules and regulations for device drivers are presented at the end of this chapter.

Chapter 3 introduces the first device driver. Although this short, rudimentary driver does not do much, it introduces the basic concepts of writing device drivers. Because the device driver is short in terms of code and small in terms of function, you will "see" more of what device drivers do.

Chapter 4 introduces the first of several real device drivers: the Console Device Driver. The Console Device Driver is a working example that controls the screen output device and the keyboard input device. We will add a feature to this device driver to distinguish it from others: the ability to sound a tone for each keystroke entered on the keyboard.

Chapter 5 presents a Printer Device Driver that, unlike the standard printer device driver, has the ability to control up to five printers. The DOS I/O control service is used to select which of the five printers should be used.

Chapter 6 describes the Clock Device Driver. This driver requires a hardware clock/calendar that is not standard equipment with the average PC but that is available as an option to most multifunction cards for the PC. This Clock Device Driver retains the DOS time and date information intact between the time the machine is turned off until the next time it is turned on. This eliminates the effort, however slight, of re-entering the time and date each time DOS is booted.

Chapter 7 covers the preliminary material needed for you to understand what disks and disk drives are all about.

Chapter 8 is devoted to a RAM Disk Device Driver. Based on the information presented in chapter 7, we will build a disk device driver that uses memory, rather than an actual physical disk device, to store data. We will see how the device driver stores file information as well as file data in memory.

Chapter 9 presents a general discussion on how to write device drivers. Each part of such a program is covered in detail, including the information that DOS expects to be present in a device driver.

Chapter 10 concludes this book by presenting some practical tips and techniques on how to debug device drivers. There is also material on advanced topics, such as making device drivers work under the various versions of DOS.

Summary

We begin our exploration into the world of device drivers by describing what you will need to use this book. You will need an IBM PC or compatible, several of the utilities that come with DOS, and a macro assembler. You will need to know about the architecture of the IBM PC and about assembly language programming. Appendix A reviews the major aspects of the 8086/8088 architecture.

Questions

1. Does it matter whether I use MS-DOS or PC-DOS?

2. I have several versions of DOS—which one should I use?

3. I have a PC at home and an AT at work. Will I have problems if I use both machines for the examples in this book?

Answers may be found in appendix E.

Chapter 2

Basic Concepts

- DOS Services
- DOS Device Management
- The DOS Device Driver
- Device Driver Commands
- Tracing a Request from Program to Device
- The Mechanics of Building Device Drivers

I n this chapter, we will cover the basic software and hardware concepts of DOS that you will need before you tackle your first device driver in chapter 3. These basic concepts include programming PC hardware devices, internal operations of DOS, and how DOS interacts with devices.

The first part of this chapter describes the various devices found on most PCs and how to access those devices through ROM BIOS. The second part presents the ways in which programs interface to DOS for services and discusses how devices are accessed through DOS. The third part begins an overview of device drivers. In this section we cover some of the basic concepts behind device drivers; what they are, what each part is, and how they interact with DOS. The fourth part describes the steps needed to build a device driver.

Controlling Devices through Software

Overview of Device Fundamentals

We begin this section with an overview of the standard hardware of the PC. We will start with what devices are, how they connect to the PC, and what the standard devices of the PC are. This summary will help you get a better understanding of how devices interface to the PC.

Devices for Your PC   You are used to the keyboard, screen, printers, and disks that are part of the PC you use on a daily basis. These devices are but a small fraction of what can be added to the PC. Table 2–1 lists some of the more important devices that can be added to the PC. These devices fall into several categories: input, input and output, and output. You will learn to write device drivers for these devices.

Type	Device	What They Do
Input	Image digitizer	Captures video images through a camera and converts the image for computer use
	CD-ROM	Compact disk systems designed to store vast libraries of data and video images
	Bar code reader	Reads computerized supermarket labels using a light-based scanner device
	Graphics digitizer	Captures complex graphics images by tracing the printed image
	Mouse/track ball	Mechanical pointing device designed to provide user-friendly computer interfaces
	A/D	Converts analog signals to digital for use in measurement
Input/ output	Local area network	Connects several PCs together to allow data and device sharing
	Tape drives	Backs up data onto tape cartridges for archival storage
	Video cassette recorder	Displays video films using tape—also stores data
	Bisync interface	Allows communication with large computers using a special communications protocol
	Multifunction board	Adds serial and parallel device ports for printers and modems
	Disk drive	Floppy and hard disks for data storage
Output	Plotter	High-resolution graphics plotting systems using vertically positioned pens
	PROM burner	Programs read-only-memory (ROM) chips
	Laser printer	Fast and high-resolution printing using laser technology
	Synthesizer	Artificial voice and sound generators that produce computer-generated music
	D/A	Converts digital signals to analog signals for control purposes

Table 2–1: Examples of add-on devices for the PC

In addition to floppy disk drives and faster hard disk drives, other examples of popular add-on devices are image digitizers, CD-ROMs, local area network controllers and interface devices, tape drives, video disk players, plotters, PROM burners, laser printers, bar code readers, music synthesizers, graphics digitizers, "mouse" devices, joysticks, track balls, bisynchronous communication interfaces, analog-to-digital (A/D) converters, and digital-to-analog (D/A) converters.

As you will see later in this book, it is the use of device drivers through DOS that make devices such as these accessible to you.

Controllers, Adapters, Interfaces   Devices need to be added to a PC in such a way that the PC will recognize them. Devices often will work with printed circuit boards that insert into a hardware slot inside your PC. These cards are given various names, such as *controllers, adapters,* or *interfaces.* The generic function of these cards is to provide an interface between the hardware device and the PC. This allows the PC to control the device through signals passed between the PC and the device on the bus. These signals are commonly called *I/O bus signals,* and they have a variety of functions. I/O ports or addresses are used to identify devices attached to the PC. Data is transferred on the portion of the bus called the *data bus.* Other control signals on the bus are used to coordinate all the devices with the PC.

Typically, controller cards are plugged directly into the PC's I/O bus on the motherboard and become an integral part of the PC. The design feature of the PC that allows controllers and devices to be added so easily is often referred to as an *open architecture.* It is this open architecture that enables the PC to make such widespread use of the variety of devices discussed earlier.

Although there are 64k I/O addresses or ports to choose from, each device has a unique set of I/O addresses. This set of I/O addresses is used by the PC to select a device for data transfer. For a given device, each I/O address performs a unique function. For example, the printer device has an I/O address for the data being transferred, an I/O address for the status of the data transfer, and an I/O address for printer control.

When the PC transfers data to the device, the OUT instruction is used to select an I/O address and a character to send. For example, to send an ASCII "A" out to the printer, the following instructions are used:

```
mov  dx,0378h      ;I/O address for printer
mov  al,41h        ;ASCII A
out  dx,al         ;send character to the printer
```

When the PC executes the *out* instruction, the I/O address is asserted on the bus (the value 378h is placed on the address bus); the value in the AL register is also placed on the bus (the value 41 is placed on the data bus). The controller for the device is constantly monitoring the (address) bus for the values associated with the device. Once it sees the value 378h on the bus, the controller will "grab" the value on the data bus and pass it to the device.

Controllers perform the basic functions of controlling devices and transferring data between the PC and those devices by recognizing signals sent by the 8086/8088 on the address and data busses.

Standard Devices for the PC   General-purpose controllers or multifunction boards are designed to handle a group of devices, such as output ports, clock, a calendar, extra memory, and game I/O. The typical PC system today often includes as standard equipment two such general-purpose controllers: the *serial device* controller and the *parallel device* controller. Earlier PCs included a game port to allow you to attach a joystick.

To allow external devices to be attached to such a controller, a connector is provided on the outside edge of the controller card. Often referred to as *ports,* these connectors merely serve as hardware-connection mechanisms. Both serial and parallel device controllers use these connectors, which are called, respectively, the *serial port* and *parallel port.*

Note that the ports described above are not the same as the I/O ports described in the overview of the 8086/8088 architecture discussed in appendix A. The I/O ports of the 8086/8088 are internal ports used to access the device controllers through the data bus using special CPU instructions (*IN* and *OUT*). The ports described in this section are external device ports (outside the bus, on the interface board), used for connecting the devices to their respective controllers.

The easiest way to attach a new device to your PC often is to connect it to your PC's serial port, parallel port, or game port. These three ports differ primarily in the type of electrical signals passed through them and in the manner in which data transfers between the devices and the controllers.

Serial Devices   The serial port is the most versatile of the three ports described above. This port is used to connect modems, mouse devices, and bar-code readers to the PC. Data can be transferred in either direction (to or from the 8086/8088), and speeds can range as high as 9600 baud. Printers, which are output devices, also may be connected to the serial port, but it is more common to use the parallel port for this purpose. The connector used to plug devices into the serial port is defined as an *RS–232–C connector* because the protocol used to communicate to the device attached to the port closely follows the EIA RS–232–C standard. Therefore, the serial port is also referred to as the RS–232 port.

Parallel Devices   The parallel port was originally designed for efficient handling of output-only devices. Its primary design objective is to serve as a printer interface. The electrical signals in this interface tend to be meaningful only to printers and special output devices. The speed of data transfer can exceed 10k bytes per second. Because the parallel port is used for output-only devices, it is a bit more limiting than the serial port. Therefore, there is a tendency to connect only printers, print-buffer devices, and special-purpose output devices to the parallel port. Originally developed by the Centronics Corporation, the parallel port is also referred to as the *Centronics port.*

The Game Port Of the three standard ports provided on PC, the game port is the most limited. It is designed to handle very simple input signals with minimal data transfer. The game port is generally used for connecting to the PC simple input devices, such as joysticks and track balls.

High-speed and DMA Controllers Some devices, such as disk drives, transfer data faster than the serial, parallel, or game device controllers can handle. Such devices cannot use general-purpose controllers.

To illustrate this, the serial controller can handle up to 9,600 bits per second (approximately 1,200 characters/bytes per second). However, the hard disk transfers data at well over 100,000 bytes per second. In addition to the requirement for high data-transfer speed, the hard disk drive also requires many control signals that the serial controller cannot provide.

For these reasons, the hard disk drive needs a controller that can access the PC's data bus directly, and data needs to be able to be transferred directly between the device and memory for maximum efficiency. This is called *Direct Memory Access* (DMA). Many other devices also require high-speed DMA: examples are the video monitor, tape drives, and clock/calendars. As will be seen later in this book, these devices, like the hard disk, require special-purpose controllers and, therefore, have unique interfaces, different from those used by the usual printers and other devices.

Character and Block Devices In the general PC environment, devices are divided into two types: character devices or block devices. This distinction is based on how these devices transfer data to and from the PC.

Character devices transfer data one character at a time. Examples of such devices include printers, modems, keyboards, and mouse devices.

Block devices, on the other hand, manage their data in groups of characters and transfer several bytes at one time in a block, such as 512 or 1,024 bytes. Examples of block devices are disks and tapes; with these devices, the basic method of storage is a group of characters. Block devices are usually chosen when high data-transfer speeds are needed. If disks were somehow made into character devices, the speed of the data transfer would be severely limited. Because the disk rotates at a high speed, by the time one character is transferred, the disk would no longer be in position to read a second character. Obviously, it would take many revolutions of the disk to transfer a group of characters. On the other hand, the block-device approach allows the disk to capture a block's worth of data under the read/write heads.

All sorts of controllers are available for the PC. These range from those found on multifunction boards to special-purpose controllers. Writing drivers for the controllers in this second category requires that the programmer have special knowledge of the way these devices work.

The Console Device When we sit down to use a PC we naturally use the keyboard to enter our commands, and we see the results displayed on the screen. We don't think anything of it; we assume that they are a part of the PC. But the keyboard and the screen are also devices. The combination of the keyboard and the screen is called the console.

The console device as the primary interface to the PC is an old concept. This concept dates back to the earliest days of computers, when the console, a teletype containing a keyboard and printer instead of a screen, was often the only means of communicating with the computer. As the primary input device for a PC, the keyboard allows commands to be input to the computer. The display, or screen, allows you to view what is typed and the results of the commands.

Although we have briefly described some of the standard devices for the PC in this section, chapter 7 covers disk devices in more detail because they are more popular devices.

Program Control of Devices

If you want to use a particular device in your programs, complex software-control routines will need to be included. Fortunately, you have a choice of two methods: you can use the routines built into the PC's Read-Only Memory or you can use the services provided by DOS.

The Differences between ROM-BIOS and DOS Services Through the ROM-based routines, collectively called the Basic Input-Output System (BIOS), you can control the serial ports, the parallel ports, the keyboard, the screen, and the disks. However, these routines provide only basic access mechanisms, such as read or write; they do not organize data in a form that is easily managed. For example, through the ROM routines, data can be written to disk sectors but the concept of organizing data into files does not exist.

DOS, on the other hand, provides higher-level processing capabilities. Instead of writing separate routines to use the BIOS services for each device, you can refer to devices by name in programs using DOS services. For disk data, programs can let DOS organize the data in files instead of managing the disk sectors in which the data resides. For transferring data to serial or parallel ports, the program using BIOS services needs to check constantly for errors in transmission. On the other hand, programs that use the DOS services for data transmission need not check as often; DOS retries each operation if there are any errors.

DOS itself uses the BIOS routines for device access and control. In doing so, DOS adds an additional layer between the program and the BIOS routines. This additional layer protects the program from the BIOS in many instances. We mentioned earlier some of the features that DOS provides in addition to those provided by BIOS services. One important reason for using DOS services is that not all PCs have compatible BIOS's. Thus, programs built to one machine's BIOS may not work on another machine. Programs using only DOS services will work on any machine that uses DOS.

To be fair to programs using BIOS routines, the additional layer between programs and the BIOS when DOS services are used causes most programs to run slower. For this reason, many programs bypass some of the DOS services and go directly to the BIOS routines.

This is particularly true for programs that need to display screen data quickly. In other cases, the DOS services cannot execute at a fast enough rate. For example, although the serial port is designed to operate at 9600 baud, this speed cannot be attained using DOS services for the serial port; the program must access the serial port directly.

For the most part, DOS uses the BIOS routines in device drivers. It is within the programs defined to DOS as device drivers that the calls to the BIOS code for the respective devices are executed.

Programs that use DOS services for device access sacrifice speed, but, in return, gain flexibility and portability.

BIOS Programming   Many powerful low-level routines are built into the PC's ROM-based BIOS to allow programs to control most of the PC's devices. Through the use of the BIOS, you can control the serial, parallel, keyboard, screen, and disk devices of the PC without having to write the code from scratch. The software routines that are built into the ROM BIOS are accessed through the 8086/8088 *interrupt* mechanism. For a review of how interrupts work, refer to appendix A.

Each device has an associated BIOS interrupt and a unique routine in ROM. The use of unique interrupts allows you to refer to these routines without having to remember the exact address of the routine.

Using the BIOS interrupts is merely one method of accessing the PC's devices. Later in this chapter, we shall also see how DOS is used to access data from devices. We describe the BIOS interrupts first because DOS also uses the BIOS interrupts for device access.

Example of Using Interrupts with the Serial Adapter   Let's look at how the serial port is controlled using BIOS. The BIOS interrupt for the serial adapter is numbered 14h. This BIOS service contains routines that allows you to control up to two serial adapters or devices (although the PC can support more than two serial adapters, the BIOS routines are limited to two; to access more than two, you would have to write your own code). The convention for identifying device number is simple: devices are numbered starting at 0. For example, the device attached to the first serial port is numbered 0, and the device attached to the second serial port is numbered 1.

A description of the features of the serial adapter BIOS interrupt (14h) is provided in table 2–2. The registers and values required are also shown. The sequence for using this interrupt is to set up the required registers for the feature desired, issue an *int* instruction specifying 14h, and check the appropriate registers upon return for any errors that occurred during the call.

This interrupt provides four subfunctions. The first subfunction (when *ah = 0)* is used to initialize the individual devices. This function is used to set the required characteristics for the serial adapter. Refer to appendix B for a full description of the parameter settings used for initialization. The second subfunction *(ah = 1)* is used to send a single character through the serial adapter to the device. The third subfunction *(ah = 2)* is used to receive one character through the serial adapter. The last subfunction *(ah = 3)* returns the status of the serial adapter so that the program can determine whether it can send another character or whether the serial adapter is ready to read another character.

Listing 2–1 shows an example of using the first serial adapter. The first lines of codes check the status of the serial adapter using subfunction 3. The first *test* instruction checks the status returned in *ah*. If the serial adapter's transfer register is empty and the Data Set Ready signal is high, a character can be sent to the serial adapter. This occurs at label *send* through the use of subfunction 1.

The serial adapter BIOS routines provide the means to transmit and receive a single character from a serial device. In addition, this interrupt is used to initialize and perform a status check on the serial adapter.

Examples of Using Interrupts To Control the Parallel Adapter   The BIOS interrupt for controlling the parallel adapter is numbered 17h. Like the serial adapter, parallel devices are numbered starting at 0. The register conventions are slightly different, however, and the parallel adapter BIOS service has only three functions. The first function (ah = 0) is used to transmit one character through the parallel adapter. The second function (ah = 1) is used to initialize the parallel port. The last function (ah = 2) is used to retrieve the printer status. As you can see, the structure of a BIOS interrupt is fairly similar: initialize, output, input, and status checking are the typical functions. Note that the parallel adapter sends and cannot receive. This is shown in table 2–3.

The parallel adapter is programmed in the same way as the serial adapter. Before each transmission of a character to the parallel adapter, you select the parallel adapter (DX = 0) and check it for readiness (ah = 2). Then you send a character out (ah = 0). Finally, you check the status register to ensure that the character made it out correctly. This process is shown in listing 2–2.

Register	Value	Description
ah	0	Initialize serial port
	1	Transmit 1 character
	2	Receive 1 character
	3	Get serial port status
al		Character received (ah = 2) or
		Character to transmit (ah = 1)
dx		Serial port to use (0 or 1)

Status is returned in ax as follows:

ah Bit	If Set, Means
7	Timeout has occurred
6	Transmission shift register is empty
5	Transmission buffer is empty
4	A break has been detected
3	A framing error has occurred
2	A parity error has occurred
1	An overrun has occurred
0	Data is ready

al Bit	If Set, Means
7	Receive line signal has been detected
6	Ring indicator has been detected
5	Data set ready asserted
4	Clear to send asserted
3	A change has occurred in receive line signal
2	A change has occurred in ring indicator
1	A change has occurred in data set ready
0	A change has occurred for clear to send

Table 2–2: The register set-up requirements for the serial adapter BIOS interrupt 14 hex. This interrupt provides both transmit and receive functions through the serial adapter.

Listing 2–1: An example of programming the serial adapter

```
;     assume that the bl register contains a character to
;     be sent out to the first serial port

;     check the first serial adapter to see whether it is
;     ready to accept a character

      mov      dx,0          ;select the first serial adapter
      mov      ah,3          ;status check subfunction for int 14h
      int      14h           ;BIOS serial adapter interrupt
                             ;returns a status value in ah
      test     ah,20h        ;is the transfer hold register empty?
      jnz      next          ;yes (not busy) - go to next check
      jmp      error         ;previous character still waiting
next:
      test     al,20h        ;is data set ready (=1) ?
      jnz      send          ;yes - ready to send
      jmp      error         ;device is not ready - process error

;     transmit the character to the first serial adapter

send:
      mov      al,bl         ;move character to al for sending
      mov      ah,1          ;transmit function
      int      14h           ;BIOS serial adapter interrupt
      test     ah,80h        ;any transmit errors?
      jnz      error         ;yes - process error
        .                    ;continue processing
        .
        .
error:
```

You will see more of this interrupt when you build the Printer Device Driver in chapter 5.

The Keyboard   Each time you type a character on the keyboard a ROM BIOS routine retrieves these keystrokes. Each keystroke can be defined by an ASCII code, a scan code, or both. A scan code is a unique code assigned to each key of the keyboard (this is still true for keys that are duplicated, such as the Shift key). For keystrokes that have no meaning, such as function key 1, F1, the ASCII code is zero and the scan code is an extended scan code. This allows the keyboard interrupt routine to distinguish between normal keystrokes, those that produce printable characters, and those that do not normally produce printable characters.

Register	Value	Description
ah	0	Transmit 1 character
	1	Initialize parallel port
	2	Get parallel port status
al		Character to transmit (ah = 0)
dx		Parallel port to use (0, 1 or 2)

Status is returned in ah as follows:

ah Bit	If Set, Means
7	Printer is not busy
6	Parallel port acknowledge
5	Printer is out of paper
4	Parallel port selected
3	An I/O error has occurred
2–1	Not used
0	A timeout has occurred

Table 2–3: The register set-up requirements for the parallel adapter BIOS interrupt 17 hex. This interrupt provides only transmit functions through the parallel adapter.

The ROM BIOS routine that captures keystrokes is known as the BIOS keyboard interrupt and is numbered 9h (see figure 2–1). Interrupt 9h is a hardware interrupt and is not issued by a program. Its purpose is to capture up to sixteen keystrokes and store them in a 32-byte buffer. A keystroke is made up of two bytes: an ASCII code and a possible scan code, so the buffer must be 32 bytes long ($16 * 2 = 32$). The buffer allows keystrokes to be captured even when the program is busy processing nonkeyboard-related information.

To get a keystroke character into your program, you must use another software interrupt call to the BIOS keyboard services routine. This BIOS keyboard services routine is numbered 16h and is responsible for retrieving characters from the buffer in which interrupt 9h has stashed these characters. This process is shown in figure 2–1.

Listing 2–2: An example of programming the parallel adapter

```
;     assume that the bl register contains a character to
;     be sent out to the first parallel port

;     check the first parallel adapter to see whether it is
;     ready to accept a character

      mov      dx,0        ;select the first parallel adapter
      mov      ah,2        ;status check function
      int      17h         ;BIOS parallel adapter interrupt
                           ;returns a status value in ah
      test     ah,80h      ;is the printer not busy?
      jne      next        ;yes (not busy) - go to send
      jmp      error       ;no - busy

;     transmit the character to the first parallel adapter

send:
      mov      al,bl       ;move character to al for sending
      mov      ah,0        ;transmit function
      int      17h         ;BIOS parallel adapter interrupt
      test     ah,09h      ;I/O Error or Timeout?
      jne      error       ;yes - process error
                           ;continue processing
      .
      .
      .
error:
```

Interrupts 9h and 16h work hand in hand. The interrupt 9h routine is always available in case you type a character on the keyboard. A program does not need to issue a request for characters from the keyboard before interrupt 9h will go into action. This allows you to type ahead, which means that you can type in characters before they are requested from a program. The interrupt 16h routine is responsible for returning the specified number of characters to the requesting program from the buffer in which interrupt 9h has stored them.

Using the Keyboard Services Interrupt (INT 16h)   Table 2–4 summarizes the services available from this BIOS interrupt.

Interrupt 16h's service is used to read a character from the keyboard buffer. Service 1 is used to determine whether there is a character in the keyboard buffer for us to retrieve. The reason for this is simply to prevent a program from waiting for a character to be struck if the buffer is empty. This saves time, but more importantly, the program is not holding up other things that DOS may

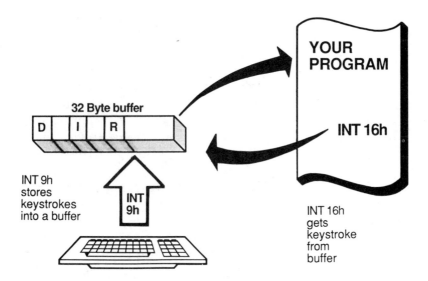

Figure 2–1: The role of the keyboard Interrupt 9h. When a key is struck on the keyboard, Interrupt 9h stores the keystroke in the keyboard buffer.

Contents of ah	Service
0	Read next keyboard character
1	Check for available character
2	Get shift status

Table 2–4: The three services for the keyboard interrupt.

need to do. Service 2 returns the status of the shift keys. Holding the Shift key down will not cause a character to be sent from the keyboard to the buffer. However, the program needs to acknowledge the use of the Shift key in conjunction with other keys. For example, lower-case characters need to be distinguished from upper-case characters. Function keys benefit from the use of the Shift function, because a second set of functions is produced by using the Shift key with the function keys.

As you can see, the BIOS calls for the keyboard, like those for serial devices, are straightforward. You will find examples of keyboard usage in the Console Device Driver of chapter 4.

The Video Screen Displaying information on the screen is accomplished through the use of BIOS interrupt 10h. This BIOS service also performs a number of functions that are not apparent to the PC user. For example, regardless of whether the PC has a color monitor, a monochrome monitor, or both, the BIOS routines will send the information out to the appropriate screen adapter.

Programming Using the Video Services Interrupt INT 10h The range of services provided by interrupt 10h covers reading and writing data to and from the screen. Table 2–5 summarizes the services available.

Many of the services listed in table 2–5 are used for special purposes. For example, services 0Bh, 0Ch, and 0Dh are used for graphics displays on color monitors. Service 4h is seldom used, because it requires a light-pen. Services 0h

ah Reg.	Service Function for 10h
0h	Set video mode
1h	Set cursor size
2h	Set cursor position
3h	Read cursor position
4h	Read light-pen position
5h	Set active display page
6h	Scroll window up
7h	Scroll window down
8h	Read character and attribute
9h	Write character and attribute
ah	Write character
bh	Set color palette
ch	Write pixel dot
dh	Read pixel dot
eh	Write character as TTY
fh	Get current video mode
13h	Write character string

Table 2–5: Summary of the functions that the video display service interrupt provides. Note that there is a break in the numbers between the Get Current Video Mode (fh) and the Write Character as String (13H) services.

and 0Fh are important when changing monitor display modes, switching from text to high-resolution modes, and vice-versa.

The video display service that is important to this book is eh, "Write Character as TTY." This service allows you to write a character out to the screen without knowing the cursor position. The character appears at the next location after the last output. All characters that are written this way are treated as simple TTY.

You will see an application for the video services interrupt in chapter 4's Console Device Driver.

Refresher Course on DOS

Since its introduction with the IBM PC, DOS has become the most popular operating system in the world. From its humble beginnings, DOS has evolved into a powerful tool, with features such as hierarchical disk structures, the ability to control just about any device, and networking capabilities.

The conceptual model for DOS as the master supervisor of resources of a computer system is shown in Figure 2-2.

At the core of DOS is the kernel. The kernel provides control functions for administrating and managing the resources of the PC. Memory management routines provide space in which programs can execute. I/O requests from application programs are managed and processed by the kernel. File-management routines within the kernel organize the data for easy access by applications programs. In addition, the kernel is responsible for initializing itself when DOS is booted.

The DOS services interface provides a path for application programs to request services from DOS. It is a defined interface mechanism that processes requests by interacting with the kernel. DOS services include file I/O to devices and disk files, time and date functions, and program control.

Strictly speaking, device drivers are part of the DOS kernel. They provide a standard interface to the devices from within the DOS kernel. As a group, the device drivers provide device management for DOS. Each device driver controls a device and uses the PC's BIOS routines. For example, the serial port device driver uses the serial port BIOS interrupt.

Programs generally use DOS services to access and control devices. However, DOS does not prevent a program from directly accessing the BIOS routines. The "back-door" approach is used by many programs to attain higher performance or to perform a task that DOS does not provide. For example, many word processors use the keyboard BIOS interrupts to speed up the keyboard input rates. Another example is programs that use the PC's built-in speaker; DOS does not provide a service for speaker control.

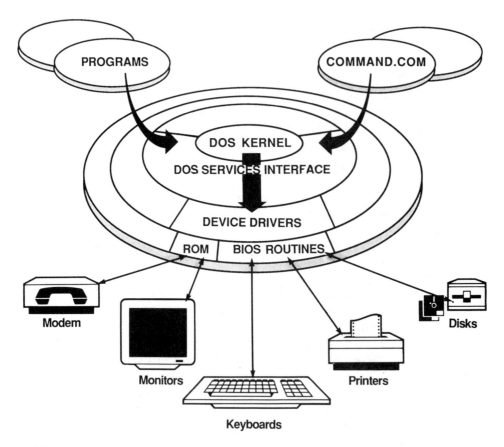

Figure 2–2: The functional parts of DOS

DOS itself is composed of several programs that assist in bringing DOS into memory when DOS is booted. There are additional external utility programs that help you when you use DOS. Among these are FORMAT, PRINT, BASIC, and CHKDSK. Although application programs are distinguished from utility programs, they both request the same services from DOS and follow the same rules that DOS expects from programs.

The most important utility program, and the one that users are most familiar with, is COMMAND.COM. This program runs automatically when DOS is booted. COMMAND.COM provides the interface for users to communicate with DOS. The commands that are entered on the keyboard are translated to services requested of DOS. For example, COMMAND.COM is used to set the time and date, to run programs, and to control the devices attached to the PC.

Lastly, application programs request the PC's resources through the DOS services interface. Without DOS, these programs would have to incorporate all of the services provided by DOS and would, in all likelihood, be incompatible with other application programs. DOS provides a common set of features and services that allows all applications programs to share the PC and its data storage. These applications programs use the services provided by the DOS kernel by requesting services through programming calls to DOS. We will discuss this topic in more detail later in this chapter.

Devices for DOS

As we have seen, DOS allows programs to control a set of standard PC devices: keyboard, screen, disks, and serial and parallel adapters. Each DOS device has a unique name assigned to it, and it is through these names that programs are able to access the devices. Table 2–6 lists the names of the standard DOS devices as they are currently defined for version 2.00 and higher.

In order to use a device in a program or DOS command, you need to specify the assigned device name in the command line or program statement that references the device. These *reserved device names* have a special meaning for DOS, and any reference to these reserved names will cause DOS to access the device. Therefore, you cannot use reserved names to access another type of device.

DOS Device Name	Standard Device
con:	Keyboard/screen
com1:	Serial port #1
aux:	Auxiliary port (identical to com1:)
com2:	Serial port #2
lpt1:	Printer port #1
lpt2:	Printer port #2
lpt3:	Printer port #3
prn:	Logical printer port (identical to lpt1:)
nul:	Null device
clock$	Software clock
A:	First diskette unit
B:	Second diskette unit
C:	Hard disk (normally)

Table 2–6: The standard device names assigned by DOS

The *con:* device name refers to the console device, which, as you've seen, is composed of the keyboard and screen that is the primary interface to the PC. When you refer to con: in a program that does output you are referring to a video device attached to the video controller.

The *aux:* is the auxiliary logical device and is assigned to the *com1:* port, which is the first of several serial adapters that may be attached to a PC. Most MS-DOS systems provide support for up to two serial ports; these are typically named *com1:* and *com2:*. Additional serial ports are numbered *com3:, com4:,* etc.

In addition to the two serial adapters noted above, most MS-DOS systems also provide support for up to three parallel adapters or ports. These are intended primarily for use with parallel printers and are assigned the names *lpt1:, lpt2:,* and *lpt3:*. The logical printer device, *prn:,* is assigned to the first printer port lpt1:, so both prn: and lpt1: may be used to refer to the same device unless prn: is changed.

The *nul:* device is a special device for DOS. This null device acts as a "bit-bucket" for output operations. If you write to this device, nothing will happen; the data is effectively thrown away (the bucket has a hole in it). This is desirable when a program generates output that should not be captured or saved in any form. By temporarily directing the output to the nul: device, the program can function in its normal fashion without worrying if it outputs garbage.

The *clock$* device is another special device defined for most MS-DOS systems. It really is not a device in the physical sense; no hardware keeps track of the date or time (there is a timer that is used to keep the clock up to date). By providing this software "device," DOS makes it possible for you to access the system time and date easily through standard I/O mechanisms.

The standard disks found on PC systems today are generally diskettes (floppy disks) and hard disks. Disks are not given reserved device names but are assigned alphabetic letters. These drive letters begin with A: and can run up to Z:. Most DOS systems come equipped with two floppy disk drives and these are assigned the drive letters A: and B:. In some cases when only a single diskette drive is supplied with a PC system, the drive letters A: and B: are used to refer to the single drive. Hard disks are usually assigned device names starting with the letter C:; that is, the first hard disk is C:, the second hard disk is D:, and so on. Although these drive letters are assigned by DOS, several PC manufacturers change DOS to reflect different drive letter assignments. Some manufacturers refer to the hard disk as E: if there are four floppy disk drives; the hard disk could be referred to as B: if there is only one floppy disk in the PC. Often a single hard disk drive may be *partitioned,* with each partition being assigned its own unique drive letter, as if the partition was itself an independent hard disk drive.

DOS Services

The DOS Interrupts

DOS provides access to devices, files, and various services through the use of the 8086/8088 software interrupt mechanism and the *int* instruction. Programs call DOS through documented interrupt numbers which are in the range of 20h to 3Fh. These interrupt numbers are reserved for use by DOS; they should not be used by your programs. These 32 interrupts are shown in table 2–7.

Eight DOS interrupts have been documented for use by programs. The remaining interrupts (28h through 3Fh) are reserved for use by DOS.

The Terminate Program interrupt (20h) terminates the current executing program as well as closing all files and flushing all data buffers to disk. It is commonly used in .COM programs.

The DOS Services interrupt (21h) is the primary interface between an application program and DOS. All requests for system services are made through this call. We will discuss these services in more detail in the next section of this chapter.

The interrupt at 22h, Terminate Address, is not an interrupt call but rather is used to store an interrupt vector (22H is the address to transfer to when a program terminates).

The interrupt defined for 23h is not an interrupt call but defines an interrupt vector at 23h to contain the address to transfer to when a user types CONTROL-C at the keyboard. Usually programs use this interrupt to define a memory address to which control should be passed when a CONTROL-C is issued.

20h	DOS	terminate program
21h	DOS	function call
22h	DOS	terminate address
23h	DOS	CTRL/break exit address
24h	DOS	vector for fatal error
25h	DOS	absolute disk read
26h	DOS	absolute disk write
27h	DOS	terminate but stay resident
28h-3fh	DOS	reserved

Table 2–7: The list of DOS interrupts (not BIOS). Note that the last 24 interrupts (28h through 3Fh) are reserved for use by DOS.

The default is to cause a break if CONTROL-C is issued at the A> prompt. The use of this interrupt allows the program to continue processing rather than being summarily aborted.

For example, figure 2–3 shows a situation in which a program intercepts a CONTROL-C interrupt and sets a flag. At a later (and safer) time, the program checks to see if the flag is set; if so, the program aborts. This allows the program to terminate in an orderly way instead of just aborting.

The Fatal Error interrupt (24h) is not an interrupt call but rather defines the address to which control should be transferred when an error occurs during disk I/O. This allows the program to continue processing instead of being aborted.

The Absolute Disk Read interrupt (25h) is used by programs to read absolute sectors on the disk. The absolute sectors are numbered from 0 to the highest available sector. Interrupt 25h allows a program to read the special sections on

CONTROL-C Processing in a Program

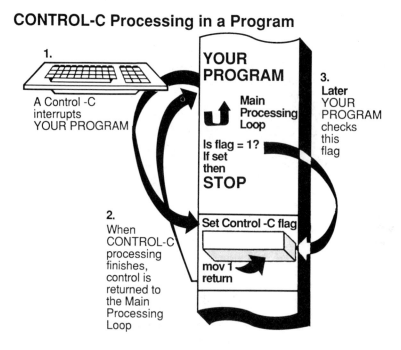

Figure 2–3: A typical example where the program sets up a CONTROL-C address. At this address a flag is set if the CONTROL-C key is struck. A flag is set and processing resumes. At some later point the flag is checked, and if set, the program is then terminated.

a disk that are not normally readable from DOS: the boot record where information on the format of the disk is kept; the file allocation table, which indicates where files are located on the disk; and the file directory which contains information about the files on the disk. Normal DOS services can read only the user data area of the disk, not the special sections. The Absolute Disk Write interrupt (26h), the counterpart to interrupt 25h, gives programs the ability to write absolute sectors on the disk, including those in the special sections of a disk.

Interrupt 27h is the Terminate but Stay Resident interrupt. This interrupt call allows the program to remain in memory but to pass control back to the calling program. It is useful in writing programs that perform a background task. The PRINT spooling program uses this interrupt to stay in memory and provide printing services.

DOS Services

By *DOS services,* we refer to the various functions for input/output, file access, device access, and program control that are accessed through DOS interrupt 21h. Each DOS service is requested by specifying the requested service in the ah register. Table 2–8 lists the DOS services available through interrupt 21h.

Using DOS Services

Programs issue requests for DOS functions through interrupt 21h. This is one of the more commonly used interrupts, because it controls so many facilities. Interrupt 21h is used to open files before reading or writing to them. Interrupt 21h lets you close files to ensure that the data is safely stored on your devices and to prevent further access of the device. In short, DOS services offer you the ability to control what you want your programs to do.

DOS Device Management

To access a device using DOS, your programs need to indicate what file or device to use; this is called *opening* the file or device. DOS requires that the name of the file or device be specified through the DOS Open service (0Fh). After this interrupt is received, DOS sets up a File Control Block (FCB), which is used as a standard mechanism to access the device. This FCB is also used to keep information regarding use of the file or device. A device such as the serial port must be opened using com1: as the device name. Then you can read or write to this device using DOS service calls.

Hex Function Number	Description
0	Terminate program
1	Read keyboard and echo
2	Display character
3	Auxiliary input
4	Auxiliary output
5	Print character
6	Direct console I/O
7	Direct console input
8	Read keyboard
9	Display string
A	Buffered keyboard input
B	Check keyboard status
C	Flush buffer, read keyboard
D	Disk reset
E	Select disk
F	Open file
10	Close file
11	Search for first entry
12	Search for next entry
13	Delete file
14	Sequential read
15	Sequential write
16	Create file
17	Rename file
19	Current disk
1A	Set disk transfer address
21	Random read
22	Random write
23	File size
24	Set relative record
25	Set vector
27	Random block read
28	Random block write

Table 2–8: DOS services

When DOS services a request that requires device access, DOS will translate this request according to a standard set of rules imbedded in code. These rules are uniform across all devices, from simple output-only parallel devices to complex input and output devices, such as disks.

These requested services, once converted to a specific command, are then passed to a certain set of routines that process the command. These routines are

Hex Function Number	Description
29	Parse file name
2A	Get date
2B	Set date
2C	Get time
2D	Set time
2E	Set/reset verify flag
2F	Get disk transfer address
30	Get DOS version number
31	Keep process
33	CONTROL-C check
35	Get interrupt vector
36	Get disk free space
38	Get country-dependent information
39	Create sub-directory
40	Write to file/device
41	Delete a directory entry
42	Move a file pointer
43	Change attributes
44	I/O Control for devices
45	Duplicate a file handle
46	Force a duplicate of a handle
47	Return text of current directory
48	Allocate memory
49	Free allocated memory
4A	Modify allocated memory blocks
4B	Load and execute a program
4C	Terminate a process
4D	Get the return code of a child
4E	Find match file
4F	Step thru directory matching files
54	Return current setting of Verify
56	Move a directory entry
57	Get/set date/time of file

Table 2–8: DOS services (*Continued*)

not common to all devices; rather, each device has a unique set of routines. These routines are the actual DOS device drivers.

DOS has device drivers for each of the devices attached to the PC. Each service request, however complex, is eventually converted by DOS into a series of simple driver commands and passed to the appropriate device driver.

Translating Service Calls to Device Driver Commands

Device drivers are designed to handle simple commands from DOS. The two most common DOS services used to access devices are interrupt 21's read (ah = 14) and write (ah = 15). These DOS services are relatively complex and may not be translatable to single device driver commands. DOS will issue as many commands to the appropriate device driver as necessary to satisfy the DOS service request.

For example, a program that writes to the disk may issue a write command—interrupt 21h (ah = 15)—that happens to append data at the end of the file. DOS may have to process this single service request by issuing several commands to the disk device driver. The first of these driver commands will need to find more space on the disk for the new data. A driver command will be issued to read the File Allocation Table in which the information on disk space is kept. Then, if there is room on the disk, DOS will write the new data to the disk file by issuing a write command to the disk device driver. Lastly, DOS will update the disk to indicate the time of last access by issuing another driver command to write to the disk. Although this scenario has been simplified, the idea here is that DOS converts a single service request into one or more device driver commands. This is shown in figure 2–4.

Now that you have seen how DOS processes requests for device access by passing the request in the form of smaller, simpler commands to the device driver, you are ready to explore device drivers themselves.

The DOS Device Driver

Device Drivers for New Devices

DOS device drivers are device-controlling software routines that actually become part of DOS. Because these programs are written to Microsoft-designed specifications, DOS can recognize these new devices and can integrate them with the rest of its standard devices. Once DOS knows about these devices through their specific device driver routines, the devices can be accessed as easily as the standard disk and screen devices.

The rules and regulations that Microsoft specifies for device drivers also allows their installation. You will see more about these rules shortly. It is these rules that make device drivers present a uniform interface to the DOS kernel. As you will see, DOS needs to know only that the device driver is controlling a

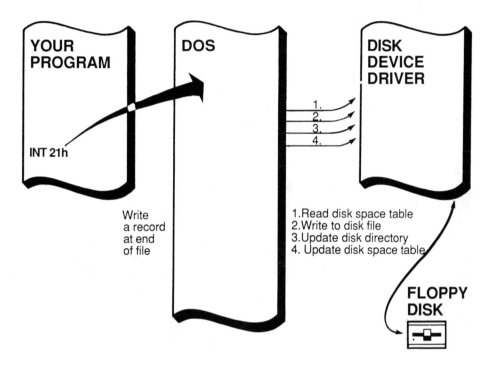

Figure 2–4: A simple service request to write data to the file converted to several possible disk device driver commands. DOS manages each request, making one or more simple driver commands until the request is complete.

particular device, identified by a device name, and that it is capable of processing standard device driver commands.

Without installable device drivers that have a uniform interface to DOS, adding a new device to DOS would be difficult. The manufacturer of the device would have to supply a custom-modified version of DOS in order for you to use the new device. This would create a number of problems. First, you could not use a newer release of DOS unless the newer version was also modified to control the new device. Second, because each device manufacturer uses different methods of modifying DOS, incompatibility problems would arise.

The DOS device driver is the most universal and meaningful method of software control for devices. New devices become standard devices in DOS, available for accessing at any time, from within programs and outside of programs, such as from the command level.

Replacement Drivers (ANSI.SYS)

Occasionally you may find that the standard device drivers built into DOS (disk, screen, etc.) do not accomplish what you need to do. For example, you may need a console driver that provides control for a color card that displays more colors and resolution than the CGA/EGA driver. To handle this situation, you can replace an existing device driver with a customized one.

This is the technique employed by the popular ANSI.SYS device driver provided with DOS. The ANSI.SYS driver is a replacement device driver for the standard console device driver. Over the past few years, the American National Standards Institute (ANSI) has designed a set of standard *escape sequences* that can be used to perform specific functions for any video monitor and keyboard (an escape sequence is a group of characters preceded by an escape character, ASCII 10h). These functions include such things as setting foreground and background colors, turning on and off reverse video display, and assigning special codes to designated keys on the keyboard. These standard escape sequences provide greater "portability" for software programs, because they allow developers to create programs that require complex control of the monitor and keyboard without any regard for the specific hardware involved.

Thus, you may add device drivers to DOS for two reasons: first, to add support to DOS for devices that are not part of the standard set of DOS devices, and second, to replace the original device driver with a new one that may have more capability or portability than the old one.

Looking at Old and New Device Drivers

As we discussed earlier in this chapter, DOS manages requests for device access from programs by issuing commands to the appropriate device driver. Each device driver contains the name of the specific device it is controlling, and DOS locates the appropriate device driver by searching through the list of installed device drivers.

DOS maintains a linked list of the device drivers starting with the nul: device. The device driver for nul: is the first in the list and contains a pointer to the next device driver. In turn, each device driver points to the next. The pointer for the last device driver will contain the value −1, thus signaling the end of the list.

DOS manages the standard, replacement, and new device drivers using a relatively simple mechanism. As shown in figure 2–5, the list of DOS standard device drivers begins with nul: and continues with con:, aux:, and so forth. These device driver programs reside in the area of the PC memory that DOS uses. Whenever a new device driver is installed, DOS inserts it in the list just after

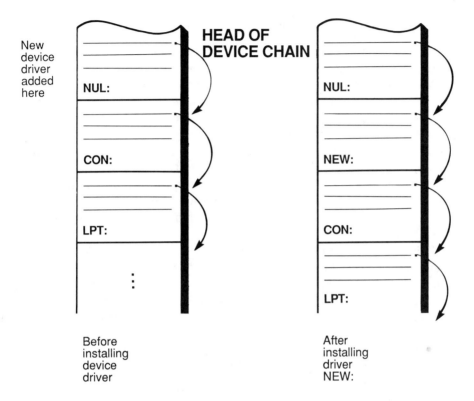

Figure 2–5: What the list of DOS device drivers looks like before and after we add a new device driver. Note that each device driver contains the device name and a field that points to the next device driver.

the nul: device. This allows you to replace a standard device driver, because any device request will cause DOS to search this list starting from the first, which is nul:. If you replace a standard device with one of your own, DOS will find the new device first and will never reach the original device of that name, which is now second in the list. Similarly, new devices with new device names will be added to this list. Thus, DOS will be able to access new, replacement, and standard device drivers simply by searching this list.

This list of DOS device drivers is called the *device chain* and is a linked list of the actual device driver programs. To access drivers all DOS needs is a pointer to the first item, the device nul:. DOS can then find the rest of the device drivers.

Customized Drivers for Standard Devices

Besides writing drivers for new devices, you can always improve upon the DOS standard device drivers. Let's explore this for a moment.

With the exception of the nul: device, which must be the first in the device chain, all of the DOS standard drivers can be replaced by alternate drivers. Improved drivers for the standard prn:, com1: and clock$ devices can be installed into DOS. The prn: driver is especially likely to be replaced, because many printers have features that are not accessible using the standard prn: driver. For example, you might need to get a status from the printer that the normal prn: driver does not handle; such a status might be used to determine whether the printer is in text or graphics mode or whether the printer is out of paper. You might also want to send special vector commands for plotting, using routines built into an intelligent printer.

Another candidate for replacement is the com1: driver. You could add your own customized version in order to change the speed of data transfer through the serial port by having your device driver detect a certain character sequence. This would greatly ease the procedures for controlling the serial port device, because it would eliminate the need to issue a special DOS command to perform this function. Your own language could be formed.

The standard PC clock driver is used to retrieve or set the time and date. You can write a driver for the clock$ device to support a special hardware device that stores the date and time (this may be integrated along with other hardware on a multifunction board). A new clock$ device driver will have to understand how the hardware clock/calendar works, be able to control the setting of the time and date, and be able to perform other tasks, such as allowing user programs to access the clock as a timer for pulses. The concepts of replacing standard DOS drivers with customized versions will be developed further in later chapters. In fact, we will develop examples of con:, prn:, and clock$ device drivers that replace the standard device drivers that DOS supplies.

The possibilities for using customized device drivers are endless. For example, one interesting use of a con: replacement would be to simulate a DVORAK keyboard, on which the keys are in different positions than on the standard QWERTY keyboard. The purpose of the DVORAK keyboard is to place the most used keys together, supposedly to facilitate faster typing. Another con: replacement could be a terminal emulator, a software program that allows the PC's normal screen and keyboard to simulate a keyboard of a specific terminal. This is useful when the PC is used to communicate to a mainframe computer. Such an emulator would solve the problem that arises when the PC's function key codes are not recognized by the mainframe computer. You could create a new keyboard/screen driver to translate the PC's function key codes to those that the mainframe computer can recognize.

Deviceless Drivers

We have discussed drivers for new peripheral hardware devices and drivers that replace standard DOS ones. Another type of drivers also exists: those that do not control real hardware devices. Commonly known as *virtual devices,* these device drivers simulate a hardware device. There are numerous examples. The RAM disk is a virtual disk that can improve the speed of "disk-bound" applications (those with lots of disk activity). The RAM disk driver reserves memory to simulate bytes on the disk and manages this memory as if it were the real disk. Reads and writes to this RAM disk do not go out to a real disk but rather are sent to the memory reserved by the RAM disk. Thus, instead of spending time waiting for a disk to access the data at disk speeds, the RAM disk can access the data at memory speeds. Later on in this book, we will devote two chapters to designing and implementing a RAM disk device driver.

Overview of a Driver's Program Structure

A device driver program consists of five parts: the Device Header, data storage and local procedures, the STRATEGY procedure, the INTERRUPT procedure, and the command-processing routines (see figure 2–6). We will discuss each of these parts in this chapter as well as in later chapters as we develop actual device drivers.

Let's look at these five sections briefly. The beginning of a device driver program does not contain code the way normal programs do. Rather, the Device Header contains information about the device driver itself. This information is used by DOS and includes the device name for the driver and the pointer to the next driver.

The second part of the driver is used to store local data variables and local routines and procedures.

The third and fourth parts of the device driver contain what Microsoft calls the STRATEGY and INTERRUPT procedures. These two procedures are integral to processing each command that is passed from DOS to the device driver. They allow DOS to pass control to the driver. We will discuss these in detail later in this section.

The last part of the driver contains the actual code routines that process each of the commands that DOS passes to the device driver.

How DOS Communicates with the Driver

Let's see how DOS and the driver work together. Figure 2–7 shows that when DOS calls the driver it passes a packet of data to the device driver. This call might be to write to a RAM disk or send some special character to a graphics

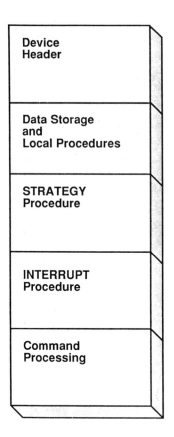

Figure 2–6: The five basic parts of the device driver.

board. This packet of data is called a Request Header and contains information for the device driver such as the data to be written to the device. DOS sets up the registers ES and BX to contain the address of the Request Header when DOS calls the device driver.

The Request Header   The Request Header is a packet of data that is passed from DOS to the driver; this data tells the driver what to do and the location of the data involved in the work to be performed. For example, if DOS wants to write a character to the serial port, it needs to specify the write command and the character (data) to write. Therefore, DOS needs to pass to the driver both a command and some data. Both of these are contained in the Request Header. (Note: Do not confuse the Request Header with the Device Header. The Device Header tells DOS about the driver program, and the Request Header contains

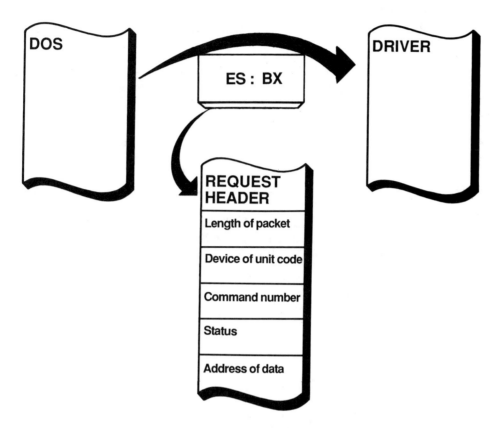

Figure 2–7: DOS calling the device driver with a pointer to the request header. Contained within the request header is the command code for the device driver. This instructs the device driver what functions to perform on the device for DOS.

the data on which the device driver works.) The Request Header is described in table 2–9.

As shown in table 2–9, the Request Header is a variable-length packet of data. Within this packet, the length of the Request Header is contained in the first entry. The second entry contains the unit code of the device. This is normally used when more than one device is attached to the controller. An example of this is the floppy disk controller, which often controls two drives. The A: drive would be unit 0, the B: drive would be unit 1, and so forth. The third entry is the command code, which tells the device driver what action to take. The fourth entry is reserved for use by DOS (its use is undocumented). Finally, the last

Entry #	Length (bytes)	Description
1	1	Length in bytes of this Request Header (varies with the amount of data in the request)
2	1	Unit code of the device
3	1	Command code
4	2	16-bit word for the status upon completion
5	8	Reserved for DOS
6	Varies	Data specific for a command

Table 2–9: Definition of the Request Header that is passed to the device driver. The Request Header contains information regarding its length, the unit code of the device, the command to be performed, and data for the command.

entry is the data field. This field varies in length depending on the command in the third field. You will see more of this data field in later chapters.

DOS automatically sets up a Request Header whenever a program makes a request to DOS that involves a device driver. This data packet resides in DOS's reserved memory space and is built with information provided from the calling program. The address of the Request Header is passed to the device driver when DOS passes control to the driver. This address is stored in the driver's local storage area. You need to specify both the segment address and the offset address of this Request Header, because the Request Header can be anywhere in the PC's 640k memory. Specifying only an offset address assumes that the packet will be in the current segment of memory in which the program is executing. DOS passes this segment and offset address in the ES and BX registers of the 8088, respectively.

You will see more of Request Headers in later chapters when you process driver commands in the various device drivers.

Driver Calls from DOS   You might assume that each command DOS passes to the driver involves a single call to the driver. Alas, this is not the case. Recall that DOS expects the device driver to have two procedures defined—the STRATEGY and the INTERRUPT procedures. Let's explore the two-step call that DOS makes to the device driver for each command request.

The Two-step Call to the Device Driver   Each time DOS asks the device driver to process a command, for example a read or write command, DOS will call the device driver twice. The first time, DOS will pass control to the STRAT-EGY procedure defined for the device driver. The second time, the device driver will be called at the address specified for the INTERRUPT procedure.

Think of the STRATEGY procedure as instructions that perform the set-up and initialization for the driver. The INTERRUPT procedure then uses the information from the STRATEGY procedure to process the command request from DOS. This process is shown in figure 2−8.

Although it is not apparent from the DOS manuals, this two-step approach allows DOS to distinguish between the request for the driver (the set-up) and the actual work to be done by the driver. You can think of this two-step process as analogous to writing a check and cashing it at a bank. You may write the check on Monday (the set-up) and not cash it (the work) until Friday. In the same way, DOS notifies the driver that there is work to be done with a call to STRAT-EGY and then calls the driver again through INTERRUPT to allow it to work.

Let's develop a scenario to see why STRATEGY and INTERRUPT are nec-essary. Assume that your PC, through DOS, can multitask, which means that

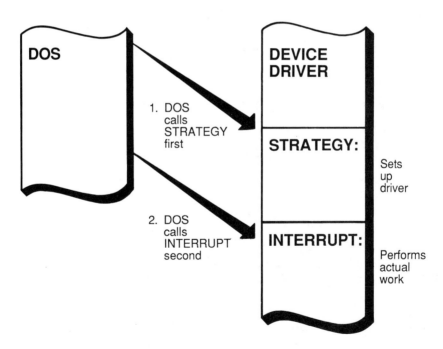

Figure 2−8: When DOS issues a request to the device driver, the device driver is actually called twice.

it can perform several tasks at one time. This permits you to do more work in a given period of time. Although DOS does not provide this capability currently, it is an important feature that future versions of DOS will have.

It is likely that the various multiple tasks will differ in importance. If you prioritize these tasks in order of importance, the calls they make to device drivers also need to be prioritized. For example, a task that is downloading a file using a modem might be higher priority than a task that is updating a collection of addresses. The two-entry point approach allows DOS to do this. DOS can process the device driver calls in the priority order of the calling task. This is accomplished by linking into a chain all driver request calls (all the calls to STRATEGY) and putting all the actual work calls (calls to INTERRUPT) into another chain in priority order. After DOS calls all the device drivers through the STRATEGY routine, it then inspects the INTERRUPT chain to see which one has the highest priority. The closer a device driver is to the beginning of the chain, the higher its priority.

Without this two-step mechanism to set up and perform the actual work, DOS would call the device drivers on a first-come, first-served basis.

To make this scenario a little easier to understand, let's use an example. Assume that there are three outstanding driver requests:

- Request A has a low priority

- Request B has a medium priority

- Request C has a high priority

The STRATEGY and INTERRUPT chains are illustrated in figure 2–9.

As this figure shows, each program request for device driver service causes DOS to place the first (set-up) call in the STRATEGY chain and the second (work) call in the INTERRUPT chain. When three programs make device driver requests, the set-up calls are linked into the STRATEGY chain in order of arrival, and the work calls are placed in the INTERRUPT chain in priority order. Think of this as writing checks in order during the week and then sending out the most important checks first on Saturday. In effect, you are handling all the incoming items as they arrive but sorting the most important items into a work list for processing.

What the STRATEGY Procedure Does   When the driver is first called, the STRATEGY routine saves the address of the Request Header, which is contained in the ES and BX registers. This is done to prepare the driver for the second call to its INTERRUPT procedure.

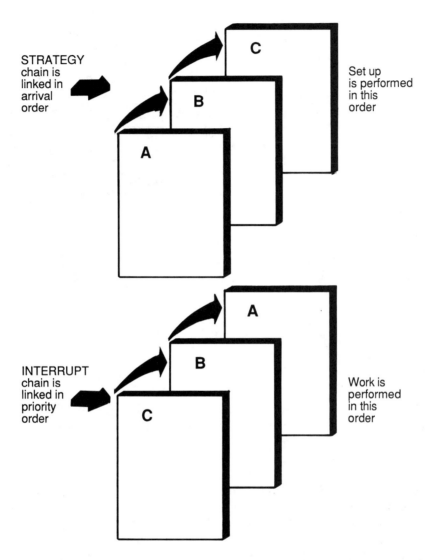

Figure 2–9: The effect of three driver requests. DOS links the three requests in the STRATEGY chain in the order of arrival. The INTERRUPT chain sorts the same three requests in order of priority.

The sequence of events is shown in figure 2–10, in which DOS prepares to call the device driver by building a Request Header, and in figure 2–11, in which DOS calls the device driver at the STRATEGY procedure.

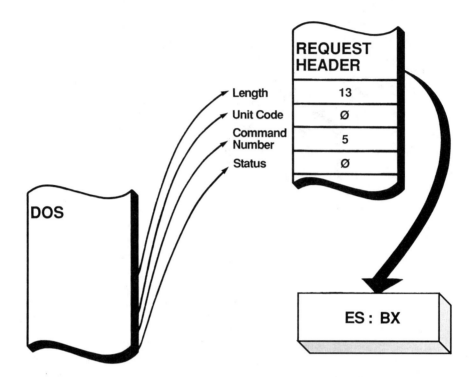

Figure 2–10: DOS preparing to call the device driver for the first time. A Request Header which contains information for the device driver to process is built. The address of this Request Header is stored in the ES and BX registers.

What the INTERRUPT Procedure Does   When DOS calls the device driver the second time, it does so through the INTERRUPT procedure. Here the real work of the device driver begins. The Request Header that contains information for the driver to process is handled by the code located in the INTERRUPT procedure. Control is then passed to the command-processing routines. This is shown in figure 2–12.

Block and Character Devices

DOS drivers need to distinguish between character and block devices. Recall that a block device transfers data in groups of characters, and character devices transfer data one character at a time. Of the control commands that the device

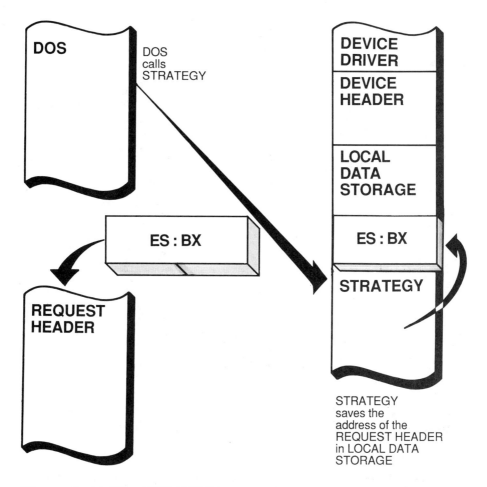

Figure 2–11: The STRATEGY procedure storing the address of the Request Header in local data storage.

driver issues to the device, some are appropriate to character devices and some to block devices. The Media Check command is one example of a block device command. Because diskettes can be formatted for single-sided or double-sided use, the DOS disk device driver needs to know which format has been used. To find out, DOS issues a Media Check command to the disk device driver, which in turn reads a block of data from the disk. From the information returned in this block of data, DOS can determine if the diskette is single- or double-sided. The Media Check command is unique to disk block devices and is not applicable to character devices.

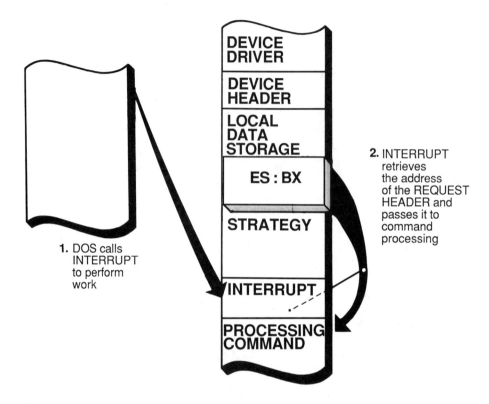

Figure 2–12: How the Request Header is retrieved by the INTERRUPT routine. Control is then passed to the command processing routines.

DOS also needs to know which type of device its driver is controlling in order to determine the appropriate commands the device driver can perform. This topic will be covered in detail in later chapters as we develop various device drivers.

Device Driver Commands

So far, we have provided a lot of material on the various parts of a device driver. The information presented so far has been on the flow of control around and in device drivers. Now we have come to the core of device drivers: command processing.

Recall that programs make service requests of DOS. Each of these service requests translates to a specific set of commands that the driver understands. These commands are common to all device drivers.

Commands defined by Microsoft for device drivers are listed by device type in table 2–10 for character devices and in table 2–11 for block devices. Note that not all of the commands are available for all versions of DOS.

In the following pages, we will review these driver commands. You can find out more about them in chapter 9.

Initialization Command

Command 0 is the Initialization command. DOS always calls the device driver with this command immediately after the driver is loaded into memory. This allows the device driver to perform its device's unique initialization functions,

Number	Command Description
0	Initialization
1–2	Not applicable
3	IOCTL Input
4	Input
5	Nondestructive Input
6	Input Status
7	Input Flush
8	Output
9	Output With Verify
10	Output Status
11	Output Flush
12	IOCTL Output
13*	Device Open
14*	Device Close
15*	Not applicable
16*	Output Til Busy
17–18**	Undefined
19*	Not applicable
20–22**	Undefined
23**	Get Logical Device
24**	Set Logical Device

$$* = \text{DOS version } 3+ \text{ only}$$
$$** = \text{DOS version } 3.2 \text{ only}$$

Table 2–10: The list of commands that are applicable for character-oriented devices. There are 25 commands, numbered from 0 through 24. Commands 13 through 16 are valid for DOS versions 3.00 or 3.10. Commands 17 through 24 are valid for DOS versions 3.20 or greater.

Number	Command Description
0	Initialization
1	Media Check
2	Get BIOS Parameter Block
3	IOCTL Input
4	Input
5	Not applicable
6	Not applicable
7	Not applicable
8	Output
9	Output With Verify
10	Not applicable
11	Not applicable
12	IOCTL Output
13*	Device Open
14*	Device Close
15*	Removable Media
16*	Not applicable
17–18**	Undefined
19**	Generic IOCTL
20–22**	Undefined
23**	Get Logical Device
24**	Set Logical Device

* = DOS version 3+ only
** = DOS version 3.2 only

Table 2–11: The list of commands that are applicable for block-oriented devices. There are 25 commands numbered from 0 through 24. Commands 13 through 16 are valid for DOS versions 3.00 or 3.10. Commands 17 through 24 are valid for DOS versions 3.20 or greater.

such as writing a message to the console, clearing registers or other set-up functions. DOS service calls can be issued from within the driver program only when the driver is processing the Initialization command. For all other commands, the driver cannot issue DOS service calls; if it attempts to do so, DOS will crash, because the driver is part of DOS and DOS cannot call itself (when the driver is processing the Initialization command it is not considered to be part of DOS). When the driver returns control to DOS, DOS will assume that the driver is ready to perform other commands.

Media Check and Get BIOS Parameter Block Commands

Commands 1 and 2 are applicable to block devices only; these will be discussed in chapters 7 and 8. You need not concern yourself about these commands at this time.

IOCTL Input Command

Command 3 is IOCTL Input. You will see IOCTL often—it stands for I/O Control. This command is used by the device driver to return control information to the program regarding the device. For example, if the device is a printer, you can have the device driver return status information, such as the baud rate at which the printer device is set to receive data. When the driver returns I/O control information to the program, it is called *input*. Although this is quite useful, it is not a normal feature of device drivers. There are many reasons for this. The first is that there is only one DOS call that allows I/O control—DOS service 44h. Most programs do not use this DOS service, because they do not expect a device driver to return this type of information. The second reason is that adding I/O control to a device driver is not easy; the device driver does not know what type of information to return. For I/O control to work properly, both the program issuing an IOCTL call and the device driver accepting IOCTL calls must agree on the information to be passed back and forth.

Input Command

Command 4 is the driver's Input command. This command instructs the driver to read data from a device. This data is then returned to DOS, which then returns it to the calling program.

Nondestructive Input Command

Command 5 is the Nondestructive Input command. This command is used to determine whether there is any data from the device without actually passing the data back to the calling program through DOS. This is often a means of testing to see whether you are ready to read from the device. If there are characters waiting to be read, you simply issue an Input command. If there are no characters, you tell DOS that there are no characters to be read. In effect, you are looking ahead to see whether there is any input.

Input Status Command

Command 6 is Input Status. This call allows DOS to check the status of a device. If the device is not ready, no Read or Input call would be issued. On the other hand, if the status of the device indicates a ready condition, a Read command for the device could be issued immediately. Note that this command is not the same as the Nondestructive Input command. The Input Status command checks the status of a device; the Nondestructive Input command checks for a character in the device's buffer.

Input Flush Command

Command 7 is the Input Flush command. This command allows you to discard any input for the device by clearing out the buffer associated with the device. This can be important in just about any program. Suppose a program asks the user if he or she wants to erase all the files on a disk. If you did not use a call to flush or get rid of all characters that had been typed ahead, you could accidentally erase all files if the type-ahead buffer happens to contain the character that the user would press to erase all the files. You should use this call to get rid of any possible extraneous characters just before you read some critical data from a device.

Output Command

Command 8 is the Output command. This command tells the driver to write a specified amount of data to the device.

Output With Verify Command

Command 9 is the Output With Verify command. This command is similar to the Output command but has one additional function: when the VERIFY switch is set ON at the DOS command level, the driver will read the data after each Write. This is a useful feature when you need to know that critical data has actually been written properly. Of course, this presumes that the device you are writing to can read the same data. This feature is not meaningful for printers and screens, because such devices cannot read what was written.

Output Status Command

Command 10 is the Output Status command. This command instructs the driver to check the status of the device you are using for output. This has no meaning for devices that can only read data.

Output Flush Command

Command 11 is the Output Flush command. This command tells the driver to send a signal to the device, informing it that any data currently still in the output device should be discarded.

IOCTL Output Command

Command 12 is the IOCTL Output command. This command is sent to the driver when DOS needs to pass data to the driver for use by the driver itself. This is not the command that DOS uses to send data to the device. If this command is implemented in the device driver, you use the data to control the device rather than to send data to the device. As mentioned previously with reference to the IOCTL Input command, programs that issue the IOCTL call must agree with the device driver on what information is to be passed.

Device Open Command

Command 13 is the Device Open command, which can be used by the driver to keep track of all the times the device is opened. This command is available in DOS versions 3.0 or later if the Device Open/Device Close/Removable Media bit in the Attribute word of the Device Header is set. You will see how this is set in a later section of this chapter. The driver can perform a number of functions when it receives this call. For example, it can reinitialize a device or prevent access to the device if another program has opened it.

Device Close Command

Command 14 is the Device Close command. You can use this command if the DOS version is 3.0 or later, the Device Open/Device Close/Removable Media bit is set, and a program closes the device. This command is used with the Device Open command to implement a count of the number of opens for the device. In turn, the driver can perform a function for the device, such as flushing any information that may be within the driver out to the device.

Removable Media Command

Command 15, the Removable Media command, is valid for block devices. This command asks the driver whether the device contains removable media.

Output Til Busy Command

Command 16 is the Output Til Busy command. This command is valid for character-oriented devices if bit 13 is set in the Attribute word of the Device Header. This command is most useful for printers that have a buffer to receive data. Instead of outputting a small number of characters, the driver would send enough data to fill the printer device's buffer. This minimizes the number of times that DOS needs to call the driver with data for the printer. The PRINT spooler program uses this feature.

Other Commands

Commands 17 through 24 are advanced commands that are available under DOS versions 3.20 or later. These commands will be treated in detail in chapter 9.

Tracing a Request from Program to Device

To finish this section, we will look at an example of what happens along the way as a program calls a device driver. Let's assume that a program has asked you to type some data from the keyboard into a file called MYFILE. Let's say the program will then write the data into a record in a disk file. Figure 2–13 shows the various steps performed by your program, DOS, the disk device driver, the BIOS, and the device itself.

When you have typed in all the data, your application program will issue a Write to a previously opened disk file named "myfile." The data to be written is contained in a record or variable block of data named "newdata." The Write is a call to a library function in the programming language used in your program. This function will take your Write command and convert it to a DOS function call. There are many DOS calls that write data to a file; for this example, we will assume that it is simply a Write Sequential File Record call. The library function is generally written in assembly language. It will set up the data for a Write Sequential File Record as DOS needs it and will then call DOS by issuing interrupt 21h.

The first part of DOS that is used is the *call handler,* which is where control goes when the interrupt 21h is executed. It is here that DOS inspects the type of function that the caller has set up (as found in the AH register). In this case the function is hex 15, which means Write Sequential File Record to DOS.

DOS then internally locates the relative position of the disk file to which your record is to be written. Next, DOS finds the starting address, relative to

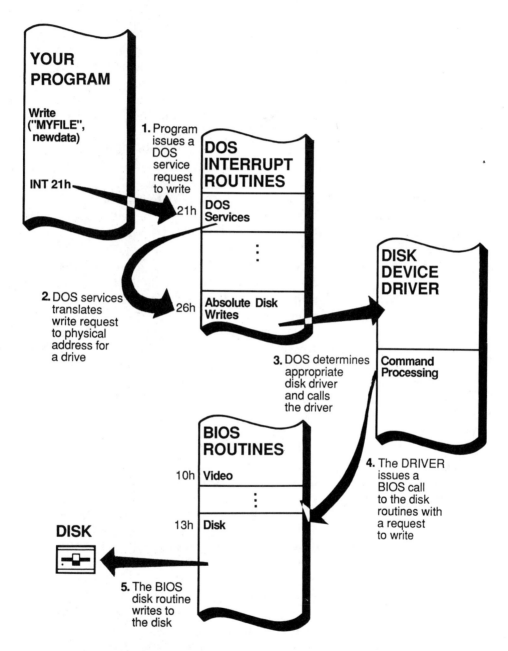

Figure 2–13: Block diagram of the paths taken to write a block of data to the disk.

the beginning of the disk, of the file "myfile." This is done by searching through the disk directory for information on where "myfile" resides. The relative position of the record to be written to is added to the position of the start of the file; this yields the absolute position on the disk at which the "newdata" record should be stored. This part of the DOS call handler is responsible for determining all the information for a given disk and all the information for the files on this particular disk.

The next step performed is that this data is sent to the general disk handler, which is also the DOS Absolute Disk Write routine (also known as interrupt 26h). This is called from the DOS kernel.

Interrupt 26h or the DOS Absolute Disk Write routine requires two basic pieces of information. The first piece of information identifies the drive to which DOS needs to write the data. The second piece defines the location of the write relative to the beginning of the disk (that is, the starting sector). The reason for this routine is that DOS treats all disks alike: all of the sectors of each disk are numbered from 0, starting at the beginning of the disk. Thus, the file handler finds the relative position of the record within the file, and the general disk handler calculates the relative position within the disk. What the DOS Absolute Disk Write routine does is to determine the actual physical address to which the data should be written, using the relative information calculated by the original int 21h service Write Sequential. The physical address referred to here is the relative physical sector on the disk to which data should be written. Finally, this information is passed to the disk device driver.

In turn, the disk device driver is responsible for converting the physical address to a track, a sector, and a surface; it also performs the actual write.

A point should be made here about the BIOS routines. The disk device driver uses the disk BIOS routines to perform the actual reads and writes to the disk. This is accomplished by executing an interrupt 13h after specifying the appropriate subfunctions for read or write.

Once the disk device driver has finished the write operation, it will return a status to the Absolute Disk Write routine, which, through the DOS call handler, will return the status to the original calling program. Just as the original write request passed through the DOS call handler, the Absolute Disk Write routine, the disk device driver, and the disk BIOS routine, the status "percolates" through the layers back to the original program.

So the device driver plays a vital role in ensuring that your data is written to the disk. This illustration of the complicated process of writing a record to the disk has involved many steps. You have seen the relative roles of the device driver, DOS, and the BIOS. The interactions for all device drivers are similar to those in the example.

The Mechanics of Building Device Drivers

In this last section of the chapter we will cover the mechanical aspects of building device drivers. We will survey the steps in building device drivers and the utility programs needed for each step.

Writing a Device Driver Program

A device driver is a program that is built using a set of rules. DOS has defined these rules in order for the device driver to work properly. We will define the various sections of code that make up a device driver. Each of these sections contains assembly language instructions or data. Instructions in 8088 assembly language are written and grouped into procedures. Variables are defined in memory and are used to store data that DOS passes to the device driver. Other variables are also needed to store text messages that will be displayed on the video screen.

A word processor is used to input the source text of a device driver. Then the text is assembled using the Macro Assembler. The object code output from the assembler is linked to create an executable file. Then this executable file is converted to a memory image file for proper execution by DOS.

Once the device driver is built, it is loaded into memory. This is done by specifying the device driver file in the CONFIG.SYS file and rebooting DOS. During its initialization phase, DOS will read the CONFIG.SYS file and copy the contents of the device driver file into DOS's memory. Then DOS will call the driver to initialize it. DOS initializes all device drivers to ensure that they are ready for use. For more information on DOS initialization, refer to appendix C.

Assembling the Device Driver

After you key in the source code of the device driver using a word processor, the device driver is ready to be assembled. Use the Macro Assembler as follows:

```
C>masm DRIVER,DRIVER,DRIVER,DRIVER
The IBM Personal Computer MACRO Assembler
Version 1.00 (C)Copyright IBM Corp 1981

Warning  Severe
Errors   Errors
0        0
```

The first command parameter to the Macro Assembler is the name of the text source file. The second command parameter specifies the name of the file that will contain the generated object; the file name extension will be .OBJ. The third command parameter specifies the name of the file that will contain the output listing from the Macro Assembler; it will have a file name extension of .LST. The fourth and last command parameter specifies the name of the cross-reference file.

Linking the Device Driver

This step will convert the object file into an executable file that is commonly called an .EXE file. These files are normally program files that are executed by DOS and are prepared by the linker when it reads the object code. However, when device drivers are .EXE files, they cannot be executed by DOS, because the device drivers must be in .COM format.

As was mentioned earlier in this section, device drivers are memory image files. This means the driver must be in .COM format. First, create the .EXE file by using the linker program, LINK:

```
C>link driver,driver,driver,null

IBM Personal Computer Linker
Version 2.00 (C)Copyright IBM Corp 1981, 1982, 1983

Warning: No STACK segment
There was 1 error detected.
```

This step will create two separate files: the .EXE file and DRIVER.MAP, which is the listing of the .EXE file in terms of variable names and addresses used. Note that there was one error detected. Do not be alarmed by this. A STACK segment can be defined within a program and is used as a storage area for variables. The LINK program has been designed to assume that all programs will define a STACK. Most device drivers do not define a STACK segment, because a device driver is part of DOS and not an ordinary program. DOS has defined a stack, so device drivers use it instead of defining one.

Convert .EXE to .COM Format

You need to convert the device driver to a .COM format program, which is a memory image of what the driver should look like when it is loaded into memory. This is a requirement of DOS and is accomplished by using the EXE2BIN.COM utility that is supplied with DOS:

```
C>exe2bin driver.exe driver.sys
```

Note here that we have named the .COM output file DRIVER.SYS. Device driver files should be named .SYS for several reasons. The first is that if they are left named .COM after the EXE2BIN conversion, there is the possibility of someone accidentally executing the driver program, causing the inevitable machine crash.

Caution: You cannot run a device driver directly the way you would a normal program!

The second reason that device drivers should be named .SYS is that .SYS has become the standard naming convention for such programs. This distinguishes the device driver files from all other files.

Installing Device Drivers into DOS

Before rebooting the machine to try out any device drivers, you will need to tell DOS to load these drivers into memory. This is done by creating a file named CONFIG.SYS that resides in the root directory of the disk from which you are booting. Assuming that you use the C: drive as your hard disk, build the CONFIG.SYS file as follows:

```
C>copy con: config.sys
break = on
device = driver.sys
^Z
1 File(s) copied
```

When DOS initializes, it will read the CONFIG.SYS file and look for any device driver files. It detects these by searching for the keyword *device*. DOS then reads this file into memory. For more information, refer to appendix C.

If you already have a CONFIG.SYS file, you can include a device driver in that file by adding the following line to your CONFIG.SYS file:

```
device = driver.sys
```

After you create a CONFIG.SYS file, you can simply warm-start your machine by depressing the CONTROL, ALT, and DEL keys. The new device driver will be loaded into memory.

Summary

In this chapter, we have covered the hardware aspects of devices and controllers, the programming of devices using BIOS interrupts, and the need for software to control devices; we have also discussed the reasons why device drivers offer the best solution to the problem of device access by DOS. In addition, we have covered how the device driver is used by DOS and how the device driver controls devices. In short, you now have enough information about the external features of device drivers to look into writing a device driver.

In the next chapter, we will present a simple device driver. You will learn about the structure of a device driver program, the Device Header that describes to DOS the type of device we are controlling, the INTERRUPT and STRATEGY routines, and the driver command processing.

Questions

1. Could I use the same device driver under PC-DOS as well as MS-DOS?

2. Are BIOS calls required in device drivers?

3. Why is DOS version 2.00 or greater required for adding device driver programs?

4. How many printer devices does DOS normally support?

5. How many serial devices does DOS support?

6. If a new device driver is added to DOS, which standard device does it follow?

7. If I add two new devices to DOS, for example, new1:, then new2:, what order would they be in after nul:?

Answers may be found in appendix E.

Chapter 3

A Simple Device Driver

This chapter will show you a real but very plain device driver program, one that makes a simple "beep" and prints a message on the screen. Although this example will not win awards for functionality and processing power, it does allow us to clearly present the various parts of a device driver and to develop the 8088 assembly code for each section. These code sections will contain the functions that DOS requires in a device driver—some that we have already covered and some new ones as well.

Because this is the first device driver in the book, we will cover each section in detail. What you will learn in this chapter will prepare you for the device drivers in the following chapters.

What Does a Device Driver Look Like?

Listing 3–1 is an empty MASM 8086/8088 assembly language listing of a program we will call the Simple Device Driver. This driver will refer to a nonexistent device named SIMPLE$. The source code is composed only of comment statements; such a source code is known in programming circles as a *skeleton*. The comment statements are grouped together in sections delineated by a banner consisting of asterisks. Each of these sections is required for a device driver. Some of the sections are definitions that are necessary to the Macro Assembler; others are necessary for the procedures you need for the device driver itself. We will describe each section in detail in this chapter. At the end of this chapter, we will present the finished result.

An Overview of the Simple Device Driver Sections

Listing 3–1 will be expanded as we go on and will form the basis for the Simple Device Driver as well as for all the other device drivers that you will encounter

---

Listing 3–1: A skeleton listing from which we will develop the simple device driver.

```
     ;*******************************************************************
1    ;* COMMENT SECTION HEADER                                         *
     ;*******************************************************************


     ;*******************************************************************
2    ;* INSTRUCTING THE ASSEMBLER                                      *
     ;*******************************************************************


     ;*******************************************************************
3    ;* MAIN PROCEDURE CODE                                            *
     ;*******************************************************************


     ;*******************************************************************
4    ;* DEVICE HEADER REQUIRED BY DOS                                  *
     ;*******************************************************************


     ;*******************************************************************
5    ;* WORK SPACE FOR THE DEVICE DRIVER                               *
     ;*******************************************************************


     ;*******************************************************************
6    ;* THE STRATEGY PROCEDURE                                         *
     ;*******************************************************************


     ;*******************************************************************
7    ;* THE INTERRUPT PROCEDURE                                        *
     ;*******************************************************************


     ;*******************************************************************
8    ;* YOUR LOCAL PROCEDURES                                          *
     ;*******************************************************************


     ;*******************************************************************
9    ;* DOS COMMAND PROCESSING                                         *
     ;*******************************************************************


     ;*******************************************************************
10   ;* ERROR EXIT                                                     *
     ;*******************************************************************


     ;*******************************************************************
11   ;* COMMON EXIT                                                    *
     ;*******************************************************************


     ;*******************************************************************
12   ;* END OF PROGRAM                                                 *
     ;*******************************************************************
```

---

in this book. Each of the various sections of this driver plays a vital role in contributing to all device drivers. These sections are described below.

Comment Section Header

All well-written programs have brief descriptions at the beginning of the program that identify what the program does, when it was created, the author's name and address, and other information. What appears obvious to the author of the program may not be clear to another person, and even the original author forgets. Other kinds of information that can be placed in this section can be a history of program modifications, including the dates of the changes made to the program as well as a description of each change.

Instructions to the Assembler

When you are writing in assembly language, you will need to include numerous commands to the Macro Assembler that are not actual instructions to the processor. Rather, these commands instruct the Macro Assembler itself to perform some functions on behalf of your program. Examples of commands include how the program will use memory, some control over the listing that the Macro Assembler produces, and definitions that the program will use.

Main Procedure Code

This is the next section within the Simple Device Driver. This section is responsible for defining to the Macro Assembler the overall organization of the program. For the Simple Device Driver, as well as for all other device drivers in this book, there is only one main procedure. The Simple Device Driver sounds a beep and then prints a string. Device driver programs are built with a single main procedure for a number of reasons. The first reason is that DOS assumes that the device driver is a single procedure. Recall from the *Macro Assembler Reference Manual* that when procedures are called, control passes to the first instruction at the beginning of the procedure; the procedure then exits through a RETURN instruction. Because the device driver begins with a Device Header table, DOS cannot call the main procedure of the device driver. Instead, DOS uses information in the Device Header table to pass control to the device driver. The second reason that there is just one procedure is that there is no reason for device drivers ever to contain more than a single procedure. Code that is modularized into procedures may always be contained within the main procedure. So, for all the device drivers in this book, you will see many procedures nested within the main procedure.

Device Header Required by DOS

This is a table of fixed values that DOS requires of all device drivers and that is located in the beginning of the program. The Device Header defines five key values to DOS. The first value tells whether there is another device driver following the Simple Device Driver. The second value tells DOS what type of device this device driver is controlling (block or character). The third and fourth entries in the Device Header are addresses of the STRATEGY and INTERRUPT procedures in the device driver. Although there two procedures are not procedures in the strictest programming sense, they behave like procedures in that they both execute RETURN instructions to exit. DOS expects each to perform according to the rules that you saw in chapter 2. Then, upon completion, they exit back to DOS through a RETURN instruction. Recall from chapter 2 that DOS uses a two-step call to request work from a device driver. The STRATEGY routine is the first routine called, and the INTERRUPT routine is the second. The last entry in the Device Header table is the name of the device for the device driver.

Work Space for the Device Driver

This is the section in the program in which data storage is defined for any variables the Simple Device Driver will need. Variables are defined here that store information for controlling the device in the Simple Device Driver. The space these variables consume is defined here as well.

The STRATEGY Procedure

This section contains code for performing the first task of the Simple Device Driver in processing DOS requests, which is usually the task of handling set-up requirements. As the name implies, the STRATEGY routine performs set-up work; it is the first of two calls from DOS.

The INTERRUPT Procedure

This section contains the code for the second part of command processing. DOS passes control to this procedure during the second call to the Simple Device Driver. The INTERRUPT procedure has a command for the device as well as the data for the device.

Your Local Procedures

This section contains any necessary procedures the Simple Device Driver will require. These local procedures support and assist the Simple Device Driver program.

DOS Command Processing

This is the heart of all the device drivers. Whenever a program uses the Simple Device Driver, a command, such as one telling the device to read or write, is passed through DOS to the Simple Device Driver. This command is then actually performed by the code in this section. We presented a summary of the standard commands that drivers process in the previous chapter in table 2–9; in this chapter we will begin to implement these commands.

Error Exit

This is the section of code in which the Simple Device Driver processes any errors that occur.

Common Exit

This is the section of code that the Simple Device Driver will execute when it is finished processing the driver request that DOS has made, such as a command to read or to write. This section of code returns status information to DOS, indicating a successful operation.

End of Program

This is the section of code that signals to the Macro Assembler the end of the Simple Device Driver.

We have seen, briefly, the twelve sections that make up an assembly language program for a device driver. Now let's take a closer look at the actual code in each of these sections.

Instructing the Assembler

Every device driver program has a certain number of assembler directives. Assembler directives are special instructions to the Macro Assembler that do not cause the Macro Assembler to generate instruction code. Such instructions merely tell the Macro Assembler to treat your code in a particular way, depending on which directive you use.

The Microsoft MASM Macro Assembler used in this book allows directives and instructions to be entered in any column. For ease of reading, we will use four basic columns (see listing 3–2). The first column is for labels and variable names. This allows you to glance at the listing to see where you have defined these labels and variables. The second column is for instruction code and directives to the Macro Assembler (think of this second column as the commands you need in the program). The third column contains required information or options for instruction code and directives; the number of options will depend on the command in the second column. The fourth and last column is an optional comment field in which you explain what a particular command is doing. Now let's examine the code.

The first thing you will see in column one of listing 3–2 is the name cseg. This is the name you choose for the label you are assigning to a *segment*. In appendix A, *segment* is the term that defines a block of memory of up to 64k. The term *segment* is also an assembler directive that tells the assembler that you are defining a block of memory. The assembler will calculate how large this segment is (up to 64k) after it assembles the program. The directive segment defines the start of the 64k-maximum segment, and the ends directive defines the end of the segment. The required ends directive is found in the End of Program section.

Listing 3–2: Assembler directives for the Simple Device Driver set the program into the segment called cseg Here.

```
;****************************************************************
;*        INSTRUCTING THE ASSEMBLER                           *
;****************************************************************


!              !        !          !
!column 1      !column 2!column 3!column 4

cseg           segment  para       public 'code'
simple         proc     far
               assume   cs:cseg,es:cseg,ds:cseg

labels         code     options   comments
               macros
```

Additional information for the segment directives follows the directive segment. The word *para* is a directive that tells the assembler to align this segment in memory on a paragraph boundary. In appendix A, a *paragraph* is defined as 16 bytes, which, in hex, is a 0 in the least-significant position. This fits in nicely, because the address of a segment assumes that the low-order address position is 0h. The next piece of information on the first line is the *public* directive, which tells the assembler that the segment containing your code can be referenced externally from another program. The last piece of information after public is *code,* which tells the assembler this segment will contain instruction code. You may notice that there is only one segment directive in this program; this indicates to the Macro Assembler that only a single block of memory is being used in your device driver program.

The second line in listing 3–2 defines to the assembler a procedure named *simple.* The directive *proc* defines the start of your main procedure (at the End of Program section, endp will signal the end of the simple procedure). The keyword *far* on this line is required and tells the assembler that this is a far procedure, which can be anywhere in memory. When DOS calls the Simple Device Driver, it will use the long form of the call instruction which is known as a *far call.* These far calls are calls to routines that cannot be assumed to be within the same 64K segment as the calling routine. Such calls take slightly longer to execute than *near calls.* The *simple* procedure will contain all of your code for the device driver. Thus, your short device driver program will have one procedure within one segment.

The *assume* directive on the third line tells the Macro Assembler that the CS, ES, and DS registers of the 8088 CPU will reference items that are defined within this one segment (see appendix A for a detailed explanation of segment usage). Your Simple Device Driver program will need to use these three registers. Thus, *cs:cseg* means that *cs* will refer to items in the current segment *cseg.* Programs can thus use the CS register to reference the code segment, the DS register to reference the data segment, and the ES register to reference the extra segment. The CS, ES, and DS registers contain the starting address of the code segment, the extra segment, and the data segment for the current segment. Because all three segments share the same segment, the addresses that are generated for these segment registers will be relative to the beginning of the *cseg* segment in your program. Normally, each of these three registers has a separate segment or block of memory assigned. In this Simple Device Driver program, each of these three segment registers will share the same block of memory in the segment named *cseg.* In other device driver programs this may not be the case.

You will find these assembler directives in every device driver program. They may differ depending on whether or not they share segments.

Main Procedure Code

The main procedure is where the Simple Device Driver program starts. Contained within this main procedure is the code that performs all the work. You must tell the Macro Assembler that the instruction code and data addresses start at this location.

The *begin* label is a label given to the start of the program:

```
;****************************************************************
;*        MAIN PROCEDURE CODE                                   *
;****************************************************************
;

begin:
```

Normally, you should use this *begin* label to instruct the assembler (by specifying this label to an *end* directive at the end of the program) that you want the program to start execution at *begin*. However, *begin* is used here more as a place-marker. Device driver programs, like many other normal programs, need not start execution at the beginning of the program. Rather, *begin* is placed at address 0 to mark the beginning of the program. Right after the *begin* label comes the data and instructions for the Simple Device Driver.

The Device Header Required by DOS

We now have our comments, main procedure, and assembler directives set up. The Device Header is a table of required data for DOS. Device drivers, as you have seen, come in different types. When DOS loads a device driver, it needs to identify the type of device driver it is, so you should specify this in the Device Header.

A device driver can replace a standard DOS device driver, such as the *con:* driver, or it can be a totally new driver also at which DOS knows nothing. In either case, DOS needs to know if it is a character-oriented driver or a block-oriented driver. Recall from chapter 2 that character devices transfer data one character at a time, and block devices transfer data in groups of characters. This identification information for DOS is contained in the Device Header, as shown in listing 3–3. Each of the entries in the table comprising the Device Header will contain varying information of varying lengths. The assembler knows the length of your entries from your use of *define* directives: define 8-bit bytes using *db*, 16-bit words using *dw*, and double 16-bit words using *dd*.

The five entries that constitute the Device Header will be examined in the next sections.

**Listing 3–3: The Device Header, which specifies the device characteristics
and driver information to DOS**

```
;*****************************************************************
;*        DEVICE HEADER REQUIRED BY DOS                          *
;*****************************************************************
next_dev        dd      -1              ;no other device drivers
attribute       dw      8000h           ;character device
strategy        dw      dev_strategy    ;address of 1st dos call
interrupt       dw      dev_int         ;address of 2nd dos call
dev_name        db      'SIMPLE$ '      ;name of the Driver
```

The Next Device

The variable *next_dev* is a double word (dd in MASM) that is used to indicate to DOS whether another device driver "follows" this one. If there is, the segment and offset addresses of the next device driver are placed in *next_dev*. As you saw in chapter 2, this is how DOS keeps track of drivers and puts them in a chain. If no driver follows this one, a −1 for both the segment and offset address indicates to DOS that there is only one device driver. The address order for *next_dev* is offset first and segment second.

The technique of using *next_dev* allows DOS to place more than one device driver program into one file; DOS saves time by having to open and read only one file instead of several. DOS uses the *next_dev* field to link the device drivers into the device chain. As was discussed in chapter 2, device drivers are linked in a chain, and new device drivers are added to the beginning of the chain after the *nul:* device driver. DOS uses this device chain to search for the appropriate device driver whenever a device access is requested.

If there is another device driver following the Simple Device Driver, you should place the segment and offset address in this field. Thus, this field tells DOS where the next device driver is. The last device driver will have the −1 in both words.

Attribute

The label *attribute* contains a 16-bit word that describes to DOS what type of driver this is. Table 3–1 summarizes the more popular bit settings. In chapter 9, we will define other bits.

As you can see from table 3–1, the *attribute* word can describe many types of devices. The entries in this table are discussed briefly in the next sections; they will be covered in greater depth in later chapters. In the Simple Device Driver example, the *attribute* word is set to 8000h. If you convert this to binary

Bits	Description for Bit Set to 1
0	Standard input device
1	Standard output device
2	Null device
3	Clock device
4	Special
5–10	Reserved (must be set to zero)
11	Device supports OPEN/CLOSE/REMOVABLE MEDIA*
12	Reserved (must be set to zero)
13	Non-IBM Format
14	IOCTL
15	Character device (set to 0 for block device)

*DOS 3.0 and later

Table 3–1: The *Attribute* bits for the Device Header

you will find that bit 15 is on, which signifies that this is a character device. Note that all other bits are set to 0 to prevent DOS from assuming that other *attribute* bits are desired.

The STRATEGY and INTERRUPT Routines

As you learned in chapter 2, a STRATEGY procedure is a set of instructions that performs the set-up for the device driver, the INTERRUPT procedure uses the information from the STRATEGY procedure to perform the required work. Recall from chapter 2 that DOS uses a two-step mechanism to pass commands to the device driver. The STRATEGY procedure is called first, followed by a call to the INTERRUPT procedure.

In listing 3–3, *strategy* and *interrupt* are the names for the addresses of the two routines that DOS uses in the device driver. These 16-bit words contain addresses that DOS uses to get to the two routines, *dev_strategy* and *dev_int*. The first time, DOS passes control to the device driver program at the address you specify at *strategy*. The second time, DOS will enter the device driver at the address you specify at *interrupt*.

Device Name

Device name is the name assigned to the character device in the device driver. You may recall from chapter 2 that character devices are named in the device driver and disk devices have drive letters assigned. Use this name in a program

---

Listing 3–4: Some local variables needed for the Simple Device Driver

---

```
;****************************************************************
;*          WORK SPACE FOR OUR DEVICE DRIVER                    *
;****************************************************************
rh_off          dw          ?          ;request header offset
rh_seg          dw          ?          ;request header segment
msg1            db          07h
                db          'The Waite Group Simple Device Driver! '
                db          0dh,0ah,07h,'$'
```

---

to make DOS call the device driver. In listing 3–3, the *dev_name* label contains the name *SIMPLE$,* which defines to DOS the name of the device driver, in the Special Device Header. You may name the device anything as long as it meets two DOS requirements. First, the name cannot be NUL, because DOS does not allow the replacement of this particular reserved name. Second, the name must be less than or equal to eight characters in length and must be padded with blanks. We have named this device *SIMPLE$.* Because the *dev_name* field is eight characters in length and *SIMPLE$* is seven characters in length, we have added a blank to the end of '*SIMPLE$* ' so that the name is '*SIMPLE$* '.

Work Space for the Device Driver

As shown in listing 3–4, Work Space for the Device Driver is the section of the Simple Device Driver that contains the local variables for procedures. The INTERRUPT procedure requires two variables, and the *initial* procedure for the Simple Device Driver, which we will present later, requires a single variable for a print message. These three variables will be referenced from within the respective procedures but we defined them here because defining the variables in one section makes it easier to find them later.

The three variables occupy memory right after the Device Header table. The variables *rh_off* and *rh_seg* will be used to store information that DOS passes to the device driver. You will see the significance of these two variables soon. The variable *msg1* will be printed when the device driver program executes. The string of bytes you define for *msg1* is composed of hex codes and of text contained within quotation marks. Hex codes allow you to control the cursor on the screen or use special functions of the PC. In this case, the *07h* is the code for a "beep" (CONTROL-G). This makes the speaker beep before the program prints the text of the message. The *0dh* and *0ah* signify that the message is followed by a carriage return and line feed to prevent other messages from writing to the same screen display line. Finally, the PC beeps again. At the end of the string of bytes you must signal to the assembler that your variable is complete by using the special symbol "$," enclosed in quotation marks.

As was mentioned in chapter 2, the Request Header is the name given to the packet of data that is passed from DOS to the device driver. You may also recall that DOS will call the device driver twice for any command requested of a device driver by an applications program. The variables *rh_seg* and *rh_ofs* are used to save the segment and offset addresses of the Request Header, which contains the information that the device driver needs in order to process a command.

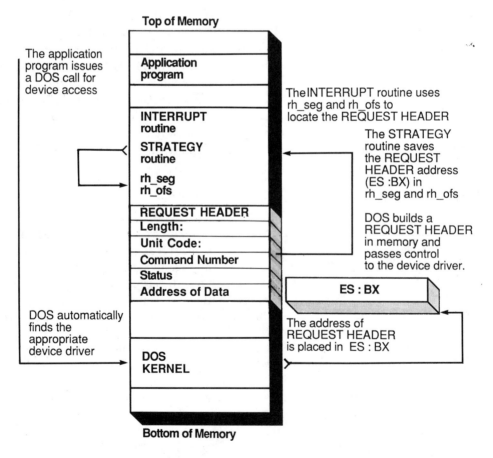

Figure 3–1: DOS builds a Request Header in memory and passes the address in ES:BX to the device driver. The strategy routine saves this address in variables rh__seg and rh__ofs.

Figure 3–1 traces the path of the Request Header from DOS through the device driver. The program requesting a service from the Simple Device Driver first passes control to DOS. DOS then takes the request and builds a Request Header that contains the request. Control is then passed to the STRATEGY routine, which saves the ES and BX registers in the variables *rh_seg* and *rh_ofs*. Lastly, the INTERRUPT routine uses these two variables to retrieve the Request Header in order to process the requested command.

The STRATEGY Procedure

The STRATEGY procedure (see listing 3–5) contains the first piece of actual program instruction code in this program. It is the code executed when DOS calls this device driver for the first time. This is called the STRATEGY procedure because this is the mechanism that DOS will use to plan or structure all the device driver requests (an initialization function).

The only task of the STRATEGY code is to save the address of the Request Header into variables we call *rh_seg* and *rh_off* so that the driver can determine what command and data it is to process. Once the address is saved in *rh_seg* and *rh_off*, control returns to DOS to allow DOS to continue processing by calling the device driver again. The device driver can now use *rh_seg* and *rh_off* to access the code for processing in the driver. This will be done with the *interrupt* call, as you will see in the following section.

A *mov* instruction is used to save the ES and BX registers. Note that the *cs* segment override tells MASM to generate addresses relative to the *cs* (code) segment and not the default *ds* (data) segment. The reason for the *cs* segment override is that the *ds* register is not valid when control passes to the device driver. If the *cs* segment override were omitted, the addresses for the two variables would be relative to some unknown value of *ds*. When the STRATEGY routine completes, control returns to DOS.

Listing 3–5: The STRATEGY procedure

```
;*****************************************************************
;*        THE STRATEGY PROCEDURE                                *
;*****************************************************************
dev_strategy:                      ;First call from DOS
        mov     cs:rh_seg,es       ;save request header ptr segment
        mov     cs:rh_off,bx       ;save request header ptr offset
        ret
```

The INTERRUPT Procedure

The INTERRUPT procedure (see listing 3–6) is the section of code that determines what command the device driver will execute and that uses the code for that command within the driver. When DOS calls the INTERRUPT procedure, control is passed to the code, which we have labeled *dev_int*.

The first part of the INTERRUPT code shown in listing 3–6 saves the state of the microprocessor registers. This is done by storing all the registers onto the stack using *push* instructions. Any or all of the registers may be used.

Listing 3–6: The INTERRUPT procedure

```
;*****************************************************************
;*       THE INTERRUPT PROCEDURE                                *
;*****************************************************************
dev_int:                       ;Second call from DOS
        cld                    ;save machine state on entry
        push    ds
        push    es
        push    ax
        push    bx
        push    cx
        push    dx
        push    di
        push    si

;perform branch based on the command passed in the req header

        mov     al,es:[bx]+2   ;get command code
        cmp     al,0           ;check for 0
        jnz     exit3          ;no - exit go to error exit
        rol     al,1           ;get offset into table
        lea     di,cmdtab      ;get address of command table
        mov     ah,0           ;clear hi order
        add     di,ax          ;add offset
        jmp     word ptr[di]   ;jump indirect

;command table
;       the command code field of the static request
;       field contains the function to be performed

cmdtab  label   byte           ;
        dw      init           ; initialization
```

At the end of the device driver, upon exit, you must be sure to restore the original values to the registers. Note that the DOS stack is not large; it will allow only about 20 *push*es. Be careful about how many bytes you push onto the stack. For the most part there is more than enough room for saving the registers.

The second part of the INTERRUPT code is used to find out what command DOS wants the device driver to perform. Recall that the driver is being called from DOS in response to a program requesting that DOS perform a specific function. A "command" code for this function is passed to the device driver in the second entry of the Request Header. Examples of commands or requests are Read, Write, and Initialize. The Simple Device Driver allows only one command to be accepted; this is the Initialize command, which is specified by the value 0.

Each command requires a procedure in the driver to carry out the operation defined for it. Because each command has a unique value associated with it, you can set up a table for all commands, and each entry in the table can contain an address of a procedure in the driver to execute the function. The first entry will contain the address of the procedure to process command code 0, the second entry will contain the address of the procedure to process command code 1, and so on. For example, for ten possible values a table of ten entries is constructed. Each entry then contains the address of the procedure to be executed for the particular ordinal value.

For each command to be processed by your driver, you must use the value of the command code in the Request Header to position into the table (this is commonly called *indexing*). Control is then passed to this address and the code in the procedure is executed. This table is also called a *jump table,* because the *jump* instruction is used to pass control to an address contained in the table.

Let's take a look at the rest of the code in listing 3–6. The first instruction references the Request Header by using the ES and BX registers. The +2 references the third byte, which is the command code for the device driver. Because the command code is a byte value, *mov* puts it into the low-order portion of the AX register, which is AL.

The next two instructions are unique to the Simple Device Driver and will not appear in subsequent device drivers. The reason is that this Simple Device Driver will accept only one command, the Initialize command. The command code (which is now in AL) is compared with 0 (which is the value for Initialize). If it is not 0 it will jump to *exit3*.

The instruction that contains *rol* starts the code to find the procedure for INITIALIZE. The table containing addresses of procedures is composed of 16-bit entries, and the command code is a byte quantity. This presents a problem. If you use the byte value of the command code to index into the table, you will be indexing by bytes. This will give half of the 16-bit address rather than the two-byte address needed. Therefore, in order to index into the table properly you must convert the byte value into a word value. This means that command value 0 gets the first 16-bit address, command value 1 gets the second 16-bit address, and so on. Do this by multiplying the command value by two using *rol*, which is a left-shift instruction.

The next instruction of listing 3–6 retrieves the address of the command table *(cmdtab)*. The *lea* (load effective address) instruction picks up the jump table for determining the proper command procedure to which the driver should jump.

Then the *add* instruction adds the converted command code to the address of the command table. In effect, we are indexing into the table. The index register *di* now contains the address of the procedure for command value 0. The instruction to *mov* a 0 to the AH register is a safety precaution, because the command values will not use AH.

Lastly, an indirect jump through the *di* register passes control to the INITIALIZE procedure and performs this driver's task.

When the INTERRUPT code is called, the device driver jumps to the appropriate routine as specified in this table. In this case, it jumps to the routine that starts at *init*, which we will cover soon. Note that the table *cmdtab* has only one entry, whereas a more complex driver would have several (one for each command).

Your Local Procedures

Local procedures are routines you write to assist in performing device driver functions. In this code you will need to use only one procedure. It is named *init* (to initialize the driver). (See listing 3–7.) Its function here is to make a "beep," display a message to the screen, and "beep" again. These procedures allow you to modularize the driver and, thus, change code without affecting the entire driver.

Listing 3–7: The procedure *Initial*

```
;****************************************************************
;*      YOUR LOCAL PROCEDURES                                  *
;****************************************************************
;
initial proc    near
        lea     dx,msg1         ;initialization
        mov     ah,9            ; message
        int     21h             ;doscall
        ret                     ;return
initial endp
```

The *initial* proc is the procedure that displays a message on the monitor when the device driver is initially loaded by DOS. The text for the message is contained in the variable *msg1,* which was defined in the section Work Space for Our Device Driver. DOS function 9 is used to display a message to the screen.

The *initial* proc is called when the driver is loaded by DOS. DOS calls the device driver with the command number 0, which is initialization. This is always done for every device driver. For this program, you will see the following message on the screen:

```
'The Waite Group Simple Device Driver!  '
```

> **Caution: DOS function calls are allowed only in processing the Initialization command. The function calls allowed are 01h through 0Ch and 30h. Because DOS has not finished initializing itself, using other function calls will cause it to crash. If DOS was reentrant, this would not be true.**

DOS Command Processing

The DOS Command Processing section of a device driver contains the procedures for processing the command codes; in our driver we process only command 0. In listing 3–8, the *init* routine contains two instructions: a call to a procedure named *initial,* which was discussed above, and a jump out to the *exit* procedure.

Few device drivers will be this simple. Most will do much more processing than this, but all will have this structure. In later chapters we will add more commands to this device driver. Each command will require code to perform the

---

Listing 3–8: The *init* procedure

```
;****************************************************************
;*      DOS COMMAND PROCESSING                                 *
;****************************************************************
;
;command = 0     initialization

init:   call    initial                 ;display a message
        jmp     exit2
```

---

requested function. As an example, to pass data to the device, DOS calls the driver with a Write command (command = 8).

The Request Header Status Word

For each command requested of the device driver, DOS expects a success/failure status indicator when the driver is finished processing. The Request Header that DOS passes to the device driver is returned to DOS with the status word set to indicate the outcome. The status word has bits that can be set on to indicate several conditions. Table 3–2 shows the various conditions and bit settings. If there is an error, a 1 in bits 0 through 7 forms the error code. Table 3–3 shows the list of standard DOS error codes.

Note that a combination of the status word bits can be used in any given status. For example, if the driver has processed a request and no error has occurred, the driver must set the DONE bit, but if an operation completes and an error has occurred, both the DONE and the ERROR bits must be set. Additionally, an error code should be returned that tells DOS (and eventually the user) what caused the error. Note that it is up to your driver program to figure out the error and set the right bits.

In the Simple Device Driver, there are only two possible conditions and, therefore, two possible status codes. The first condition is when DOS calls the device driver with command = 0 (Initialization) when the device driver is loaded. The second condition is when DOS has called the device driver with a command other than 0. This can happen in several ways.

For example, assume that you make an attempt to copy the contents of a

Name	Bits	Description
ERROR	15	Set by driver to indicate error—see ERROR_CODE in table 3–3
DONE	8	Must be set by device driver upon exit
BUSY	9	Set by device driver, if needed, to prevent further operations
ERROR_CODE	0–7	Standard DOS error code; see table 3–3
	10–14	Reserved

Table 3–2: Description of the status word. The ERROR, DONE, and BUSY bits may be set.

Hex Code	Description of Error Code
0	Write protect violation
1	Unknown unit
2	Drive not ready
3	Unknown command
4	CRC error
5	Bad drive request structure length
6	Seek error
7	Unknown media
8	Sector not found
9	Printer out of paper
A	Write fault
B	Read fault
C	General failure

Table 3–3: The error codes listed here form the standard error codes for DOS device drivers.

file to *SIMPLE$* (which DOS assumes to be a device) using the following DOS command-level statement.

```
A> Copy simple.asm simple$
```

This statement will cause DOS to call the device driver with command number 8, which is Output or Write (one of sixteen possible device driver commands). Because the Simple Device Driver does not process any commands other than 0 (Initialization), this causes an error.

The following two sections describe the processing for error conditions and normal conditions.

The ERROR EXIT Procedure

In the event of an error, you must provide a means for the device driver to exit the program and tell DOS that something has gone wrong. DOS can then return this error message to the program that requested the device driver. The program might then retry the operation after displaying a message indicating the error. A typical error for a disk might be attempting to write to a diskette that has a write-protect tab. The error that you will see from DOS is:

```
Write protect error writing drive A
Abort, Retry, Ignore?
```

Listing 3–9: The fourth field of the Request Header, a 16-bit status word that contains the value 8103h

---

```
;*************************************************************
;*        ERROR EXIT                                         *
;*************************************************************
;
;Set the Done flag, error flag, and unknown command error code

exit3:  mov     es:word ptr 3[bx],8103h
        jmp     exit1           ;restore environment
```

When the Simple Device Driver encounters an error, control is passed to *exit3*. The error caused by a write to *SIMPLE$* via the copy described above is one such path to *exit3*. As listing 3–7 shows, the command code of 8 will fail the compare with the legal command code 0 in the code of the INTERRUPT procedure. This will cause a jump to *exit3*.

The code for processing errors in the Simple Device Driver is shown in listing 3–9.

As shown in listing 3–10, ES and BX refer to the Request Header, and the fourth byte (relative byte 3) begins the word used to store a status. This 16-bit word returns a code to DOS indicating the outcome of the work performed by the driver. If your program has code that causes a branch to *exit3*, this will set bits in this status field to indicate certain information, such as the fact that an error has occurred, and the type of error encountered. The value *8103h* shown in listing 3–10 is broken down as follows: the DONE bit (bit 8) is set on, the ERROR bit (bit 15) is set indicating an error has occurred, and the ERROR_CODE bit is set to 3 (bits 0 and 1 set on). An ERROR_CODE of 3 is used to tell DOS that an unknown command has been encountered in the Simple Device Driver.

By returning this status to DOS through the Request Header, you ensure that DOS has information concerning the command processed by the driver. In turn, DOS returns this information to the calling program, which can use it to decide how to display an error. We shall examine driver completion without errors in the following section.

The COMMON EXIT Procedure

Upon exit from the device driver, you will need to restore the state of the microprocessor registers as they were before your device driver took control (see listing 3–10).

Listing 3–10: Common exit

```
;****************************************************************
;*        COMMON EXIT                                          *
;****************************************************************
;
;common exits    fall thru code
;        2 sets status to done and noerror
;        1 restore callers es:bx
;        0 restore machine state and exit
;
exit2:                               ; Set done flag and no error
        mov     es:word ptr 3[bx],0100h
exit1:  mov     bx,cs:rh_off    ;restore req hdr to bx and es
        mov     es,cs:rh_seg    ;as saved by dev_strategy
exit0:  pop     si              ;restore all registers
        pop     di
        pop     dx
        pop     cx
        pop     bx
        pop     ax
        pop     es
        pop     ds
        ret
```

The first step in restoring the environment is to set the status value for DOS, because DOS expects to know the status of the operation in the device driver. If the program branched to the *exit3* routine because of an error condition, as described in the preceding section, then it does not need to set the status.

The first instruction at label *exit2* of listing 3–11 sets the Request Header Status word to indicate DONE—*0100h.*

The second step in restoring the environment is to restore the ES and BX register. As you may recall from the section on the STRATEGY procedure, the ES and BX registers were saved in variables *rh_seg* and *rh_off.* These variables held the address of the Request Header; the driver needed to use those registers to process the command and data in your device driver program. Now you must reverse the process and set ES and BX so that DOS gets a status indicator regarding what occurred in the program.

The third step in restoring the environment is to restore all the registers saved on the stack using the *pop* instruction. Keep in mind that the order in which you saved the registers must be reversed when you restore them. Lastly, the *ret* instruction returns control to DOS.

Listing 3–11: The end of program processing consists of the assembler directives that tell the assembler that you are defining the end of the *simple* procedure, as well as the end of the *cseg* segment.

```
;****************************************************************
;*            END OF PROGRAM                                   *
;****************************************************************

simple   endp
cseg     ends
         end      begin

; that's all folks
```

The End of Program Section

This final section (see listing 3–11) is where you ensure that the driver ends properly using MASM directives. You should declare the end of the *simple* procedure, as well as the end of the *cseg* segment, with *endp* and *ends*. On the *end* assembler directive, specify the label *begin*. This tells the Macro Assembler that your device driver begins execution at the *begin* label. The Macro Assembler does this by generating a program start address at *begin*.

The Entire Simple Device Driver

Listing 3–12 is a complete listing of all the code we have developed for the Simple Device Driver.

Building the Simple Device Driver

Listing 3–12 shows the source assembly code for the entire driver. To build the Simple Device Driver, you first need to enter the source code into a file using a word processor. Then you must assemble, link, and convert the code to .COM format. The normal output from the LINK utility is in .EXE format, which contains relocation information and is not usable. DOS does not have the ability to load relocatable code at initialization time. To tell DOS to use the Simple

Listing 3–12: A Simple Device Driver

```
;***********************************************************
;*     This is a simple Device Driver                      *
;***********************************************************


;***********************************************************
;*        INSTRUCTING THE ASSEMBLER                        *
;***********************************************************

cseg            segment para    public  'code'
simple          proc    far
                assume  cs:cseg,es:cseg,ds:cseg

;***********************************************************
;*        MAIN PROCEDURE CODE                              *
;***********************************************************

begin:

;***********************************************************
;*        DEVICE HEADER REQUIRED BY DOS                    *
;***********************************************************

next_dev        dd      -1              ;no other Device drivers
attribute       dw      2000h           ;character device
strategy        dw      dev_strategy    ;address of 1st dos call
interrupt       dw      dev_int         ;address of 2nd dos call
dev_name        db      'SIMPLE$ '      ;name of the Driver

;***********************************************************
;*        WORK SPACE FOR OUR DEVICE DRIVER                 *
;***********************************************************

rh_off          dw      ?       ;request header offset
rh_seg          dw      ?       ;request header segment
msg1            db      07h
                db      'The Waite Group Simple Device Driver! '
                db      0dh,0ah,07h,'$'

;***********************************************************
;*        THE STRATEGY PROCEDURE                           *
;***********************************************************

dev_strategy:                   ;First call from DOS
        mov     cs:rh_seg,es    ;save request header ptr segment
        mov     cs:rh_off,bx    ;save request header ptr offset
        ret
```

Listing 3–12: A Simple Device Driver *(cont.)*

```
;****************************************************************
;*       THE INTERRUPT PROCEDURE                               *
;****************************************************************

dev_int:                    ;Second call from DOS
        cld                 ;save machine state on entry
        push    ds
        push    es
        push    ax
        push    bx
        push    cx
        push    dx
        push    di
        push    si

;perform branch based on the command passed in the req header

        mov     al,es:[bx]+2    ;get command code
        cmp     al,0            ;check for 0
        jnz     exit3           ;no - exit go to error exit
        rol     al,1            ;get offset into table
        lea     di,cmdtab       ;get address of command table
        mov     ah,0            ;clear hi order
        add     di,ax           ;add offset
        jmp     word ptr[di]    ;jump indirect

;command table
;       the command code field of the static request
;       field contains the function to be performed

cmdtab  label   byte            ;
        dw      init            ; initialization


;****************************************************************
;*       YOUR LOCAL PROCEDURES                                 *
;****************************************************************

initial proc    near
        lea     dx,msgl         ;initialization
        mov     ah,9            ; message
        int     21h             ;doscall
        ret                     ;return
initial endp


;****************************************************************
;*       DOS COMMAND PROCESSING                                *
;****************************************************************
```

Listing 3–12: A Simple Device Driver *(cont.)*

```
;command = 0     initialization

init:   call    initial                 ;display a message
        jmp     exit2


;****************************************************************
;*      ERROR EXIT                                             *
;****************************************************************

;Set the Done flag, error flag, and unknown command error code

exit3:  mov     es:word ptr 3[bx],8103h
        jmp     exitl                   ;restore environment


;****************************************************************
;*      COMMON EXIT                                            *
;****************************************************************

;common exits    fall thru code
;       2 sets status to done and noerror
;       1 restore callers es:bx
;       0 restore machine state and exit
;

exit2:                                  ; Set done flag and no error
        mov     es:word ptr 3[bx],0100h
exitl:  mov     bx,cs:rh_off    ;restore req hdr to bx and es
        mov     es,cs:rh_seg    ;as saved by dev_strategy
exit0:  pop     si              ;restore all registers
        pop     di
        pop     dx
        pop     cx
        pop     bx
        pop     ax
        pop     es
        pop     ds
        ret


;****************************************************************
;*      END OF PROGRAM                                         *
;****************************************************************

simple  endp
cseg    ends
        end     begin

; that's all folks
```

Device Driver, you must add a *DEVICE* = command in your CONFIG.SYS file. Note that the CONFIG.SYS file must be in the root directory of your boot disk.

If you already have a CONFIG.SYS file, for the time being, rename your CONFIG.SYS file to another name. You could also include this driver in your CONFIG.SYS file by adding the following line to your CONFIG.SYS file:

```
device = simple.sys
```

Using the Simple Device Driver

After you create a CONFIG.SYS file, you can simply warm-start your machine by depressing the CONTROL, ALT, and DEL keys. DOS will begin loading and you will hear a tone and see the following message:

```
The Waite Group Simple Device Driver!
```

Congratulations! You have just loaded the Simple Device Driver!

What You Can Try

You can customize the Simple Device Driver by changing the contents of *msg1* to any string you desire. As a suggestion, try using your name in the message that is displayed.

If It Does Not Work

Because this driver is very simple, you should not encounter any problems installing it. However, there is always the possibility of making mistakes along the way. Here are a few things to look for if problems develop.

First, look for any typing mistakes. Most of the time, the Macro Assembler will catch mistyped variable names, but any values that were keyed in incorrectly will not be caught by MASM. Print out a copy of the MASM listing output and compare it with the source in listing 3–12. Reassemble the driver if you make any changes to the source.

Second, if there are no apparent source errors, look for errors in the LINK stage. Note that there will be one error message ("Warning: No Stack Segment") from a normal LINK of a device driver. Any other error will require going back to the source to see how the error was generated. Normally, errors from the LINK step occur when the segment definitions are out of order or incorrect.

Check to see that the order and the sequence of the assembler directives *segment, assume, proc, endp, ends,* and *end* match those in listing 3–12.

Next, check to see that EXE2BIN has been used to convert the driver into .COM format. This is important, because DOS does not expect any code or data relocation information in the device driver file.

Lastly, ensure that the name of the file has been correctly specified in the *device* command for the CONFIG.SYS file.

Summary

The Simple Device Driver presented in this chapter is the simplest device driver imaginable. It does nothing but beep at you when it initializes. The material you have seen in this chapter is very important, however. You can build on it because it has all of the sections necessary for a complex device driver.

We have looked at a sample device driver and have broken it down into pieces that are more manageable and understandable. You should now understand the reasons for each of the various sections and why DOS expects each one in a certain format.

Questions

1. Are DOS calls allowed in a device driver?

2. What instruction would DOS use to call your device driver?

3. What is the purpose of the STRATEGY procedure?

4. Within the Device Header, there is an entry that tells DOS if it is the only device driver. Which entry is this? What is the reason for this?

5. When is the device driver initialized?

6. How many characters in length could the name of a device be in a device driver?

Answers may be found in appendix E.

Chapter 4

A Console Device Driver

In the last chapter, we developed a simple device driver in a step-by-step fashion. The new simple driver became part of DOS. In this chapter, we will develop a console device driver that will control the keyboard and screen. This driver, called *con:*, will replace the standard DOS device driver for the console, which is also called *con:*. When the device name of a user-supplied driver matches the name of an existing device, as it does in this case, the new driver effectively replaces the old one. This is what we will be doing in this chapter: replacing the standard console driver *con:* with a new enhanced driver, also called *con:*.

The Console Device Driver

The standard driver that controls the keyboard and screen for the PC is known as the *con:* device. This device is an integral part of DOS and is the primary interface between the user and the PC. Almost all programs use the *con:* device in this manner. As we develop our Console Device Driver, you will see what happens when a program requests keyboard input, how a character is displayed on the screen, and some of the control functions that are largely invisible to you but that you may have wondered about.

For example, you may have noticed that you can type ahead in DOS (this is the ability to type characters faster than the program can accept them). The type-ahead function is handled by the BIOS interrupt routine for the keyboard (9h). Occasionally, you may have noticed that certain programs cannot use your type-ahead characters. Within DOS, there is a command to "flush" out the contents of the keyboard buffer (the storage area in which your type-ahead characters were stored). The console driver is responsible for flushing characters from the keyboard buffer when the DOS service Ch is used from within a program.

In developing our Console Device Driver, we will expand many of the sections that were used in writing the Simple Device Driver in chapter 3. Like all device drivers, this one will contain some sections that are common to all device drivers and other sections that are tailored to this driver. Many of the sections that were summarized in a rather quick manner in chapter 2 will be treated in more detail in this and following chapters. Our goal is to bring you closer to how drivers work in an input/output mode.

Designing Our Console Device Driver

Before you can write a program, you need to determine how it should be implemented. This is true of writing a console device driver. The two questions that arise in determining how to implement this driver are: How should you write the code to control the console and what features do you want the Console Device Driver to have.

Design Issue #1: ROM BIOS vs. Input/Output Instructions

The first design issue for a console driver concerns the types of instructions to use for input and output. You have a choice of using ROM BIOS calls or direct access via IN/OUT instructions. Note that the console driver cannot use DOS calls, because it is considered part of DOS.

Should you use ROM BIOS calls or direct I/O calls? If a driver makes use of ROM BIOS calls, other machines that use that driver will also have to contain identical, or functionally identical, ROM BIOS routines. This may rule out some PC clones. If a device driver uses direct I/O calls, other machines must have similar devices and must address them in the same manner.

It is important to understand that the ROM BIOS routines also use IN/OUT instructions to control a particular device. Device drivers that use direct I/O calls rather than BIOS do so for speed or because there are no ROM BIOS routines that access the device.

For the Console Device Driver in this chapter, we decided to use the ROM BIOS method for device control. This decision allows the Console Device Driver to be used on a wide variety of PCs, regardless of the particular keyboard or screen attached. By using the ROM BIOS for I/O, we are, in effect, masking or hiding a great deal of the machine-dependent programming from the user.

In this and future chapters we will be noting differences between using BIOS for I/O and using direct I/O calls.

Design Issue #2: Features of the Console Device Driver

The second issue in designing a Console Device Driver is deciding what features should be included. Because DOS supplies a console device driver as part of its standard complement of drivers, we chose to make our replacement console device driver somewhat unusual (or else why replace it?). Because one of the features of the PC is the ability to produce sounds, we can use this built-in ability to produce sounds whenever a keystroke is entered using the keyboard. In effect, we are going to design a device driver for a musical keyboard.

Characters that users type in will cause the PC's speaker to sound with short tones. Numbers will have high pitches, letters will have very high pitches, and the function keys will have low pitches.

ROM BIOS Calls for the Console Device Driver

You may recall from chapter 2 that the console device is actually composed of two parts that must be controlled: the keyboard and the screen. The keyboard ROM BIOS routines are referenced through interrupt 16h and are described in table 4−1. The video-services ROM BIOS routines are referenced through interrupt 10h and are described in table 4−2. For more details on what each of the interrupt services are, refer to chapter 2 or to appendix B.

In summary, the standard console device driver is composed of a keyboard device handler as well as a screen device handler. We use standard ROM BIOS interrupts to control these two devices.

Assembly Language Conventions

In the previous chapter, we used assembly language instructions to get information from and return it to the Request Header. Let's examine the code we used in the Simple Device Driver and see how we can make it easier to understand.

Examine the following *mov* instruction:

```
mov es: word pointer[bx]3,8100h
```

ah	Service
0h	Read next keyboard character
1h	Check for available character
2h	Get shift status

Table 4−1: The three services for the keyboard interrupt. In this chapter, we will be using only the first two services of this BIOS interrupt.

ah	Service
0h	Set video mode
1h	Set cursor size
2h	Set cursor position
3h	Read cursor position
4h	Read light-pen position
5h	Set active display page
6h	Scroll window up
7h	Scroll window down
8h	Read character and attribute
9h	Write character and attribute
ah	Write character
bh	Set color palette
ch	Write pixel dot
dh	Read pixel dot
eh	Write character as TTY
fh	Get current video mode
13h	Write character string

Table 4–2: The services provided by the video display service interrupt 10h.

Its purpose is to store 8100 hex into what DOS has defined as the status word of the Request Header. The location in memory at which this value must be stored has an offset address of the contents of the BX register incremented by three. The segment in which the Request Header is located is contained in the ES register. The assembler phrase *word pointer* is used to indicate to the assembler that the memory location being referenced is a word and not a byte.

There are two problems with the use of this assembler construction. The first problem is that the word pointer phrase is annoying, for it breaks up the flow of the instruction. The second problem is that if DOS changes the location of the status word in the Request Header, we will have to go through the program line by line, changing all references from 3 to the new location of the status word. For the current versions of DOS, the status word is located at offset 3, but this could be changed in future versions, although it is not likely.

We can eliminate this problem by using equates in our program, as follows:

```
status field    equ  3
          .
          .
          .
mov ES:word pointer status_field[BX],8100h
```

However, note that this type of construction still includes the *word pointer* phrase. The next section describes a method that can be used to eliminate this problem.

Structures

The macro assembler (MASM) has a definition type called *struc,* which is short for *structure*. Structures are used to define a group of data fields in a certain sequence. The size of each of the fields in this data group is also specified. Thus, *struc* is used to tell the assembler the location and size of each field. After *struc* is defined, when you reference these fields in an instruction you need not instruct the assembler for each instruction. Listing 4–1 shows an example of the Request Header and the fields contained in it defined as a structure.

Structures allow you to build templates for your data. As is true for equates, the assembler does not allocate storage when you define *strucs*. You use these field names to define the relative offset of each field you reference. In addition, these templates save you the effort of specifying to the assembler whether you are using bytes, words, or double words in your instruction references. The assembler has a definition of the variable from the use of the *struc* name.

The *mov* instruction in the section above can now be made easier to read:

```
mov  es:[bx].entry1,8100h
```

The *word pointer* phrase in the instruction has been eliminated, which saves space on the line that can be used more profitably for comments. This

---

Listing 4–1: A structure defined for the Request Header. The *struc* name is rh, and there are four fields of data defined within it. Each of the fields has a define data statement that tells the assembler the size of that field. The *struc* ends with an *ends* phrase.

```
rh         struc    table

rh_len     db       ?

rh_unit    dw       ?

rh_cmd     dd       ?

rh_status  dw       ?

rh         ends
```

---

instruction also eliminates the need to change instruction coding when a variable changes in size. Simply change the size within the definition in the *struc*.

DOS Requests and Console Device Driver Commands

The Simple Device Driver in the previous chapter was capable of processing only one command, the Initialization command. When DOS loads the device driver into memory, it immediately calls the device driver with the initialization command. This allows the device driver to set itself up to handle further calls from DOS. The process of initialization tells DOS that the device driver is ready to process requests.

With the exception of the Initialization command, other commands that device drivers process are on behalf of programs that request device access. Recall from chapter 2 that programs that use a device will issue an appropriate DOS service call through INT 21h. Typically, these are calls to read from or write to a device. DOS translates these requests into one or more commands to the device driver. These commands are contained in the Request Header that is passed to the device driver. The command information is in the form of a number that identifies to the device driver the type of command that DOS expects the device driver to perform.

The commands that DOS expects device drivers to handle are defined by Microsoft and include commands for both character-oriented and block-oriented devices. For the purposes of our Console Device Driver, we will concentrate on the commands that are valid for character devices. These are shown in table 4–3. For a description of each command, refer to chapter 2.

For the Console Device Driver, we will implement only six out of the 25 commands. These six are required for a full-function device driver.

The first command that will be used is the Initialization command (0), which allows the Console Device Driver to perform initialization tasks, such as writing a message to the console and setting up hardware registers.

The second command is the Input command (4), which instructs the Console Device Driver to read data from the keyboard. This data is then returned to DOS, which returns it to the calling program.

The third command is the Nondestructive Input command (5), which is used by the Console Device Driver to test whether the keyboard has any data to be read. In effect, this command is used to look ahead to see whether there is any input.

The fourth command is the Input Flush command (6), which allows the Console Device Driver to discard any data in the keyboard buffer. This is important to Console Device Drivers in situations in which a program does not want

Number	Command Description
0	**Initialization**
1–2	Not applicable
3	IOCTL Input
4	**Input**
5	**Nondestructive Input**
6	Input Status
7	**Input Flush**
8	**Output**
9	**Output With Verify**
10	Output Status
11	Output Flush
12	IOCTL Output
13*	Device Open
14*	Device Close
15*	Not Applicable
16*	Output Til Busy
17–18**	Undefined
19**	Not Applicable
20–22**	Undefined
23**	Get Logical Device
24**	Set Logical Device

```
 * = DOS version 3+ only
** = DOS version 3.2+ only
```

Table 4–3: The list of commands that are applicable for character-oriented devices. Bold-faced commands are those that the Console Device Driver will use.

old keyboard data. In short, this command flushes all characters that had been typed ahead by the user to prevent unwanted characters from being returned to a program.

The fifth command is the Output command (8), which causes the Console Device Driver to write a specified amount of data to the screen.

Finally, the sixth and last command is the Output With Verify command (9). This is similar to the Output command but has one additional function. When the VERIFY switch is set ON at the DOS command level, the driver will read the data after each write. This is useful to ensure that critical data has actually been written. However, the Console Device Driver cannot read back in what was written; this command would make more sense for a disk device driver.

An Overview of Writing a Console Device Driver

Listing 4–2 is the skeleton that we used in chapter 3 to develop the Simple Device Driver. We use it again here to review the various parts of code that need to be written.

Listing 4–2: The skeleton from which we will develop the Console Device Driver.

```
;*******************************************************************
;*      This is a Console Device Driver                           *
;*      Author:   Robert S. Lai                                   *
;*      Date:     2 November 1986                                 *
;*      Purpose: To replace the standard console driver           *
;*******************************************************************


;*******************************************************************
;*         ASSEMBLER DIRECTIVES                                   *
;*******************************************************************


;*******************************************************************
;*         MAIN PROCEDURE CODE                                    *
;*******************************************************************


;*******************************************************************
;*         DEVICE HEADER REQUIRED BY DOS                          *
;*******************************************************************
                                                              ..

;*******************************************************************
;*         WORK SPACE FOR OUR DEVICE DRIVER                       *
;*******************************************************************


;*******************************************************************
;*         THE STRATEGY PROCEDURE                                 *
;*******************************************************************


;*******************************************************************
;*         THE INTERRUPT PROCEDURE                                *
;*******************************************************************


;*******************************************************************
;*         YOUR LOCAL PROCEDURES                                  *
;*******************************************************************


;*******************************************************************
;*         DOS COMMAND PROCESSING                                 *
;*******************************************************************
```

Listing 4–2: (*cont.*)

```
;****************************************************************
;*        ERROR EXIT                                          *
;****************************************************************
;
;****************************************************************
;*        COMMON EXIT                                         *
;****************************************************************
;
;****************************************************************
;*        END OF PROGRAM                                      *
;****************************************************************
;
```

This Is a Console Device Driver

This section describes the device driver, the author, the date written and the purpose of the driver. The Console Device Driver replaces the standard DOS console driver.

Assembler Directives

In this section we will be expanding the assembler directives that you saw in chapter 2. We will add structures called *strucs* for the various requests that DOS will pass to the Console Device Driver (see listing 4–3). Structures relieve us of the burden of remembering numerical offsets which can cause typing errors. They also streamline the amount of code needed by eliminating extraneous words.

Listing 4–3 shows only one segment in our program, the segment named *cseg*. It is to begin on a paragraph *(para)* boundary, it is available to other programs *(public)* and it contains code *('code')*.

We define only one procedure in our program, and it is named *console*. It is a *far* procedure, which means that any routine calling our Console Device Driver must use a long call, one that assumes it is not necessarily in the same segment as the caller. Because this program can sit anywhere in memory, we must use a segment address as well as the offset address.

We define *strucs* for only the commands that are applicable to our Console Device Driver. These are listed below:

- Initialization
- Input
- Nondestructive Input

Listing 4–3: The assembler directives that we will be using for the Console Device Driver. We name our main procedure *console*. All segment registers used (CS, ES, DS) are to have addresses relative to the beginning of *cseg*, which is our only defined segment.

```
;****************************************************************
;*        ASSEMBLER DIRECTIVES                                 *
;****************************************************************

        cseg        segment   para public    'code'
        console     proc      far
                    assume    cs:cseg, es:cseg, ds:cseg

;request header structures

rh              struc     ;fixed request header structure
rh_len          db        ?       ;len of packet
rh_unit         db        ?       ;unit code (block devices only)
rh_cmd          db        ?       ;device driver command
rh_status       dw        ?       ;returned by the device driver
rh_res1         dd        ?       ;reserved
rh_res2         dd        ?       ;reserved
rh              ends      ;

rh0             struc     ;request header for Initialization (command 0)
rh0_rh          db        size rh dup (?) ;fixed request header portion
rh0_nunits      db        ?       ;number of units (block devices only)
rh0_brk_ofs     dw        ?       ;offset address for break
rh0_brk_seg     dw        ?       ;segment address for break
rh0_bpb_tbo     dw        ?       ;offset address of pointer to BPB array
rh0_bpb_tbs     dw        ?       ;segment address of pointer to BPB array
rh0_drv_ltr     db        ?       ;first available drive (DOS 3+) (block only)
rh0             ends      ;

rh4             struc     ;request header for INPUT          (command 4)
rh4_rh          db        size rh dup(?)  ;fixed request header portion
rh4_media       db        ?       ;media descriptor from DPB
rh4_buf_ofs     dw        ?       ;offset address of data transfer area
rh4_buf_seg     dw        ?       ;segment address of data transfer area
rh4_count       dw        ?       ;transfer count (sectors for block)
                                  ;(bytes for character)
rh4_start       dw        ?       ;start sector number (block only)
rh4             ends      ;

rh5             struc     ;request header for ND_INPUT (command 5)
rh5_rh          db        size rh dup (?) ;fixed request header portion
rh5_return      db        ?       ;character returned
rh5             ends      ;
```

Listing 4–3: (*cont.*)

```
rh7             struc    ;request header Input_Flush (command 7)
rh7_len         db    ?     ;len of packet
rh7_unit        db    ?     ;unit code (block devices only)
rh7_cmd         db    ?     ;device driver command
rh7_status      dw    ?     ;returned by the device driver
rh7_resl        dd    ?     ;reserved
rh7_res2        dd    ?     ;reserved
rh7             ends        ;

rh8             struc    ;request header for OUTPUT        (command 8)
rh8_rh          db    size rh dup(?)  ;fixed request header portion
rh8_media       db    ?     ;media descriptor from DPB
rh8_buf_ofs     dw    ?     ;offset address of data transfer area
rh8_buf_seg     dw    ?     ;segment address of data transfer area
rh8_count       dw    ?     ;transfer count (sectors for block)
                            ;(bytes for character)
rh8_start       dw    ?     ;start sector number (block only)
rh8             ends        ;

rh9             struc    ;request header for OUTPUT_VERIFY (command 9)
rh9_rh          db    size rh dup(?)  ;fixed request header portion
rh9_media       db    ?     ;media descriptor from DPB
rh9_buf_ofs     dw    ?     ;offset address of data transfer area
rh9_buf_seg     dw    ?     ;segment address of data transfer area
rh9_count       dw    ?     ;transfer count (sectors for block)
                            ;(bytes for character)
rh9_start       dw    ?     ;start sector number (block only)
rh9             ends        ;
```

- Input Flush
- Output
- Output With Verify

These *strucs* define the fields required for each of the various headers. The assembler pseudo-ops used are *define byte (db), define word (dw),* and *define double (dd).* Each of the Request Headers is named *rhx*, where x is the command number associated with the Request Header. Each field within a Request Header is assigned the name *rhx_y*, where y is the name of the field within the header.

You will notice that some of the Request Headers have a field name *media* with a comment describing it as the media descriptor from DPB. The media descriptor is valid for block devices, such as disks, and is passed to device drivers from a table that DOS maintains regarding the disk. DOS names this internal table the Disk Parameter Block (DPB), and it is used to keep track of the various disks DOS uses.

Main Procedure Code

The main procedure code is simply a label named *begin:*

```
begin:
```

The Device Header

The first code that must be written is the device header for the Console Device Driver. It is not code in the form of instructions, with which you are familiar, but a table of values. This table informs DOS of the particular characteristics that your Console Device Driver will have. Table 4–4 contains the definition of the Device Header; the five required data fields are discussed below.

Name	Start	Length	Description
next_dev	0	8	The offset and segment address of the next device driver (if any) following our Console Device Driver
attribute	8	2	Bit field that defines our Console Device Driver
strategy	10	2	Address of the strategy routine in our Device Driver
interrupt	12	2	Address of the interrupt routine in our Device Driver
dev_name	14	8	The name of our Console Device Driver

Table 4–4: The Device Header fields. The Device Header table must be defined at the very beginning of the device driver program.

Next_dev   Because our program will contain only one device driver, we will set the *next_dev* field to a value that tells DOS there are no other device drivers following this one. We do this by setting both the offset and the segment addresses to −1.

If there were device drivers following the Console Device Driver, we would set the segment address to the current segment, which is *cseg,* and the offset address would be the label that begins the next device driver.

Attribute   The attribute field is a single-word field that has bits set to indicate to DOS the characteristics of the Console Device Driver. Basically, it is the driver's fingerprint. Most of the important attribute bit settings are defined in table 4–5. The other attribute bits will be discussed in later chapters as we build other device drivers.

For our Console Device Driver, we will set bits 15, 1, and 0 to 1. This tells DOS that our device driver is a character device, it is the replacement for the standard DOS output device, and it is also the replacement for the standard DOS input device.

Bit	Value	Description
15	0	Block device driver
	1	Character device driver
14	1	Supports IOCTL DOS call (44h)
13	1	Allows output until busy driver commands for character devices (DOS 3+ only)
12	0	Not used; must be set to 0
11	1	Device Open/Close and Removable Media calls to the device driver allowed (DOS 3+ only)
10–9	0	Not used; must be set to 0
4	1	Special; allows special writes to the screen thru interrupt 29h
3	1	If set, this device driver is the current clock device and replaces the standard DOS clock device driver
2	1	If set, this is the current NUL: device
1	1	If set, this device driver is the standard output device and replaces the standard DOS output device
0	1	If set, this device driver is the standard input device and replaces the standard DOS input device

Table 4–5: The attribute field and the various bits defined. Each bit, if set, will inform DOS of a special characteristic of our device driver. Unused bits must be set to 0.

Strategy and Interrupt The two words that contain the addresses of the STRATEGY and INTERRUPT routines will be represented by the variables *dev_strategy* and *dev_interrupt,* respectively.

Dev_name The device name we will be using is *con,* which is the same as the DOS console driver that we are replacing. We fill the field with *con* and pad out the rest of the field with blanks. Note that we do not add a colon to the name; DOS requires the colon to distinguish *con* as a device name at the operator and program level, not in the device name field.

Here is the Device Header for our Console Device Driver:

```
;*************************************************************
;        DEVICE HEADER REQUIRED BY DOS                      *
;*************************************************************

next_dev      dd    -1                ;no other drivers following
attribute     dw    8003h             ;character,output,input
strategy      dw    dev_strategy      ;Strategy routine address
interrupt     dw    dev_interrupt     ;Interrupt routine address
dev_name      db    'CON    '         ;name of our Console driver
```

Work Space for Our Console Device Driver

Work space is where we put the variables for our driver. The Console Device Driver will require very little work space, because it needs only three variables. The first two variables, *rh_ofs* and *rh_seg,* are used to store the ES and BX registers that are passed to our device driver. The third variable is used to save the character that we will be getting from the keyboard. Here is the filled-in work space code:

```
;*************************************************************
;*       WORK SPACE FOR OUR DEVICE DRIVER                   *
;*************************************************************

rh_ofs    dw    ?    ;offset address of the request header
rh_seg    dw    ?    ;segment address of the request header

char      db    0    ;character saved from the keyboard
```

The STRATEGY Procedure

The code for the STRATEGY procedure is quite simple. DOS expects the Console Device Driver to save the segment and offset address of the Request Header for future references. DOS passes this in the ES and BX registers, respectively. We store these two registers in *rh_seg* and *rh_ofs*. The use of the segment override, *cs:*, insures that when we execute these instructions we refer to the variables through the CS register rather than through the DS register. We do this for several reasons. First, we cannot assume that the DS register is properly pointing to our data when control passes to our Console Device Driver. Second, and more important, we originally set up this program to use only one segment. We reference both code and data through the CS register; data storage shares the same segment as the instruction code.

Because the STRATEGY procedure is called from DOS with a CALL instruction, we use a return *(ret)* instruction to exit to DOS:

```
;*********************************************************************
;*          THE STRATEGY PROCEDURE                                  *
;*********************************************************************

dev_strategy:    mov   cs:rh_seg,es    ;save the segment address
                 mov   cs:rh_ofs,bx    ;save the offset address
                 ret                   ;return to DOS
```

The INTERRUPT Procedure

The INTERRUPT procedure is called by DOS immediately after the STRATEGY procedure. It is this procedure that performs all the work that DOS requests of our Console Device Driver.

DOS passes commands and data relating to the command in the Request Header. The driver must use the Request Header to find out what command it is to perform.

To find the command that DOS expects our Console Device Driver to perform, we retrieve the segment and offset address of the Request Header that we stored during the STRATEGY call. Next, we jump to the routine that is appropriate for the command. Listing 4–4 shows the code that accomplishes this.

In the section called "Instructing the Assembler," we mentioned that we will not be processing all of the possible device driver commands. For the sake of completeness, however, we specify all routines in the command table, *CMTAB*, although we do not write code for all of the routines listed.

Your Local Procedures

For this section, we have only one main routine because we are only implementing one command. Each character that we read from the keyboard will be used to make a different frequency sound on the speaker. This routine is named TONE and is shown in listing 4–5.

Listing 4–4: The INTERRUPT routine and the command table that follows

```
;******************************************************************
;*        THE INTERRUPT PROCEDURE                                *
;******************************************************************


;device interrupt handler - 2nd call from DOS

dev_interrupt:
        cld                             ;save machine state on entry
        push    ds
        push    es
        push    ax
        push    bx
        push    cx
        push    dx
        push    di
        push    si

        mov     ax,cs:rh_seg    ;restore ES as saved by STRATEGY call
        mov     es,ax           ;
        mov     bx,cs:rh_ofs    ;restore BX as saved by STRATEGY call

;jump to appropriate routine to process command

        mov     al,es:[bx].rh_cmd   ;get request header command
        rol     al,1                ;times 2 for index into word table
        lea     di,cmdtab           ;function (command) table address
        mov     ah,0                ;clear hi order
        add     di,ax               ;add the index to start of table
        jmp     word ptr[di]        ;jump indirect

;CMDTAB is the command table that contains the word address
;for each command. The request header will contain the
;command desired. The INTERRUPT routine will jump through an
;address corresponding to the requested command to get to
;the appropriate command processing routine.

CMDTAB  label   byte                ;* = char devices only
        dw      INITIALIZATION  ; initialization
        dw      MEDIA_CHECK     ; media check (block only)
        dw      GET_BPB         ; build bpb
        dw      IOCTL_INPUT     ; ioctl in
        dw      INPUT           ; input (read)
        dw      ND_INPUT        ;*non destructive input no wait
        dw      INPUT_STATUS    ;*input status
        dw      INPUT_FLUSH     ;*input flush
        dw      OUTPUT          ; output (write)
        dw      OUTPUT_VERIFY   ; output (write) with verify
```

Listing 4–4: (*cont.*)

```
dw      OUTPUT_STATUS    ;*output status
dw      OUTPUT_FLUSH     ;*output flush
dw      IOCTL_OUT        ; ioctl output
dw      OPEN             ; device open
dw      CLOSE            ; device close
dw      REMOVABLE        ; removable media
dw      OUTPUT_BUSY      ;*output til busy
```

The TONE routine uses the PC's programmable timer chip, the 8253–5 (the AT uses a different chip for this purpose). Each key retrieved from the keyboard buffer will be sent to this routine. We set up the timer-chip control word by sending the value *0b6h* to the port numbered 43h. This sets up the 8253–5 chip to produce sounds at a later point. We generate a sound with an audible frequency of less than 14000 cycles per second. Because most keys will be represented by values that range from 0 to 127 or so, we divide 14000 by each key's value. This key-dependent frequency is loaded into port 42h. Then we turn on the speaker and timer by setting bits 0 and 1 in port 61h. This allows us to hear the sound from the speaker. At label *d1* we loop for approximately 50 milliseconds, which allows us to hear the sound without slowing down the keystroke input rate excessively. Finally, we turn off the speaker and timer by setting bits 0 and 1 to 0 in port 61h just before we exit from the TONE routine.

DOS Command Processing

DOS Command Processing is the heart of the Console Device Driver. Listing 4–1 shows that there are 17 commands for device drivers, numbered from 0 to 16. Each command provides a unique but standard action with the driver. Some commands are required to return a *busy* and a *done* indication or just a *done* indication in the status word, even though the command is not applicable.

Command 0—Initialization   DOS will always call our Console Device Driver with the Initialization command immediately after the driver is loaded into memory. This allows the device driver to set up its program code and data. DOS assumes that the device driver is ready for further commands once it returns control to DOS.

Initialization is called only once. We can use only certain DOS services inside the Initialization procedure. These permitted services are numbered 1

Listing 4–5: The code for the only local procedure, TONE

```
;*****************************************************************
;*        YOUR LOCAL PROCEDURES                                 *
;*****************************************************************

TONE    proc    near            ;tone
        mov     ah,0            ;clear ah
        push    ax              ;save ax
        mov     al,0b6h         ;timer chip control word
        out     43h,al          ;send to timer
        mov     dx,0            ;clear dividend (hi)
        mov     ax,14000        ;frequency
        pop     cx              ;restore key value as divisor
        inc     cx              ;add 1 to prevent div by 0
        div     cx              ;quotient is ax
        out     42h,al          ;output lo order byte
        xchg    ah,al           ;reverse
        out     42h,al          ;output hi order byte
        in      al,61h          ;get speaker/timer value
        or      al,3            ;turn on timer & speaker
        out     61h,al          ;set timer chip
        mov     cx,15000        ;value for 50 milliseconds
dl:     loop    dl              ;loop
        in      al,61h          ;get timer chip value
        and     al,0fch         ;turn off speaker & timer
        out     61h,al          ;set timer chip
        ret                     ;return to caller
Tone    endp                    ;end of tone
```

---

through c hex, and 30 hex. The reason for this limitation is that DOS is still in the process of initializing itself, and not all of the services are available for use.

Keep in mind that once we exit from the device driver, we can no longer use DOS services. After DOS calls our device driver with the Initialization command, the driver is part of DOS and cannot issue DOS calls.

One question that is often asked involves the fact that some of the DOS services a driver can issue involve the use of the keyboard and screen. How can that be if the new driver is the replacement for the console device? The answer is simple—DOS loads the standard console device driver before the driver replacement is installed. The DOS service calls issued by the driver use the standard console device driver, but once the driver is finished with the Initialization phase and control returns to DOS, requests for the console are handled by the new Console Device Driver.

Here is the code for the initialization procedure:

```
;****************************************************************
;*        DOS COMMAND PROCESSING                               *
;****************************************************************

;command 0       Initialization
Initialization:

        call    initial                 ;display message
        lea     ax,initial              ;set Break Addr. at initial
        mov     es:[bx].rh0_brk_ofs,ax  ;store offset address
        mov     es:[bx].rh0_brk_seg,cs  ;store segment address
        jmp     done                    ;set done status and exit
```

The Break Address referred to in this procedure tells DOS the next available memory location after our code; this address must be provided by DOS. DOS uses this address to determine where to load other device drivers or operating-system code after the new driver has been installed.

The driver can also specify a Break Address that is within the Console Device Driver. This tells DOS to overwrite some of our code. We may do this to take advantage of the fact that the Initialization is called only once. If, during the Initialization command, we call a routine that is used only once, and we place the code at the end of our Console Device Driver, we can set the Break Address to the starting address of this routine. In effect, we save space by allowing DOS to reuse some of our memory locations. For this example, we will place a procedure called *initial* at the end of our program. This procedure will display a message and return to the Initialization code.

If there is some condition that prevents the Console Device Driver from working properly, the driver signals DOS to abort the device driver. This is done by specifying a Break offset address of 0 and a Break segment address of our current code segment register, CS. This tells DOS that the next available location in memory is the beginning of our device driver, in effect, ignoring our device driver.

In the Initialization code, the driver will display a message on the console, set the Break Address in the Request Header, and exit.

Commands 1 through 3 The commands *Media_Check, Get_BPB,* and *IOCTL_Input* are not implemented in our Console Device Driver. The DONE bit is set in the status word of the Request Header for *Media_Check* and *Get_BPB*. For the *IOCTL_Input* command, the driver jumps to *unknown* to set the ERROR bit. The code is as follows:

```
;command 1          Media_Check
Media_Check:

        jmp         done                    ;set done bit and exit

;command 2          Get_BPB
Get_BPB:

        jmp         done                    ;set done bit and exit

;command 3          IOCTL_Input
IOCTL_Input:

        jmp         unknown                 ;set error bit/code and exit
```

Command 4—Input   Our Console Device Driver uses the Input command to input characters from the keyboard buffer via *int 16h*. See listing 4–6.

DOS passes through the Request Header to the driver the count of the number of characters to be input, as well as the address at which the characters are to be stored.

The keyboard BIOS interrupt 16h returns an ASCII value of the character in al and the corresponding scan code in ah. Recall that the scan code is a number, one of which is assigned to each key on the keyboard. For example, the Shift key on the left side of the keyboard generates a scan code of 42, whereas the Shift key on the right side of the keyboard generates a scan code of 54. This allows programs to distinguish which Shift key was used if necessary.

Most of the PC's keys will generate both an ASCII value and a scan code. However, some keys will not generate an ASCII value. For these keys, which are called the *extended keys, int 16h* returns an ASCII value of 0 in al and the scan code in ah. For example, the function keys (F1–F10) and their variations (using Shift and Alt) will not generate ASCII values; scan codes are required to figure out what key is pressed.

This presents an interesting situation. When a key that has an ASCII value is struck, only the ASCII value is returned to DOS from the keyboard buffer. When an extended key is struck, however, DOS expects two values: first, the ASCII code of 0, and second, the key value of the scan code.

Therefore, in our Console Device Driver we must return to DOS, in the Request Header, the ASCII value of a key for every key and its scan code if it is an extended key. In listing 4–6 this is accomplished with the variable *sav*. The program checks the value of *sav* and passes it back to DOS if it is not 0. If it is 0, ah is saved into *sav*. In short, we save the scan code of an extended key in *sav* and pass it back to DOS at the next request for a character from the device driver.

Listing 4–6: The code for the Input command. Interrupt 16h is used to retrieve characters from the keyboard buffer and pass them back to DOS in the buffer specified by the Request Header. Each character that is retrieved will cause a distinct sound on the speaker.

```
;command 4        Input
Input:

        mov     cx,es:[bx].rh4_count    ;load input count
        mov     di,es:[bx].rh4_buf_ofs  ;load offset address
        mov     ax,es:[bx].rh4_buf_seg  ;load segment address
        mov     es,ax                   ; move to es
read1:  mov     ax,0                    ;clear ax
        xchg    al,sav                  ;pick up saved character
        cmp     al,0                    ;is it 0?
        jne     read3                   ;no - we return it
read2:  mov     ah,0                    ;service = read
        int     16h                     ;Keyboard BIOS call
        cmp     ax,0                    ;is key = 0?
        je      read2                   ;yes - go get another
        cmp     al,0                    ;is it an extended key?
        jne     read3                   ;no - we return it
        mov     sav,ah                  ;save scan code
read3:  mov     es:[di],al              ;store key value in buffer
        inc     di                      ;point to next buffer loc
        push    cx                      ;save cx
        call    tone                    ;sound a tone
        pop     cx                      ;restore for loop control
        loop    read1                   ;continue til count = 0
        mov     ax,cs:rh_seg            ;restore es
        mov     es,ax                   ; from rh_seg
        mov     bx,cs:rh_ofs            ;restore bx
        jmp     done                    ;set done bit and exit
```

In listing 4–6, the basic code to retrieve characters from the keyboard buffer is placed in a loop for a count of the number of characters or keys that DOS requires to be passed back from the device driver. DOS does not request more than one character at a time.

Once a character has been retrieved by issuing an *int 16h*, the character is stored in the DOS data buffer and the TONE procedure is called. TONE will convert the value of the key into a sound with a frequency below 14,000 cycles per second. This sound will last for approximately 50 milliseconds.

The driver ends after the tone has been generated. The driver will restore ES and BX, because these registers are needed to point back to the data buffer in which DOS expects to find the retrieved characters. The driver then jumps to *done* to set the DONE bit in the status word and exits back to DOS.

Command 5—Nondestructive Input   This command allows DOS to look ahead one character without actually retrieving a character from the keyboard buffer. It is included because a program can issue the DOS service for Input Device Check (0Bh). The driver uses the ah = 1 service of *int 16h* to perform a status check of the keyboard buffer. It tells DOS that the keyboard buffer is empty or it passes back the next character in the buffer without actually removing it from the buffer.

We have one situation where we need to read a character from the keyboard. This is when the status check returns a 0 for both the ASCII value and the scan code, which occurs when the keyboard buffer is exhausted.

The instructions that check the scan code for a possible value are shown in listing 4–7. If there is a nonzero value, it is passed back to DOS. Otherwise, the driver issues a status check call to *int 16h (ah = 1)*. The only tricky part of this call is that the Zero Flag (ZF) is set to 1 if there are no characters in the buffer. If this is so, we set the *busy* bit in the status word and return to DOS.

Command 6—Input Status   Command 6 is the Input Status command and is not applicable to the Console Device Driver. It is typically used for character-

---

Listing 4–7: The code for the Nondestructive Input command, which allows DOS to look at the next character in the keyboard buffer without actually removing the character from the buffer.

```
;command 5          ND_Input
ND_Input:

          mov       al,sav                  ;pickup saved character
          cmp       al,0                    ;is it 0?
          jne       ndl                     ;no - return it to DOS
          mov       ah,1                    ;service = status check
          int       16h                     ;Keyboard BIOS call
          jz        busy                    ;ZF=1 means no key in buffer
          cmp       ax,0                    ;is key = 0?
          jne       ndl                     ;no - return it to DOS
          mov       ah,0                    ;service = read
          int       16h                     ;Keyboard BIOS call
          jmp       ND_Input                ;check again
ndl:      mov       es:[bx].rh5_return,al   ;return key to DOS
          jmp       done                    ;set done bit and exit
```

---

oriented input devices that maintain a status that a program can request through this command. For the Console Device Driver, we simply set the *done* bit and exit:

```
;command 6        Input_Status
Input_Status:

        jmp       done                      ;set done bit and exit
```

Command 7—Input Flush The Input Flush command allows DOS to flush the contents of the keyboard buffer. This typically is used to prevent characters that are typed ahead from being used by a program. In some cases, such accidentally entered characters may affect critical input responses. For example, the FORMAT program flushes all keyboard input when asking whether to format the disk. This prevents the existence of a character in the buffer from starting an unwanted format.

The code for this command is shown in listing 4–8 and is relatively simple. Calls are issued by the driver to BIOS interrupt 16h to check the status of the keyboard buffer. If there is a character in the buffer, it is retrieved but not passed back to DOS. This process is repeated until the buffer is empty of any characters.

Command 8—Output The Output command is used to write characters to the screen and must be implemented by our *con:* replacement driver. The video BIOS interrupt 10h is used to do this. The code shown in listing 4–9 shows the use of the output character count in a loop which calls Video BIOS routine 10h with ah = 0Eh. The 0eh is the service called Write Character as TTY. When the driver is done, it restores the es and bx registers, which were used to retrieve the characters in the DOS data buffer.

Listing 4–8: The code for flushing the keyboard input buffer

```
;command 7        Input_Flush
Input_Flush:

        mov       sav,0                     ;clear saved key
IF1:    mov       ah,1                      ;service = check status
        int       16h                       ;Keyboard BIOS call
        jz        done                      ;ZF=1 means buffer empty
        mov       ah,0                      ;service = read
        int       16h                       ;Keyboard BIOS call
        jmp       IF1                       ;loop until buffer empty
```

Listing 4–9: The processing of an Output command

```
;command 8       Output
Output:

        mov     cx,es:[bx].rh8_count      ;load output count
        mov     di,es:[bx].rh8_buf_ofs    ;load offset address
        mov     ax,es:[bx].rh8_buf_seg    ;load segment address
        mov     es,ax                     ; into es
        mov     bx,0                      ;clear bx
out1:   mov     al,es:[di]                ;pick up character to output
        inc     di                        ;point to next location
        mov     ah,0eh                    ;service = write char as tty
        int     10h                       ;Video BIOS call
        loop    out1                      ;loop til count = 0
        mov     ax,cs:rh_seg              ;restore request header
        mov     es,ax                     ; segment adress as es
        mov     bx,cs:rh_ofs              ;restore bx
        jmp     done                      ;set done bit and exit
```

Command 9—Output With Verify This command is identical to the Output command except that it is sent to our Console Device Driver when the VERIFY switch is set ON at the DOS command level.

Normally, the Output With Verify command is used for devices that can read the data that was just written. It is typically used to ensure that the data has been correctly written to the device. Here is the code for processing the Output With Verify command:

```
;command 9       Output_Verify
Output_Verify:

        jmp     output                              ;same as output
```

Command 10 through 16 Commands 10 through 16 are not required by the *con:* replacement driver, but the code must be included in case they are accidentally sent to the driver. Note that each command will jump to either *done* or *unknown*. See listing 4–10.

Error and Common Exits

In this section of code, the driver will set the status word in the Request Header to inform DOS of the outcome of the driver's work. DOS always expects the

---

Listing 4–10: The processing of commands 10 through 16

```
;command 10      Output_Status
Output_Status:

        jmp      done                    ;set done bit and exit

;command 11      Output_Flush
Output_Flush:

        jmp      done                    ;set done bit and exit

;command 12      IOCTL_Out
IOCTL_Out:

        jmp      unknown                 ;set error bit/code and exit

;command 13      Open
Open:

        jmp      done                    ;set done bit and exit

;command 14      Close
Close:

        jmp      done                    ;set done bit and exit

;command 15      Removable
Removable:

        jmp      unknown                 ;set error bit/code and exit

;command 16      Output Til Busy
Output_Busy:

        jmp      unknown                 ;set error bit/code and exit
```

DONE bit to be set. In addition, other bits can be set to indicate other conditions, such as BUSY and ERROR. Refer to table 3–3 for a detailed layout of the status word.

Listing 4–11 shows the code for setting the status word to UNKNOWN, BUSY, or DONE. For UNKNOWN, bit 15 is set to indicate an error, and the error code in bits 0 through 7 is set to a 3, which is the Unknown command. For BUSY, bit 9 is set. For DONE, bit 8 is set.

Listing 4–11: The code for processing errors and exiting from the Console Device Driver. The DONE bit is set in the status word, the registers are popped from the stack, and control returns to DOS.

```
;*****************************************************************
;*         ERROR EXIT                                           *
;*****************************************************************
;
unknown:
        or      es:[bx].rh_status,8003h ;set error bit and error code
        jmp     done                    ;set done and exit

;*****************************************************************
;*         COMMON EXIT                                          *
;*****************************************************************
busy:   or      es:[bx].rh_status,0200h ;set busy bit

done:   or      es:[bx].rh_status,0100h ;set done

        pop     si                      ;restore all registers
        pop     di
        pop     dx
        pop     cx
        pop     bx
        pop     ax
        pop     es
        pop     ds
        ret                             ;return to DOS
```

To exit from the Console Device Driver, the registers are popped from the stack and the code executes a return *(ret)* instruction.

End of Program

In the End of Program section is the procedure *initial,* which displays a message on the screen when the Console Device Driver is first loaded into memory by DOS. Earlier, the driver informed DOS that the Break Address or the address of the next available location is at the same location as *initial.* Because the driver calls the *initial* procedure only once and never needs it again, DOS overwrites this area after the driver exits from the Initialization command processing.

Listing 4–12 shows the code for the End of Program section.

Listing 4–12: The code for the End of Program section. The procedure *initial* is placed here. The message it displays on the screen occurs at Initialization time, just after DOS loads our Console Device Driver.

```
;*****************************************************************
;*        END OF PROGRAM                                        *
;*****************************************************************

;this procedure is called from the Initialization command and
;is executed only once. We can tell DOS that the next available
;memory location (Break Address) is here. This allows DOS to over
;write this code; we save space.

initial proc    near     ;display message on console
        lea     dx,msg1  ;message to be displayed
        mov     ah,9     ;display
        int     21h      ;DOS call
        ret              ;return to caller
initial endp

msg1    db     'The Waite Group Console Driver',0dh,0ah,'$'

console endp             ;end of console procedure
cseg    ends             ;end of cseg segment
        end     begin    ;end of program
```

A Complete Look at the Console Device Driver

In the previous sections, we have discussed the various parts of a device driver and what we need in order to build our Console Device Driver. We are now finished with our tour of inspection, and the complete Console Device Driver is shown in listing 4–13.

Listing 4–13: The complete listing for the Console Device Driver

---

```
;*****************************************************************
;*    This is a Console Device Driver                           *
;*    Author:   Robert S. Lai                                   *
;*    Date:     2 November 1986                                 *
;*    Purpose: To replace the standard console driver           *
;*****************************************************************
```

Listing 4–13: (*cont.*)

```
;****************************************************************
;*         ASSEMBLER DIRECTIVES                                *
;****************************************************************

        cseg    segment   para public   'code'
        console proc      far
                assume    cs:cseg, es:cseg, ds:cseg

;structures

rh              struc   ;fixed request header structure
rh_len          db      ?       ;len of packet
rh_unit         db      ?       ;unit code (block devices only)
rh_cmd          db      ?       ;device driver command
rh_status       dw      ?       ;returned by the device driver
rh_res1         dd      ?       ;reserved
rh_res2         dd      ?       ;reserved
rh              ends    ;

rh0             struc   ;request header for Initialization (command 0)
rh0_rh          db      size rh dup (?) ;fixed request header portion
rh0_nunits      db      ?       ;number of units (block devices only)
rh0_brk_ofs     dw      ?       ;offset address for break
rh0_brk_seg     dw      ?       ;segment address for break
rh0_bpb_tbo     dw      ?       ;offset address of pointer to BPB array
rh0_bpb_tbs     dw      ?       ;segment address of pointer to BPB array
rh0_drv_ltr     db      ?       ;first available drive (DOS 3+) (block only)
rh0             ends    ;

rh4             struc   ;request header for INPUT        (command 4)
rh4_rh          db      size rh dup(?)  ;fixed request header portion
rh4_media       db      ?       ;media descriptor from DPB
rh4_buf_ofs     dw      ?       ;offset address of data transfer area
rh4_buf_seg     dw      ?       ;segment address of data transfer area
rh4_count       dw      ?       ;transfer count (sectors for block)
                                ;(bytes for character)
rh4_start       dw      ?       ;start sector number (block only)
rh4             ends    ;

rh5             struc   ;request header for ND_INPUT (command 5)
rh5_rh          db      size rh dup (?) ;fixed request header portion
rh5_return      db      ?       ;character returned
rh5             ends    ;

rh7             struc   ;request header Input_Flush (command 7)
rh7_len         db      ?       ;len of packet
rh7_unit        db      ?       ;unit code (block devices only)
rh7_cmd         db      ?       ;device driver command
rh7_status      dw      ?       ;returned by the device driver
rh7_res1        dd      ?       ;reserved
```

Listing 4–13: (*cont.*)

```
rh7_res2        dd      ?           ;reserved
rh7             ends                ;

rh8             struc   ;request header for OUTPUT        (command 8)
rh8_rh          db      size rh dup(?)  ;fixed request header portion
rh8_media       db      ?           ;media descriptor from DPB
rh8_buf_ofs     dw      ?           ;offset address of data transfer area
rh8_buf_seg     dw      ?           ;segment address of data transfer area
rh8_count       dw      ?           ;transfer count (sectors for block)
                                    ;(bytes for character)
rh8_start       dw      ?           ;start sector number (block only)
rh8             ends                ;

rh9             struc   ;request header for OUTPUT_VERIFY (command 9)
rh9_rh          db      size rh dup(?)  ;fixed request header portion
rh9_media       db      ?           ;media descriptor from DPB
rh9_buf_ofs     dw      ?           ;offset address of data transfer area
rh9_buf_seg     dw      ?           ;segment address of data transfer area
rh9_count       dw      ?           ;transfer count (sectors for block)
                                    ;(bytes for character)
rh9_start       dw      ?           ;start sector number (block only)
rh9             ends                ;

;***************************************************************
;*      MAIN PROCEDURE CODE                                    *
;***************************************************************

    begin:

;***************************************************************
;*      DEVICE HEADER REQUIRED BY DOS                          *
;***************************************************************

next_dev        dd      -1              ;no other drivers following
attribute       dw      8003h           ;character,output,input
strategy        dw      dev_strategy    ;Strategy routine address
interrupt       dw      dev_interrupt   ;Interrupt routine address
dev_name        db      'CON     '      ;name of our Console driver

;***************************************************************
;*      WORK SPACE FOR OUR DEVICE DRIVER                       *
;***************************************************************

rh_ofs  dw      ?       ;offset address of the request header
rh_seg  dw      ?       ;segment address of the request header

sav     db      0       ;character saved from the keyboard

;***************************************************************
;*      THE STRATEGY PROCEDURE                                 *
;***************************************************************
```

Listing 4–13: (*cont.*)

```
dev_strategy:   mov   cs:rh_seg,es    ;save the segment address
                mov   cs:rh_ofs,bx    ;save the offset address
                ret                   ;return to DOS

;******************************************************************
;*        THE INTERRUPT PROCEDURE                                 *
;******************************************************************

;device interrupt handler - 2nd call from DOS

dev_interrupt:

                cld                   ;save machine state on entry
                push  ds
                push  es
                push  ax
                push  bx
                push  cx
                push  dx
                push  di
                push  si

                mov   ax,cs:rh_seg    ;restore ES as saved by STRATEGY call
                mov   es,ax           ;
                mov   bx,cs:rh_ofs    ;restore BX as saved by STRATEGY call

;jump to appropriate routine to process command

                mov   al,es:[bx].rh_cmd    ;get request header header command
                rol   al,1                ;times 2 for index into word table
                lea   di,cmdtab           ;function (command) table address
                mov   ah,0                ;clear hi order
                add   di,ax               ;add the index to start of table
                jmp   word ptr[di]        ;jump indirect

;CMDTAB is the command table that contains the word address
;for each command. The request header will contain the
;command desired. The INTERRUPT routine will jump through an
;address corresponding to the requested command to get to
;the appropriate command processing routine.

CMDTAB  label   byte              ;* = char devices only
        dw      INITIALIZATION    ; initialization
        dw      MEDIA_CHECK       ; media check (block only)
        dw      GET_BPB           ; build bpb
        dw      IOCTL_INPUT       ; ioctl in
        dw      INPUT             ; input (read)
        dw      ND_INPUT          ;*non destructive input no wait
        dw      INPUT_STATUS      ;*input status
        dw      INPUT_FLUSH       ;*input flush
```

Listing 4-13: (cont.)

```
        dw      OUTPUT          ; output (write)
        dw      OUTPUT_VERIFY   ; output (write) with verify
        dw      OUTPUT_STATUS   ;*output status
        dw      OUTPUT_FLUSH    ;*output flush
        dw      IOCTL_OUT       ; ioctl output
        dw      OPEN            ; device open
        dw      CLOSE           ; device close
        dw      REMOVABLE       ; removable media
        dw      OUTPUT_BUSY     ;*output til busy

;****************************************************************
;*      YOUR LOCAL PROCEDURES                                  *
;****************************************************************

TONE    proc    near            ; tone
        mov     ah,0            ; clear ah
        push    ax              ; save ax
        mov     al,0b6h         ; timer chip control word
        out     43h,al          ; send to timer
        mov     dx,0            ; clear dividend (hi)
        mov     ax,14000        ; frequency
        pop     cx              ; restore key value as divisor
        inc     cx              ; add 1 to prevent div by 0
        div     cx              ; quotient is ax
        out     42h,al          ; output lo order byte
        xchg    ah,al           ; reverse
        out     42h,al          ; output hi order byte
        in      al,61h          ; get speaker/timer value
        or      al,3            ; turn on timer & speaker
        out     61h,al          ; set timer chip
        mov     cx,15000        ; value for 50 milliseconds
dl:     loop    dl              ; loop
        in      al,61h          ; get timer chip value
        and     al,0fch         ; turn off speaker & timer
        out     61h,al          ; set timer chip
        ret                     ; return to caller
Tone    endp                    ; end of tone

;****************************************************************
;*      DOS COMMAND PROCESSING                                 *
;****************************************************************

;command 0      Initialization
Initialization:

        call    initial                 ; display message
        lea     ax,initial              ; set Break Addr. at initial
        mov     es:[bx].rh0_brk_ofs,ax  ; store offset address
        mov     es:[bx].rh0_brk_seg,cs  ; store segment address
        jmp     done                    ; set done status and exit
```

125

Listing 4−13: (*cont.*)

```
;command 1        Media_Check
Media_Check:

        jmp       done                    ;set done bit and exit

;command 2        Get_BPB
Get_BPB:

        jmp       done                    ;set done bit and exit

;command 3        IOCTL_Input
IOCTL_Input:

        jmp       unknown                 ;set error bit/code and exit

;command 4        Input
Input:

        mov       cx,es:[bx].rh4_count    ;load input count
        mov       di,es:[bx].rh4_buf_ofs  ;load offset address
        mov       ax,es:[bx].rh4_buf_seg  ;load segment address
        mov       es,ax                   ; move to es
read1:  mov       ax,0                    ;clear ax
        xchg      al,sav                  ;pick up saved character
        cmp       al,0                    ;is it 0?
        jne       read3                   ;no − we return it
read2:  mov       ah,0                    ;service = read
        int       16h                     ;Keyboard BIOS call
        cmp       ax,0                    ;is key = 0?
        je        read2                   ;yes − go get another
        cmp       al,0                    ;is it an extended key?
        jne       read3                   ;no − we return it
        mov       sav,ah                  ;save scan code
read3:  mov       es:[di],al              ;store key value in buffer
        inc       di                      ;point to next buffer loc
        push      cx                      ;save cx
        call      tone                    ;sound a tone
        pop       cx                      ;restore for loop control
        loop      read1                   ;continue til count = 0
        mov       ax,cs:rh_seg            ;restore es
        mov       es,ax                   ; from rh_seg
        mov       bx,cs:rh_ofs            ;restore bx
        jmp       done                    ;set done bit and exit

;command 5        ND_Input
ND_Input:

        mov       al,sav                  ;pickup saved character
        cmp       al,0                    ;is it 0?
        jne       nd1                     ;no − return it to DOS
```

Listing 4–13: (*cont.*)

```
        mov     ah,1                    ;service = status check
        int     16h                     ;Keyboard BIOS call
        jz      busy                    ;ZF=1 means no key in buffer
        cmp     ax,0                    ;is key = 0?
        jne     nd1                     ;no - return it to DOS
        mov     ah,0                    ;service = read
        int     16h                     ;Keyboard BIOS call
        jmp     ND_Input                ;check again
nd1:    mov     es:[bx].rh5_return,al   ;return key to DOS
        jmp     done                    ;set done bit and exit

;command 6      Input_Status
Input_Status:

        jmp     done                    ;set done bit and exit

;command 7      Input_Flush
Input_Flush:

        mov     sav,0                   ;clear saved key
IF1:    mov     ah,1                    ;service = check status
        int     16h                     ;Keyboard BIOS call
        jz      done                    ;ZF=1 means buffer empty
        mov     ah,0                    ;service = read
        int     16h                     ;Keyboard BIOS call
        jmp     IF1                     ;loop until buffer empty

;command 8      Output
Output:

        mov     cx,es:[bx].rh8_count    ;load output count
        mov     di,es:[bx].rh8_buf_ofs  ;load offset address
        mov     ax,es:[bx].rh8_buf_seg  ;load segment address
        mov     es,ax                   ; into es
        mov     bx,0                    ;clear bx
out1:   mov     al,es:[di]              ;pick up character to output
        inc     di                      ;point to next location
        mov     ah,0eh                  ;service = write char as tty
        int     10h                     ;Video BIOS call
        loop    out1                    ;loop til count = 0
        mov     ax,cs:rh_seg            ;restore request header
        mov     es,ax                   ; segment adress as es
        mov     bx,cs:rh_ofs            ;restore bx
        jmp     done                    ;set done bit and exit

;command 9      Output_Verify
Output_Verify:

        jmp     output                  ;same as output
```

Listing 4–13: (*cont.*)

```
;command 10     Output_Status
Output_Status:

        jmp     done                    ;set done bit and exit

;command 11     Output_Flush
Output_Flush:

        jmp     done                    ;set done bit and exit

;command 12     IOCTL_Out
IOCTL_Out:

        jmp     unknown                 ;set error bit/code and exit

;command 13     Open
Open:

        jmp     done                    ;set done bit and exit

;command 14     Close
Close:

        jmp     done                    ;set done bit and exit

;command 15     Removable
Removable:

        jmp     unknown                 ;set error bit/code and exit

;command 16     Output Til Busy
Output_Busy:

        jmp     unknown                 ;set error bit/code and exit

;******************************************************************
;*      ERROR EXIT                                               *
;******************************************************************

unknown:
        or      es:[bx].rh_status,8003h ;set error bit and error code
        jmp     done                    ;set done and exit

;******************************************************************
;*      COMMON EXIT                                              *
;******************************************************************

busy:   or      es:[bx].rh_status,0200h ;set busy bit
```

Listing 4–13: (*cont.*)

```
done:   or      es:[bx].rh_status,0100h ;set done

        pop     si                      ;restore all registers
        pop     di
        pop     dx
        pop     cx
        pop     bx
        pop     ax
        pop     es
        pop     ds
        ret                             ;return to DOS


;****************************************************************
;*      END OF PROGRAM                                         *
;****************************************************************
;
;this procedure is called from the Initialization command and
;is executed only once. WE can tell DOS that the next available
;memory location (Break Address) is here. This allows DOS to over
;write this code; we save space.

initial proc    near    ;display message on console
        lea     dx,msgl ;message to be displayed
        mov     ah,9    ;display
        int     21h     ;DOS call
        ret             ;return to caller
initial endp

msgl    db      'The Waite Group Console Driver',0dh,0ah,'$'

console endp            ;end of console procedure
cseg    ends            ;end of cseg segment
        end     begin   ;end of program
```

A Note about DOS Versions

Although the Console Device Driver was built to handle the 17 basic commands for DOS version 3.0, the five command-processing sections are also valid for version 2.0. The Attribute bits defined for DOS version 3.0 were not set, and as a result, the additional command functions of version 3.0 will not be sent to the Console Device Driver.

Building the Replacement Console Device Driver

Before you can use this Console Device Driver, you will need to enter the source code of listing 4–13, assemble that code, and link it. Use your favorite word processor to enter the source code and name the file *console.asm*. Then use the Macro Assembler to assemble the source file. The next step is to LINK the object files to produce an executable file. Then convert the .EXE file into a .COM file using the EXE2BIN utility. Lastly, rename the .COM file into a .SYS file.

For DOS to be able to use the Console Device Driver, you will need to specify to DOS that you have a device driver to be loaded at boot time. This is done by specifying the device driver .SYS file in a CONFIG.SYS file using the *device =* command:

```
device = console.sys
```

After you boot DOS with a CONFIG.SYS file that specifies the Console Device Driver, you will see on the screen:

```
The Waite Group Console Driver
```

This message lets you know that the driver was successfully installed. The next characters you type in will cause the speaker to sound with short musical tones.

Summary

In this chapter, we have built a device driver that replaces the standard DOS console device driver. Our replacement driver will do everything the standard driver does, and, in addition, each key struck will generate a tone from the speaker. The Console Device Driver will work on versions 2.0 and 3.0 of DOS. We have seen the various commands that DOS might send to the device driver and what actions we should take for each of these commands. We have seen the requirements of the Device Header, the STRATEGY procedure, the INTERRUPT procedure, the device driver command processing, and lastly, the setting of the various bits of the status word.

Questions

1. Are all DOS service calls allowed in the Initialization command?
2. Are there other examples of a console device driver?

3. Can I customize the Console Device Driver to display color characters?

4. Why does the Console Device Driver use the ROM BIOS routines?

5. Why does the Console Device Driver use only the Write Character as TTY service (0Eh) of the video ROM BIOS interrupt?

6. Why is the colon in CON: not included in the device name field of the Device Header?

7. I find that the Console Device Driver is too long to type in. Can I condense some of the code, particularly in the areas of unimplemented commands?

Answers may be found in appendix E.

Chapter 5

A Printer Device Driver

I n this chapter, we will develop a printer device driver. Instead of building a driver that just replaces the DOS version, as we did in our Console Device Driver example, we will develop one that has many more bells and whistles than a standard printer device driver.

In the previous two chapters, we have learned how to build device drivers that essentially perform simple functions. The Printer Device Driver presented in this chapter will be more powerful and will use more of the features of DOS.

Specifically, in this chapter we will build a device driver for *prn:* that will support both the parallel and serial printers. DOS supplies several printer drivers; each will support either the serial or the parallel port. The dual-role driver developed here allows one DOS device name to be used to access different printers at different times. You save time by not having to change printer device names in your programs when you direct the output to different printers.

To allow the device driver to switch between printers, we will implement the I/O Control command within the Printer Device Driver. I/O Control is a driver feature that, though rarely used, allows programs to communicate directly with device drivers. Normally, data is passed to drivers only for outputting to a device. With I/O Control, special commands can also be sent; these can be used by the device driver to perform special functions.

Printer Types

Printers are commonly connected to a PC using a serial or a parallel interface. DOS supports up to three printers, attached to parallel adapters called LPT1:, LPT2:, and LPT3:. PRN: is used to refer to the printer attached as LPT1:. In addition, two additional printers may be attached to the PC through serial adapters; these adapters are called COM1: and COM2:. This allows us a maximum of five printers we could use. The MODE command can be used to redirect the parallel printer output to another device. For example, MODE is used to specify printer output to either COM1: or COM2:.

Selecting one of these five possible printers from DOS or from a program is tedious at best. Programs need to be changed each time a different printer is desired. MODE commands may be placed in batch files to select printers before a program executes. The print-spooling TSR program, PRINT, does allow the selection of the output device (once PRINT starts executing, however, selecting another printer for output is not possible until PRINT is terminated and restarted with another type of printer specified). The most convenient place to select printers is within the printer device driver itself.

Printers and DOS

DOS supplies four standard printer device drivers. These are PRN:, LPT1:, LPT2:, and LPT3:. These control the three parallel ports. PRN: references the same parallel port as LPT1:. Therefore, there are three parallel printers and four possible names.

The Printer Device Driver we will build in this chapter will not be restricted to one of these three choices. Rather, our Printer Device Driver will have the ability to control up to five printers: three using the parallel ports and two using the serial ports. Of course, if we do not have five printers attached to the PC, we can control only those that are attached.

Controlling printers is simple. First, we create a device driver with the device name of PRN: and we write the code to send data to both the parallel and serial adapters. Then we need a method of selecting the appropriate output port.

We will use the I/O Control Write commands to select the printer and the I/O Control Read commands to determine which printer was selected. This special code needs to be built into the Printer Device Driver along with a special program to send and receive I/O Control strings to and from the Printer Device Driver. The process of controlling printers this way is shown in figure 5–1.

I/O Control and IOCTL Calls

I/O Control, abbreviated IOCTL, is a feature of DOS device drivers that allows control information to be sent to the device driver without being passed through to the device. This control information, also called I/O Control strings, can be read from or written to the device driver. This allows us to communicate with the device driver to pass information back and forth between a program and the device driver. Think of this as a special communication link between DOS and

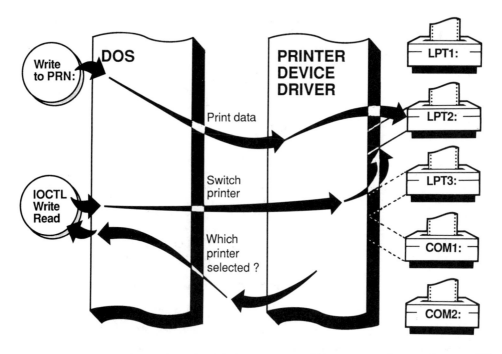

Figure 5–1: Printer Device Driver controlling up to five printers. The IOCTL program is used to send I/O Control strings to select a printer and to receive I/O Control strings to determine which printer was selected. I/O Control strings are written to and read from the device driver and are not treated as data.

a driver, handling information that does not get sent to the device. Without this feature, we would not be able to direct or control the device driver.

We need to look at both sides of the IOCTL feature: programs that read and write control strings and the actions the device driver must take when it encounters these control strings.

The I/O Control for Devices Call

DOS provides a service through interrupt 21h that allows a program to perform I/O Control with its driver. With this service (44h), we can request a number of functions that pass data to and from the device driver. Table 5–1 shows the various operations of the I/O Control for Devices service routine, called IOCTL

Register	Value	Description
ah	44h	Service = I/O Control
al		I/O operation requested
	0	Get device information
	1	Set device information
	2	Read
	3	Write
	4	Read from disk drive
	5	Write to disk drive
	6	Get input status
	7	Get output status
	8	Is device media removable?
	9	Is drive local or remote?
	10	Is file handle local or remote?
	11	Changing the retry of a shareable entry
bx		File handle returned from open a file handle call
cx		Count of the number of bytes to be transferred
dx		With DS this is the address of the data transfer buffer

Table 5–1: The DOS I/O Control service call. Each of the operations requested will require different uses of the various registers.

from here on. Some of the operations require the registers to be set up differently than described in table 5–1. Refer to the *DOS Programmer's Reference Manual* for more details.

Our program will use only two of the eleven possible operations of IOCTL. Operation 2, IOCTL Read, is used to read an IOCTL string from the driver, and operation 3, IOCTL Write, is used to write an IOCTL string to the driver. IOCTL Read allows us to determine which printer was last selected. IOCTL Write (operation 3) allows us to select a printer.

When we select a printer, we indicate that any output written to PRN: will be directed to that printer. All subsequent writes to PRN: will continue to use this printer until we select another printer. Conversely, an IOCTL Read operation allows our program to determine which printer is in use.

The IOCTL program is used to select one of five printers for program access using the name prn:. This removes the requirement that programs change their printer output names to reflect the different printer desired.

The IOCTL Program

The IOCTL program will be used to control which printer the Printer Device Driver will write to when programs use the device name PRN:.

When IOCTL operations are used to read and write, the format of the IOCTL string must be determined. We cannot just write a string of data and expect the device driver to understand what it means; a convention of what the data should look like—a common language—must be established.

Fortunately, this can be done easily. We can set up an arbitrary convention, or protocol, that requires only two bytes. The first byte indicates which type of printer adapter should be used. A *P* indicates the parallel printer adapter; an *S* indicates the serial printer adapter. With this first byte, the IOCTL program will tell the driver which printer adapter to select. The driver will use this byte to return the printer adapter selected.

The second byte contains the adapter number—that is, the device number for that particular type of adapter. For parallel printers, we can use 0, 1 or 2 to indicate LPT1:, LPT2:, or LPT3:. For serial printers, we can specify 0 or 1 to represent COM1: or COM2:. The second byte is used by the IOCTL program to tell the driver which device number to select and by the driver to return the device number selected.

The IOCTL program is simple in concept. Basically, we select which type of printer adapter to use by indicating a *P* or an *S*. Then we select the device number for that particular adapter by specifying a 0, 1, or 2. Next, we open PRN:, using the DOS service for opening a file. Then we select the appropriate IOCTL operation, either Write or Read. Finally, we display the IOCTL string before we exit from the program. The listing of the IOCTL program is shown in listing 5–1.

Listing 5–1: The code for the IOCTL program. We use standard DOS services to write to the console, read from the keyboard, open files, and perform I/O Control for Devices.

```
title    IOCTL Program

;This program is designed to use the I/O Control (IOCTL)
;commands of the The Waite Group Printer Device Driver
;(PRN:). The DOS service 44h provides a read and write function
;for I/O Control strings to device drivers that allow IOCTL.

code     segment                        ;define segment as code
         assume  cs:code, ds:code       ;COM file DS=CS
         org     100h                   ;COM file start
```

Listing 5–1: (*cont.*)

```
main      proc                          ;main procedure
start:                                  ; start

;display a message to the console
          lea     dx,msg1             ; banner
          call    display             ;console display

;Determine if it is a Serial or a Parallel printer
ptype:    lea     dx,msg2             ;prompt for printer type
          call    display             ;console display
          call    input               ;get input character
          cmp     al,'P'              ;is it a [P]arallel printer?
          je      ptype1              ;yes - store it
          cmp     al,'S'              ;is it a [S]erial printer?
          je      ptype1              ;yes - store it
          lea     dx,msg2e            ;error message
          call    display             ;console display
          jmp     ptype               ;its neither - go back
ptype1:   mov     buf,al              ;store the 'P' or 'S'

;get the device number: 1, 2, or 3
;convert this to 0, 1, or 2 for use by the BIOS.
pdev:     lea     dx,msg3             ;prompt for device number
          call    display             ;console display
          call    input               ;get input character
          cmp     al,'3'              ;is it greater than 3?
          ja      perr1               ;yes - too large
          cmp     al,'1'              ;is it below 1?
          jb      perr1               ;yes - too small
          sub     al,30h              ;convert ASCII to binary
          dec     al                  ;subtract one for driver use
          mov     buf+1,al            ;store device number
          jmp     fopen               ;go open PRN: file
perr1:    lea     dx,msg2e            ;incorrect selection message
          call    display             ;console display
          jmp     pdev                ;go back & try again

;open PRN using file handle call
fopen:    mov     al,2                ;read/write access
          mov     ah,3dh              ;open file handle
          lea     dx,file             ;address of filename
          int     21h                 ;DOS call
          jc      openerr             ;error (carry set)?
          push    ax                  ;save file handle
          lea     dx,filemsg          ;no error - tell user
          call    display             ;console display
          jmp     ioctl               ;get IOCTL function
openerr:  lea     dx,msg5             ;error message
          jmp     exit                ;exit - problem in program
```

Listing 5–1: (*cont.*)

```
;get function type: Write IOCTL or Read IOCTL
ioctl:  lea     dx,msg4         ;Read or Write IOCTL
        call    display         ;console display
        call    input           ;get input character
        cmp     al,'R'          ;is it [R]ead?
        je      ioread          ;yes - process it
        cmp     al,'W'          ;is it [W]rite?
        je      iowrite         ;yes - process it
        lea     dx,msg2e        ;no - error message
        call    display         ;console display
        jmp     ioctl           ;try again

ioread: mov     al,2            ;read IOCTL string from driver
        jmp     doioctl         ;process it
iowrite:mov     al,3            ;write IOCTL string to driver

doioctl:pop     bx              ;restore file handle to bx
        mov     ah,44h          ;service = IOCTL
        mov     cx,2            ;count = 2 bytes
        lea     dx,buf          ;address of buffer
        int     21h             ;DOS call
        jc      chkerr          ;error (carry set)?
        or      al,30h          ;make count ASCII
        mov     msg6a,al        ;store count
        mov     al,buf+1        ;get device unit number
        or      al,30h          ;make it ASCII
        mov     buf+1,al        ;store it back
        lea     dx,msg6         ;display results
        call    display         ;console display
        jmp     exit            ;we are done!

;check error from IOCTL call
chkerr: cmp     ax,1            ;invalid function number?
        jne     err1            ;no
        lea     dx,emsg1        ;yes
        jmp     err             ;display & exit
err1:   cmp     ax,4            ;no handle?
        jne     err2            ;no
        lea     dx,emsg2        ;yes
        jmp     err
err2:   cmp     ax,5            ;access denied?
        jne     err3            ;no
        lea     dx,emsg3        ;yes
        jmp     err             ;display & exit
err3:   cmp     ax,6            ;invalid handle or not open?
        jne     err4            ;no
        lea     dx,emsg4        ;yes
        jmp     err             ;display & exit
```

Listing 5–1: (*cont.*)

```
err4:    cmp     ax,0dh           ;invalid data?
         jne     err5             ;no
         lea     dx,emsg5         ;yes
         jmp     err              ;display & exit
err5:    cmp     ax,0fh           ;invalid drive?
         jne     err6             ;no
         lea     dx,emsg6         ;yes
         jmp     err              ;display & exit
err6:    lea     dx,emsg7         ;unknown error
err:     call    display          ;display

exit:    lea     dx,msg7          ;goodbye message
         call    display          ;console display
         int     20h              ;exit back to DOS

display proc     near             ;display message on screen
         mov     ah,9             ;service = display
         int     21h              ;DOS call
         ret                      ;return to caller
display endp                      ;

input   proc     near             ;get 1 character from the keyboard
         mov     ah,1             ;service = keyboard input
         int     21h              ;DOS call
         ret                      ;return to caller
input   endp                      ;

msg1    db      'IOCTL PROGRAM',0dh,0ah,'$'
msg2    db      0dh,0ah,'Select Printer type ',0dh,0ah,
        db      ' "S" for serial or "P" for parallel :','$'
msg2e   db      0dh,0ah,'bad selection — try again!',0dh,0ah,'$'
msg3    db      0dh,0ah,'Enter printer number [1,2,3] :$'
msg4    db      0dh,0ah,'IOCTL type [W]rite or [R]ead :$'
msg5    db      0dh,0ah,'cannot open PRN!',0dh,0ah,'$'
msg6    db      0dh,0ah,'IOCTL call OK',0dh,0ah,' count transferred = ',
msg6a   db      '0',0dh,0ah,' IOCTL string = ',
buf     db      'S',0h,0dh,0ah,'$'
msg7    db      'Goodbye for now',0dh,0ah,'$'
filemsg db      0dh,0ah,
file    db      'PRN',0h,
        db      ' has been opened!',0d,0ah,'$'
emsg1   db      0dh,0ah,'invalid function number',0dh,0ah,'$'
emsg2   db      0dh,0ah,'no file handle',0dh,0ah,'$'
emsg3   db      0dh,0ah,'access denied',0dh,0ah,'$'
emsg4   db      0dh,0ah,'invalid handle or not open',0dh,0ah,'$'
emsg5   db      0dh,0ah,'invalid data',0dh,0ah,'$'
emsg6   db      0dh,0ah,'invalid drive number',0dh,0ah,'$'
emsg7   db      0dh,0ah,'unknown error number',0dh,0ah,'$'
```

Listing 5–1: (*cont.*)

```
main    endp                ;end of main procedure
code    ends                ;end of code segment
        end     start       ;
```

Building and Using the IOCTL Program

Use your favorite word processor to enter the text as shown in listing 5–1. Name the source file IOCTL.

Running the IOCTL program requires that an S be entered to specify a serial interface or a P to specify a parallel interface. In addition, the number 1, 2, or 3 must be entered to indicate which printer should be enabled. Any previously enabled printer will be disabled. The number 1, 2, or 3 is called the *adapter number,* and the S or P is called the *adapter type.* The IOCTL program will translate the printer numbers (1, 2, 3) to the required internal designations (0, 1, 2). Here is a sample execution:

```
C>ioctl
IOCTL PROGRAM

Select Printer type
 "S" for serial or "P" for parallel :S
Enter printer number [1,2,3] :1
PRN has been opened!

IOCTL type [W]rite or [R]ead :W
IOCTL call OK
 count transferred = 2
 IOCTL string = SO
Goodbye for now
```

Note that the program does not automatically convert lower-case input to upper-case input. All keyboard input must be upper-case.

BIOS Services for Serial and Parallel Adapters

As was discussed in chapters 1 and 2, the BIOS routines for the serial and parallel adapters are found in the ROMs of IBM and IBM-compatible PCs. Programs can use either DOS services or BIOS services to access devices on the serial or the parallel adapters. Using the ROM BIOS routines means bypassing DOS and losing some of the extensive services available. However, using the ROM BIOS routines provides greater control over the device and faster response times. In addition, once a driver is installed, it becomes part of DOS; because DOS is not reentrant, the driver cannot call DOS and therefore cannot use those DOS services in any case.

The ROM BIOS routines allow us to send data to the device, to check the status of the adapter, and, in the case of the serial adapter, to receive data (the serial adapter may have a modem). The Printer Device Driver uses the ROM BIOS routines for the serial and parallel adapters to access the serial and parallel printers.

The specific BIOS interrupts we will be using are 14h, which controls the serial adapters, and 17h, which controls the parallel adapters. These two BIOS interrupts perform similar functions, but they have different register conventions. For both interrupts, all devices are numbered starting at 0. At the DOS level, these device numbers start at 1; therefore, the IOCTL program subtracts 1 from the device number to get the BIOS device number.

The functions provided by the serial adapter BIOS interrupt (14h) are shown in table 5–2. The Printer Device Driver will use only two of the four functions provided by this BIOS service: the Transmit function (ah = 1) and the Get Status function (ah = 3). For more complete descriptions, refer to the *IBM Technical Reference* manual.

The parallel port BIOS interrupt (17h) is shown in table 5–3. The Printer Device Driver will use the Transmit function (ah = 0) and the Get Status function (ah = 2) of this interrupt. For further information, refer to chapter 2 and appendix B.

In summary, the Printer Device Driver will use only two services provided by the two BIOS interrupts; the transmit function and the retrieve status function.

Inside the Printer Device Driver

The Printer Device Driver takes the same format as the Console Device Driver in chapter 4. The overall framework for device drivers will not change, except for items that are specific to each device driver. In many cases, when you are creating a new driver, you can use the code from another driver with little modification.

The first three sections are shown in listing 5–2. There are only two differences between these sections and those in the Console Device Driver. The first change is the name of the main procedure, which is now *printer*. The second is within the assembler directives. We no longer need the *struc*s for commands

Register	Value	Description
ah	0	Initialize serial port
	1	Transmit 1 character
	2	Receive 1 character
	3	Get serial port status
al		Character received (ah = 2) or
		Character to transmit (ah = 1)
dx		Serial port to use (0 or 1)

Status is returned in ax as follows:

ah Bit	If Set, Means
7	Timeout has occurred
6	Transmission shift register is empty
5	Transmission buffer is empty
4	A break has been detected
3	A framing error has occurred
2	A parity error has occurred
1	An overrun has occurred
0	Data is ready

al Bit	If Set, Means
7	Receive line signal has been detected
6	Ring indicator has been detected
5	Data set ready asserted
4	Clear to send asserted
3	A change has occurred in receive line signal
2	A change has occurred in ring indicator
1	A change has occurred in data set ready
0	A change has occurred for clear to send

Table 5–2: The register set-up requirements for the serial adapter BIOS interrupt 14h. This interrupt provides both transmit and receive functions through the serial adapter.

Register	Value	Description
ah	0	transmit 1 character
	1	initialize parallel port
	2	get parallel port status
al		character to transmit (ah = 0)
dx		parallel port to use (0, 1 or 2)

Status is returned in ah as follows:

ah Bit	If Set, Means
7	printer is not busy
6	parallel port acknowledge
5	printer is out of paper
4	parallel port selected
3	an I/O error has occurred
2–1	not used
0	a timeout has occurred

Table 5–3: The register set-up requirements for the parallel adapter BIOS interrupt 17h. This interrupt provides only transmit functions through the parallel adapter.

4 (Input), 5 (Nondestructive Input), and 7 (Input Flush); these have been deleted. For the Printer Device Driver, we add the *strucs* for commands 3 (IOCTL Input), 10 (Output Status), 12 (IOCTL Output), and 16 (Output Til Busy). We will use these *strucs* in the DOS command processing section.

The Device Header

The next section is the Device Header. Normally, this section sets the appropriate bits in the Attribute word to describe the type of driver this is and changes the name of the device driver to the new name. In this case, however, we have a decision to make with respect to the command functions that the Printer Device Driver will support.

The decision to be made involves the DOS version with which we wish the Printer Device Driver to work. With DOS versions 3.0 or higher, four additional

Listing 5–2: The code for the first part of the Printer Device Driver. Note that the main procedure is now called *printer*. Also note that the *strucs* have been changed to reflect the requirements of the Printer Device Driver.

```
;******************************************************************
;*      This is a Printer Device Driver                          *
;*      Author:   Robert S. Lai                                  *
;*      Date:     15 November 1986                               *
;*      Purpose: to replace the standard printer driver          *
;******************************************************************


;******************************************************************
;*        ASSEMBLER DIRECTIVES                                    *
;******************************************************************

        cseg        segment    para public    'code'
        printer     proc       far
                    assume     cs:cseg, es:cseg, ds:cseg

;Request Header structures

rh              struc               ;request header
rh_len          db        ?         ;len of packet
rh_unit         db        ?         ;unit code
                                    ;(block devices only)
rh_cmd          db        ?         ;device driver command
rh_status       dw        ?         ;returned by device driver
rh_res1         dd        ?         ;reserved
rh_res2         dd        ?         ;reserved
rh              ends                ;

rh0             struc               ;Initialization (command 0)
rh0_rh          db        size rh dup (?) ;fixed portion
rh0_nunits      db        ?         ;number of units
                                    ;(block devices only)
rh0_brk_ofs     dw        ?         ;offset address for break
rh0_brk_seg     dw        ?         ;segment address for break
rh0_bpb_tbo     dw        ?         ;offset address of pointer
                                    ;to BPB array
rh0_bpb_tbs     dw        ?         ;segment address of pointer
                                    ;to BPB array
rh0_drv_ltr     db        ?         ;first available drive
                                    ;(DOS 3+) (block only)
rh0             ends                ;

;*** The following is a new struc ***

rh3             struc               ;IOCTL_INPUT (command 3)
rh3_rh          db        size rh dup(?)  ;fixed portion
rh3_media       db        ?         ;media descriptor from DPB
```

Listing 5-2: (*cont.*)

```
rh3_buf_ofs     dw      ?           ;offset address of
                                    ;data transfer area
rh3_buf_seg     dw      ?           ;segment address of
                                    ;data transfer area
rh3_count       dw      ?           ;transfer count
                                    ;(sectors for block)
                                    ;(bytes for character)
rh3_start       dw      ?           ;start sector number
                                    ;(block only)
rh3             ends                ;

rh8             struc               ;OUTPUT (command 8)
rh8_rh          db      size rh dup(?)  ;fixed portion
rh8_media       db      ?           ;media descriptor from DPB
rh8_buf_ofs     dw      ?           ;offset address of
                                    ;data transfer area
rh8_buf_seg     dw      ?           ;segment address of
                                    ;data transfer area
rh8_count       dw      ?           ;transfer count
                                    ;(sectors for block)
                                    ;(bytes for character)
rh8_start       dw      ?           ;start sector number
                                    ;(block only)
rh8             ends                ;

rh9             struc               ;OUTPUT_VERIFY (command 9)
rh9_rh          db      size rh dup(?)  ;fixed portion
rh9_media       db      ?           ;media descriptor from DPB
rh9_buf_ofs     dw      ?           ;offset address of
                                    ;data transfer area
rh9_buf_seg     dw      ?           ;segment address of
                                    ;data transfer area
rh9_count       dw      ?           ;transfer count
                                    ;(sectors for block)
                                    ;(bytes for character)
rh9_start       dw      ?           ;start sector number (block only)
rh9             ends                ;

;*** The following is a new struc ***

rh10            struc               ;Output_Status (command 10)
rh10_len        db      ?           ;len of packet
rh10_unit       db      ?           ;unit code
                                    ;(block devices only)
rh10_cmd        db      ?           ;device driver command
rh10_status     dw      ?           ;returned by device driver
rh10_res1       dd      ?           ;reserved
rh10_res2       dd      ?           ;reserved
rh10            ends                ;
```

Listing 5–2: (cont.)

```
;*** The following is a new struc ***

rh12            struc                   ;IOCTL_OUTPUT (command 12)
rh12_rh         db      size rh dup(?)  ;fixed portion
rh12_media      db      ?               ;media descriptor from DPB
rh12_buf_ofs    dw      ?               ;offset address of
                                        ;data transfer area
rh12_buf_seg    dw      ?               ;segment address of
                                        ;data transfer area
rh12_count      dw      ?               ;transfer count
                                        ;(sectors for block)
                                        ;(bytes for character)
rh12_start      dw      ?               ;start sector number
                                        ;(block only)
rh12            ends                    ;

;*** The following is a new struc ***

rh16            struc                   ;OUTPUT_BUSY (command 16)
rh16_rh         db      size rh dup (?) ;fixed portion
rh16_media      db      ?               ;media descriptor
rh16_buf_ofs    dw      ?               ;offset address of
                                        ;data transfer area
rh16_buf_seg    dw      ?               ;segment address of
                                        ;data transfer area
rh16_count      dw      ?               ;byte count returned
                                        ;from device driver
rh16            ends                    ;

;commands that do not have unique portions to the request header:
;       INPUT_STATUS    (command 6)
;       INPUT_FLUSH     (command 7)
;       OUTPUT_STATUS   (command 10)
;       OUTPUT_FLUSH    (command 11)
;       OPEN            (command 13)
;       CLOSE           (command 14)
;       REMOVABLE       (command 15)
;


;****************************************************************
;*      MAIN PROCEDURE CODE                                     *
;****************************************************************

    begin:
```

---

device driver commands are available: 13 (Device Open), 14 (Device Close), 15 (Removable Media), and 16 (Output Til Busy). For this driver, we would like the ability to use the Output Til Busy command. This requires the Attribute word to have the appropriate bit (13) set. Unfortunately, this is not acceptable for DOS versions 2.0.

To allow you to experiment with the new DOS 3.0 driver calls, we present two versions of this driver, one with and one without code for the Output Til Busy command. Two different versions of the Device Header are provided; the first version will work for both versions of DOS and the second version will work only with DOS 3.0. Therefore, there will be two Printer Device Drivers, differing only in the Device Header used. If you use the second Device Header, you will need to have DOS 3.0. In chapter 10, you will see how to make a single version of the Printer Device Driver that will adapt itself to either version of DOS without sacrificing features.

Changes are made to the Attribute word in the Device Header to distinguish the two versions. Interestingly enough, DOS has redefined the Attribute word over the years. Both versions of the Waite Group Printer Device Driver Attribute words are shown in table 5–4. The two Device Headers are shown in listing 5–3.

Device Driver	DOS Version	Attribute	Description
DOS PRN:	2.0	8000h	Character device
DOS PRN:	3.0	8800h	Character device (open/close/removable)
DOS PRN:	3.1	a000h	Character device (Output Til Busy)
The Waite Group	2.0, 3.0	c000h	Character device (supports IOCTL)
The Waite Group	3.0	e000h	Character device (supports IOCTL Output Til Busy)

Table 5–4: The various Attribute words for the printer device drivers. Note that the Printer Device Driver in this chapter will have two versions, one that works under DOS 2.0 and 3.0, and one that works only under DOS 3.0.

Listing 5–3: The two versions of the Device Header. The first version is for use in DOS versions 2.0 and 3.0. The second version is used with DOS version 3.0 only. You will use only one of these Device Headers.

```
;*****************************************************************
;*        DEVICE HEADER REQUIRED BY DOS 2                       *
;*****************************************************************

next_dev        dd    -1                ;no other drivers following
attribute       dw    0c000h            ;char,IOCTL
strategy        dw    dev_strategy      ;Strategy routine address
interrupt       dw    dev_interrupt     ;Interrupt routine address
dev_name        db    'PRN     '        ;name of our Console driver


;*****************************************************************
;*        DEVICE HEADER REQUIRED BY DOS 3                       *
;*****************************************************************

next_dev        dd    -1                ;no other drivers following
attribute       dw    0e000h            ;char,IOCTL,output til busy
strategy        dw    dev_strategy      ;Strategy routine address
interrupt       dw    dev_interrupt     ;Interrupt routine address
dev_name        db    'PRN     '        ;name of our Console driver
```

Work Space for Our Device Driver

The Printer Device Driver retains the familiar variables *rh_seg* and *rh_ofs*, which hold the ES and BX registers that point to the Request Header that DOS passes to the device. In addition to these two variables, we declare two more variables. The first variable is *device,* which contains a value that indicates which type of adapter will be used; *device* will contain a 0 to use the parallel adapters and a 1 to use the serial adapters. The second variable added is *dev_num,* which contains the number of the adapter to use. The range of values for this variable will be 0 to 2 for parallel adapters and 0 to 1 for serial adapters. This is shown in listing 5–4.

The STRATEGY, INTERRUPT and Local Procedures

The STRATEGY and INTERRUPT procedures used in the Console Device Driver do not change for the Printer Device Driver. The TONE procedure has been removed from the Console Device Driver, because there is no need for it. This is shown in listing 5–5.

Listing 5−4: The declarations for the variables we will be using in the Printer Device Driver

---

```
;****************************************************************
;*       WORK SPACE FOR OUR DEVICE DRIVER                      *
;****************************************************************
;

rh_ofs  dw      ?       ;offset address of the request header
rh_seg  dw      ?       ;segment address of the request header

device  db      0       ;0=parallel, 1= serial
dev_num db      0       ;0,1,2 depending on configuration
```

Listing 5−5: The code for the STRATEGY, INTERRUPT, and local procedures used by the printer driver

---

```
;****************************************************************
;*       THE STRATEGY PROCEDURE                               *
;****************************************************************
;

dev_strategy:   mov     cs:rh_seg,es    ;save the segment address
                mov     cs:rh_ofs,bx    ;save the offset address
                ret                     ;return to DOS

;****************************************************************
;*       THE INTERRUPT PROCEDURE                              *
;****************************************************************
;

;device interrupt handler - 2nd call from DOS

dev_interrupt:

        cld                     ;save machine state on entry
        push    ds
        push    es
        push    ax
        push    bx
        push    cx
        push    dx
        push    di
        push    si

        mov     ax,cs:rh_seg    ;restore ES as saved by STRATEGY call
        mov     es,ax           ;
        mov     bx,cs:rh_ofs    ;restore BX as saved by STRATEGY call
```

Listing 5–5: (*cont.*)

```
;jump to appropriate routine to process command

        mov     al,es:[bx].rh_cmd       ;get request header command
        rol     al,1                    ;times 2 for index into word table
        lea     di,cmdtab               ;function (command) table address
        mov     ah,0                    ;clear hi order
        add     di,ax                   ;add the index to start of table
        jmp     word ptr[di]            ;jump indirect

;CMDTAB is the command table that contains the word address
;for each command. The request header will contain the
;command desired. The INTERRUPT routine will jump through an
;address corresponding to the requested command to get to
;the appropriate command processing routine.

CMDTAB  label   byte            ;* = char devices only
        dw      INITIALIZATION  ; initialization
        dw      MEDIA_CHECK     ; media check (block only)
        dw      GET_BPB         ; build bpb
        dw      IOCTL_INPUT     ; ioctl in
        dw      INPUT           ; input (read)
        dw      ND_INPUT        ;*nondestructive input no wait
        dw      INPUT_STATUS    ;*input status
        dw      INPUT_FLUSH     ;*input flush
        dw      OUTPUT          ; output (write)
        dw      OUTPUT_VERIFY   ; output (write) with verify
        dw      OUTPUT_STATUS   ;*output status
        dw      OUTPUT_FLUSH    ;*output flush
        dw      IOCTL_OUT       ; ioctl output
        dw      OPEN            ; device open
        dw      CLOSE           ; device close
        dw      REMOVABLE       ; removable media
        dw      OUTPUT_BUSY     ;*output til busy

;******************************************************************
;*         YOUR LOCAL PROCEDURES                                 *
;******************************************************************
```

DOS Command Processing

Of the 17 commands for DOS version 3.0 device drivers, only a few will actually be implemented for a particular device driver. The Printer Device Driver will implement commands 0 (Initialization), 3 (IOCTL Input), 8 (Output), 9 (Output With Verify), 10 (Output Status), 12 (IOCTL Output), and 16 (Output Til Busy).

The rest of the commands require the Printer Device Driver to return in the Status word either the BUSY or the ERROR bit set in addition to the DONE bit. Table 5–5 shows the Status word bits set for commands that are not applicable in our Printer Device Driver.

The code for the commands listed in table 5–5 that are not used by our Printer Device Driver (those marked "**" in table 5–5) is shown in listing 5–6.

The code needed to implement the new device driver commands, such as IOCTL Input, IOCTL Output, Output, Output With Verify, Output Til Busy, and Initialization, is presented in the next sections.

Command 0—Initialization   The Initialization command does not change much. The driver calls the *initial* procedure to display a banner and information about

Number	Command Description	Status Bits Set
0	Initialization	**
1	Media Check	DONE
2	Build BPB	DONE
3	IOCTL Input	**
4	Input	**
5	Nondestructive Input	BUSY
6	Input Status	DONE
7	Input Flush	DONE
8	Output	**
9	Output With Verify	**
10	Output Status	**
11	Output Flush	DONE
12	IOCTL Output	**
13	Device Open	DONE
14	Device Close	DONE
15	Removable Media	ERROR
16	Output Til Busy	**
**		The printer driver performs some processing for these commands. The Status word setting will depend on the outcome of the processing. The balance of unused commands will jump to DONE or UNKNOWN.

Table 5–5: The Status word bit setting for those commands that have no meaning in our Printer Device Driver

Listing 5–6: The code for commands that have no meaning in the Printer Device Driver

```
;********************************************************************
;*        DOS COMMAND PROCESSING FOR UNUSED COMMAND                 *
;********************************************************************
;

;command 1      Media_Check
Media_Check:

        jmp     done            ;set done bit and exit

;command 2      Get_BPB
Get_BPB:

        jmp     done            ;set done bit and exit

;command 4      Input
Input:

        jmp     done              ;set done bit and exit

;command 5      ND_Input
ND_Input:

        jmp     busy              ;set busy bit and exit

;command 6      Input_Status
Input_Status:

        jmp     done              ;set done bit and exit

;command 7      Input_Flush
Input_Flush:

        jmp     done              ;set done bit and exit

;command 11     Output_Flush
Output_Flush:

        jmp     done              ;set done bit and exit

;command 13     Open
Open:

        jmp     done              ;set done bit and exit
```

Listing 5–6: (*cont.*)

```
;command 14      Close
Close:

        jmp      done                   ;set done bit and exit

;command 15      Removable
Removable:

        jmp     ·unknown                ;set error bit/code and exit
```

---

the serial and parallel adapters. You will see more of this procedure in a later section of this chapter. Again, the driver destroys the space occupied by the Initialization procedure, and the driver specifies this. The memory used is returned to DOS. The Break Address, which signals the last memory location that the Printer Device Driver uses, is returned to DOS. Recall that the Break Address is used to tell DOS where the next available location is following the Printer Device Driver. This is shown in listing 5–7.

Command 3—IOCTL Input The IOCTL Input command instructs the Printer Device Driver to return to the calling program an I/O Control string. As was discussed earlier, the IOCTL data is two bytes in length, with the first byte indicating the printer adapter type and the second byte indicating the adapter number.

Listing 5–7: The Initialization command processing. We call the *initial* procedure to display information about the Printer Device Driver. Then we return the Break Address to DOS.

```
;command 0       Initialization
Initialization:

        call     initial                 ;display message
        lea      ax,initial              ;set Break Addr. at initial
        mov      es:[bx].rh0_brk_ofs,ax  ;store offset address
        mov      es:[bx].rh0_brk_seg,cs  ;store segment address
        jmp      done                    ;set done status and exit
```

Listing 5–8 shows that the address of the data transfer area is contained in *rh3_buf_seg* and *rh3_buf_ofs* and is used to store two protocol bytes received by the driver. The variable *device* is checked with a compare *(cmp)* instruction to determine whether the lower byte specifies a parallel adapter (value is 0) or a serial one (value is 1); the driver stores a 'P' or an 'S' in the data transfer area. This value is subsequently returned to the IOCTL program. Similarly, the driver returns the variable *dev_num,* which contains the adapter number.

Before the driver exits and sets the DONE bit of the Status word, the ES and BX registers, which were used to store our IOCTL information, are restored.

Command 8—Output   This command is the heart of the Printer Device Driver. Data sent to PRN: to be printed by a program calling our driver is processed in this section. Each character is output to the selected printer one byte at a time. See listing 5–9. Note that this is not related to IOCTL Output, but deals with data to be printed.

The initial part of the Output procedure sets up the various registers used to retrieve data from the DOS buffer pointed to by the address contained in *rh8_buf_seg* and *rh9_buf_ofs.* This particular buffer was defined in the *struc* section and will be the output buffer.

Listing 5–8: The code for the IOCTL Input command. This command instructs the Printer Device Driver to return an IOCTL string.

```
;command 3          IOCTL_Input
IOCTL_Input:

          mov       di,es:[bx].rh3_buf_ofs   ;get buffer offset
          mov       ax,es:[bx].rh3_buf_seg   ;get buffer
          mov       es,ax                    ; segment to es
          cmp       cs:device,0              ;is it currently parallel?
          jne       iniol                    ;no — check for serial
          mov       al,'P'                   ;yes — ASCII P
          jmp       inioctl                  ;store it
iniol:    mov       al,'S'                   ;assume [S]erial
inioctl:  mov       es:[di],al               ;Store printer type
          inc       di                       ;next location
          mov       al,cs:dev_num            ;get device number
          mov       es:[di],al               ;store it
          mov       cx,cs:rh_seg             ;restore request header
          mov       es,cx                    ; segment to es
          mov       bx,cs:rh_ofs             ;same for offset
          jmp       done                     ;set done bit and exit
```

The program then determines the printer adapter number and the printer adapter type. Based on the value for the printer adapter, contained in the variable *device,* the program branches to either the parallel or the serial output routines.

The section of the driver labeled *pout* outputs data using the parallel adapter BIOS interrupt 17h. The basic loop checks the status of the parallel adapter (ah = 2) before transmitting 1 character (ah = 0). Normally, we do not need to check the status before sending a character. DOS issues an Output Status (command 10) and checks to see if the Printer Device Driver is ready to output more characters. If so, DOS will call the Printer Device Driver with an Output command.

A status check is performed by the Printer Device Driver for two reasons. First, some programs bypass the DOS Printer Device Driver by issuing interrupt 17h calls directly. This can cause the printer to become busy when our Printer Device Driver attempts to write to it. The Printer Device Driver then waits, unnecessarily, until the device is no longer busy. The status check code detects the possibility of this condition. Instead of having the Printer Device Driver wait until the printer is ready, we will detect the fact that the device is busy, and return a busy indication to DOS. This allows DOS to check the status (through an Output Status command) and when the device is not busy, resend the character to the Printer Device Driver for printing. Thus, we prevent a "hung" situation, which occurs when the printer is too busy to accept more characters.

The second, perhaps more convoluted, reason for a status check is that the same output code can then be used for the Output Til Busy command. If the driver uses the same code for processing the Output Til Busy command but does not have the status check code, the driver can wait endlessly for the printer to free up when passing a stream of characters. In short, the status check is doubly justified when the Output Til Busy command shares the same code as the Output command; the chance of the printer being busy is greatly increased if the driver sends a block of characters to be printed. In either case, the status check code is important in minimizing the time spent by the driver waiting for the printer to be free.

The driver section labeled *pout2* checks for errors that occur in the status check and the output sections for the parallel adapter. If an error arises, the program sets the ERROR bit and stores an appropriate error number in the status word before exiting.

The section labeled *sout* transmits print data through the serial adapter interface using interrupt 14h. The code first checks the status to ensure that the serial adapter and the printer are ready to receive a character from the Printer Device Driver. If there are any errors, the driver will exit with a *write fault* error. DOS does not distinguish among the different error conditions returned from the serial adapter; the *write fault* error is intended to represent all such errors.

A status check is performed before a character is transmitted to the serial adapter for the same reasons as described for the parallel adapter output. Any busy conditions are returned to DOS, and DOS keeps checking, waiting until the printer is ready before resending the character to the Printer Device Driver. This code is also used to process the Output Til Busy command.

The Output command code is shown in listing 5–9.

Command 9—Output With Verify The Output With Verify command is called from DOS when print output is desired and the command-level switch VERIFY

Listing 5–9: The code for the Printer Driver Output command. The code determines the adapter type and number and branches to the appropriate serial or parallel output routines.

```
;command 8       Output
Output:

          mov     cx,es:[bx].rh8_count      ;load output count
          mov     di,es:[bx].rh8_buf_ofs    ;load offset address
          mov     ax,es:[bx].rh8_buf_seg    ;load segment address
          mov     es,ax                     ; into es

          mov     dl,cs:dev_num             ;load printer #
          mov     dh,0                      ;clear hi-order DX
          mov     bx,0                      ;set current count to 0

;check for device type
          cmp     cs:device,0               ;to parallel device?
          je      pout                      ;yes
          jmp     sout                      ;no - assume serial


;process output to parallel printer
pout:     cmp     bx,cx                     ;is current = output?
          je      pout2                     ;yes - we are done
          mov     al,es:[di]                ;get output character
          inc     di                        ;point to next byte
          mov     ah,2                      ;service = status check
          int     17h                       ;Printer BIOS call
          test    ah,80h                    ;not busy (=1)?
          jne     pout1                     ;yes - continue
          jmp     pout3                     ;no - exit with error
pout1:    mov     ah,0                      ;service = print
          int     17h                       ;Printer BIOS call
          test    ah,9h                     ;I/O error or Timeout?
          jne     perrl                     ;yes
          inc     bx                        ;increment current count
          jmp     pout                      ;go back for more
```

Listing 5-9: (*cont.*)

```
;process printer errors

pout2:  mov     ax,0                ;no error
        jmp     load_status         ;load status & exit
pout3:  mov     ax,8002h            ;set error bit & 'not ready'
        jmp     load_status         ;load status & exit

perr1:  test    ah,1                ;Timeout?
        jz      perr2               ;no - go to next test
        mov     ax,8002h            ;set error bit & not ready
        jmp     load_status         ;go to cleanup
perr2:  test    ah,8                ;I/O Error?
        jz      perr3               ;no - go to next test
        mov     ax,800ah            ;set error bit & Write Fault
        jmp     load_status         ;go to cleanup
perr3:  test    ah,20h              ;No Paper (printer off)?
        jz      perr4               ;no - go to last step
        mov     ax,8009h            ;set error bit & No Paper
        jmp     load_status         ;go to cleanup
perr4:  mov     ax,800ch            ;set error bit & General Failure
        jmp     load_status         ;go to cleanup

;process output to serial printer

sout:   cmp     bx,cx               ;is current = request count?
        je      sout2               ;yes - set status & exit
        mov     ah,3                ;service = status check
        int     14h                 ;RS232 BIOS call
        test    ah,20h              ;xfer hold register empty?
        jnz     st1                 ;yes (implies not busy)
        jmp     sout3               ;no - set error & exit
st1:    test    al,20h              ;is data set ready =1?
        jnz     sout1               ;yes (implies not busy)
        jmp     sout3               ;no - set error & exit
sout1:  mov     al,es:[di]          ;get output character
        inc     di                  ;increment for next char
        mov     ah,1                ;service = transmit 1 char
        int     14h                 ;RS232 BIOS call
        test    ah,80h              ;transmit error?
        jnz     sout3               ;yes - set error & exit
        inc     bx                  ;no - increment output count
        jmp     sout                ;go back for more

sout2:  mov     ax,0                ;no errors - we are done
        jmp     load_status         ;load status word & exit
sout3:  mov     ax,800ah            ;set error bit & 'write fault'
        jmp     load_status         ;set status word & exit
```

is set ON. This command is the same as an Output command and is processed by jumping to the Output routine. The code for this command is shown below:

```
;command 9        Output_Verify
Output_Verify:

        jmp     output                      ;same as output
```

Command 10—Output Status The Output Status command is sent to the Printer Device Driver whenever DOS is about to send an Output command to print data. DOS needs to know the status of the output device before it sends an Output command to the device driver. (From an efficiency viewpoint, it is better to let DOS check and wait for a ready indication than it is for the device driver to keep checking.) This is particularly true if DOS has other work to perform; it could not do so if the device driver was in a loop waiting for a device to become ready to accept data. DOS can also retry an operation several times before displaying an error message on the console.

The Output Status routine determines the adapter type and number before issuing an appropriate BIOS status check interrupt. The DOS BUSY bit is set in the Status word if the device is not ready. Note that the parallel adapter status bit returned by the BIOS call is reversed in meaning from the BUSY bit in the device driver's Status word. When interrupt 17h returns bit 7 in the ah register, the device is not busy. Therefore, if this bit is set we do not set the BUSY bit of the Status word. The code for this command is illustrated in listing 5–10.

Command 12—IOCTL Output The IOCTL Output command is sent to the Printer Device Driver whenever a program issues a 44h service call to DOS via interrupt 21h with a Write Request operation (al = 3). This command is processed by inspecting the data buffer specified by DOS in the address *rh12_buf_seg* and *rh12_buf_ofs*.

As defined earlier in this chapter, the IOCTL data used by both the device driver and the program issuing an IOCTL service follows a set format. It has two bytes, the first of which is a P or an S which indicates the parallel or the serial adapter, and the second of which is the adapter number (0–2).

The IOCTL Output section of code converts the adapter ASCII letter P to a 0 for a parallel adapter and the S to a 1 for the serial adapter. This value is stored in the variable *device*. Similarly, the second byte in the data buffer is saved in the variable *dev_num*.

If the first byte in the data buffer is not a P or an S, the driver returns to DOS with an error. Otherwise, the driver sets the DONE bit of the Status word and exits. The code for this command is shown in listing 5–11.

Listing 5–10: The code for processing the Output Status command. The driver sets the BUSY bit of the Status word if the device is not ready for more output.

```
;command 10      Output_Status
Output_Status:

;The DOS BUSY bit of the status word is set to indicate to DOS
;that DOS should wait. If BUSY is not set (eg DONE bit only),
;this means that device is ready for more output.

;determine device type and unit number
         mov     dl,cs:dev_num            ;load printer #
         mov     dh,0                     ;clear hi-order DX

;check for device type
         cmp     cs:device,0              ;to parallel device?
         je      pstatus                  ;yes
         jmp     sstatus                  ;no - assume serial

;get status from parallel device
; if bit 7 in ah is set this means device is not busy
; so we do not set BUSY in status word.
pstatus:
         mov     ah,2                     ;service = status check
         int     17h                      ;Printer BIOS call
         test    ah,80h                   ;not busy or other?
         jne     pstat1                   ;yes
         jmp     busy                     ;no (not busy) - set BUSY!
pstat1:  test    ah,9h                    ;I/O Error or Timeout?
         jz      pstat2                   ;no - exit with BUSY not set!
         mov     es:[bx].rh_status,8009h  ;set error bit & 'No Paper'
pstat2:  jmp     done                     ;set done bit and exit

;get serial printer status
sstatus:
         mov     ah,3                     ;service = status check
         int     14h                      ;RS232 BIOS call
         test    ah,20h                   ;xfer hold register empty?
         jz      sstat                    ;no - set BUSY!
         test    al,20h                   ;data set ready?
         jz      sstat                    ;no - set BUSY!
         jmp     done                     ;device is ready!
sstat:   jmp     busy                     ;device is not ready!
```

Command 16—Output Til Busy The Output Til Busy command, which is valid only when DOS 3.0 is used, is sent to the Printer Device Driver when it is desirable to send an entire buffer of characters to the printer rather than one

Listing 5–11: The processing for the IOCTL Output command. The driver converts and stores the adapter type and number.

```
;command 12         IOCTL_Out
IOCTL_Out:
          mov       cx,es:[bx].rh12_count      ;load output count
          mov       di,es:[bx].rh12_buf_ofs    ;load offset address
          mov       ax,es:[bx].rh12_buf_seg    ;load segment address
          mov       es,ax                      ; into es

          mov       al,es:[di]                 ;pickup Device
          cmp       al,'P'                     ;is it parallel?
          jne       IOCTL1                     ;no - test for serial
          mov       cs:device,0                ;yes - move 0
          jmp       IOCTL2                     ;now get device number
IOCTL1:   cmp       al,'S'                     ;is it serial?
          jne       IOCTL3                     ;no - wrong IOCTL data
          mov       cs:device,1                ;yes - move 1
IOCTL2:   inc       di                         ;next character
          mov       al,es:[di]                 ;pickup device number
          mov       cs:dev_num,al              ;store it
          mov       ax,0                       ;no error
          jmp       IOCTL4                     ;load status & exit

IOCTL3:   mov       ax,8003                    ;not P or S - error

IOCTL4:   mov       cx,cs:rh_seg               ;restore request header
          mov       es,cx                      ; segment to es
          mov       bx,cs:rh_ofs               ;restore offset also
          mov       es:[bx].rh_status,ax       ;return status
          jmp       done                       ;set done bit and exit
```

character at a time. The command sends data until the printer device is busy and cannot accept any more. It finds out when the printer is busy by checking the printer's status before sending out each character. This speeds processing, because DOS normally calls the Printer Device Driver each time there is a character to be printed.

Most printers today have an internal RAM buffer that holds many characters and that acts as a temporary storage area to moderate between the relatively fast speeds of transferring data to the printer and the slower speeds of printing characters. The Output Til Busy command uses this feature of printers to fill up the buffer in one shot before returning to DOS with a busy indication.

The Output Til Busy command is processed by the Output command code. The Output command section sends characters to the printer until either the count of output characters is exhausted or the status check code indicates the printer is busy. If the printer returns a busy status, the driver returns to DOS with the Status word set and the number of characters transferred. The code for processing the Output Til Busy command is simply a jump to the Output routine.

Error Exit   This section sets the Error bit of the Status word, sets the error number, and then exits. This code has not changed from the previous chapter's driver and is shown in the listing of the complete Printer Device Driver at the end of this chapter.

Common Exit   This section completes the Output command processing by restoring the ES and BX registers and returning the error code and the number of bytes transferred to the printer adapter.

The BUSY bit is set if needed. For the Printer Device Driver, this bit needs to be set if the Output Status command processing code finds the printer busy. Lastly, the DONE bit of the Status word is set before returning to DOS. Listing 5–12 illustrates the code required by the Common Exit routines.

Listing 5–12: The Common Exit processing. The Output command results are processed at the label *load_status*.

```
;*************************************************************
;*         COMMON EXIT                                      *
;*************************************************************
load_status:
          mov     cx,cs:rh_seg          ;restore request header
          mov     es,cx                 ; segment to es
          mov     cx,cs:rh_ofs          ;restore offset also
          xchg    bx,cx                 ;switch them
          mov     es:[bx].rh_status,ax  ;return status
          mov     es:[bx].rh8_count,cx  ;return output count
          jmp     done                  ;set done bit and exit

busy:     or      es:[bx].rh_status,0200h ;set busy bit

done:     or      es:[bx].rh_status,0100h ;set done

          pop     si                    ;restore all registers
          pop     di
          pop     dx
          pop     cx
          pop     bx
          pop     ax
          pop     es
          pop     ds
          ret                           ;return to DOS
```

End of Program We finally have reached the end of the Printer Device Driver! The driver simply displays a banner indicating the number of serial and parallel adapters that the Printer Device Driver will support. The Equipment Check interrupt (11h) is used to return the number of serial and parallel adapters supported by the PC. Because the driver cannot tell if printers are attached to these adapters, it only indicates what adapters are present.

The *initial* procedure is executed only once by the Initialization command, so the routine is placed at the end of the device driver instead of in the section called "Local Procedures." This is done so that DOS can reuse these memory locations once the Initialization phase is complete. Listing 5–13 shows the code for the End of Program processing.

Listing 5–13: The code required for the End of Program processing. The *initial* procedure is placed at the end of the Printer Device Driver so that we can tell DOS to overwrite it. We do this by specifying the Break Address at the *initial* procedure.

```
;******************************************************************
;*        END OF PROGRAM                                         *
;******************************************************************
;
;this procedure is called from the Initialization command and
;is executed only once. We tell DOS that the next available
;memory location (Break Address) is here. This allows DOS to over
;write this code; we save space.

initial proc     near      ;display message on console
        int      11h       ;equipment check
        push     ax        ;save for parallel calculation
        mov      cl,9      ;shift count
        shr      ax,cl     ;get serial ports
        and      al,7      ;keep 3 right bits
        add      al,30h    ;make it an ASCII number
        mov      msglb,al  ;store it
        pop      ax        ;restore for parallel calculation
        mov      cl,14     ;shift count
        shr      ax,cl     ;get parallel ports
        and      al,3      ;keep 2 right bits
        add      al,30h    ;make it an ASCII number
        mov      msglc,al  ;store it
        lea      dx,msgl   ;message to be displayed
        mov      ah,9      ;display
        int      21h       ;DOS call
        ret                ;return to caller
initial endp
```

Listing 5–13: (*cont.*)

```
msg1     db          'The Waite Group Printer Driver',0dh,0ah,
         db          ' supporting',0dh,0ah,' ',
msg1b    db          '0 parallel printers',0dh,0ah,' ',
msg1c    db          '0 serial printers',0dh,0ah,'$'

printer  endp           ;end of printer procedure
cseg     ends           ;end of cseg segment
         end     begin  ;end of program
```

Building the Printer Device Driver

To build the Printer Device Driver discussed in this chapter, use a word processor to enter the text shown in listing 5–14, which is the complete listing of the Printer Device Driver. Name the text file *printer.asm*.

Listing 5–14: The complete listing for the Printer Device Driver.

```
        page    60,132
        title   A Printer Device Driver

;*****************************************************************
;*      This is a Printer Device Driver                         *
;*      Author:   Robert S. Lai                                 *
;*      Date:     15 November 1986                              *
;*      Purpose: to replace the standard printer driver         *
;*****************************************************************


;*****************************************************************
;*          ASSEMBLER DIRECTIVES                                *
;*****************************************************************

        cseg        segment   para public    'code'
        printer     proc      far
                    assume    cs:cseg, es:cseg, ds:cseg

;Request Header structures

rh                  struc                ;request header
rh_len              db        ?          ;len of packet
rh_unit             db        ?          ;unit code
                                         ;(block devices only)
```

Listing 5–14: (cont.)

```
rh_cmd          db      ?               ;device driver command
rh_status       dw      ?               ;returned by device driver
rh_res1         dd      ?               ;reserved
rh_res2         dd      ?               ;reserved
rh              ends                    ;

rh0             struc                   ;Initialization (command 0)
rh0_rh          db      size rh dup (?) ;fixed portion
rh0_nunits      db      ?               ;number of units
                                        ;(block devices only)
rh0_brk_ofs     dw      ?               ;offset address for break
rh0_brk_seg     dw      ?               ;segment address for break
rh0_bpb_tbo     dw      ?               ;offset address of pointer
                                        ;to BPB array
rh0_bpb_tbs     dw      ?               ;segment address of pointer
                                        ;to BPB array
rh0_drv_ltr     db      ?               ;first available drive
                                        ;(DOS 3+) (block only)
rh0             ends                    ;

;*** The following is a new struc ***

rh3             struc                   ;IOCTL_INPUT (command 3)
rh3_rh          db      size rh dup(?)  ;fixed portion
rh3_media       db      ?               ;media descriptor from DPB
rh3_buf_ofs     dw      ?               ;offset address of
                                        ;data transfer area
rh3_buf_seg     dw      ?               ;segment address of
                                        ;data transfer area
rh3_count       dw      ?               ;transfer count
                                        ;(sectors for block)
                                        ;(bytes for character)
rh3_start       dw      ?               ;start sector number
                                        ;(block only)
rh3             ends                    ;

rh8             struc                   ;OUTPUT (command 8)
rh8_rh          db      size rh dup(?)  ;fixed portion
rh8_media       db      ?               ;media descriptor from DPB
rh8_buf_ofs     dw      ?               ;offset address of
                                        ;data transfer area
rh8_buf_seg     dw      ?               ;segment address of
                                        ;data transfer area
rh8_count       dw      ?               ;transfer count
                                        ;(sectors for block)
                                        ;(bytes for character)
rh8_start       dw      ?               ;start sector number
                                        ;(block only)
rh8             ends                    ;
```

Listing 5–14: (*cont.*)

```
rh9             struc               ;OUTPUT_VERIFY (command 9)
rh9_rh          db      size rh dup(?)  ;fixed portion
rh9_media       db      ?           ;media descriptor from DPB
rh9_buf_ofs     dw      ?           ;offset address of
                                    ;data transfer area
rh9_buf_seg     dw      ?           ;segment address of
                                    ;data transfer area
rh9_count       dw      ?           ;transfer count
                                    ;(sectors for block)
                                    ;(bytes for character)
rh9_start       dw      ?           ;start sector number (block only)
rh9             ends                ;

;*** The following is a new struc ***

rh10            struc               ;Output_Status (command 10)
rh10_len        db      ?           ;len of packet
rh10_unit       db      ?           ;unit code
                                    ;(block devices only)
rh10_cmd        db      ?           ;device driver command
rh10_status     dw      ?           ;returned by device driver
rh10_res1       dd      ?           ;reserved
rh10_res2       dd      ?           ;reserved
rh10            ends                ;

;*** The following is a new struc ***

rh12            struc               ;IOCTL_OUTPUT (command 12)
rh12_rh         db      size rh dup(?)  ;fixed portion
rh12_media      db      ?           ;media descriptor from DPB
rh12_buf_ofs    dw      ?           ;offset address of
                                    ;data transfer area
rh12_buf_seg    dw      ?           ;segment address of
                                    ;data transfer area
rh12_count      dw      ?           ;transfer count
                                    ;(sectors for block)
                                    ;(bytes for character)
rh12_start      dw      ?           ;start sector number
                                    ;(block only)
rh12            ends                ;

;*** The following is a new struc ***

rh16            struc               ;OUTPUT_BUSY (command 16)
rh16_rh         db      size rh dup (?) ;fixed portion
rh16_media      db      ?           ;media descriptor
rh16_buf_ofs    dw      ?           ;offset address of
                                    ;data transfer area
rh16_buf_seg    dw      ?           ;segment address of
                                    ;data transfer area
```

Listing 5-14: (*cont.*)

```
rh16_count      dw      ?           ;byte count returned
                                    ;from device driver
rh16            ends                ;

;commands that do not have unique portions to the request header:
;        INPUT_STATUS     (command 6)
;        INPUT_FLUSH      (command 7)
;        OUTPUT_STATUS    (command 10)
;        OUTPUT_FLUSH     (command 11)
;        OPEN             (command 13)
;        CLOSE            (command 14)
;        REMOVABLE        (command 15)
;


;*****************************************************************
;*        MAIN PROCEDURE CODE                                    *
;*****************************************************************

    begin:

;*****************************************************************
;*        DEVICE HEADER REQUIRED BY DOS                          *
;*****************************************************************

next_dev        dd      -1              ;no other drivers following
attribute       dw      0e000h          ;char,IOCTL,output til busy
strategy        dw      dev_strategy    ;Strategy routine address
interrupt       dw      dev_interrupt   ;Interrupt routine address
dev_name        db      'PRN    '       ;name of our Console driver

;*****************************************************************
;*        WORK SPACE FOR OUR DEVICE DRIVER                       *
;*****************************************************************

rh_ofs  dw      ?           ;offset address of the request header
rh_seg  dw      ?           ;segment address of the request header

device  db      0           ;0=parallel, 1= serial
dev_num db      0           ;0,1,2 depending on configuration

;*****************************************************************
;*        THE STRATEGY PROCEDURE                                 *
;*****************************************************************

dev_strategy:   mov     cs:rh_seg,es    ;save the segment address
                mov     cs:rh_ofs,bx    ;save the offset address
                ret                     ;return to DOS
```

Listing 5–14: (*cont.*)

```
;****************************************************************
;*      THE INTERRUPT PROCEDURE                                *
;****************************************************************

;device interrupt handler - 2nd call from DOS

dev_interrupt:

        cld                             ;save machine state on entry
        push    ds
        push    es
        push    ax
        push    bx
        push    cx
        push    dx
        push    di
        push    si

        mov     ax,cs:rh_seg    ;restore ES as saved by STRATEGY call
        mov     es,ax           ;
        mov     bx,cs:rh_ofs    ;restore BX as saved by STRATEGY call

;jump to appropriate routine to process command

        mov     al,es:[bx].rh_cmd       ;get request header command
        rol     al,1                    ;times 2 for index into word table
        lea     di,cmdtab               ;function (command) table address
        mov     ah,0                    ;clear hi order
        add     di,ax                   ;add the index to start of table
        jmp     word ptr[di]            ;jump indirect

;CMDTAB is the command table that contains the word address
;for each command. The request header will contain the
;command desired. The INTERRUPT routine will jump through an
;address corresponding to the requested command to get to
;the appropriate command processing routine.

CMDTAB  label   byte            ;* = char devices only
        dw      INITIALIZATION  ; initialization
        dw      MEDIA_CHECK     ; media check (block only)
        dw      GET_BPB         ; build bpb
        dw      IOCTL_INPUT     ; ioctl in
        dw      INPUT           ; input (read)
        dw      ND_INPUT        ;*non destructive input no wait
        dw      INPUT_STATUS    ;*input status
        dw      INPUT_FLUSH     ;*input flush
        dw      OUTPUT          ; output (write)
        dw      OUTPUT_VERIFY   ; output (write) with verify
        dw      OUTPUT_STATUS   ;*output status
```

Listing 5–14: (*cont.*)

```
        dw      OUTPUT_FLUSH    ;*output flush
        dw      IOCTL_OUT       ; ioctl output
        dw      OPEN            ; device open
        dw      CLOSE           ; device close
        dw      REMOVABLE       ; removable media
        dw      OUTPUT_BUSY     ;*output til busy

;******************************************************************
;*      YOUR LOCAL PROCEDURES                                     *
;******************************************************************
;


;******************************************************************
;*      DOS COMMAND PROCESSING                                    *
;******************************************************************

;command 0      Initialization
Initialization:

        call    initial                 ;display message
        lea     ax,initial              ;set Break Addr. at initial
        mov     es:[bx].rh0_brk_ofs,ax  ;store offset address
        mov     es:[bx].rh0_brk_seg,cs  ;store segment address
        jmp     done                    ;set done status and exit

;command 1      Media_Check
Media_Check:

        jmp     done                ;set done bit and exit

;command 2      Get_BPB
Get_BPB:

        jmp     done                ;set done bit and exit

;command 3      IOCTL_Input
IOCTL_Input:

        mov     di,es:[bx].rh3_buf_ofs  ;get buffer offset
        mov     ax,es:[bx].rh3_buf_seg  ;get buffer
        mov     es,ax                   ; segment to es
        cmp     cs:device,0             ;is it currently parallel?
        jne     iniol                   ;no — check for serial
        mov     al,'P'                  ;yes — ASCII P
        jmp     inioctl                 ;store it
iniol:  mov     al,'S'                  ;assume [S]erial
inioctl:mov     es:[di],al              ;Store printer type
        inc     di                      ;next location
        mov     al,cs:dev_num           ;get device number
```

Listing 5–14: (*cont.*)

```
        mov     es:[di],al              ;store it
        mov     cx,cs:rh_seg            ;restore request header
        mov     es,cx                   ; segment to es
        mov     bx,cs:rh_ofs            ;same for offset
        jmp     done                    ;set done bit and exit

;command 4      Input
Input:

        jmp     done                    ;set done bit and exit

;command 5      ND_Input
ND_Input:

        jmp     busy                    ;set busy bit and exit

;command 6      Input_Status
Input_Status:

        jmp     done                    ;set done bit and exit

;command 7      Input_Flush
Input_Flush:

        jmp     done                    ;set done bit and exit

;command 8      Output
Output:

        mov     cx,es:[bx].rh8_count    ;load output count
        mov     di,es:[bx].rh8_buf_ofs  ;load offset address
        mov     ax,es:[bx].rh8_buf_seg  ;load segment address
        mov     es,ax                   ; into es

        mov     dl,cs:dev_num           ;load printer #
        mov     dh,0                    ;clear hi-order DX
        mov     bx,0                    ;set current count to 0

;check for device type
        cmp     cs:device,0             ;to parallel device?
        je      pout                    ;yes
        jmp     sout                    ;no - assume serial

;process output to parallel printer
pout:   cmp     bx,cx                   ;is current = output?
        je      pout2                   ;yes - we are done
        mov     al,es:[di]              ;get output character
        inc     di                      ;point to next byte
        mov     ah,2                    ;service = status check
```

Listing 5-14: (*cont.*)

```
        int     17h             ;Printer BIOS call
        test    ah,80h          ;not busy (=1)?
        jne     pout1           ;yes - continue
        jmp     pout3           ;no - exit with error
pout1:  mov     ah,0            ;service = print
        int     17h             ;Printer BIOS call
        test    ah,9h           ;I/O error or Timeout?
        jne     perr1           ;yes
        inc     bx              ;increment current count
        jmp     pout            ;go back for more

;process printer errors

pout2:  mov     ax,0            ;no error
        jmp     load_status     ;load status & exit
pout3:  mov     ax,8002h        ;set error bit & 'not ready'
        jmp     load_status     ;load status & exit

perr1:  test    ah,1            ;Timeout?
        jz      perr2           ;no - go to next test
        mov     ax,8002h        ;set error bit & not ready
        jmp     load_status     ;go to cleanup
perr2:  test    ah,8            ;I/O Error?
        jz      perr3           ;no - go to next test
        mov     ax,800ah        ;set error bit & Write Fault
        jmp     load_status     ;go to cleanup
perr3:  test    ah,20h          ;No Paper (printer off)?
        jz      perr4           ;no - go to last step
        mov     ax,8009h        ;set error bit & No Paper
        jmp     load_status     ;go to cleanup
perr4:  mov     ax,800ch        ;set error bit & General Failure
        jmp     load_status     ;go to cleanup

;process output to serial printer

sout:   cmp     bx,cx           ;is current = request count?
        je      sout2           ;yes - set status & exit
        mov     ah,3            ;service = status check
        int     14h             ;RS232 BIOS call
        test    ah,20h          ;xfer hold register empty?
        jnz     st1             ;yes (implies not busy)
        jmp     sout3           ;no - set error & exit
st1:    test    al,20h          ;is data set ready =1?
        jnz     sout1           ;yes (implies not busy)
        jmp     sout3           ;no - set error & exit
sout1:  mov     al,es:[di]      ;get output character
        inc     di              ;increment for next char
        mov     ah,1            ;service = transmit 1 char
        int     14h             ;RS232 BIOS call
```

Listing 5-14: (*cont.*)

```
        test    ah,80h                  ;transmit error?
        jnz     sout3                   ;yes - set error & exit
        inc     bx                      ;no - increment output count
        jmp     sout                    ;go back for more

sout2:  mov     ax,0                    ;no errors - we are done
        jmp     load_status             ;load status word & exit
sout3:  mov     ax,800ah                ;set error bit & 'write fault'
        jmp     load_status             ;set status word & exit

;command 9       Output_Verify
Output_Verify:

        jmp     output                  ;same as output

;command 10      Output_Status
Output_Status:

;The DOS BUSY bit of the status word is set to indicate to DOS
;that DOS should wait. If BUSY is not set (eg DONE bit only),
;this means that device is ready for more output.

;determine device type and unit number
        mov     dl,cs:dev_num           ;load printer #
        mov     dh,0                    ;clear hi-order DX

;check for device type
        cmp     cs:device,0             ;to parallel device?
        je      pstatus                 ;yes
        jmp     sstatus                 ;no - assume serial

;get status from parallel device
; if bit 7 in ah is set this means device is not busy
; so we do not set BUSY in status word.
pstatus:
        mov     ah,2                    ;service = status check
        int     17h                     ;Printer BIOS call
        test    ah,80h                  ;not busy or other?
        jne     pstat1                  ;yes
        jmp     busy                    ;no (not busy) - set BUSY!
pstat1: test    ah,9h                   ;I/O Error or Timeout?
        jz      pstat2                  ;no - exit with BUSY not set!
        mov     es:[bx].rh_status,8009h ;set error bit & 'No Paper'
pstat2: jmp     done                    ;set done bit and exit

;get serial printer status
sstatus:
        mov     ah,3                    ;service = status check
        int     14h                     ;RS232 BIOS call
```

Listing 5-14: (*cont.*)

```
            test    ah,20h                      ;xfer hold register empty?
            jz      sstat                       ;no — set BUSY!
            test    al,20h                      ;data set ready?
            jz      sstat                       ;no — set BUSY!
            jmp     done                        ;device is ready!
sstat:      jmp     busy                        ;device is not ready!

;command 11         Output_Flush
Output_Flush:

            jmp     done                        ;set done bit and exit

;command 12         IOCTL_Out
IOCTL_Out:
            mov     cx,es:[bx].rh12_count       ;load output count
            mov     di,es:[bx].rh12_buf_ofs     ;load offset address
            mov     ax,es:[bx].rh12_buf_seg     ;load segment address
            mov     es,ax                       ; into es

            mov     al,es:[di]                  ;pickup Device
            cmp     al,'P'                      ;is it parallel?
            jne     IOCTL1                      ;no — test for serial
            mov     cs:device,0                 ;yes — move 0
            jmp     IOCTL2                      ;now get device number
IOCTL1:     cmp     al,'S'                      ;is it serial?
            jne     IOCTL3                      ;no — wrong IOCTL data
            mov     cs:device,1                 ;yes — move 1
IOCTL2:     inc     di                          ;next character
            mov     al,es:[di]                  ;pickup device number
            mov     cs:dev_num,al               ;store it
            mov     ax,0                        ;no error
            jmp     IOCTL4                      ;load status & exit

IOCTL3:     mov     ax,8003                     ;not P or S — error

IOCTL4:     mov     cx,cs:rh_seg                ;restore request header
            mov     es,cx                       ; segment to es
            mov     bx,cs:rh_ofs                ;restore offset also
            mov     es:[bx].rh_status,ax        ;return status
            jmp     done                        ;set done bit and exit

;command 13         Open
Open:

            jmp     done                        ;set done bit and exit

;command 14         Close
Close:

            jmp     done                        ;set done bit and exit
```

Listing 5–14: (*cont.*)

```
;command 15      Removable
Removable:

        jmp     unknown                 ;set error bit/code and exit

;command 16      Output Til Busy
Output_Busy:

        jmp     output                  ;use Output code to process

;*****************************************************************
;*      ERROR EXIT                                               *
;*****************************************************************

unknown:
        or      es:[bx].rh_status,8003h ;set error bit and error code
        jmp     done                    ;set done and exit

;*****************************************************************
;*      COMMON EXIT                                              *
;*****************************************************************
load_status:
        mov     cx,cs:rh_seg            ;restore request header
        mov     es,cx                   ; segment to es
        mov     cx,cs:rh_ofs            ;restore offset also
        xchg    bx,cx                   ;switch them
        mov     es:[bx].rh_status,ax    ;return status
        mov     es:[bx].rh8_count,cx    ;return output count
        jmp     done                    ;set done bit and exit

busy:   or      es:[bx].rh_status,0200h ;set busy bit

done:   or      es:[bx].rh_status,0100h ;set done

        pop     si                      ;restore all registers
        pop     di
        pop     dx
        pop     cx
        pop     bx
        pop     ax
        pop   · es
        pop     ds
        ret                             ;return to DOS

;*****************************************************************
;*      END OF PROGRAM                                           *
;*****************************************************************

;this procedure is called from the Initialization command and
;is executed only once. We tell DOS that the next available
```

Listing 5–14: (*cont.*)

```
;memory location (Break Address) is here. This allows DOS to over
;write this code; we save space.

initial proc    near      ;display message on console
        int     11h       ;equipment check
        push    ax        ;save for parallel calculation
        mov     cl,9      ;shift count
        shr     ax,cl     ;get serial ports
        and     al,7      ;keep 3 right bits
        add     al,30h    ;make it an ASCII number
        mov     msglb,al  ;store it
        pop     ax        ;restore for parallel calculation
        mov     cl,14     ;shift count
        shr     ax,cl     ;get parallel ports
        and     al,3      ;keep 2 right bits
        add     al,30h    ;make it an ASCII number
        mov     msglc,al  ;store it
        lea     dx,msgl   ;message to be displayed
        mov     ah,9      ;display
        int     21h       ;DOS call
        ret               ;return to caller
initial endp

msgl    db      'The Waite Group Printer Driver',0dh,0ah,
        db      ' supporting',0dh,0ah,' ',
msglb   db      '0 parallel printers',0dh,0ah,' ',
msglc   db      '0 serial printers',0dh,0ah,'$'

printer endp              ;end of printer procedure
cseg    ends              ;end of cseg segment
        end     begin     ;end of program
```

Remember to use the Device Header that matches the version of DOS being used. Then assemble, link, and convert the driver to a .COM format. To install the driver, build a CONFIG.SYS file, specifying the Printer Device Driver file in a *device* = command.

Using the Printer Device Driver

The Printer Device Driver normally will access the printer attached to the first parallel adapter interface when it is first booted. When you wish to use another printer, use the IOCTL program again to change the printer selection.

Summary

In this chapter, we have built a Printer Device Driver that takes advantage of the PC's ability to support up to five printers. Additional device driver commands, such as IOCTL Input and IOCTL Output, have been explored. In addition, we have also provided a quick overview of the powerful I/O Control commands from both the program's viewpoint and the Printer Device Driver's viewpoint. Some of the differences between DOS 2.0 and 3.0 that affect device drivers have also been discussed. The Printer Device Driver in this chapter has more features than are available with the standard DOS device drivers. In the next chapter, we will continue this idea and build an even more powerful Clock Device Driver.

Questions

1. Are there practical reasons for using printers on parallel ports rather than on serial ports?

2. Why does the Printer Device Driver support only two serial printers?

3. Can you put printer initialization code into the Printer Device Driver?

4. In the section "Command 8—Output," the discussion on status checking indicated that one program using BIOS interrupts to the printer can interfere with another program using the Printer Device Driver. How is this possible? I thought DOS could only execute one program at a time.

5. What other functions can be added to I/O Control processing?

6. Why does the IOCTL program ask for adapter type first, rather than for IOCTL Read or Write?

Answers may be found in appendix E.

Chapter 6

A Clock Device Driver

I n this chapter, we will build a Clock Device Driver. This driver will be used to set the system time and date automatically. The driver will also display the time continually on the PC's screen. The standard clock driver that is built into DOS can program a standard clock; our driver will replace it.

Unlike the device drivers of chapters 3 and 4, which used standard PC hardware, the Clock Device Driver will require nonstandard add-on hardware— a clock/calendar chip. You may already have this chip on a multifunction card that also provides additional memory, a parallel and/or a serial port, and perhaps a modem.

The clock driver will contain code to determine where the address of the clock chip is on the PC bus. The driver will also illustrate how the time and date is retrieved from the clock chip to set the DOS time and date. Finally, to keep the time on screen continuously, we will add Terminate but Stay Resident code to the driver.

The Clock/Calendar Chip

The Clock Device Driver is based on the National Semiconductor clock/calendar chip MM58167A. This chip is present on many multifunction cards made by third-party manufacturers, such as AST Research.

When the PC is turned off, the MM58167A chip maintains the time and date by drawing power from a battery. The Clock Device Driver will read the chip for the time and date, display it on the screen, and write a new time and date to the chip when requested. Although the Clock Device Driver in this chapter will be written to program the MM58167A, it can be changed easily to suit other types of clock chips.

The Clock Device Driver Functions

The Clock Device Driver will replace the standard DOS Clock Device Driver. Whenever you boot the PC, DOS will request the time and date via the standard

Clock Device Driver, which is normally set to midnight of January 1, 1980. Thus, when using the standard clock driver, you will need to set the time and date through the TIME and DATE commands.

The Clock Device Driver in this chapter will read the MM58167A chip upon a read command from DOS. The read command is requested only once of the driver, during the boot phase. Whenever you use the TIME and DATE command to set the time and date, DOS will send a write command to the Clock Device Driver. This write command signals the driver to set the MM58167A chip with the time and date passed by DOS.

When DOS sends a read command, the Clock Device Driver will read the time and date stored in the MM58167A clock chip and return it to DOS, which stores it in a special location. Whenever the time and date is set by the user, DOS sends a write command to the Clock Device Driver, which causes the new time to be written into the MM58167A clock chip.

In addition to normal clock and calendar functions, we will build into the Clock Device Driver the ability to display the time on the screen. This is accomplished through a feature of DOS that allows programs to "terminate but stay resident." These programs are loaded into memory like ordinary programs, but when they have finished, they do not exit and are not removed from memory. Instead, they reside in memory and can perform a function on demand regardless of what other programs may be running. For example, a key press, a timer interrupt, or a call to a special interrupt may activate the resident program. This ability to perform a function on demand is used in the Clock Device Driver to display the time on the screen.

Another feature we will build into the Clock Device Driver is the ability to find the hardware address of the clock calendar chip. Normally when clock calendars are available as options on a PC bus card, they can be set to several addresses using tiny DIP switches. This prevents conflicts if another device already uses a certain address. Because most clock calendars have this selectable-address feature, we will build the Clock Device Driver so that it can address the correct clock chip ports. To do so, the driver searches through typical clock chip ports, storing the address of a valid port determined through testing, and writing the code to reference this port. In effect, the software is matched to the hardware settings. Without this feature, the Clock Device Driver software would have to be modified each time the hardware address changes.

Overview of PC Clocks and Timing Signals

There are literally dozens of clocks within the software and hardware of the PC. You will need to understand the function of these clocks in order to write and use the Clock Device Driver.

The most basic of all clocks is the system clock, which is a simple circuit that generates a 14.31818-MHz frequency. This frequency is used to control the color video adapter. It is divided by 3 to generate a 4.772727-MHz frequency that drives the Intel 8088 microprocessor, and the frequency that drives the 8088 is divided by 4 (producing 1.1931817 MHz) and fed to the 8253−5 timer chip. The PC uses the timer chip to perform a variety of functions, such as memory refresh and generating a timer interrupt. Every 64K cycles, the 8253−5 timer chip, running at 1.19 MHz, will generate a hardware interrupt to interrupt 8h at a rate of 18.2 times per second. Thus, the basic clock for DOS is through interrupt 8h and occurs 18.2 times per second. As you will see shortly, this is important to software clock functions. Figure 6−1 ties all of these clocks together.

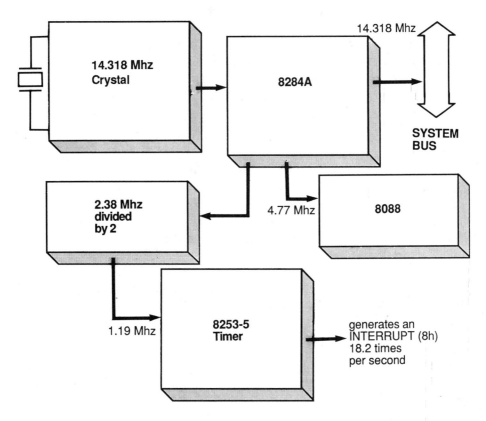

Figure 6−1: The major hardware clocks within the PC. We will need the timer interrupt that is generated from the 8253−5 timer chip 18.2 times per second.

The Timer Interrupt

The timer interrupt, 8h, is important to the clock functions within the PC. It is generated 18.2 times per second by the 8253–5 timer chip and is used by DOS to update a time-of-day counter in low memory (locations 46Ch through 46Fh). This counter contains the number of timer ticks since midnight of the starting day. The value of this counter will range from 0 (start of day) to 1,573,040 (1800B0h), which represents midnight of the starting day. DOS uses this time-of-day counter to calculate the hours, minutes, and seconds that you use through programs.

The time-of-day counter can be read or set from a program by using the 1Ah interrupt. However, it is not recommended that you use this interrupt, because once you use interrupt 1A, you must process the rollover from one day to another. Doing so is unnecessary and a lot of work.

In addition to setting the time-of-day counter, interrupt 8h will generate an interrupt (1C) 18.2 times per second. Many programs take advantage of this interrupt to perform some time-dependent function. We will use this particular interrupt to refresh the time on our screens.

Figure 6–2 shows the relationships among the 8h, 1Ah, and 1Ch interrupts.

Programming the MM58167A Clock Chip

The MM58167A clock/calendar chip contains counters for the various parts of the time and date. Each counter is referenced by an offset relative to the port address that has been selected by DIP switches for the clock chip. In table 6–1, you can see that the counter for 1/10,000ths of a second is assigned to the first port address (0) of the clock chip. The second port address (1) is used for tenths and hundredths of a second, the third port is used for seconds, and so on.

RAM locations on the chip are used to store certain information for which the chip does not provide a counter (see ports 8–F). For example, port 9 can be used to store the previous month, and port ah can be used to store the year. This feature of the MM58167A chip will be used by our driver to retain information. The battery that is part of the clock chip circuit will maintain the contents of the RAM after the PC is turned off. This allows the Clock Device Driver to determine whether the month or year has changed since you last used the PC.

We program the MM58167A chip using IN and OUT instructions like this:

```
mov    dx,340h        ;base address of our clock board is 340h
add    dx,2           ;+2 to access the seconds counter
in     al,dx          ;get the seconds count from the chip
```

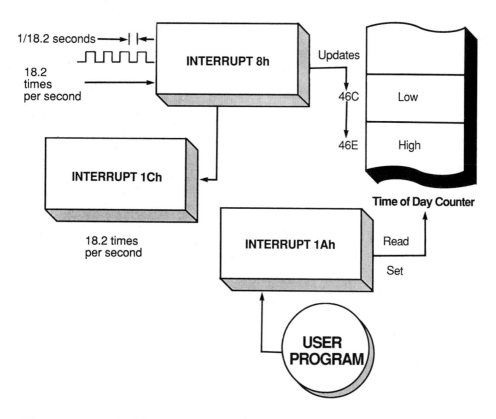

Figure 6–2: The 8h, 1Ch, and 1Ah interrupts. The 1Ch interrupt is used in the Clock Device Driver to display the time on the screen. 8h updates the time of day counter and 1A can be used by a user program to read or set the time of day counter.

Binary Coded Decimal Values

Unfortunately, you cannot just read or set the MM58167A chip using binary data. The chip has been designed for use with Binary Coded Decimal (BCD) values.

BCD numbers are simply binary numbers that occupy four bits and contain a value from 0 to 9. An 8-bit byte contains two such BCD numbers: the left four-bit BCD number represents the ten's value and the right four bits represent the one's value.

The MM58167A chip used BCD values in the counters that keep track of time. You decide whether the RAM locations will use BCD or plain binary values.

Base Port Address	Description
+0	1/10,000ths counter
+1	1/100 +1/10 counter
+2	Seconds counter
+3	Minutes counter
+4	Hours counter
+5	Day-of-week counter
+6	Day-of-month counter
+7	Month counter
+8	1/10,000ths RAM
+9	1/100 + 1/10ths RAM
+a	Seconds RAM
+b	Minutes RAM
+c	Hours RAM
+d	Day-of-week RAM
+e	Day-of-month RAM
+f	Months RAM
+10	Interrupt status register
+11	Interrupt control register
+12	Counter reset
+13	RAM reset
+14	Status bit
+15	GO command
+16	Standby interrupt
+1f	Test mode

Table 6–1: The port addresses for the counters and RAM locations within the MM58167A clock/calendar chip.

For the Clock Device Driver, some procedures must be developed in order to convert BCD values to hex and vice versa. The point here is that when you read or write the chip counters you have to be careful of the data that you use.

Where Is the Clock?

As mentioned earlier, the Clock Device Driver will contain a procedure that will determine the port location of the clock chip automatically. It is important to be careful in doing this, because arbitrary poking around in port addresses may disturb other devices.

The wrong way to check for a clock chip would be to write values to all the ports, and to wait for one of the ports to be updated because it is a clock port.

Doing so would destroy valuable control-status information for most of the devices that are part of the PC.

The best method for finding the clock is to read some commonly assigned port addresses at which the clock chip usually resides, checking for a valid number in one of them. This method takes advantage of the fact that when an IN instruction is used, ports that do not have associated hardware will return FEh or FCh. For example, if the counter for seconds is checked, the values returned cannot be higher than 59. If they are, then there are two assurances that the procedure for determining the clock chip address is correct.

Resident Programs

In order for the Clock Device Driver to display the time on the screen, the Terminate but Stay Resident programming feature is used. Programs that use this feature do so by issuing a DOS interrupt (21h) for the 31h service. This allows the program to continue residing in memory after it has passed control back to DOS. Because it is in memory it can be activated at any time, without the delay normally associated with reading a program from a disk.

Once they have given control back to DOS, resident programs never get control again unless the program itself takes over an interrupt. Taking over an interrupt involves changing the address of a procedure to which an interrupt points. Instead of pointing to some original procedure, the interrupt would point to the resident program. Thus, whenever a particular interrupt occurs, the interrupt would point to the new procedure within the resident program, thus causing the resident program to become active. Figure 6–3 shows the use of an interrupt to pass control to a resident program.

The timer interrupt (1Ch) is one of the most popular interrupts to steal for a resident program. This is because this interrupt always occurs at a rate of 18.2 times per second. Therefore, your resident program has a chance to be activated often. For example, the DOS PRINT utility is actually a resident program, and it uses the timer interrupt to print characters in the print buffer by passing them to the BIOS routines.

Using the Timer Interrupt for Time Displays

As we have said, a feature of the Clock Device Driver is the ability to display the time on the screen. You can, of course, write a resident program just to do this function, but you will have the unnecessary nuisance of two programs to write and maintain.

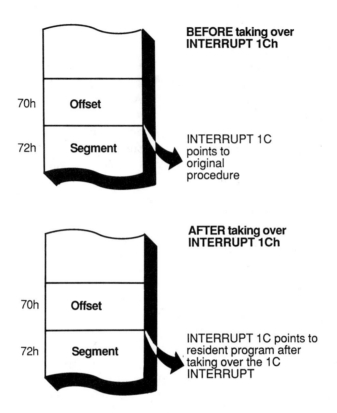

BEFORE taking over
INTERRUPT 1Ch

70h **Offset**

72h **Segment**

INTERRUPT 1C
points to
original
procedure

AFTER taking over
INTERRUPT 1Ch

70h **Offset**

72h **Segment**

INTERRUPT 1C points to
resident program after
taking over the 1C
INTERRUPT

Figure 6–3: The 1C interrupt containing the segment and offset
address that points to the resident program.

The basic task in displaying the time on the screen is simply writing to the screen whenever an interrupt 1Ch passes control to our Clock Device Driver, which occurs 18.2 times a second. Our driver reads the MM58167A chip for the time stored, converts the BCD values it reads to ASCII values, and then writes those values to the screen.

As you have seen, writing to the screen is normally performed through BIOS or DOS function calls. The Clock Device Driver will not use this technique, because DOS function calls are not permitted in device drivers except when processing the Initialization command.

Most video controllers are designed using the technique of memory-mapping in which the video controller and the PC share a part of memory. *Memory-mapping* is the term that defines a memory address that, when referenced, actually "maps" or accesses a controller's memory. In this case, a chunk of the

PC's main memory is used to store the data that is displayed on the screen. Any access of this memory by a program is also an access of the screen's contents. Writes to this area are immediately shown on the screen.

To display the time and date on the screen, two basic functions are performed by the Clock Device Driver. First, it changes the data read from the clock to a format needed to write to the display. This is done during the initialization phase of the Clock Device Driver and before any writing to the screen. Second, whenever the 1Ch interrupt passes control to the Clock Device Driver (18.2 times per second), the time is read from the chip and displayed on the screen.

Understanding the Clock Device Driver Program

The Clock Device Driver will be presented in the same style used in chapters 3, 4, and 5. Because it has only the Read and Write commands to process, the Clock Device Driver is simple compared to the previous console and printer drivers. However, more code is used for these two commands than was present in previous device drivers, because more processing of the clock chip is required. The resident portion of the driver also makes it more complex.

One reason this driver is more complex than others is that the Clock Device Driver is processing several pieces of information (hours, minutes, seconds, month, day, and year). Drivers that process only one byte at a time, such as a console driver, are far less complicated.

The Beginnings

In listing 6–1, you can see that the first three sections have as the basis the code that you have seen in previous chapters. However, there are some differences. First, the main procedure is called *clock*. Second, and more important, the Assembler Directives section has several additional declarations. The first is another segment declaration named *timer*. The Clock Device Driver needs to refer to this segment when processing the 1Ch interrupt, because control is passed to the original timer interrupt routine.

Notice that there is an *org* statement that declares *1ch*4*. This is how *timer* is translated to the 1Ch interrupt vector. The statement *1ch*4* uses the correct form for referencing the segment and offset address associated with a particular interrupt. Because each interrupt location is composed of a 2-byte segment address and a 2-byte offset address, the addresses of a particular interrupt are calculated by simply multiplying the interrupt value by 4. The 1ch interrupt defined as *timer* will point to a procedure *(clkint)* within the Clock Device Driver; control will pass to it 18.2 times per second to allow the time to be displayed on the screen.

Listing 6–1: The beginning of the Clock Device Driver. Note that there is an additional segment definition for *timer,* which is used to take over interrupt 1C so that the timer interrupt passes control to the Clock Device Driver.

```
            page    60,132
            title   A Clock Device Driver

;*****************************************************************
;*      This is a Clock Device Driver                           *
;*      Author:    Robert S. Lai                                *
;*      Date:      27 November 1986                             *
;*      Purpose:   A Clock Driver based on the MM58167A clock chip *
;*****************************************************************


;*****************************************************************
;*          ASSEMBLER DIRECTIVES                                *
;*****************************************************************

timer           segment at      0h          ;int 1c segment
                org     1ch*4
timer_ofs       label   word
timer_seg       label   word
timer           ends

cseg            segment para public    'code'
clock           proc    far
                assume  cs:cseg, es:cseg, ds:cseg

;structures for the Device Driver

dosdate struc               ;DOS DATE structure
dos_day dw      ?           ;days since 1/1/80
dos_min db      ?           ;minutes
dos_hr  db      ?           ;hours
dos_hun db      ?           ;hundredths of a second
dos_sec db      ?           ;seconds
dosdate ends                ;end of struc

;structures

rh              struc                   ;request header
rh_len          db      ?               ;len of packet
rh_unit         db      ?               ;unit code
                                        ;(block devices only)
rh_cmd          db      ?               ;device driver command
rh_status       dw      ?               ;returned by device driver
rh_res1         dd      ?               ;reserved
rh_res2         dd      ?               ;reserved
rh              ends                    ;
```

Listing 6–1: (*cont.*)

```
rh0             struc                   ;Initialization (command 0)
rh0_rh          db      size rh dup (?) ;fixed portion
rh0_nunits      db      ?               ;number of units
                                        ;(block devices only)
rh0_brk_ofs     dw      ?               ;offset address for break
rh0_brk_seg     dw      ?               ;segment address for break
rh0_bpb_tbo     dw      ?               ;offset address of pointer
                                        ;to BPB array
rh0_bpb_tbs     dw      ?               ;segment address of pointer
                                        ;to BPB array
rh0_drv_ltr     db      ?               ;first available drive
                                        ;(DOS 3+) (block only)
rh0             ends                    ;

rh4             struc                   ;INPUT (command 4)
rh4_rh          db      size rh dup(?)  ;fixed portion
rh4_media       db      ?               ;media descriptor from DPB
rh4_buf_ofs     dw      ?               ;offset address of
                                        ;data transfer area
rh4_buf_seg     dw      ?               ;segment address of
                                        ;data transfer area
rh4_count       dw      ?               ;transfer count
                                        ;(sectors for block)
                                        ;(bytes for character)
rh4_start       dw      ?               ;start sector number
                                        ;(block only)
rh4             ends                    ;

rh8             struc                   ;OUTPUT (command 8)
rh8_rh          db      size rh dup(?)  ;fixed portion
rh8_media       db      ?               ;media descriptor from DPB
rh8_buf_ofs     dw      ?               ;offset address of
                                        ;data transfer area
rh8_buf_seg     dw      ?               ;segment address of
                                        ;data transfer area
rh8_count       dw      ?               ;transfer count
                                        ;(sectors for block)
                                        ;(bytes for character)
rh8_start       dw      ?               ;start sector number
                                        ;(block only)
rh8             ends                    ;

rh9             struc                   ;OUTPUT_VERIFY (command 9)
rh9_rh          db      size rh dup(?)  ;fixed portion
rh9_media       db      ?               ;media descriptor from DPB
rh9_buf_ofs     dw      ?               ;offset address of
                                        ;data transfer area
rh9_buf_seg     dw      ?               ;segment address of
                                        ;data transfer area
```

Listing 6–1: (*cont.*)

```
rh9_count        dw        ?          ;transfer count
                                      ;(sectors for block)
                                      ;(bytes for character)
rh9_start        dw        ?          ;start sector number (block only)
rh9              ends                 ;

;commands that do not have unique portions to the request header:
;         INPUT_STATUS      (command 6)
;         INPUT_FLUSH       (command 7)
;         OUTPUT_STATUS     (command 10)
;         OUTPUT_FLUSH      (command 11)
;         OPEN              (command 13)
;         CLOSE             (command 14)
;         REMOVABLE         (command 15)
;


;*****************************************************************
;*        MAIN PROCEDURE CODE                                    *
;*****************************************************************

begin:
```

A new *struc, dosdate,* has been added right after the *cseg* and *clock* declarations. This *struc* is used to access the time and date from within the Clock Device Driver. The read command will use this structure to set the clock chip time and date. A write command sent to the Clock Device Driver will read the clock chip and use the *struc* to pass the time and date back to DOS.

Notice, however, that the *struc* does not define the date in the normal form of month, day, and year. Instead, the date is defined as the number of days since January 1, 1980. This is the format that DOS uses to pass the date to and from clock drivers. Most of the code in the Clock Device Driver is devoted to conversions from one format to the other.

Some *strucs* have been removed. The only ones we use are for commands 0 (Initialization), 4 (Input), 8 (Output), and 9 (Output With Verify). Recall that the Input command is used to pass data from the device back to DOS, and the Output command is used to pass data from DOS to the device.

The Device Header

The Device Header is shown in listing 6–2. For the Clock Device Driver, the bits in the Attribute word are set to indicate a character device (bit 15). Bit (3)

Listing 6–2: The Device Header section. Note that the Attribute and the device name are the only entries that change in the various device drivers in this book.

```
;************************************************************
;*        DEVICE HEADER REQUIRED BY DOS                    *
;************************************************************
next_dev        dd    -1               ;no other drivers following
attribute       dw    8008h            ;char,clock device
strategy        dw    dev_strategy     ;Strategy routine address
interrupt       dw    dev_interrupt    ;Interrupt routine address
dev_name        db    'CLOCK$  '       ;name of our Clock driver
```

---

is set to indicate to DOS that the device is a clock. The device name is set to *CLOCK$*.

Work Space for the Clock Device Driver

A number of variables are defined in the Work Space to support the Clock Device Driver. Listing 6–3 shows the variables declared.

The familiar variables *rh_ofs* and *rh_seg* are first. Recall that you will use these variables to store the ES and BX registers that point to the address at which the Request Header is stored in DOS's memory space.

The next variable is a table suitably named *table,* which is used to store the number of days for each month of the year, one day (28, 30, or 31) per byte. The driver will use this table to calculate two items: the number of days since the beginning of the year, given the month and day, and the month and day, given the number of days since the beginning of the year.

The word variable *clock_port* is used to store the 16-bit port address of the clock chip in the procedure that finds the clock chip hardware address.

The label *old1c* and the two word variables *old1c_ofs* and *old1c_seg* are used to reference the offset and segment address of the original timer interrupt (1Ch) procedure. This address is used to store the address of the original procedure, so that the driver can call that procedure before passing control to the code that displays the time on the screen. This allows the 1Ch interrupt to be used by others.

The balance of the Work Space variables are used when the time is displayed on the screen. The *mode* variable is used to store a flag that indicates whether the screen is controlled by a monochrome or a color adapter. This flag displays the type of monitor adapter used in the initialization code.

Listing 6–3: The work space variable allocated for the Clock Device Driver.
Note that the order of the variables is not important.

```
;****************************************************************
;*        WORK SPACE FOR CLOCK DEVICE DRIVER                   *
;****************************************************************

rh_ofs    dw      ?          ;offset address of the request header
rh_seg    dw      ?          ;segment address of the request header

table     label   byte
jan       db      31
feb       db      28
mar       db      31
apr       db      30
may       db      31
jun       db      30
jul       db      31
aug       db      31
sep       db      30
oct       db      31
nov       db      30
decm      db      31

dosdays           dw      0        ;DOS date (days since 1/1/80)
clock_port        dw      0        ;clock chip base address
oldlc             label   dword    ;old timer interrupt 1C
oldlc_ofs         dw      ?        ; offset
oldlc_seg         dw      ?        ; segment
refresh           dw      0        ;screen update indicator
mode              db      0        ;color = 0, mono = 1
scn_pos           dw      144      ;column 72 (includes attribute)
scn_port          dw      03dah    ;video status port for color
                                   ;03bah for mono
scn_seg           dw      0b800h   ;video memory address for color
                                   ;0b000h for mono
time              dw      8 dup (003ah)   ;time display
```

The variable *scn_pos* is the number of the column in which the time is displayed. The actual number (144) reflects the fact that each column is composed of two bytes, the first containing the data to be displayed and the second containing the screen attribute for the data byte. Screen attributes are used to color or highlight the data byte. The time display starts at column 72 of the top line.

The variable *scn_port* is used to store the video adapter status port for the particular type of monitor adapter. This status port is used to determine when to write a byte to the screen.

The variable *scn_seg* is used to store the segment address of the screen memory for the particular type of monitor adapter being used. The default is the color adapter (the color and monochrome adapters have different segment addresses).

As we said earlier, rather than use BIOS calls to display the time, we chose to use a write to the screen memory segment. Because the screen memory is mapped to the screen display, when you write to the screen memory segment the data will appear on the screen.

Lastly, the variable *time* is used to store the time you wish to display on the screen in a suitable format. Eight words are declared. Each word will contain a data byte and a byte for the screen attribute. Eight data bytes will be displayed: two bytes for the hours, two for the minutes, two for the seconds, and two for the colons in between.

The STRATEGY and INTERRUPT Procedures

The STRATEGY and INTERRUPT procedures for the Clock Device Driver have not changed from those for the printer driver; they will remain unchanged for the rest of the device drivers in this book. The code for these procedures is contained in listing 6–4.

Local Procedures for the Clock Device Driver

As shown in listing 6–5, there are five local procedures for the Clock Device Driver: *hex2bcd, bcd2hex, cvt2asc, display,* and *clkint*. All of these are *near* procedures, because they are defined and referenced from within the same segment.

The first two procedures, *hex2bcd* and *bcd2hex,* are used to convert a hexadecimal number to Binary Coded Decimal (BCD) format and vice versa. (The MM58167A chip uses BCD values, and the Clock Device Driver needs to convert them to hex for calculations and then back to BCD for setting the clock chip.)

The third procedure, *cvt2asc,* is used by the fourth procedure display. Procedure *cvt2asc* ("convert to ASCII") is used to input a value from a particular clock chip port and to convert the two BCD digits into two ASCII display bytes for the screen.

The *display* procedure is used to build a string that contains the time the Clock Device Driver displays on the screen. The variable *time* is used to store the hours, minutes, and seconds, which are separated by colons. Each piece of

---

Listing 6–4: The code for the STRATEGY and INTERRUPT procedures

```
;*****************************************************************
;*        THE STRATEGY PROCEDURE                                *
;*****************************************************************

dev_strategy:   mov   cs:rh_seg,es     ;save the segment address
                mov   cs:rh_ofs,bx     ;save the offset address
                ret                    ;return to DOS

;*****************************************************************
;*        THE INTERRUPT PROCEDURE                               *
;*****************************************************************

;device interrupt handler - 2nd call from DOS

dev_interrupt:

        cld                         ;save machine state on entry
        push    ds
        push    es
        push    ax
        push    bx
        push    cx
        push    dx
        push    di
        push    si

        mov     ax,cs:rh_seg        ;restore ES as saved by STRATEGY call
        mov     es,ax               ;
        mov     bx,cs:rh_ofs        ;restore BX as saved by STRATEGY call

;jump to appropriate routine to process command

        mov     al,es:[bx].rh_cmd   ;get request header command
        rol     al,1                ;times 2 for index into word table
        lea     di,cmdtab           ;function (command) table address
        mov     ah,0                ;clear hi order
        add     di,ax               ;add the index to start of table
        jmp     word ptr[di]        ;jump indirect

;CMDTAB is the command table that contains the word address
;for each command. The request header will contain the
;command desired. The INTERRUPT routine will jump through an
;address corresponding to the requested command to get to
;the appropriate command processing routine.

CMDTAB  label   byte                ;* = char devices only
        dw      INITIALIZATION      ; initialization
```

Listing 6–4: (cont.)

```
        dw      MEDIA_CHECK       ; media check (block only)
        dw      GET_BPB           ; build bpb
        dw      IOCTL_INPUT       ; ioctl in
        dw      INPUT             ; input (read)
        dw      ND_INPUT          ;*non destructive input no wait
        dw      INPUT_STATUS      ;*input status
        dw      INPUT_FLUSH       ;*input flush
        dw      OUTPUT            ; output (write)
        dw      OUTPUT_VERIFY     ; output (write) with verify
        dw      OUTPUT_STATUS     ;*output status
        dw      OUTPUT_FLUSH      ;*output flush
        dw      IOCTL_OUT         ; ioctl output
        dw      OPEN              ; device open
        dw      CLOSE             ; device close
        dw      REMOVABLE         ; removable media
        dw      OUTPUT_BUSY       ; output til busy
```

Listing 6–5: The five local procedures for the Clock Device Driver

```
;*****************************************************************
;*      YOUR LOCAL PROCEDURES                                   *
;*****************************************************************

hex2bcd proc    near    ;convert AL from Hex to BCD
;uses   ax,cx
        push    cx
        mov     cl,10   ;divide by 10
        mov     ah,0    ;setup for divide
        div     cl      ;get 10's digits
        mov     cl,4    ;shift count
        shl     al,cl   ;place 10's in left half
        or      al,ah   ;add back 1's
        pop     cx
        ret     •       ;return to caller
hex2bcd endp

bcd2hex proc    near    ;convert AL from BCD to hex
;uses ax,cx
        push    cx
        mov     ah,0    ;setup for divide
        push    ax      ;save for 1's processing
        mov     cl,16   ;divide for left half of byte
        div     cl      ; to get 10's digits
        mov     ah,0    ;have 10's digits
        mov     cl,10   ;convert to base 10
```

Listing 6–5: (*cont.*)

```
        mul     cl          ; by multiplying by 10
        pop     cx          ;process 1's digits
        and     cl,0fh      ;keep 1's only
        add     al,cl       ;add 1's to 10's
        pop     cx
        ret                 ;return to caller
bcd2hex endp

cvt2asc proc    near        ;gets chip data & converts to ASCII
        in      al,dx           ;get (BCD) chip data
        mov     ah,0            ;clear high
        mov     cl,10h          ;separate 10's digits
        div     cl              ;al=10's, ah=1's
        or      ax,3030h        ;convert to ascii
        ret                     ;return to caller
cvt2asc endp                    ;

display proc    near            ;calculates time for display
        push    ax              ;save registers used
        push    bx
        push    cx
        push    dx
        mov     dx,cs:clock_port;get chip's base address
        add     dx,4            ;base+4 = hours
        call    cvt2asc         ;get hours and convert
        lea     bx,cs:time      ;move to Time string
        mov     cs:[bx],al      ;tens of hrs
        mov     cs:[bx+2],ah    ;hrs
        dec     dx              ;base+3 = minutes
        call    cvt2asc         ;get minutes and convert
        mov     cs:[bx+6],al    ;tens of minutes
        mov     cs:[bx+8],ah    ;ones
        dec     dx              ;base+2 = seconds
        call    cvt2asc         ;get seconds and convert
        mov     cs:[bx+12],al   ;tens of seconds
        mov     cs:[bx+14],ah   ;ones
        pop     dx              ;restore saved registers
        pop     cx
        pop     bx
        pop     ax
        ret                     ;return to caller
display endp

;Clock Driver's replacement code for interrupt 1Ch

clkint  proc    near        ;new timer interrupt code
        push    ax              ;save registers used
        push    cx
        push    di
```

Listing 6–5: (*cont.*)

```
          push    si
          push    es
          pushf                       ;must push flags
          call    cs:oldlc            ;call old timer int
          mov     cx,cs:refresh       ;get refresh counter
          inc     cx                  ;increment
          cmp     cx,18               ;18th time?
          jb      notime              ;no need to recalc time
          call    display             ;yes we do
          mov     cx,0                ;reset counter
notime:   mov     cs:refresh,cx       ;store it
          mov     dx,cs:scn_port      ;screen status port
          mov     di,cs:scn_pos       ;screen display position
          lea     si,cs:time          ;time string source
          mov     cx,cs:scn_seg       ;screen segment
          mov     es,cx               ; in es
          mov     cx,10               ;move 10 bytes
          cli                         ;clear interrupts
hlow:                                 ;wait for horizontal scan
          in      al,dx               ;get video port status
          test    al,1                ;wait for low = 1
          jnz     hlow                ;back   .
          mov     ah,cs:[si]          ;get byte to be displayed
hhigh:
          in      al,dx               ;status must go hi after lo
          test    al,1                ; before a screen write
          jz      hhigh               ;wait til high = 0
          mov     es:[di],ah          ;1 byte at any one time
          inc     di                  ;increment screen position
          inc     si                  ;increment source position
          loop    hlow                ;loop thru all bytes
          sti                         ;restore interrupts
          pop     es                  ;restore all saved registers
          pop     si
          pop     di
          pop     cx
          pop     ax
          iret                        ;interrupt return
clkint    endp
```

---

data is read from the clock chip by calling the *cvt2asc* procedure, which also converts the data to ASCII.

The procedure *clkint* is not called as part of the processing that the Clock Device Driver performs. It is the procedure that is called when the timer interrupt (1Ch) is invoked. Every 55 milliseconds, or 18.2 times per second, control is passed to the timer interrupt. It contains the address of *clkint,* which displays the *time* string on the screen. See figure 6–4 for a summary of how the 1Ch interrupt passes control to the Clock Device Driver to display the time.

In *clkint,* the first check is to see whether this is the 18th time the timer interrupt has passed control to the driver. The number 18 is used as an approximate countdown for determining when to reread the time from the clock chip. If it is the 18th time, the *display* procedure is called. Then the fun begins: displaying the time on the screen.

Because of the design of the color monitor adapter, you cannot simply write the time to the screen. This would cause the screen to *flicker,* or *snow. Snow* is caused by interference with the hardware display functions. When the color monitor adapter performs line scans in displaying information on the screen, the screen memory it is reading from needs to be dedicated to the operation. When your program writes directly to this same screen memory, you are disturbing this parallel hardware operation. To avoid this problem, you should write to screen memory only when the color adapter status port indicates that a horizontal retrace is being performed. This is the time when the screen's electron beam has reached the right edge and is turned off, returning to the left side and

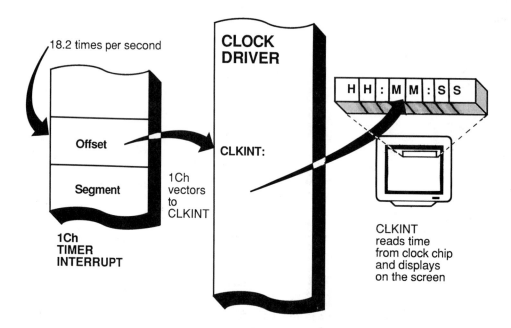

Figure 6–4: The 1Ch interrupt passes control to the Clock Driver.

the next line down on the screen. You can write to the screen memory during this horizontal retrace without causing snow by interference.

In listing 6–5 above, you will notice the code at labels *hlow* and *hhigh*. This code handles the actual screen writes. Writes are allowed when the video port status bit 0 is high. Even when it is high, however, there may not be enough time to perform a write, because we are selecting a random point during the retrace. To handle this situation, two loops are provided: the first loop, the label *hlow,* catches the first high status (a retrace), and the second loop, at *hhigh,* waits out the low status. When this second loop finishes, the start of a new high status occurs. If the write begins at the start of this high status, there will be enough time to write out a single character without interference.

Remember that this snow-protection code is necessary only for writing text characters using the color monitor adapter. If you are in color graphics mode or if you are using the monochrome monitor adapter, such code is unnecessary; instead, you can use the horizontal-retrace time to update screen memory without harm. Because the Clock Device Driver is written for both color and monochrome adapters, the special code for snow-free display will remain.

Our driver writes to the screen memory by specifying the screen memory segment address *(scn_seg)* and the offset address *(scn_pos)* at which you want the time displayed. Because the screen is memory-mapped, these addresses specify a screen cell. Interrupts are turned off during the two wait loops and turned back on after a byte is moved to the screen memory. This on/off pattern is used because there is enough time to display only one byte (one character or attribute) during the horizontal retrace period. Thus, during this time we do not want any interference from interrupts. Simply put, while we are trying not to interfere with the color adapter, we do not want to be interfered with!

So far you have seen how the *clkint* procedure takes control when a timer interrupt occurs. The last section in this chapter discusses how to actually divert the timer interrupt to run our procedure.

DOS Command Processing

Of the 17 allowable commands that DOS passes to the device drivers, only four commands are processed by the Clock Device Driver. The Initialization command is always one of them. In addition, the Clock Device Driver will process the Input, Output, and Output With Verify commands. Let's see how these routines work.

Command 0—Initialization The Initialization command will, once again, call the procedure *initial*. However, the driver will need to check the results from the call to *initial,* because the code that determines the address of the clock chip may not find such an address. If no address is found, you cannot allow DOS to load this device driver. If the variable *clock_port* contains a 0, the driver tells DOS not to use this device driver by simply placing the address of the Clock Device Driver as the next available address. Thus, by setting the Break Address to the beginning of this driver, DOS overwrites the Clock Device Driver's memory space upon return to DOS. In effect, the Clock Device Driver has not been loaded at all. However, if the *clock_port* contains a value other than 0, indicating that a clock chip address has been found, the Break Address is set to the memory address of *initial* and the driver returns to DOS. The code for the Initialization command is shown in listing 6–6.

Commands Not Applicable to the Clock Device Driver   The Media Check, Get BIOS Parameter Block, and IOCTL Input commands are not applicable to the Clock Device Driver, because the device is not a disk device. Here is the code for these sections:

```
;command 1     Media_Check
Media Check:

        jmp     done              ;set done bit and exit

;command 2     Get_BPB
Get_BPB:

        jmp     done              ;set done bit and exit

;command 3     IOCTL_Input
IOCTL_Input:

        jmp     unknown           ;set error bit/code and exit
```

Command 4—Input   The Input command is sent to the Clock Device Driver by DOS whenever DOS needs to read the time and date. This usually occurs from the command level when the TIME and DATE commands are issued by a user or from within programs that request DOS services.

The basic function of the Input command is to read the clock chip and pass the time and date back to DOS, which then stores it. As you saw earlier, the clock chip's data, which is in BCD format, needs to be converted to hex.

At label *Input* in listing 6–7, there is code that points to the data in which DOS expects the time and date to be returned. The registers ES and BX are used to point to the beginning of the data-transfer area. The *struc dosdate* is used to index into the table when the time is returned. The time is retrieved from the clock chip by reading into al the respective time counters. The hundredths of a

---

Listing 6–6: The code for the Initialization command. If the procedure *initial* does not find a valid clock chip port address, DOS is allowed to overwrite the Clock Device Driver. This is accomplished by setting the Break Address to the beginning of the device driver.

```
;*****************************************************************
;*        DOS COMMAND PROCESSING                                 *
;*****************************************************************
;command 0      Initialization
Initialization:

        call    initial                 ;display message
;determine whether we found a clock chip
        cmp     cs:clock_port,0         ;is chip base = 0?
        jne     init1                   ;no - there is a chip
;no chip found - we must abort loading this driver
        mov     ax,0                    ;set address to beginning
        jmp     init2                   ;store break offset
init1:  lea     ax,initial              ;set Break Addr. at initial
init2:  mov     es:[bx].rh0_brk_ofs,ax  ;store offset address
        mov     es:[bx].rh0_brk_seg,cs  ;store segment address
        jmp     done                    ;set done status and exit
```

---

second, the seconds, the minutes, and the hours are read from the clock chip and converted from BCD to hex values.

At the label *incheck* there is a check to see whether the month has changed since the clock chip was last read during a similar Read command. This check is performed because you may have used the PC past midnight of the last day of a month or you may not have used the PC since the end of the last month. The RAM memory location on the clock chip is used to store the month in which you last accessed the clock chip. This allows the driver to check the clock chip months-counter against the last time the driver read the clock chip. If the driver finds that the clock chip months-counter has been incremented, further calculations may determine that it is a new year. If the clock chip had an automatic counter for years, all this work would not be required.

Next, the driver reads the months-counter and checks the number returned against the number that was last stored in the months RAM location. If the months-counter has been incremented by 1, the driver stores the new count in the months RAM location. However, if the months-counter is less than the last value stored in the months RAM location, the driver assumes that the month has changed from December 12 to January 1; the years count is then incre-

Listing 6–7: The code for the Input command. The clock chip time and date is read and these values are returned to DOS. The date needs to be converted from month, day, and year into days since 1/1/80.

```
;command 4        Input    Read clock chip and return to DOS
Input:

;Read and convert clock chip date and time to DOS date format
        mov       dx,es:[bx].rh4_buf_ofs  ;get dos date data area
        mov       ax,es:[bx].rh4_buf_seg  ;
        mov       es,ax                   ;set up es
        mov       bx,dx                   ;set up bx
;ES:BX points to the DOS date buffer
        push      es                      ;save segment for later
        push      bx                      ;save offset for later
;first read the clock chip for time
        mov       dx,cs:clock_port        ;get the clock base address
        inc       dx                      ;base+1
        in        al,dx                   ;get hundredths
        call      bcd2hex                 ;convert data
        mov       es:[bx].dos_hun,al      ;store hundredths
        inc       dx                      ;base+2
        in        al,dx                   ;get seconds
        call      bcd2hex                 ;convert data
        mov       es:[bx].dos_sec,al      ;store seconds
        inc       dx                      ;base+3
        in        al,dx                   ;get minutes
        call      bcd2hex                 ;convert data
        mov       es:[bx].dos_min,al      ;store minutes
        inc       dx                      ;base+4
        in        al,dx                   ;get hours
        call      bcd2hex                 ;convert data
        mov       es:[bx].dos_hr,al       ;store hours
;now convert chip date (BCD format) to DOS date format (hex)

;first check to see if month (and therefore year) has changed
;by comparing the months COUNTER against the month RAM location
incheck:
        mov       dx,cs:clock_port        ;get base clock address
        add       dx,7                    ;base+7
        in        al,dx                   ;get chip's month counter
        call      bcd2hex                 ;convert to hex
        mov       bl,al                   ;save in bl
        add       dx,2                    ;base+9
        in        al,dx                   ;get RAM version of month
        call      bcd2hex                 ;convert to hex
        cmp       al,bl                   ;is RAM & counter same?
        jg        newyear                 ;last month > current ( 12>1 )
        jl        updatemonth             ;last month < current
        jmp       prev_days               ;same month
```

Listing 6–7: (*cont.*)

```
;December rolled over to January - update the Year count in RAM
newyear:
        inc     dx                      ;base+10
        in      al,dx                   ;get year (stored in RAM)
        inc     al                      ;add 1 year
        out     dx,al                   ;store in RAM year
        dec     dx                      ;make it base+9
;now update month in RAM
updatemonth:
        mov     al,bl                   ;set current month
        call    hex2bcd                 ;convert for clock chip
        out     dx,al                   ;update month RAM


;determine days in previous years
prev_days:
        inc     dx                      ;base+10 (RAM)
        in      al,dx                   ;get years since 1980
        mov     ah,0                    ;set up for multiply
        push    ax                      ;save for leap year processing
        mov     bx,365                  ;days per year
        mul     bx                      ;times years - AX has days
        xchg    bx,ax                   ;save days in BX
        mov     cl,4                    ;leap divisor
        pop     ax                      ;get year count again
        div     cl                      ;divide for leap years elapsed
        mov     cl,ah                   ;save leap year indicator
;BX has total days and cl has leap year indicator
        mov     ah,0                    ;set up for add
        add     bx,ax                   ;add leap days to total

;we have days since 1/1/80 for all previous years including
; the extra days in leap years past
curr_days:
        push    bx                      ;save total days past
        mov     dx,cs:clock_port        ;get base clock chip address
        add     dx,7                    ;base+7
        in      al,dx                   ;get month counter
        call    bcd2hex                 ;convert to hex
        mov     ah,0                    ;set up for index
        push    cs                      ;days per month table
        pop     es                      ; addressed by ES
        lea     di,cs:table             ; and DI
        mov     cx,0                    ;clear current year day count
        xchg    ax,cx                   ;month loop count in cx
        push    cx                      ;save for leap year check
        mov     bh,0                    ;clear hi-order
cvt2days:
        mov     bl,es:[di]              ;days in this month
        inc     di                      ;increment for next month
```

Listing 6–7: (*cont.*)

```
        add     ax,bx                       ;add to total days
        loop    cvt2days                    ;until month count exhausted
        pop     cx                          ;restore months
        pop     bx                          ;total days past
        add     ax,bx                       ;add to days in current year
        cmp     cl,3                        ;past March?
        jl      leapyr                      ;no
        inc     ax                          ;yes - add 1 for 2/29
leapyr: pop     bx                          ;restore DOS date offset
        pop     es                          ;restore DOS date segment
        mov     es:[bx].dos_day,ax          ;return days since 1/1/80
        mov     ax,0                        ;status ok
        mov     bx,6                        ;count of 6
        jmp     load_status                 ;restore es:bx exit
```

---

mented and stored in the years RAM location, and the new month is stored in the months' RAM location.

Once the driver has the correct count of the months and years, it can calculate the number of days since January 1, 1980, up to the beginning of the current year. This calculation, which is performed at the label *prev_days,* involves multiplying the number of years by 365 and adding one day for each of the previous years that were leap years.

Finally, at the label *curr_days,* the days in the current year are added to the total. If the date is past March 1 and the current year is a leap year, one day is added to the total days since January 1, 1980. This number is returned to DOS through the *struc* that points to the data transfer area. The Clock Device Driver then returns control to DOS. The code for the Input command is shown in listing 6–7.

Other Input Commands The Clock Device Driver does not need to process the other Input commands, Nondestructive Input, Input Status, and Input Flush. These commands are not applicable, so the driver jumps to the BUSY and DONE routines to exit. The code for these commands are shown as follows:

```
;command 5      ND Input
ND Input:

        jmp     busy                        ;set busy bit and exit

;command 6      Input Status
```

```
Input Status:

        jmp     done                    ;set done bit and exit

;command 7      Input Flush
Input Flush:

        jmp     done                    ;set done bit and exit
```

Command 8—Output The Output command is used to set the clock chip time and date. DOS passes to the Clock Device Driver the time and days since January 1, 1980. The driver converts these values to time, month, day, and year. In listing 6–8, you will see each of the calculations needed to perform this conversion.

At the label *Output,* the registers ES and BX are set up to point to the data-transfer area in which DOS has passed the time and date. The *struc dosdate* is used to reference each piece of data. First, the value for the number of days since January 1, 1980, is moved to the local variable *dosdays.* This variable is needed later on, when the driver converts its value to month, day, and year.

At the label *outchip,* the time is retrieved. These values are stored in the clock chip after a hexadecimal-to-BCD conversion is performed for each of the values.

At the label *out_years,* the number of years since 1980 is calculated, given the days since 1/1/80. The loop at *out1* simply subtracts 365 from the total days and increments the BX register for the count of years elapsed. Upon completion, the driver has the number of years elapsed since 1980 and the count of the days in the current year.

At the label *out2,* the driver calculates the number of extra days resulting from the number of leap years passed. The number of these extra days is subtracted from the days left in the current year. If the number of extra days is greater than the number of days in the current year, the driver needs to adjust the days-left count and the number of years since 1980.

At the label *out3,* the driver tests for the number of days left in the current year against the leap year indicator. If the current year is a leap year, the driver needs to determine whether the current date is before, at, or after February 29. If the current date is before February 29, the driver needs to add back the one day that was subtracted earlier when it was determined that the current year is a leap year. If the current date is February 29, the month and day is set accordingly.

At the label *out5,* the driver uses the days left in the current year and calculates the month and day by using the days-per-month table named *table.* The code loops, subtracting each time, the number of days per month for each month in *table* from the days left in current year, until the remainder is less

---

Listing 6–8: The code for the Output command, which sets the time and date on the MM58167A clock chip

---

```
;command 8        Output  Set the Clock Chip Time and Date
Output:

;Convert the date in DOS date format to clock chip format
; for writing to the clock chip

;let ES:BX point to beginning of the DOS date
        mov     si,es:[bx].rh8_buf_ofs  ;get data offset
        mov     ax,es:[bx].rh8_buf_seg  ;get data segment
        mov     ds,ax                   ;to DS for (DS:SI use)
        push    si                      ;save offset
        push    ds                      ;save segment
        push    cs                      ;
        pop     es                      ;ES points to here
        lea     di,cs:dosdays           ;destination address
        mov     cx,2                    ;move count = 2
        cld                             ;direction is forward
        rep     movsb                   ;  from DOS to us
        push    cs                      ;restore DS
        pop     ds                      ;  by using CS
;update clock chip with time from DOS date data
outchip:
        pop     es                      ;restore DOS date segment
        pop     bx                      ;restore DOS date offset
        mov     dx,cs:clock_port        ;get clock port
        inc     dx                      ;base+1
        mov     al,es:[bx].dos_hun      ;get hundredths
        call    hex2bcd                 ;convert for clock use
        out     dx,al                   ;send to clock chip
        inc     dx                      ;base+2
        mov     al,es:[bx].dos_sec      ;get seconds
        call    hex2bcd                 ;convert for clock use
        out     dx,al                   ;send to clock chip
        inc     dx                      ;base+3
        mov     al,es:[bx].dos_min      ;get minutes
        call    hex2bcd                 ;convert for clock use
        out     dx,al                   ;send to clock chip
        inc     dx                      ;base+4
        mov     al,es:[bx].dos_hr       ;get hours
        call    hex2bcd                 ;convert for clock use
        out     dx,al                   ;send to clock chip

;chip loaded with time - now calc chip date from DOS date
out_years:
        mov     ax,cs:dosdays           ;get days since 1/1/80
        cmp     ax,0                    ;date not set?
        je      out8                    ;skip everything
        mov     bx,0                    ;BX = year count
```

Listing 6–8: (*cont.*)

```
out1:   cmp     ax,365              ;day count within a year?
        jle     out2                ;yes
        sub     ax,365              ;no - subtract 365
        inc     bx                  ;increment year count
        jmp     out1                ;continue until w/i 1 yr
;BX has years since 1980 - now adjust for leap years
out2:   push    ax                  ;save leftover days
        mov     ax,bx               ;AX now has years
        mov     cl,4                ;divisor for leap years
        div     cl                  ;al=leaps, ah=remainder
        mov     cl,ah               ;remainder=0 is leap itself
        mov     ah,0                ;set up for subtract
        inc     ax                  ;add 1 to leap year count
        mov     dx,ax               ;DX has 1 day/leap yr passed
        pop     ax                  ;restore days remaining
        sub     ax,dx               ;subtract 1 day for each leap yr
        cmp     ax,0                ;are we negative?
        jg      out3                ;no - we are ok
        add     ax,365              ;add back 365 days
        dec     bx                  ;subtract 1 year
out3:   push    bx                  ;save year count
        cmp     cl,0                ;leap year if 0
        jne     out5                ;not a leap year
        cmp     ax,59               ;Feb 29?
        je      out4                ;yes - set and exit
        jg      out5                ;past Feb 29
        inc     ax                  ;before - reverse subtraction
        jmp     out5                ;
out4:   mov     cx,2                ;Feb
        mov     ax,29               ; 29
        jmp     out7                ;exit
;AX has days left in current year - now find month and day
out5:   mov     cx,1                ;month count
        lea     di,cs:table         ;days per month
        mov     bh,0                ;clear hi-order
out6:   mov     bl,es:[di]          ;get days in each month
        inc     di                  ;increment to next month
        cmp     ax,bx               ;less than last day?
        jle     out7                ;yes (in current month)
        sub     ax,bx               ;no subtract days in month
        inc     cx                  ;increment month count
        jmp     out6                ;continue until month found
;AX has days, CX has month - now get years since 1980
out7:   pop     bx                  ;restore year count
        jmp     out9                ;go load chip
;no date set (special case)
out8:   mov     bx,0                ;1980
        mov     cx,1                ;Jan
        mov     ax,1                ; 1st
```

Listing 6–8: (*cont.*)

```
;BX = years since 1980, CX = month, AX = days - now load clock chip
out9:   mov     dx,cs:clock_port        ;get chip base address
        add     dx,6                    ;base+6
        push    cx                      ;Hex2bcd destroys cx
        call    hex2bcd                 ;convert for chip use
        out     dx,al                   ;set days counter
        inc     dx                      ;base+7
        pop     ax                      ;restore month count
        call    hex2bcd                 ;convert for chip use
        out     dx,al                   ;set months counter
        add     dx,2                    ;base+9
        out     dx,al                   ;set months RAM
        inc     dx                      ;base+10
        xchg    al,bl                   ;move years to al
        out     dx,al                   ;set years since 1980 RAM
        mov     ax,0                    ;status ok
        mov     bx,6                    ;count of 6
        jmp     load_status             ;set status word & exit
```

---

than the number of days in the next month in the table. Finally we have the month, day, and years since 1980.

At the label *out9,* the date is converted from hex to BCD and the clock chip is loaded with these values.

The Rest of the Commands   Listing 6–9 contains the code for the rest of the driver commands. Output With Verify (command 9) is processed by the same code as Output, so the driver jumps to the Output procedure. The commands Output Status (10), Output Flush (11), I/O Control Output (12), Device Open (13), Device Close (14), Removable Media (15), and Output Til Busy (16) are not applicable, so the Clock Device Driver jumps to the appropriate routine, sets DONE or ERROR, and exits.

The Error Exit Section

The Error Exit section for the Clock Device Driver is the same as that for the device drivers of the previous chapters. Control is passed to the Error Exit routine from the commands Removable Media and Output Til Busy if the Clock Device Driver receives these commands. The ERROR bit of the Request Header

Listing 6–9: The code for the commands following the Output command (8).

```
;command 9     Output_Verify
Output_Verify:

        jmp     output              ;same as output

;command 10    Output_Status
Output_Status:

        jmp     done                ;set done bit and exit

;command 11    Output_Flush
Output_Flush:

        jmp     done                ;set done bit and exit

;command 12    IOCTL_Out
IOCTL_Out:

        jmp     unknown             ;set error bit/code and exit

;command 13    Open
Open:

        jmp     done                ;set done bit and exit

;command 14    Close
Close:

        jmp     done                ;set done bit and exit

;command 15    Removable
Removable:

        jmp     unknown             ;set error bit/code and exit

;command 16    Output Til Busy
Output_Busy:

        jmp     unknown             ;set error bit/code and exit
```

status word is set. The error code is set to 3, which indicates an Unknown command. Here is the code for the Error Exit section:

```
;****************************************************************
;*        ERROR EXIT                                            *
;****************************************************************
unknown:
        or      es:[bx].rh_status,8003h ;set error bit and error code
        jmp     done                    ;set done and exit
```

The Common Exit Section

The Clock Device Driver passes control from the Input and Output commands to the Common Exit routine at the label *load_status*. The status in the AX register and the count in the BX register are set before the program jumps to this section. The status word is set to 0 to indicate that there are no errors, and the count is always set to 6.

Next, the driver restores the ES and BX registers, which point to the Request Header; the status and count are stored before the Clock Device Driver exits. In addition, commands that jump to BUSY are processed here. The Common Exit code is shown in listing 6–10.

The End of Program

The code contained in the *initial* procedure, which is called from the Initialization command, is placed at the end of the device driver because it is used only once. As you have seen in previous examples, the driver allows DOS to overwrite the memory used by this procedure by setting the Break Address to point to this memory space. The amount of memory for other DOS code is thus increased.

In listing 6–11, you will see that the first function that the *initial* procedure performs is to find the MM58167A clock chip hardware port address. The driver uses a table named *clock_table* that contains the typical values of the base port addresses used for the MM58167A chip.

The Clock Device Driver uses a simple algorithm to find the clock chip port address. Because the counter for seconds is at location 2 relative to the base port address, this counter is read using the base chip ports from the *clock_table*. The driver also assumes that the MM58167A chip will return a BCD value in the range from 0 to 59. Therefore, if a clock chip exists at the base port address, any seconds values that are read in will not have the high-order bit (8) set, and the values will be less than 80h. If the driver finds that the seconds value does not have this high-order bit set, it assumes that a clock chip has been found at the base port address.

Listing 6–10: The code for the Common Exit processing. The ES and BX registers are restored, the status and count are saved, and the driver exits.

```
;*****************************************************************
;*        COMMON EXIT                                           *
;*****************************************************************
load_status:
        mov     cx,cs:rh_seg        ;restore request header
        mov     es,cx               ; segment to es
        mov     cx,cs:rh_ofs        ;restore offset also
        xchg    bx,cx               ;switch them
        mov     es:[bx].rh_status,ax ;return status
        mov     es:[bx].rh8_count,cx ;return output count
        jmp     done                ;set done bit and exit

busy:   or      es:[bx].rh_status,0200h ;set busy bit

done:   or      es:[bx].rh_status,0100h ;set done

        pop     si                  ;restore all registers
        pop     di
        pop     dx
        pop     cx
        pop     bx
        pop     ax
        pop     es
        pop     ds
        ret                         ;return to DOS
```

The base port address is saved in the variable *clock_port,* which will be used by the rest of the Clock Device Driver to determine how to read from and write to the MM58167A clock chip. If a base port address is not found, then the driver returns to the Initialization command, whose code will check for a valid *clock_port* and will abort the loading of the Clock Device Driver.

Once the clock chip base port address is found, the driver continues by determining the type of video display adapter that is present in the PC. A BIOS interrupt (10h) is issued and the value returned in al is checked. Based on the type of display adapter, the driver will set the screen memory segment address (B000h for monochrome or B800h for color), the screen status port address (3BAh for monochrome or 3DAh for color), and the variable *mode* to indicate if the driver found a monochrome adapter (1) or a color adapter (0).

At the label *calc,* the driver calls the procedure *display* to initialize the time display that will appear on the screen. The timer interrupt (1Ch) is changed to

---

Listing 6–11: The End of Program section. This section is used only once; DOS is permitted to overwrite this code after it has been executed. The code finds the base port address of the clock chip, determines the type of video adapter being used, sets up the timer interrupt, and displays a console message in two parts.

```
;******************************************************************
;*         END OF PROGRAM                                        *
;******************************************************************
;
;this procedure is called from the Initialization command and
;is executed only once. We tell DOS that the next available
;memory location (Break Address) is here. This allows DOS to over
;write this code; we save space.

initial proc    near                        ;display message on console
        lea     dx,cs:msg1                   ;part 1 of message
        mov     ah,9                         ;display on console
        int     21h                          ;DOS call
;First find clock chip base address
        lea     si,cs:clock_table            ;get address of table
        mov     cx,3                         ;three addressess
find1:  mov     dx,cs:[si]                   ;get 1st address
        add     dx,2                         ;base+2 = seconds
        in      al,dx                        ;get seconds
        test    al,80h                       ;high order bit set?
        jz      find2                        ;no - not empty port
        add     si,2                         ;next address
        loop    find1                        ;search thru clock table
;no port found - don't continue with setup
        lea     dx,cs:msg4                   ;no port found
        mov     ah,9                         ;display on console
        int     21h                          ;DOS call
        ret                                  ;exit
;Clock Chip port found
find2:  mov     dx,3                         ;convert back to port #
        sub     dx,cx                        ;port position
        shl     dx,1                         ;double it
        lea     di,cs:clock_table            ;address of chip table
        add     di,dx                        ;word index
        mov     dx,cs:[di]                   ;get port
        mov     cs:clock_port,dx             ;save it
        lea     di,cs:msg2a                  ;convert to ASCII
        call    hex2asc                      ;for later display
;Determine type of Video Display adapter in system
        mov     ah,0fh                       ;get video mode
        int     10h                          ;Video BIOS call
        cmp     al,7                         ;mono?
        jne     calc                         ;no - assume color
        mov     cs:mode,1                    ;mono = 1
        mov     cs:scn_port,3bah             ;mono video port
        mov     cs:scn_seg,0b000h            ;mono screen address
```

Listing 6–11: (*cont.*)

```
;Calculate time string
calc:     call      display             ;setup initial time
          cli                           ;clear interrupts
          assume    es:timer            ;new directive
          mov       ax,timer            ;get segment addr
          mov       es,ax               ;set ES
          mov       ax,es:timer_ofs     ;get old timer offset
          mov       cs:oldlc_ofs,ax     ;save it
          mov       ax,es:timer_seg     ;get old timer segment
          mov       cs:oldlc_seg,ax     ;save it
          lea       ax,clkint           ;get new offset
          mov       es:timer_ofs,ax     ;set new offset
          mov       es:timer_seg,cs     ;also segment
          assume    es:cseg             ;restore directive
          sti                           ;restore interrupts
          lea       dx,cs:msg2          ;part 2 of message
          mov       ah,9                ;display on console
          int       21h                 ;DOS call
          cmp       cs:mode,1           ;mono?
          jne       exit2               ;no
          lea       dx,cs:msg3a         ;yes
          jmp       exit3               ;go print mono message
exit2:    lea       dx,cs:msg3b         ;color
exit3:    mov       ah,9                ;display on console
          int       21h                 ;DOS call
          mov       bx,cs:rh_ofs        ;restore BX
          mov       ax,cs:rh_seg        ;restore segment
          mov       es,ax               ; to ES
          ret                           ;return to caller
initial endp

msg1      db        'The Waite Group Clock Device Driver',0dh,0ah,'$'
msg2      db        ' using device address '
msg2a     db        '0000H',0dh,0ah,'$'
msg3a     db        ' with monochrome adapter',0dh,0ah,'$'
msg3b     db        ' with color adapter',0dh,0ah,'$'
msg4      db        ' No Clock Found - Driver Aborted',0dh,0ah,'$'

clock_table         label     byte      ;table of possible chip addresses
                    dw        0240h     ;
                    dw        02c0h     ;
                    dw        0340h     ;

hex2asc proc

;requires:
;                   dx = binary number
;                   di = address of ASCII string
;uses:
;                   ax - for character conversion
```

Listing 6–11: (*cont.*)

```
;                       cx - loop control
;returns:
;                       nothing

          push    cx        ;save cx
          push    ax        ;save ax
          mov     cx,4      ;number of hex digits
h1:       push    cx        ;save cx inside this loop
          mov     cl,4      ;shift count (bits/hex digit)
          rol     dx,cl     ;rotate left 1 hex digit
          mov     al,dl     ;move hex digit to al
          and     al,0fh    ;mask off desired hex digit
          cmp     al,0ah    ;is it above 9h?
          jge     h2        ;yes
          add     al,30h    ;numeric hex digit
          jmp     h3        ;skip
h2:       add     al,37h    ;alpha hex digit
h3:       mov     cs:[di],al       ;store hex digit in string
          inc     di        ;next string address
          pop     cx        ;get saved loop count
          loop    h1        ;loop start
          pop     ax        ;restore ax
          pop     cx        ;restore cx
          ret               ;return to caller
hex2asc   endp

clock     endp              ;end of clock procedure
cseg      ends              ;end of cseg segment
          end     begin     ;end of program
```

---

point to our *clkint* procedure. This is done by saving the segment *(timer_seg)* and offset *(timer_ofs)* address of the original timer interrupt in the variables *old1c_seg* and *old1c_ofs*. Then the driver sets the timer interrupt segment and offset addresses to the segment and offset address of the *clkint* procedure.

Note: A good programming practice is to turn interrupts off when swapping interrupt addresses. An interrupt cannot be allowed to disturb you while you are changing interrupt addresses. More importantly, you do not want a timer interrupt to occur when you are changing the timer interrupt itself. Unfortunately, because DOS restricts the use of DOS services to those numbered 1 through 0Ch and 30h (in device drivers only during Initialization command processing), the proper DOS services cannot be used. Get Interrupt Vector (35h) and Set Interrupt Vector (25h) are the correct ways to determine and set interrupt vectors. Although it is a good practice to turn interrupts off when you are changing interrupt addresses, it is not the approved method. However, it is the only way you can do so from within a device driver.

As a last note, the display of the console message during the driver initialization process is split into two parts. The first part is displayed when the *initial* procedure is first executed. The second part of the message is displayed at the label *exit2* upon exit from the procedure. Splitting the display code in this way is a good practice when there is a lot of code in the initialization procedure. If there are any problems with this code, the second part of the console display will not be displayed. This will alert you that there is a problem with the code.

The procedure *hex2asc* is used to convert the base port address of the MM58167A chip to ASCII for display on the console.

Building the Clock Device Driver

To build the Clock Device Driver in this chapter, enter the source code of the driver into a file using a word processor. Name the file *clock.asm*. The listing of the entire Clock Device Driver is shown in listing 6–12.

Listing 6–12: The entire listing of the Clock Device Driver.

```
        page    60,132
        title   A Clock Device Driver

;*****************************************************************
;*      This is a Clock Device Driver                          *
;*      Author:   Robert S. Lai                                *
;*      Date:     27 November 1986                             *
;*      Purpose:  A Clock Driver based on the MM58167A clock chip *
;*****************************************************************
;

;*****************************************************************
;*      ASSEMBLER DIRECTIVES                                    *
;*****************************************************************
;
timer           segment at      0h      ;int 1c segment
                org     1ch*4
timer_ofs       label   word
timer_seg       label   word
timer           ends

cseg            segment para public     'code'
clock           proc    far
                assume  cs:cseg, es:cseg, ds:cseg

;structures for the Device Driver
```

Listing 6-12: (*cont.*)

```
dosdate struc               ;DOS DATE structure
dos_day dw      ?           ;days since 1/1/80
dos_min db      ?           ;minutes
dos_hr  db      ?           ;hours
dos_hun db      ?           ;hundredths of a second
dos_sec db      ?           ;seconds
dosdate ends                ;end of struc

;structures

rh              struc       ;request header
rh_len          db      ?   ;len of packet
rh_unit         db      ?   ;unit code
                            ;(block devices only)
rh_cmd          db      ?   ;device driver command
rh_status       dw      ?   ;returned by device driver
rh_resl         dd      ?   ;reserved
rh_res2         dd      ?   ;reserved
rh              ends        ;

rh0             struc       ;Initialization (command 0)
rh0_rh          db      size rh dup (?) ;fixed portion
rh0_nunits      db      ?   ;number of units
                            ;(block devices only)
rh0_brk_ofs     dw      ?   ;offset address for break
rh0_brk_seg     dw      ?   ;segment address for break
rh0_bpb_tbo     dw      ?   ;offset address of pointer
                            ;to BPB array
rh0_bpb_tbs     dw      ?   ;segment address of pointer
                            ;to BPB array
rh0_drv_ltr     db      ?   ;first available drive
                            ;(DOS 3+) (block only)
rh0             ends        ;

rh4             struc       ;INPUT (command 4)
rh4_rh          db      size rh dup(?)  ;fixed portion
rh4_media       db      ?   ;media descriptor from DPB
rh4_buf_ofs     dw      ?   ;offset address of
                            ;data transfer area
rh4_buf_seg     dw      ?   ;segment address of
                            ;data transfer area
rh4_count       dw      ?   ;transfer count
                            ;(sectors for block)
                            ;(bytes for character)
rh4_start       dw      ?   ;start sector number
                            ;(block only)
rh4             ends        ;

rh8             struc       ;OUTPUT (command 8)
rh8_rh          db      size rh dup(?)  ;fixed portion
```

Listing 6–12: (*cont.*)

```
rh8_media       db      ?       ;media descriptor from DPB
rh8_buf_ofs     dw      ?       ;offset address of
                                ;data transfer area
rh8_buf_seg     dw      ?       ;segment address of
                                ;data transfer area
rh8_count       dw      ?       ;transfer count
                                ;(sectors for block)
                                ;(bytes for character)
rh8_start       dw      ?       ;start sector number
                                ;(block only)
rh8             ends            ;

rh9             struc           ;OUTPUT_VERIFY (command 9)
rh9_rh          db      size rh dup(?)  ;fixed portion
rh9_media       db      ?       ;media descriptor from DPB
rh9_buf_ofs     dw      ?       ;offset address of
                                ;data transfer area
rh9_buf_seg     dw      ?       ;segment address of
                                ;data transfer area
rh9_count       dw      ?       ;transfer count
                                ;(sectors for block)
                                ;(bytes for character)
rh9_start       dw      ?       ;start sector number (block only)
rh9             ends            ;

;commands that do not have unique portions to the request header:
;       INPUT_STATUS    (command 6)
;       INPUT_FLUSH     (command 7)
;       OUTPUT_STATUS   (command 10)
;       OUTPUT_FLUSH    (command 11)
;       OPEN            (command 13)
;       CLOSE           (command 14)
;       REMOVABLE       (command 15)
;

;******************************************************************
;*      MAIN PROCEDURE CODE                                       *
;******************************************************************

begin:

;******************************************************************
;*      DEVICE HEADER REQUIRED BY DOS                             *
;******************************************************************

next_dev        dd      -1              ;no other drivers following
attribute       dw      8008h           ;char,clock device
strategy        dw      dev_strategy    ;Strategy routine address
interrupt       dw      dev_interrupt   ;Interrupt routine address
dev_name        db      'CLOCK$  '      ;name of our Clock driver
```

Listing 6–12: (*cont.*)

```
;****************************************************************
;*        WORK SPACE FOR CLOCK DEVICE DRIVER                   *
;****************************************************************

rh_ofs    dw      ?              ;offset address of the request header
rh_seg    dw      ?              ;segment address of the request header

table     label   byte
jan       db      31
feb       db      28
mar       db      31
apr       db      30
may       db      31
jun       db      30
jul       db      31
aug       db      31
sep       db      30
oct       db      31
nov       db      30
decm      db      31

dosdays     dw      0            ;DOS date (days since 1/1/80)
clock_port  dw      0            ;clock chip base address
oldlc       label   dword        ;old timer interrupt 1C
oldlc_ofs   dw      ?            ; offset
oldlc_seg   dw      ?            ; segment
refresh     dw      0            ;screen update indicator
mode        db      0            ;color = 0, mono = 1
scn_pos     dw      144          ;column 72 (includes attribute)
scn_port    dw      03dah        ;video status port for color
                                 ;03bah for mono
scn_seg     dw      0b800h       ;video memory address for color
                                 ;0b000h for mono
time        dw      8 dup (003ah)    ;time display

;****************************************************************
;*        THE STRATEGY PROCEDURE                               *
;****************************************************************

dev_strategy:   mov  cs:rh_seg,es    ;save the segment address
                mov  cs:rh_ofs,bx    ;save the offset address
                ret                  ;return to DOS

;****************************************************************
;*        THE INTERRUPT PROCEDURE                              *
;****************************************************************

;device interrupt handler - 2nd call from DOS
```

Listing 6–12: (*cont.*)

```
dev_interrupt:

        cld                             ;save machine state on entry
        push    ds
        push    es
        push    ax
        push    bx
        push    cx
        push    dx
        push    di
        push    si

        mov     ax,cs:rh_seg    ;restore ES as saved by STRATEGY call
        mov     es,ax           ;
        mov     bx,cs:rh_ofs    ;restore BX as saved by STRATEGY call

;jump to appropriate routine to process command

        mov     al,es:[bx].rh_cmd       ;get request header command
        rol     al,1                    ;times 2 for index into word table
        lea     di,cmdtab               ;function (command) table address
        mov     ah,0                    ;clear hi order
        add     di,ax                   ;add the index to start of table
        jmp     word ptr[di]            ;jump indirect

;CMDTAB is the command table that contains the word address
;for each command. The request header will contain the
;command desired. The INTERRUPT routine will jump through an
;address corresponding to the requested command to get to
;the appropriate command processing routine.

CMDTAB  label   byte            ;* = char devices only
        dw      INITIALIZATION  ; initialization
        dw      MEDIA_CHECK     ; media check (block only)
        dw      GET_BPB         ; build bpb
        dw      IOCTL_INPUT     ; ioctl in
        dw      INPUT           ; input (read)
        dw      ND_INPUT        ;*non destructive input no wait
        dw      INPUT_STATUS    ;*input status
        dw      INPUT_FLUSH     ;*input flush
        dw      OUTPUT          ; output (write)
        dw      OUTPUT_VERIFY   ; output (write) with verify
        dw      OUTPUT_STATUS   ;*output status
        dw      OUTPUT_FLUSH    ;*output flush
        dw      IOCTL_OUT       ; ioctl output
        dw      OPEN            ; device open
        dw      CLOSE           ; device close
        dw      REMOVABLE       ; removable media
        dw      OUTPUT_BUSY     ; output til busy
```

Listing 6–12: (*cont.*)

```
;****************************************************************
;*      YOUR LOCAL PROCEDURES                                  *
;****************************************************************

hex2bcd proc    near        ;convert AL from Hex to BCD
;uses    ax,cx
        push    cx
        mov     cl,10       ;divide by 10
        mov     ah,0        ;setup for divide
        div     cl          ;get 10's digits
        mov     cl,4        ;shift count
        shl     al,cl       ;place 10's in left half
        or      al,ah       ;add back 1's
        pop     cx
        ret                 ;return to caller
hex2bcd endp

bcd2hex proc    near        ;convert AL from BCD to hex
;uses ax,cx
        push    cx
        mov     ah,0        ;setup for divide
        push    ax          ;save for 1's processing
        mov     cl,16       ;divide for left half of byte
        div     cl          ; to get 10's digits
        mov     ah,0        ;have 10's digits
        mov     cl,10       ;convert to base 10
        mul     cl          ; by multiplying by 10
        pop     cx          ;process 1's digits
        and     cl,0fh      ;keep 1's only
        add     al,cl       ;add 1's to 10's
        pop     cx
        ret                 ;return to caller
bcd2hex endp

cvt2asc proc    near        ;gets chip data & converts to ASCII
        in      al,dx           ;get (BCD) chip data
        mov     ah,0            ;clear high
        mov     cl,10h          ;separate 10's digits
        div     cl              ;al=10's, ah=1's
        or      ax,3030h        ;convert to ascii
        ret                     ;return to caller
cvt2asc endp                    ;

display proc    near            ;calculates time for display
        push    ax              ;save registers used
        push    bx
        push    cx
        push    dx
        mov     dx,cs:clock_port;get chip's base address
```

Listing 6-12: (*cont.*)

```
          add       dx,4                  ;base+4 = hours
          call      cvt2asc               ;get hours and convert
          lea       bx,cs:time            ;move to Time string
          mov       cs:[bx],al            ;tens of hrs
          mov       cs:[bx+2],ah          ;hrs
          dec       dx                    ;base+3 = minutes
          call      cvt2asc               ;get minutes and convert
          mov       cs:[bx+6],al          ;tens of minutes
          mov       cs:[bx+8],ah          ;ones
          dec       dx                    ;base+2 = seconds
          call      cvt2asc               ;get seconds and convert
          mov       cs:[bx+12],al         ;tens of seconds
          mov       cs:[bx+14],ah         ;ones
          pop       dx                    ;restore saved registers
          pop       cx
          pop       bx
          pop       ax
          ret                             ;return to caller
display   endp

;Clock Driver's replacement code for interrupt 1Ch

clkint    proc      near      ;new timer interrupt code
          push      ax                    ;save registers used
          push      cx
          push      di
          push      si
          push      es
          pushf                           ;must push flags
          call      cs:old1c              ;call old timer int
          mov       cx,cs:refresh         ;get refresh counter
          inc       cx                    ;increment
          cmp       cx,18                 ;18th time?
          jb        notime                ;no need to recalc time
          call      display               ;yes we do
          mov       cx,0                  ;reset counter
notime:   mov       cs:refresh,cx         ;store it
          mov       dx,cs:scn_port        ;screen status port
          mov       di,cs:scn_pos         ;screen display position
          lea       si,cs:time            ;time string source
          mov       cx,cs:scn_seg         ;screen segment
          mov       es,cx                 ; in es
          mov       cx,10                 ;move 10 bytes
          cli                             ;clear interrupts
hlow:                                     ;wait for horizontal scan
          in        al,dx                 ;get video port status
          test      al,1                  ;wait for low = 1
          jnz       hlow                  ;back
          mov       ah,cs:[si]            ;get byte to be displayed
```

Listing 6–12: (*cont.*)

```
hhigh:
        in      al,dx           ;status must go hi after lo
        test    al,1            ; before a screen write
        jz      hhigh           ;wait til high = 0
        mov     es:[di],ah      ;1 byte at any one time
        inc     di              ;increment screen position
        inc     si              ;increment source position
        loop    hlow            ;loop thru all bytes
        sti                     ;restore interrupts
        pop     es              ;restore all saved registers
        pop     si
        pop     di
        pop     cx
        pop     ax
        iret                    ;interrupt return
clkint  endp


;******************************************************************
;*        DOS COMMAND PROCESSING                                  *
;******************************************************************
;command 0      Initialization
Initialization:

        call    initial                 ;display message
;determine whether we found a clock chip
        cmp     cs:clock_port,0         ;is chip base = 0?
        jne     init1                   ;no - there is a chip
;no chip found - we must abort loading this driver
        mov     ax,0                    ;set address to beginning
        jmp     init2                   ;store break offset
init1:  lea     ax,initial              ;set Break Addr. at initial
init2:  mov     es:[bx].rh0_brk_ofs,ax  ;store offset address
        mov     es:[bx].rh0_brk_seg,cs  ;store segment address
        jmp     done                    ;set done status and exit

;command 1      Media_Check
Media_Check:

        jmp     done                    ;set done bit and exit

;command 2      Get_BPB
Get_BPB:

        jmp     done                    ;set done bit and exit

;command 3      IOCTL_Input
IOCTL_Input:

        jmp     unknown                 ;set error bit/code and exit
```

Listing 6–12: (*cont.*)

```
;command 4        Input    Read clock chip and return to DOS
Input:

;Read and convert clock chip date and time to DOS date format
        mov     dx,es:[bx].rh4_buf_ofs  ;get dos date data area
        mov     ax,es:[bx].rh4_buf_seg  ;
        mov     es,ax                   ;set up es
        mov     bx,dx                   ;set up bx
;ES:BX points to the DOS date buffer
        push    es                      ;save segment for later
        push    bx                      ;save offset for later
;first read the clock chip for time
        mov     dx,cs:clock_port        ;get the clock base address
        inc     dx                      ;base+1
        in      al,dx                   ;get hundredths
        call    bcd2hex                 ;convert data
        mov     es:[bx].dos_hun,al      ;store hundredths
        inc     dx                      ;base+2
        in      al,dx                   ;get seconds
        call    bcd2hex                 ;convert data
        mov     es:[bx].dos_sec,al      ;store seconds
        inc     dx                      ;base+3
        in      al,dx                   ;get minutes
        call    bcd2hex                 ;convert data
        mov     es:[bx].dos_min,al      ;store minutes
        inc     dx                      ;base+4
        in      al,dx                   ;get hours
        call    bcd2hex                 ;convert data
        mov     es:[bx].dos_hr,al       ;store hours
;now convert chip date (BCD format) to DOS date format (hex)

;first check to see if month (and therefore year) has changed
;by comparing the months COUNTER against the month RAM location
incheck:
        mov     dx,cs:clock_port        ;get base clock address
        add     dx,7                    ;base+7
        in      al,dx                   ;get chip's month counter
        call    bcd2hex                 ;convert to hex
        mov     bl,al                   ;save in bl
        add     dx,2                    ;base+9
        in      al,dx                   ;get RAM version of month
        call    bcd2hex                 ;convert to hex
        cmp     al,bl                   ;is RAM & counter same?
        jg      newyear                 ;last month > current ( 12>1 )
        jl      updatemonth             ;last month < current
        jmp     prev_days               ;same month
;December rolled over to January — update the Year count in RAM
newyear:
        inc     dx                      ;base+10
```

Listing 6–12: (*cont.*)

```
        in      al,dx                   ;get year (stored in RAM)
        inc     al                      ;add 1 year
        out     dx,al                   ;store in RAM year
        dec     dx                      ;make it base+9
;now update month in RAM
updatemonth:
        mov     al,bl                   ;set current month
        call    hex2bcd                 ;convert for clock chip
        out     dx,al                   ;update month RAM

;determine days in previous years
prev_days:
        inc     dx                      ;base+10 (RAM)
        in      al,dx                   ;get years since 1980
        mov     ah,0                    ;set up for multiply
        push    ax                      ;save for leap year processing
        mov     bx,365                  ;days per year
        mul     bx                      ;times years - AX has days
        xchg    bx,ax                   ;save days in BX
        mov     cl,4                    ;leap divisor
        pop     ax                      ;get year count again
        div     cl                      ;divide for leap years elapsed
        mov     cl,ah                   ;save leap year indicator
;BX has total days and cl has leap year indicator
        mov     ah,0                    ;set up for add
        add     bx,ax                   ;add leap days to total

;we have days since 1/1/80 for all previous years including
; the extra days in leap years past
curr_days:
        push    bx                      ;save total days past
        mov     dx,cs:clock_port        ;get base clock chip address
        add     dx,7                    ;base+7
        in      al,dx                   ;get month counter
        call    bcd2hex                 ;convert to hex
        mov     ah,0                    ;set up for index
        push    cs                      ;days per month table
        pop     es                      ;  addressed by ES
        lea     di,cs:table             ;  and DI
        mov     cx,0                    ;clear current year day count
        xchg    ax,cx                   ;month loop count in cx
        push    cx                      ;save for leap year check
        mov     bh,0                    ;clear hi-order
cvt2days:
        mov     bl,es:[di]              ;days in this month
        inc     di                      ;increment for next month
        add     ax,bx                   ;add to total days
        loop    cvt2days                ;until month count exhausted
        pop     cx                      ;restore months
```

Listing 6–12: (*cont.*)

```
        pop     bx                      ;total days past
        add     ax,bx                   ;add to days in current year
        cmp     cl,3                    ;past March?
        jl      leapyr                  ;no
        inc     ax                      ;yes - add 1 for 2/29
leapyr: pop     bx                      ;restore DOS date offset
        pop     es                      ;restore DOS date segment
        mov     es:[bx].dos_day,ax      ;return days since 1/1/80
        mov     ax,0                    ;status ok
        mov     bx,6                    ;count of 6
        jmp     load_status             ;restore es:bx exit

;command 5      ND_Input
ND_Input:

        jmp     busy                    ;set busy bit and exit

;command 6      Input_Status
Input_Status:

        jmp     done                    ;set done bit and exit

;command 7      Input_Flush
Input_Flush:

        jmp     done                    ;set done bit and exit

;command 8      Output  Set the Clock Chip Time and Date
Output:

;Convert the date in DOS date format to clock chip format
; for writing to the clock chip

;let ES:BX point to beginning of the DOS date
        mov     si,es:[bx].rh8_buf_ofs  ;get data offset
        mov     ax,es:[bx].rh8_buf_seg  ;get data segment
        mov     ds,ax                   ;to DS for (DS:SI use)
        push    si                      ;save offset
        push    ds                      ;save segment
        push    cs                      ;
        pop     es                      ;ES points to here
        lea     di,cs:dosdays           ;destination address
        mov     cx,2                    ;move count = 2
        cld                             ;direction is forward
        rep     movsb                   ; from DOS to us
        push    cs                      ;restore DS
        pop     ds                      ; by using CS
;update clock chip with time from DOS date data
```

Listing 6–12: (*cont.*)

```
outchip:
        pop     es                      ;restore DOS date segment
        pop     bx                      ;restore DOS date offset
        mov     dx,cs:clock_port        ;get clock port
        inc     dx                      ;base+1
        mov     al,es:[bx].dos_hun      ;get hundredths
        call    hex2bcd                 ;convert for clock use
        out     dx,al                   ;send to clock chip
        inc     dx                      ;base+2
        mov     al,es:[bx].dos_sec      ;get seconds
        call    hex2bcd                 ;convert for clock use
        out     dx,al                   ;send to clock chip
        inc     dx                      ;base+3
        mov     al,es:[bx].dos_min      ;get minutes
        call    hex2bcd                 ;convert for clock use
        out     dx,al                   ;send to clock chip
        inc     dx                      ;base+4
        mov     al,es:[bx].dos_hr       ;get hours
        call    hex2bcd                 ;convert for clock use
        out     dx,al                   ;send to clock chip

;chip loaded with time - now calc chip date from DOS date
ou_years:
        mov     ax,cs:dosdays           ;get days since 1/1/80
        cmp     ax,0                    ;date not set?
        je      out8                    ;skip everything
        mov     bx,0                    ;BX = year count
out1:   cmp     ax,365                  ;day count within a year?
        jle     out2                    ;yes
        sub     ax,365                  ;no - subtract 365
        inc     bx                      ;increment year count
        jmp     out1                    ;continue until w/i 1 yr
;BX has years since 1980 - now adjust for leap years
out2:   push    ax                      ;save leftover days
        mov     ax,bx                   ;AX now has years
        mov     cl,4                    ;divisor for leap years
        div     cl                      ;al=leaps, ah=remainder
        mov     cl,ah                   ;remainder=0 is leap itself
        mov     ah,0                    ;set up for subtract
        inc     ax                      ;add 1 to leap year count
        mov     dx,ax                   ;DX has 1 day/leap yr passed
        pop     ax                      ;restore days remaining
        sub     ax,dx                   ;subtract 1 day for each leap yr
        cmp     ax,0                    ;are we negative?
        jg      out3                    ;no - we are ok
        add     ax,365                  ;add back 365 days
        dec     bx                      ;subtract 1 year
out3:   push    bx                      ;save year count
```

Listing 6-12: (cont.)

```
            cmp     cl,0                ;leap year if 0
            jne     out5                ;not a leap year
            cmp     ax,59               ;Feb 29?
            je      out4                ;yes - set and exit
            jg      out5                ;past Feb 29
            inc     ax                  ;before - reverse subtraction
            jmp     out5                ;
out4:       mov     cx,2                ;Feb
            mov     ax,29               ; 29
            jmp     out7                ;exit
;AX has days left in current year - now find month and day
out5:       mov     cx,1                ;month count
            lea     di,cs:table         ;days per month
            mov     bh,0                ;clear hi-order
out6:       mov     bl,es:[di]          ;get days in each month
            inc     di                  ;increment to next month
            cmp     ax,bx               ;less than last day?
            jle     out7                ;yes (in current month)
            sub     ax,bx               ;no subtract days in month
            inc     cx                  ;increment month count
            jmp     out6                ;continue until month found
;AX has days, CX has month - now get years since 1980
out7:       pop     bx                  ;restore year count
            jmp     out9                ;go load chip
;no date set (special case)
out8:       mov     bx,0                ;1980
            mov     cx,1                ;Jan
            mov     ax,1                ; 1st
;BX = years since 1980, CX = month, AX = days - now load clock chip
out9:       mov     dx,cs:clock_port    ;get chip base address
            add     dx,6                ;base+6
            push    cx                  ;Hex2bcd destroys cx
            call    hex2bcd             ;convert for chip use
            out     dx,al               ;set days counter
            inc     dx                  ;base+7
            pop     ax                  ;restore month count
            call    hex2bcd             ;convert for chip use
            out     dx,al               ;set months counter
            add     dx,2                ;base+9
            out     dx,al               ;set months RAM
            inc     dx                  ;base+10
            xchg    al,bl               ;move years to al
            out     dx,al               ;set years since 1980 RAM
            mov     ax,0                ;status ok
            mov     cx,6                ;count of 6
            jmp     load_status         ;set status word & exit

;command 9       Output_Verify
```

Listing 6–12: (*cont.*)

```
Output_Verify:

        jmp     output              ;same as output

;command 10     Output_Status
Output_Status:

        jmp     done                ;set done bit and exit

;command 11     Output_Flush
Output_Flush:

        jmp     done                ;set done bit and exit

;command 12     IOCTL_Out
IOCTL_Out:

        jmp     unknown             ;set error bit/code and exit

;command 13     Open
Open:

        jmp     done                ;set done bit and exit

;command 14     Close
Close:

        jmp     done                ;set done bit and exit

;command 15     Removable
Removable:

        jmp     unknown             ;set error bit/code and exit

;command 16     Output Til Busy
Output_Busy:

        jmp     unknown             ;set error bit/code and exit
;****************************************************************
;*      ERROR EXIT                                             *
;****************************************************************
unknown:
        or      es:[bx].rh_status,8003h ;set error bit and error code
        jmp     done                ;set done and exit

;****************************************************************
;*      COMMON EXIT                                            *
;****************************************************************
```

Listing 6–12: (*cont.*)

```
load_status:
        mov     cx,cs:rh_seg        ;restore request header
        mov     es,cx               ; segment to es
        mov     cx,cs:rh_ofs        ;restore offset also
        xchg    bx,cx               ;switch them
        mov     es:[bx].rh_status,ax ;return status
        mov     es:[bx].rh8_count,cx ;return output count
        jmp     done                ;set done bit and exit

busy:   or      es:[bx].rh_status,0200h ;set busy bit

done:   or      es:[bx].rh_status,0100h ;set done

        pop     si                  ;restore all registers
        pop     di
        pop     dx
        pop     cx
        pop     bx
        pop     ax
        pop     es
        pop     ds
        ret                         ;return to DOS

;*******************************************************************
;*      END OF PROGRAM                                            *
;*******************************************************************
;this procedure is called from the Initialization command and
;is executed only once. We tell DOS that the next available
;memory location (Break Address) is here. This allows DOS to over
;write this code; we save space.

initial proc    near                ;display message on console
        lea     dx,cs:msg1          ;part 1 of message
        mov     ah,9                ;display on console
        int     21h                 ;DOS call
;First find clock chip base address
        lea     si,cs:clock_table   ;get address of table
        mov     cx,3                ;three addressess
find1:  mov     dx,cs:[si]          ;get 1st address
        add     dx,2                ;base+2 = seconds
        in      al,dx               ;get seconds
        test    al,80h              ;high order bit set?
        jz      find2               ;no - not empty port
        add     si,2                ;next address
        loop    find1               ;search thru clock table
;no port found - don't continue with setup
        lea     dx,cs:msg4          ;no port found
        mov     ah,9                ;display on console
```

Listing 6–12: (*cont.*)

```
        int     21h                 ;DOS call
        ret                         ;exit
;Clock Chip port found
find2:  mov     dx,3                ;convert back to port #
        sub     dx,cx               ;port position
        shl     dx,1                ;double it
        lea     di,cs:clock_table   ;address of chip table
        add     di,dx               ;word index
        mov     dx,cs:[di]          ;get port
        mov     cs:clock_port,dx    ;save it
        lea     di,cs:msg2a         ;convert to ASCII
        call    hex2asc             ;for later display
;Determine type of Video Display adapter in system
        mov     ah,0fh              ;get video mode
        int     10h                 ;Video BIOS call
        cmp     al,7                ;mono?
        jne     calc                ;no - assume color
        mov     cs:mode,1           ;mono = 1
        mov     cs:scn_port,3bah    ;mono video port
        mov     cs:scn_seg,0b000h   ;mono screen address
;Calculate time string
calc:   call    display             ;setup initial time
        cli                         ;clear interrupts
        assume  es:timer            ;new directive
        mov     ax,timer            ;get segment addr
        mov     es,ax               ;set ES
        mov     ax,es:timer_ofs     ;get old timer offset
        mov     cs:oldlc_ofs,ax     ;save it
        mov     ax,es:timer_seg     ;get old timer segment
        mov     cs:oldlc_seg,ax     ;save it
        lea     ax,clkint           ;get new offset
        mov     es:timer_ofs,ax     ;set new offset
        mov     es:timer_seg,cs     ;also segment
        assume  es:cseg             ;restore directive
        sti                         ;restore interrupts
        lea     dx,cs:msg2          ;part 2 of message
        mov     ah,9                ;display on console
        int     21h                 ;DOS call
        cmp     cs:mode,1           ;mono?
        jne     exit2               ;no
        lea     dx,cs:msg3a         ;yes
        jmp     exit3               ;go print mono message
exit2:  lea     dx,cs:msg3b         ;color
exit3:  mov     ah,9                ;display on console
        int     21h                 ;DOS call
        mov     bx,cs:rh_ofs        ;restore BX
        mov     ax,cs:rh_seg        ;restore segment
        mov     es,ax               ; to ES
        ret                         ;return to caller
initial endp
```

Listing 6–12: (*cont.*)

```
msg1        db          'The Waite Group Clock Device Driver',0dh,0ah,'$'
msg2        db          ' using device address '
msg2a       db          '0000H',0dh,0ah,'$'
msg3a       db          ' with monochrome adapter',0dh,0ah,'$'
msg3b       db          ' with color adapter',0dh,0ah,'$'
msg4        db          ' No Clock Found — Driver Aborted',0dh,0ah,'$'

clock_table label       byte        ;table of possible chip addresses
            dw          0240h   ;
            dw          02c0h   ;
            dw          0340h   ;

hex2asc proc

;requires:
;                       dx = binary number
;                       di = address of ASCII string
;uses:
;                       ax — for character conversion
;                       cx — loop control
;returns:
;                       nothing

            push        cx      ;save cx
            push        ax      ;save ax
            mov         cx,4    ;number of hex digits
h1:         push        cx      ;save cx inside this loop
            mov         cl,4    ;shift count (bits/hex digit)
            rol         dx,cl   ;rotate left 1 hex digit
            mov         al,dl   ;move hex digit to al
            and         al,0fh  ;mask off desired hex digit
            cmp         al,0ah  ;is it above 9h?
            jge         h2      ;yes
            add         al,30h  ;numeric hex digit
            jmp         h3      ;skip
h2:         add         al,37h  ;alpha hex digit
h3:         mov         cs:[di],al      ;store hex digit in string
            inc         di      ;next string address
            pop         cx      ;get saved loop count
            loop        h1      ;loop start
            pop         ax      ;restore ax
            pop         cx      ;restore cx
            ret                 ;return to caller
hex2asc endp

clock       endp                ;end of clock procedure
cseg        ends                ;end of cseg segment
            end         begin   ;end of program
```

After you have entered the Clock Device Driver into a file, you will need to assemble, link, and convert it to .COM format. In addition, you will need a CONFIG.SYS file that specifies the Clock Device Driver as a user-installable device driver.

The Clock Device Driver in Action

When you first boot DOS with the Clock Device Driver, you will get a strange date. This is because the driver has not set the time and date on the MM58167A clock chip. Once you have used the TIME and DATE commands to set the proper time and date, you will see the correct time and date on the next boot of DOS. Notice that the time is shown in the upper right-hand corner. This is the resident program displaying the time on the screen.

Summary

In this chapter, we have examined a Clock Device Driver. The standard DOS clock driver has been replaced with one that has many features. It will find the port address of the MM58167A clock chip, determine the video monitor adapter type, and periodically display the time on the screen. You have seen how to abort the loading of a device driver if the driver cannot find the base port address of the clock chip. Finally, you have seen how to take over an interrupt for your own use.

Device drivers are not just programs that control devices. You can use drivers for creative programming efforts, adding almost any feature you desire.

In the next two chapters we will look at a different type of device driver—the block-oriented device driver. In chapter 7 you will learn about disks—how they work, what is contained on disks, and what disks do in terms of device drivers. In chapter 8, you will build a RAM Disk Device Driver with a special feature that will allow you to hear the device driver working.

Questions

1. What happens if I ran the Clock Device Driver and the clock chip was missing from the PC?

2. Of what use are the RAM locations in the clock chip?

3. I notice a lot of code for determining leap years. Why is that?

4. I do not want to display the time on the screen. What do I do?

Answers may be found in appendix E.

Chapter 7

Introducing Disk Internals

- Technical Details of DOS Disk Support
- The Boot/Reserved Area, FAT, and Clusters
- The File Directory
- Disk Sizing
- Critical Disk Parameters
- DOS Disk Device Drivers
- Disk Device Driver Commands

In order to learn how to write a disk device driver, which we present in the next chapter, you should review the topic of disk internals. DOS supports a variety of disks, with storage capacities ranging from a hundred thousand bytes to hundreds of megabytes. In this chapter, we will describe how DOS manages different types of disk storage. You will need this information when you begin writing the powerful block device driver in chapter 8 that simulates a disk but that has much faster read and write times.

Starting with basic definitions, we will show how data is written to a disk (*disk* here means both hard [fixed] disk and floppies), how DOS organizes the data on the disks, and how DOS determines the disk type. We will distinguish between floppy and hard disk drives and look at some of the special features of hard disk drives. Lastly, we will describe the internal information that is contained on each disk drive and how disk device drivers interact with DOS to access disks.

The Physical Side of Disks

Disks are storage devices that are based on a rotating disk with magnetically alterable surfaces. The surfaces store digital information. Read/Write heads are built into the disk drive to retrieve and store data to the disk drive. Disk drives are also known as *random access devices,* because you can independently position the read/write head to any spot on the disk.

Disk drives come in two different forms. Floppy disks, or diskettes, are those types of disks that can be removed from the drive unit. Hard disk drives are fixed and cannot be removed.

Disk Types

Floppy disks are built using flexible materials and are usually made in three sizes: 3½ inches, 5¼ inches, and 8 inches in diameter. Information is recorded on one or both surfaces; most floppy disks use both surfaces.

Hard disks are built with one or more platters mounted on a spindle driven by a small motor. Each of the platters is magnetically coated on both sides for storing information. A read/write head is assigned to each surface of a platter. These disk heads are mounted on arms that move together and are controlled by another motor.

Connected to every disk drive through a cable is a disk controller; a PC add-on circuit board that provides electrical signals to control the disk and read/write head. The disk-controller board is inserted in a slot on the PC's motherboard, which connects it to the main bus and allows the board to receive instructions from the CPU. The controller is responsible for transferring data to and from the PC and for positioning the read/write head to a desired position on the disk.

Organizing Data on Disk Drives

In this section, we will examine organizing data on disks, storage capacities, sector sizing and numbering, and formatting.

Tracks on a Disk

Each surface of a disk is divided into tracks on which information is recorded. The read/write head assigned to a disk surface is positioned to one of these tracks before a read or write is performed.

Most 5¼-inch floppy disks or diskettes have either 40 or 80 tracks. There is also an emerging format based on 3½-inch diskettes. Diskettes that contain 40 tracks are commonly called *double density disks*. Historically, the original diskettes for the PC could record at half this density and were called *single density disks*. With improving technology, the density has increased to 80 tracks; such disks are known as *quad density disks*.

Because the surfaces are rigid and easier to control to tighter tolerances, hard disks can have many times the number of tracks on a floppy disk. A 10-Mb fixed disk for the IBM PC typically has 305 tracks. When there are two or more platters in a disk drive (the spinning surface is called a *platter*), the term *cylinder* is used to refer to all tracks that are identically numbered.

Tracks are numbered from 0 to the highest track number for the disk. Each recording surface of the disk is also numbered in this manner.

Raw Storage Calculations

Often you need to calculate just how much capacity there is on a disk. Several specifications can be used to determine the amount of storage. First, you will need the amount of data that can be recorded in one track, which is usually specified in bytes per track. Next, you will need the number of tracks per disk surface, which is determined by the track density (usually specified as tracks per inch, or *tpi*) multiplied by the circumference of the recording surface that contains tracks. Finally, you will need the number of recording surfaces. This is usually 1 for a single-sided disk and 2 for a double-sided one. For hard disks, this number is usually twice the number of platters.

The total amount of "raw" storage on a disk is calculated with the following formula:

```
Total storage = storage/track * tracks/surface * surfaces
```

Not all of this storage area is available for your use, because the overhead needed to manage the data stored on the disk is not taken into consideration in this calculation. *Overhead* is a term used to describe the additional information recorded onto the individual tracks that is required for the disk controller to find each track.

Disk tracks are further subdivided into sectors for ease of management; we will describe why this is done shortly. Table 7–1 summarizes the various types of disks and the amount of data that can be stored.

Size	3½	3½	5¼	5¼	5¼	5¼
Type	floppy	floppy	floppy	floppy	floppy	hard
Density Type	—	—	double	double	quad	—
Density (Tracks/Inch)	135	135	48	48	96	720
Tracks/Surface	80	80	40	40	80	305
Surfaces	1	2	1	2	2	4
Bytes/Track	5,120	5,120	5,120	5,120	5,120	10,416
Total Storage Size	400kb	800kb	200kb	400kb	800kb	12mb

Table 7–1: The amount of raw storage available for different types of disks

Organizing Data into Sectors

Sectors are subdivisions of a circular track; they form the basic unit of storage for disk drives. Using sectors allows you to use a common method for storing data for disk drives of varying sizes.

Whenever a disk is called upon to pass data back to the CPU, the read/ write head of the disk is first positioned to a particular track. Then, as the track rotates under the head, the disk controller will scan the sectors that pass by, searching for the desired sector. Once the desired sector is found, the disk controller reads the contents of the sector and returns the data.

The number of sectors in a track sometimes varies. This number depends on the amount of data that can be stored on a track. Version 1.0 of PC-DOS supported only floppy disks, and these were formatted for 8 sectors per track. PC-DOS version 3.0 allows 8, 9, and 15 sectors per track for floppy disks. Some machines, such as the Victor 9000, have formats that put more sectors per outer track than per inner tracks. This is because the larger outer tracks can contain more data than the smaller inner tracks.

For hard disks, the standard number of sectors per track is 17. However, as you will see in the section on the BIOS Parameter Block, DOS can handle just about any number of sectors per track.

Sector Numbering and Sizing

In general, for both PC-DOS and MS-DOS, the physical-sector numbering starts at 1. Therefore, for a disk with 9 sectors per track, the sectors are numbered from 1 thru 9; for a hard disk with 17 sectors per track, the sectors are numbered from 1 to 17.

Caution: Physical sectors are numbered starting at 1. This scheme is used when the disk BIOS routines are used to format, read, or write sectors. DOS uses a different scheme that numbers sectors beginning with 0. You will see this later, in the section on the BIOS Parameter Block.

As you saw above, the amount of data stored in each sector depends on the amount of storage per track and the number of sectors per track (assuming a fixed density for all the tracks). Because the amount of storage per track is fixed, the sector size can be varied by varying the number of sectors per track. Usually, the sector size is fixed at so many bytes per sector, and the number of sectors per track is calculated by dividing the amount of storage per track by the desired sector size (plus some overhead). When a track is divided into sectors, some storage is lost in defining management and location overhead for each of the sectors. Defining sectors on a track is performed by the formatting process. The formatting information, or *overhead,* reduces the amount of storage available for your use.

The DOS Standard for Sector Sizing

The DOS standard sector size is 512 bytes; however, DOS disk support allows sector sizes of 128, 256, 512, and 1,024 bytes per sector. Sector sizes other than 512 bytes are rare. Because many parts of DOS have been written to assume a sector size of 512 bytes, other sector sizes may not be used under all conditions without modifying DOS. Table 7–2 shows the number of sectors for the typical disk types that are supported by DOS.

Formatting Disks

A special program is used to create tracks and sectors within tracks on a disk. This program is known as FORMAT.COM, and it performs a number of additional tasks. The first task is to create a number of sectors on a track. This is repeated for all the tracks of a disk. The second task is to test each sector to ensure that data can be written to and read from the sector. The FORMAT.COM program will create a table for DOS that identifies which sectors are good or

Size	3½	3½	5¼	5¼	5¼	5¼
Type	floppy	floppy	floppy	floppy	floppy	hard
Density Type	—	—	double	double	quad	—
Raw Storage	400kb	800kb	200kb	400kb	800kb	12mb
Bytes/Sector	512	512	512	512	512	512
Sectors/Track	9	9	9	9	8	17
Tracks/Surface	80	80	40	40	80	305
Surfaces	1	2	1	2	2	4
Total Sectors	720	1,440	360	720	1,440	20,740
Formatted Storage	360kb	720kb	180kb	360kb	720kb	10.37mb

Table 7–2: Some of the disk formats supported by DOS

bad, so that bad sectors can be ignored. You will see more of this later in the section on File Allocation Tables.

When the data is organized by sectors, the overhead of identifying each sector results in a small loss of total storage. Typically, this is about 10 percent.

Technical Details of DOS Disk Support

In this section, we will discuss how DOS accesses the various parts of a disk, the File Allocation Tables, and File Directory, and the parameters in the Boot Record that describe the disk to DOS.

Disks Supported by DOS

The earliest versions of DOS (1.0) supported only single-sided disks. The next version (1.1) supported double-sided diskettes. Hard-disk support began with MS-DOS version 1.25 and PC-DOS version 2.00. Prior to these versions, hard-disk support was largely a matter of the disk manufacturer providing custom software routines to access the hard disk. Today, hard disks of all sizes may be added to IBM and IBM-compatible PCs without requiring special software. The use of drivers facilitates the task of adding support for a large number of disks. Table 7–3 summarizes the types of disks supported by PC-DOS for the IBM PC.

DOS Version	Single Side 5¼	Double Side 5¼	3½	1.2mb Floppy	Hard Disk 10mb	Hard Disk Size
1.0	x					
1.1	x	x				
2.0	x	x			x	
2.1	x	x			x	
3.0	x	x		x	x	10mb +
3.1	x	x		x	x	10mb +
3.2	x	x	x	x	x	10mb +
3.3	x	x	x	x	x	10mb +

Table 7–3: The types of disks supported by the various versions of PC-DOS. with each new version of DOS, support of new disk types was added

Special mention should be made of disk types supported by other vendors for non-IBM PCs. MS-DOS can be tailored to just about any machine that uses an 8086/8088 microprocessor, so the number of disk types for non-IBM compatible machines is large. Table 7–4 shows other types of PCs and the disk types supported by MS-DOS.

How Disks Are Organized

DOS is capable of supporting more than one type of disk. This is made possible by requiring that information regarding a disk's specific storage and access capabilities be stored right on the disk itself in a specific area defined by DOS.

Each disk must also have additional information stored on it indicating the amount of storage currently used, names of existing files, and other information required for managing the files and disk space. This information is invisible to the user but is a necessary component of all disks.

DOS expects the information on the disk to be defined in a certain sequence; therefore, all DOS disks are organized in a uniform fashion. This allows DOS to obtain information about the use of the disk, how space is to be allocated on the disk, and the files in use on the disk.

There are four components to a disk layout. The first is the reserved area commonly referred to as the *boot record*. The second component is the File Allocation Table (FAT), which is used to indicate the usage of space on the disk. The third component is the File Directory, which is used to store the size, location, date, and time information about files on the disk. Finally, the last component is the user data area, in which the user files are actually stored. The relationships among these four components are shown in figure 7–1.

PC	Disk Type	Size	Description
HP 150	3½ floppy	270kb	Single-sided diskettes
Tandy 2000	5¼ floppy	720kb	Double-sided 96 tpi diskettes
DEC Rainbow	5¼ floppy	720kb	2 single-sided 96 tpi diskettes
Victor 9000	5¼ floppy	1.2mb	Double-sided 96 tpi diskettes

Table 7–4: Diskette sizes for other types of PCs using MS-DOS

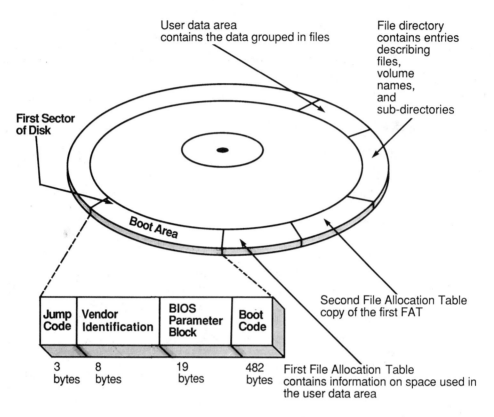

User data area
contains the data grouped in files

File directory
contains entries
describing
files,
volume
names,
and
sub-directories

First Sector
of Disk

Boot Area

Jump Code	Vendor Identification	BIOS Parameter Block	Boot Code

| 3 bytes | 8 bytes | 19 bytes | 482 bytes |

Second File Allocation Table
copy of the first FAT

First File Allocation Table
contains information on space used in
the user data area

Figure 7–1: The relative positions of the four components of a typical formatted disk, with an exploded view of a typical boot area

The Boot/Reserved Area, FAT, and Clusters

The *boot* or *reserved area* is the first section on the disk. Because disks vary in their number of sides, tracks, and sectors, DOS needs to determine these disk characteristics the first time it accesses a disk.

DOS assumes that this information describing the disk is always in a certain physical location, usually track 0, surface 0, and sector 1—the first sector of the disk. Although the boot area is usually only one sector in length, it can be larger. For this reason, this area is now more generally referred to as the *reserved sectors area*.

Figure 7–1 shows the boot area's four parts: a jump code instruction, the vendor identification code, the BIOS Parameter Block, and the boot code area.

The first part of the boot area contains a jump *(jmp)* instruction. If the disk is a DOS system disk, booting it causes the PC to load the data in the boot area into memory and to execute this jump instruction, which skips over the vendor identification and BIOS Parameter Block areas directly to the boot code.

The second part of the boot area is an 8 byte field that contains the vendor identification. This field is not used or required by DOS. Normally, a PC manufacturer will fill this field with the name of the vendor plus the DOS version on the disk. Examples of vendor identification fields are:

```
IBM  3.1      PC-DOS supplied by IBM
PSA 1.04      MS-DOS supplied by ATT (6300)
PC88 2.0      MS-DOS supplied by popular clone manufacturer
CCC  2.1      MS-DOS supplied by Compaq
```

The third part of the boot area is the BIOS Parameter Block. This is a table of special disk parameters that DOS requires to determine the size of the disk and the relative locations of the FAT and the File Directory. The BIOS Parameter Block is often called the BPB and is always present on every disk. We will describe the contents of the BPB later in this chapter.

The fourth and last part of the reserved boot area is called the *boot code area* because it contains the actual code for the bootstrap program that starts the PC. This bootstrap program has the job of "pulling itself up by the bootstraps;" in the case of DOS, this means getting DOS to bring itself into memory. Although this bootstrap code is always present in the reserved boot area, regardless of whether the disk contains the DOS system files, it is meaningful only when the disk has been set up as a system disk.

Typically, a system disk is created by the FORMAT program supplied with MS-DOS. If the FORMAT command is executed with a special command switch (usually /S), two additional files will be copied to the disk. These files (typically IO.SYS and MSDOS.SYS) contain the code for the MS-DOS operating system and are hidden from you; they do not appear in a directory listing of the disk. However, the bootstrap program knows they are there and will load them into memory when the disk is accessed at system start-up time. When a disk has been set up to make it possible to boot from that disk, the disk is referred to as a *system disk*.

Whenever any disk is formatted for use by the DOS FORMAT program, the four sections comprising the boot area are written to the reserved area of the disk, which always begins at the first sector of the disk.

Clusters as the Unit of Storage for a File

Before we describe the File Allocation Table, you need to know how sectors are used to hold data. When your program writes new data to a disk file, DOS needs to find an unused sector on the disk in which to store the new data. Conversely, when your program reads from a disk file, DOS needs to locate the sector on the disk in which the data is stored. DOS requires each disk to have a File Allocation Table in order to keep track of where sectors for a file are located.

Keeping track of files on a sector-by-sector basis can be inefficient, however. For example, a 10 Mb hard disk has more than 20,000 sectors, and keeping the location of each would make the File Allocation Table very large. Searching this table would take a relatively long time. If the File Allocation Table were smaller, the searches would be faster, and, as a result, the file accesses would be faster. A better solution would be to group sectors together in a pool so that when a new space on the disk is required, a group of sectors is allocated for the file. This concept of grouping is called *clustering* sectors; it allows DOS to be more efficient in terms of the memory required to manage the File Allocation Table. A cluster is simply a fixed number of sectors; clusters add a second layer of organization and make access easier.

Whenever a file requires disk space, DOS allocates a single cluster and marks the File Allocation Table to indicate this. Clusters (also called *allocation units*) are the basis units of storage for disk files. The number of sectors per cluster is determined by the disk type and is established by the FORMAT program when the disk is formatted. Table 7–5 shows the cluster sizes for different disk types.

The File Allocation Table

Let's learn how the File Allocation Table works.

The File Allocation Table (FAT) is the section of the disk that stores information on disk-file space usage. This table contains information on all the clusters that are unassigned (free for allocating to files), assigned (those that are in use by a particular disk file), or marked as bad (not usable because of media defects).

Note that although the FAT records information on disk space used by your files, the boot area, the two FATs, and the File Directory areas are not themselves represented by clusters in the FAT.

Within the FAT there is an entry for each available cluster on the disk. A floppy might have over 700 clusters. These entries indicate whether the cluster is in use, free, or bad. Bad clusters are found through the FORMAT program during the formatting process; sectors that cannot be used because of problems

Disk Type	Sectors per Cluster
3½ double-sided floppy	2
5¼ single-sided floppy	1
5¼ double-sided floppy	2
10mb hard disk	8
20mb hard disk (AT)	4

Table 7–5: The typical cluster sizes for different types of disks

in reading or writing cause the entire cluster to be marked bad. This means that some good sectors are lost.

As we said earlier, there are two identical copies of the FAT. The second copy provides some insurance against the possibility of the first copy being damaged. This is an old trick that has been borrowed from other operating systems. However, DOS does not use the second copy to fix the first if it is damaged.

Recording Clusters in the File Allocation Table

As you saw earlier in this chapter, when a disk file grows, DOS allocates space on the disk in clusters rather than one sector at a time. This causes the FAT to be updated to indicate that a previously free cluster is now in use. Conversely, when a file is deleted, the clusters once occupied by data are marked in the FAT as being free again.

As a file grows, DOS allocates clusters of disk space, and the use of these clusters is marked in the FAT. The list of clusters that form the disk space used by the file is called a *chain,* because of the way that DOS stores the cluster information in the FAT. You will see more of this shortly.

FAT entries contain a value to indicate the status of each cluster. The cluster may be reserved for use by DOS, free for allocation, bad, or in use. A cluster is in use when it is part of a chain. The values for the FAT entries are listed in table 7–6.

For disk sizes of 10 Mb or smaller, the size of the FAT entry is 12 bits in length, or 3 hex digits. For disks larger than 10 Mb, the FAT entry is 16 bits long, or 4 hex digits.

The first available space in the user-data area of the disk is the first cluster, which is assigned a cluster number of 2. The reason it is not called 0 or 1 is that the first two entries in the FAT, normally cluster 0 and 1, are reserved for a media descriptor. A media descriptor is a value that uniquely identifies a par-

12-bit Entry	16-bit Entry	Cluster Description
000h	0000h	Free
001h-fefh	0001h-ffefh	In-use
ff0h-ff6h	fff0h-fff6h	Reserved
ff7h	fff7h	Bad
ff8h-fffh	fff8h-ffffh	End of cluster chain

Table 7–6: The various FAT entries and what they mean

ticular type of disk and allows DOS to distinguish a single-sided 5¼-inch diskette from a double-sided one. You will see more of this media descriptor in the section on the BIOS Parameter Block. Figure 7–2 shows the entries in the FAT that point to or represent the clusters in the user data area.

Clusters, Chains, and the FAT

Suppose a file were large enough to require two clusters of disk space. DOS could simply mark each of two entries in the FAT with a value to indicate which clusters were in use, but this would not allow DOS to determine which cluster was first and which was second in the table. It would also be difficult to distinguish this particular file's use of the disk from that of another file. It follows that just marking used clusters via the FAT is insufficient for keeping track of what files exist where on the disk; we need a better method.

Consider the following: when the first cluster is allocated to the file, we could store the cluster number outside the FAT, in the File Directory. (We will explain later in this chapter what the exact format of the File Directory entry is for each file, but let it suffice now to say that the disk directory will maintain, for each file on the disk, information about the file, including its name and starting cluster number.) Then, as the file grows and the second cluster is allocated, we could use the FAT entry for the first cluster to note which cluster was assigned as the second cluster. For example, if the file used clusters 5 and 10, we would note (outside the FAT) that the file's first cluster was cluster 5; then, in the fifth entry of the FAT, we would store the number 10 to indicate that the next cluster in the file was cluster 10. It follows that if the file grew larger, thus requiring another cluster, we would find a free (unallocated) cluster in the FAT and store its number in the 10th entry of the FAT. This could continue indefinitely, or at least until there were no more available clusters to be found. In all cases, the last cluster allocated to the file would always have a special value in

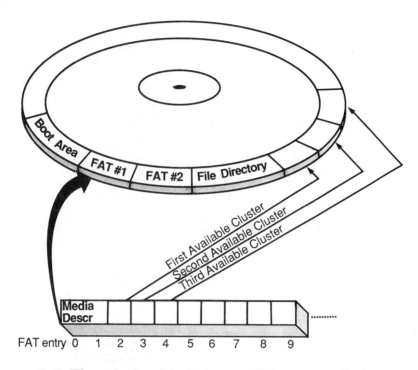

FAT entry 0 1 2 3 4 5 6 7 8 9

Figure 7–2: The relationship between FAT entry and cluster. Each cluster is assigned a position in the FAT and will indicate whether the cluster is part of a chain (in use), free, bad, or reserved. Note that clusters are numbered starting at 2.

it to indicate that there were no more clusters following it. This value would represent the end of the file.

The concept of having each cluster essentially point to the next cluster in use by a file is called a *cluster chain*. The idea is that the contents of each FAT entry in use contains a value (also called a *pointer*) that points to the next cluster, unless the FAT entry represents the last cluster for a file, in which case it would contain an end-of-file indicator. The only thing we would then have to know for a file to find all its sectors is the number of the first cluster assigned to it.

As mentioned earlier, the first cluster assigned to a file is stored in the most sensible place: the File Directory.

Figure 7–3 shows how each FAT entry points to the next, thus forming a chain. The start of the chain, or the first cluster, is kept in the File Directory with the entry for the file *myfile*. It contains the value of 4, which means that

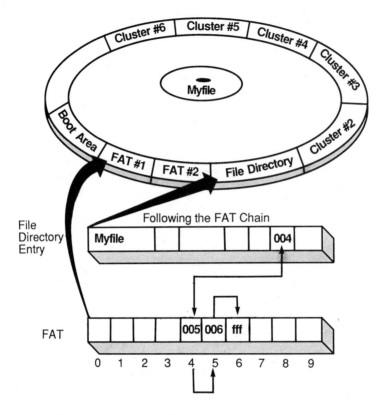

Figure 7–3: The clusters used by Myfile

the first cluster of the file in the FAT is cluster number 4. The entry in the fourth FAT position contains the value 5, which indicates that the next cluster is cluster number 5. At the entry for cluster number 5 we find the value 6, which points to cluster number 6 as the next cluster. Finally, at entry number 6, we find it contains an *fffh*. This marks the end of the clusters allocated for *myfile*. Thus, *myfile* is composed of clusters 4, 5, and 6 and is three clusters in length.

The Number of FATs Is (Almost) Always Two

The number of FATs is normally two, as shown in figure 7–3. When DOS updates the FAT, the first copy is updated, and then the second copy. As we said earlier, using a second identical copy of the FAT provides insurance against the first copy being damaged. The theory is that if the first copy is bad, then the operating system will use the second copy. Without this mechanism, a damaged FAT would render the disk inaccessible. In practice however, with a PC, if the first copy of the FAT is damaged, DOS does not use the second copy of the FAT to access file information, and the entire disk is not usable. The authors of DOS simply forgot to implement a means to fix the FATs.

Because DOS really uses only one FAT, disks can be built with only one of them. To build disks with only one FAT, you cannot use the standard DOS FORMAT program, which builds two FATs on each disk to be formatted. You will need to write a special FORMAT program to build only one FAT on each disk.

The specification of the number of FATs is defined in the BIOS Parameter Block. The overhead of a second copy and the necessity of always updating this second copy can be eliminated if you specify only one copy of the FAT.

The FATs are built for each disk during the formatting process using the FORMAT program. Each entry in the FAT is set to 0 if the corresponding cluster is available for data storage. A FAT entry is marked bad if the corresponding cluster has one or more sectors that are not usable. This occurs when read or write errors are found during the formatting of the disk.

The File Directory

As shown in figure 7–3, the File Directory follows the boot area and the FATs and contains the names for all disk files, names for subdirectories, and the volume label.

The File Directory itself is a variable number of sectors that will depend on the number of entries specified for the disk. Every File Directory entry requires 32 bytes; thus, a 512-byte sector will have 16 such directory entries. The exact number of directory sectors is the number of files or entries divided by 16 and rounded up by 1 if the number of sectors is 0. Thus, the number of files a File Directory can have is dependent on the type of disk used. Table 7–7 lists the disk types and the number of file entries possible. Popular double-sided diskettes allow 112 entries in the directory, and the hard disk allows 512.

The fields for each File Directory Entry are described in table 7–8.

Filename The *filename* field contains a file name that is up to 8 bytes (or characters) in length and is left-justified in the field. DOS expects file names that are less than 8 bytes to be filled out with blanks. If a file has been deleted, the first byte of its *filename* field is changed to a hex E5. This signifies to DOS that the entry is available for reuse. When a directory entry has never been used, the first byte of the file name field will contain a hex 00.

The distinction between a deleted file name entry and an unused entry is that during directory searches DOS will stop when it encounters the first hex 00 in the first byte of any *filename* field but continues when it encounters a hex

Directory Entries	Directory Sectors	Description
64	4	Single-sided diskettes
112	7	Double-sided diskettes
224	14	AT high-density diskettes
512	32	Hard disks

Table 7–7: The number of File Directory entries and the number of directory sectors for each type of disk

E5, which is merely a deleted entry. If a deleted entry contained a hex 00 in the first position, DOS would have to search all the directory sectors, because it could not distinguish between a deleted file and an entry that had never been used.

Filename **Extension**   The file-name extension is an optional field; files may or may not have extensions. File-name extensions are up to 3 bytes in length and, like the *filename* field, must be left-justified in the field and right-filled with spaces.

File Attributes   File attributes tell what kind of file this is: read/write, read-only, hidden, etc. Table 7–9 describes each of the attributes that are possible for a File Directory entry.

Start	Length	Description
0	8	File name
8	3	File name extension
11	1	File attribute
12	10	DOS reserved
22	2	Time of last update or creation
24	2	Date of last update or creation
26	2	Initial allocation unit/cluster
28	4	File size

Table 7–8: The File Directory entry consists of eight fields.

Value	Description
00h	Normal read/write file
01h	Read-only file
02h	Hidden
04h	System file
08h	Volume label
10h	Subdirectory
20h	Archive bit

Table 7–9: The various attribute bits that can exist for File Directory entries

Setting the attribute for read-only prevents a modification of the file name through DOS standard file write calls. The hidden attribute will prevent a display of the entry when the DIR command is issued. The attribute for system file is set for the special DOS files that reside on a system disk (IO.SYS and MSDOS.SYS). These two files are brought into memory during a boot of the PC. The attribute for volume label indicates to DOS that the File Directory entry is not a file name but a volume name. The attribute for subdirectory indicates that the file name and extension entry is the name of a subdirectory. The archive bit indicates to DOS that when the BACKUP.COM utility is used to off-load files from the disk, the contents of this particular entry are to be written out. Once the file is backed up, the archive bit is turned off.

Time of Last Update or Creation   Whenever a file is created, the time of creation of the file is entered into the File Directory entry. This includes all directory entries, such as file names, subdirectories, and the volume label. If a file has been updated, this file directory will be updated to reflect the time of the last update. This is not true for subdirectory entries; additions within the subdirectory do not cause an update of the time for the entry. The 2-byte time field is described in table 7–10.

Date of Last Update or Creation   The date of last update or creation is set with the file-creation date or the date of the last modification. This 2-byte field is similar to the time field but for the date. Table 7–11 describes the 2-byte date field.

Initial Allocation Unit/Cluster   The initial allocation unit or cluster field contains the cluster number of the first cluster allocated to the file. For subdi-

Field	Hex Offset	Decimal Offset	Bits within Offset
Hours	17h	23	7 thru 3
Minutes	17h	23	2 thru 0
	16h	22	7 thru 5
Seconds	16h	22	4 thru 0

```
Byte   <--23--> <--22-->
Bits    1       11
        5       10    54    0
Value  hhhhhmmmmmmssssss
```

Table 7–10: How to decode the 2-byte time field

rectories, this is the cluster that will contain the File Directory for the entries in the subdirectory. Table 7–12 indicates the format for the start cluster number.

File Size The file-size field contains the size of the file in bytes. It is a double-word entry with the words reversed and the bytes within each word reversed. This double word allows file sizes of up to 32 bits, which is much larger than the DOS limit of 32 Mb. You will see why DOS has this limit in a later section of this chapter. Table 7–13 describes the file-size field.

Field	Hex Offset	Decimal Offset	Bits within Offset
Year	19H	25	7 thru 1
Month	19H	25	0
	18H	24	7 thru 5
Day	18H	24	4 thru 0

```
Byte   <--25--> <--24-->
Bits    1
        5       98  65   0
Value  yyyyyyymmmmmddddd
```

* Year is years since 1980

Table 7–11: How to decode the 2-byte date field

Hex Offset	Decimal Offset	Description
1AH	26	Least significant
1BH	27	Most significant
Byte	<-27-> <-26->	
Hex value	0X XX	

Table 7–12: How to interpret the start cluster number for the File Directory entry

Disk Sizing

In previous sections of this chapter, you have seen the different sections that comprise a DOS disk. We will now cover the various aspects of DOS disk sizing, including 12- or 16-bit FAT entries. Then we will describe how to calculate the number of the clusters for a disk. Lastly, you will see how DOS limits the size of disks.

Hex Offset	Decimal Offset	Description
1CH	28	Low-order word Least-significant byte
1DH	29	Low-order word Most-significant byte
1EH	30	High-order word Least-significant byte
1FH	31	High-order word Most-significant byte
Byte	<-31-> <-30-> <-29-> <-28->	
Hex value	XX XX XX XX	

Table 7–13: The 4-byte file-size field. Note that the bytes are reversed in each field and the words are reversed.

FAT Entries: 12 or 16 bits?

As we saw earlier, FAT entries are either 12 or 16 bits in length. That length will depend on two factors: the capacity of the disk and the cluster size. You will need the size of the disk in sectors and the cluster size in number of sectors per allocation unit.

Disks will use 12-bit FAT entries until it is no longer possible to store cluster numbers in a 12-bit quantity. FAT entries of 12 bits can contain a number up to 4,096 (0 to fffh). Subtracting the 16 values that constitute reserved, bad, and end-of-file indicators (see table 7-6) yields a maximum of 4,080 clusters. Because clusters are numbered from 2, this results in a range of 2 to 4,080 or 4,079 clusters. If the number of clusters exceeds 4079, 16-bit FAT entries are used to mark each cluster.

For example, if a disk used 8 sectors of 512 bytes each per cluster, and the maximum number of clusters is 4,079, the largest disk using 12-bit FATs would be 16 Mb (512 bytes * 8 sectors/cluster * 4079 clusters). Therefore, to make life easier, disks larger than 10 Mb use 16-bit FATs.

Note that, whether 12- or 16-bit FATs are used, the FAT, File Directory, and the Boot Record are not counted in the total number of clusters available. See table 7–14 for a summary of the typical cluster and overhead values for various types of disks.

DOS Disk Size Limits

PCs have grown in every way, and disk storage is no exception. The original hard disks of 10 Mb have given way to 20- and 30-Mb drives as standard equipment. DOS is extremely versatile in its handling of disks, but there are some limits built into the software.

The critical number that limits the amount of disk storage per disk drive is the total number of sectors per drive. This number is contained in a single word that allows for a maximum of 64k sectors. With a sector size of 512 bytes, this yields a maximum disk size of 32 Mb.

DOS can provide support for disks that are larger than 32Mb in two ways. The first way is to use a larger sector size. For example, using a sector size of 1,024 bytes moves the disk size limit up to 64 Mb. However, this requires special software that changes the DOS system files to override the default 512 bytes per sector. The second method is much easier. DOS offers the capability to divide the hard disk into one or more partitions. Each partition of the disk is treated as if it were a separate and distinct physical drive. Thus, you can have multiple 32-Mb partitions on one disk. You will see more of disk partitions in the next sections.

Disk size	5¼	5¼	5¼	5¼
Disk type	Floppy	Floppy	Hard	Hard
Surfaces	1	2	Varies	Varies
Disk capacity	180 kb	360 kb	10 mb	20 mb
Total # sectors	360	720	20k	40k
Sectors/cluster	1	2	8	4
Maximum clusters	360	360	2560	10k
12/16-bit FATs	12	12	12	16
Boot area sectors	1	1	1	1
FAT sectors	2	2	8	40
# FATs	2	2	2	2
Total FAT sectors	4	4	16	80
Directory entries	64	112	512	512
Directory sectors	4	7	32	32
Overhead sectors	9	12	49	113

Table 7–14: The various calculations for determining the size of the FAT entries and the amount of overhead the disks can have

Critical Disk Parameters

With a large variety of disks to support, DOS needs a mechanism to determine the logical and physical characteristic of each disk in the PC. These disk parameters must be recorded on the disk and read by DOS before the first access. The best location is within the Boot Record, because it is common to all disks and is always at the beginning of the disk.

We will examine the disk parameters stored on each disk by taking a closer look at the Boot Record.

The Boot Area Revisited

As you may recall, the boot area is the first part of a disk or, in the case of a partitioned hard disk, the first area in the partition. As we discussed earlier, the boot area contains a 3-byte jump instruction, the vendor identification, the BIOS Parameter Block, and the boot code (see figure 7–1).

The BIOS Parameter Block

The 19 bytes that make up the BIOS Parameter Block (BPB) contain more information that allows DOS to understand how the disk has been built. The BPB contains physical information about the disk media, as well as the location and sizes of the FATs, the File Directory, and the user data area.

Table 7–15 shows the format of the BPB. Names or labels are assigned to each field to make it easier to refer to these fields when we develop the RAM Disk Device Driver in the following chapter.

The BPB is read off each disk by DOS before the very first access. As you will see, the values of the BPB allow DOS to translate physical to logical sectors and vice versa. Additionally, the FATs, File Directory, and the user data area can be found using the BPB.

Let's examine each of these fields one at a time.

Sector Size (SS)   The sector size field contains the number of bytes per sector for this media. Although possible sector sizes are 128, 256, 512, and 1024 bytes per sector, DOS does not make full use of this parameter. There are numerous places in the BIOS and within DOS itself that assume sector sizes are 512 bytes per sector.

Allocation Unit Size (AU)   As we mentioned above, a cluster, or allocation unit, is the basic unit of DOS disk storage and represents a certain number of sectors.

Name	Start	Length	Description
SS	0	2	Sector Size in bytes
AU	2	1	Allocation Unit size (sectors per cluster)
RS	3	2	Number of Reserved Sectors
NF	5	1	Number of FATs on this disk
DS	6	2	Directory Size (number of files)
TS	8	2	Number of Total Sectors
MD	10	1	Media Descriptor
FS	11	2	FAT Sectors (each FAT)
ST	13	2	Number of Sectors per Track
NH	15	2	Number of Heads
HS	17	2	Number of Hidden Sectors

Table 7–15: The fields that comprise the BIOS Parameter Block (BPB)

Reserved Sectors (RS)   This field contains the number of reserved sectors for the disk. Recall that each diskette or hard-disk partition has a reserved or boot area. This parameter specifies to DOS how many sectors are reserved as the boot area. This field generally contains a value of 1 and is always at the beginning of the disk or the partition.

An important point to note here is that in DOS, sectors are numbered starting at 0. You may recall that the BIOS routines use a sector-numbering scheme that starts at 1. You will see how DOS uses sector numbering in the section called "Hidden Sectors."

Number of FATs (NF)   The number of FATs for a disk, usually two, is contained in this field.

Directory Size (DS)   This field contains the maximum number of files in the File Directory. The size of the File Directory in sectors will be dependent on the number of files and the size of each sector. Because each file requires a 32-byte entry in the File Directory, and because the number of bytes per sector is contained in the sector size (SS) field, dividing the sector size by 32 gives the number of directory entries per sector. Then dividing the directory size by the number of directory entries per sector will give the number of directory sectors. This number is rounded up if necessary.

Normally, 512-byte sectors are used, so 16 directory entries are available per directory sector.

Total Sectors (TS)   The number of total sectors is the total size of the disk in sectors. This number must include the sectors in the boot or reserved area, the two FATs, the File Directory, and the user data area. Because this word can contain a number equal to 64k, the largest disk that DOS can support is 32 Mb using 512-byte sectors. For hard disks, this number is the same as the number that appears in the partition table as the last entry.

Media Descriptor (MD)   The media descriptor field is a single byte that describes the disk for DOS. Table 7–16 explains the various media descriptor bytes.

FAT Sectors (FS)   The FAT sectors field contains the number of sectors in each FAT. DOS will use this number to calculate the total number of sectors occupied by the reserved sectors (boot area) and the FATs to determine the start of the File Directory.

Hex Value	Description
f8h	Hard disk
f9h	Double-sided 5¼-inch diskette (15 sector HD)
	Double-sided 3½-inch diskette
fah	Ram disk (used by Columbia Data Products)
fch	Single-sided 5¼-inch diskette (9 sector)
	Double-sided 8-inch diskette (single density)
fdh	Double-sided 5¼-inch diskette (9 sector)
feh	Single-sided 5¼-inch diskette (8 sector)
	Single-sided 8-inch diskette (single density)
	Single-sided 8-inch diskette (double density)
ffh	Double-sided 5¼-inch diskette (8 sector)

Table 7–16: The various values for the media descriptor field

Sectors per Track (ST)   This field contains the number of sectors per track for a disk. For diskettes, this number is 8, 9, or 15. For hard disks, this number is usually 17.

Number of Heads (NH)   This field contains the number of heads or usable recording surfaces for the disk. This value is 1 for single-sided disks and 2 for double-sided disks. The value for hard disks will vary depending on the hard-disk drive. Typical values range from 2 to 6.

Hidden Sectors   The field that contains the number of hidden sectors for the disk typically is used for partitioning hard disks. Hard disks have the ability to be partitioned into several independent logical drives (for more information, refer to appendix D). In order for DOS to locate the start of a partition, it needs to know the number of sectors from the beginning of the disk to the start of the partition that is being used. The sectors preceding the active partition are known as the hidden sectors, because they are invisible to the active partition. The number of hidden sectors is an offset that is added to the number that is calculated for file operations that are within the active partition to derive the precise physical location on the disk. This is shown in figure 7–4.

Each of the partitions is treated by DOS as a contiguous block of sectors starting with sector 0, even though it is not the absolute 0th sector. Do not confuse this with the physical sector scheme, in which sectors are numbered starting at 1. The difference is that each track has physical sectors numbered

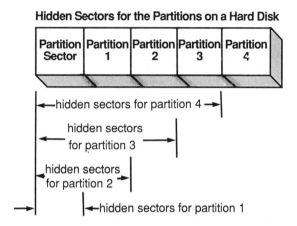

Hidden Sectors for the Partitions on a Hard Disk

Figure 7–4: The number of hidden sectors for the four partitions of a hard disk

starting at 1, repeating the sector numbering for each track. DOS partitions start at sector 0 and do not repeat any of the sector numbers.

The number of hidden sectors is always 0 for diskettes, because there is no partition. For hard disks, the number of hidden sectors for each partition will depend on the size of the preceding partitions (each partition has its own BPB). The first partition will generally have 17 hidden sectors, because the first track is occupied by the partition sector and the first partition must start on a track boundary; therefore, the existence of the partition sector forces the first partition to be on the second track, or 17 sectors from the beginning of the disk.

Using the BPB to Find Information

The BPB that must exist on each disk allows DOS to find the important and necessary parameters about the physical characteristics of the disk. For example, DOS can divide the total sector count (TS) by the number of sectors per track (ST) to determine the total number of tracks for the disk or partition.

In addition, the BPB contains enough information for DOS to determine where the FATs, the File Directory, and the user data area are located. Because the sizes of each of these sections of the disk can be found in the BPB or calculated, it is a simple matter for DOS to add up the space occupied by previous sections to arrive at the location of the FATs, the File Directory, or the user data area. This is shown in figure 7–5.

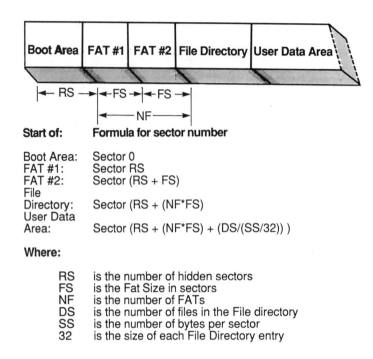

Start of: **Formula for sector number**

Boot Area: Sector 0
FAT #1:   Sector RS
FAT #2:   Sector (RS + FS)
File
Directory: Sector (RS + (NF*FS)
User Data
Area: Sector (RS + (NF*FS) + (DS/(SS/32)))

Where:

RS   is the number of hidden sectors
FS   is the Fat Size in sectors
NF   is the number of FATs
DS   is the number of files in the File directory
SS   is the number of bytes per sector
32   is the size of each File Directory entry

Figure 7–5: How DOS calculates the start sectors for the FATs, the File Directory, and the User Data Area. Note that the size of the File Directory is not stored in the BPB but is calculated using the number of files in the File Directory (DS), the sector size (SS), and the size of each File Directory entry (32).

Table 7–17 shows typical values that are found in the vendor identification and the BPB for a 5¼-inch single-sided diskette.

DOS Disk Device Drivers

You are probably wondering why we have gone to such detail in describing the FATs, BPBs, and so on. This detail is required to help you understand how DOS interacts with a disk media, so that our RAM Disk Driver in the next chapter will make sense. It is also necessary to look at the other side of the disk interface, from DOS and the device driver. This is done in the next sections.

Field	Typical Value
Vendor Identification	IBM 2.0
BIOS Parameter Block (BPB)	
Sector Size in bytes (SS)	512
Allocation Unit size (AU)	1
Number of Reserved Sectors (RS)	1
Number of FATs (NF)	2
Directory Size in files (DS)	64
Total Sectors for disk(TS)	360
Media Descriptor (MD)	fc
FAT Size in sectors (FS)	2
Sectors per Track (ST)	9
Number of Heads (NH)	1
Number of Hidden Sectors (HS)	0

Table 7–17: The typical values found in the vendor identification field and the BIOS Parameter Block for a single-sided 5¼-inch diskette

DOS and the Disk Device Driver

Whenever DOS needs to read or write to the disk, the standard disk device driver (the one that is loaded into memory with DOS) is called. In addition to read or write calls, DOS makes some calls to the disk device driver to get answers to questions about the disk.

Which Disk Is It?

DOS recognizes that disks fall into two categories: those that are removable and those that are not. Removable disks are the familiar diskettes that can be removed and replaced easily. Nonremovable disks are, for the most part, hard or fixed disks. Another type of nonremovable disk is a RAM disk, one of which we will be writing in the next chapter. A RAM disk uses memory to store data.

During disk operations, DOS always checks to see whether the disk has been changed. For nonremovable disks, there are fewer checks than for disk units that contain removable disks. DOS performs this check through a call to the DOS Media Check function. Recall from the previous sections of this chapter that all disks have a media descriptor. DOS uses this to identify the disk and to check whether the disk has changed. For example, if you have been using a single-sided diskette, the media descriptor would be fch. Then, if you swapped a double-sided diskette for a single-sided diskette, DOS would update the media descriptor and it would contain fdh. However, this is not a fool-proof method of determining if the diskette has changed—you could fool DOS by changing to another single-sided diskette! Therefore, you cannot rely on the media descriptor as the only method of determining whether a disk has changed.

The only place to determine whether a disk has changed is within the disk device driver. DOS will pass the media descriptor of the disk it has worked on to the disk device driver. The disk device driver, in turn, will determine whether the disk has changed by comparing the particular disk parameters; it then will return this information to DOS.

If the disk has been changed, DOS cannot assume that the FATs, the File Directory, and the user data area are still in the same relative locations. Recall that single- and double-sided disks have different numbers of sectors for the FATs and the File Directory. Thus, another function of the disk device driver is to return to DOS the BPB for any newly inserted disk. This allows DOS to calculate the positions of the FATs and the File Directory for the new disk.

In short, each disk access by an application can cause DOS to perform a media check on the disk. If the disk has changed, DOS will request the BPB for the new disk from the disk device driver so that it can know where everything is stored.

At this point, a real-life example might help illustrate what happens between DOS and the disk device driver. Let's assume that you have inserted into the B: drive a disk that has just been formatted. Then you issue the following DOS command:

```
DIR
```

Here is the output that appears on the screen:

```
A>DIR b:

 Volume in drive B has no label
 Directory of B:\

File not found

A>
```

Even for this tiny amount of information, DOS has to perform many steps. After the DIR command is issued, DOS has to check whether the disk in drive B: has been changed since the last time B: was accessed. Then DOS has to read the directory sectors for the volume label and the file information. Note that the

File Directory sectors may be read twice; pass 1 searches for the volume label, which does not have to be in the first directory sector; pass 2 retrieves the file names. Lastly, DOS reads the FAT for the amount of space used on the disk. This process is shown in figure 7–6.

So far, the simple DIR command has DOS reading many sectors of the disk. What other calls can the disk device driver expect? Recall that DOS always checks to determine whether the disk has changed. This is reflected in the fact that each disk read requested of the disk device driver is preceded by a Media Check call.

Let's take the example above—the DIR of a freshly formatted disk—and expand the steps DOS has to take to arrive at the message "file not found." The typical calls that DOS makes to the disk device driver to perform this task and the responses it receives are shown in table 7–18.

Note that, in table 7–18, there are a lot of Media Check and Get BPB calls to ensure that the disk has not been changed. There are generally fewer of these calls for hard disks. This is because the disk device driver knows that the hard disk is nonremovable and can tell DOS the media has not changed. Therefore, DOS will not request the BPB except when the hard disk is initially accessed.

Now that we have covered the amount of work that a disk device driver has to do on request from DOS, we can review the commands that a device driver has to perform. This will help us understand what is expected of our RAM Disk Device Driver.

Disk Device Driver Commands

As you have learned, when DOS requires a service from a device driver, the packet of data that is passed to the device driver with the call is referred to as the Request Header. Contained within this packet of data is a command number that corresponds to the service required by DOS. This command number instructs the device driver to perform a certain action. You have seen several different commands (Input, Output, and Initialization) in previous chapters.

There are 17 commands for device drivers in DOS version 3.0; only the first 13 are legal for DOS 2.0. We will now describe each of these commands and what is required to write code especially for disk device drivers. The list of applicable commands is shown in table 7–19.

The Initialization Command

The Initialization command is the first command issued to the disk device driver after it has been loaded into memory. This call is issued because DOS needs

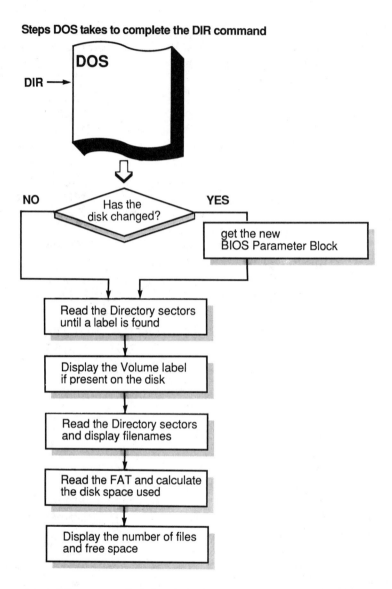

Steps DOS takes to complete the DIR command

DIR →

DOS

NO   Has the disk changed?   **YES**

get the new BIOS Parameter Block

Read the Directory sectors until a label is found

Display the Volume label if present on the disk

Read the Directory sectors and display filenames

Read the FAT and calculate the disk space used

Display the number of files and free space

Figure 7–6: The steps DOS takes to display the contents of the disk on a DIR command. Note that the File Directory sectors may be read twice; the first pass searches for the volume label which does not have to be in the first Directory sector; the second pass retrieves the file names.

DOS	Disk Device Driver
Media check ------------>	Has the disk changed?
Yes <------------	Newly formatted disk in B: therefore the disk has changed.
Get BPB ------------>	DOS needs the new BIOS Parameter Block for the new disk to determine where the Directory starts.
Read ------------>	DOS requests the first Directory sector in order to find the volume label.
Media check Get BPB ------------>	DOS may make these requests several times depending on the amount of memory DOS has available to store information on the disk.
Read ------------>	Read the Directory sector for file Name and size information.
Media check Get BPB ------------>	Retrieve the current BPB if needed for calculating where the File Directory is.
Read ------------>	Read the Directory sector for calculating number of files on the disk.
Media check Get BPB ------------>	Retrieve the current BPB if needed for determining where the FAT resides.
Read ------------>	Read the FAT sector to calculate the amount of space available on the disk.

Table 7–18: The typical calls DOS makes to the disk device driver in order to process the DIR command on a newly formatted diskette. The calls depicted are typical because the type and amount of calls will depend on the DOS configuration used and whether it is the first time the DIR is issued.

several pieces of information from the device driver. The first is how many disk drive units this particular disk device driver will be supporting. For diskettes, this number is usually read through switches set on the PC motherboard.

The next piece of information that the device driver must return to DOS is the Break Address, which is the next available memory location after the driver. Because the driver knows its location, it can easily return this information. DOS then knows where to load the next device driver, if there is one; if not, DOS continues loading other routines.

The next item returned to DOS is the address of a table of BPBs. Five types of diskettes can be used by 5¼-inch diskette units: single-sided disks of 8 or 9

Number	Command Description
0	Initialization
1	Media Check
2	Build BPB
3	IOCTL Input
4	Input
5–7	Not Applicable
8	Output
9	Output With Verify
10–11	Not Applicable
12	IOCTL Output
13	Device Open
14	Device Close
15	Removable Media
16	Not Applicable

Table 7–19: All of the applicable commands for block device drivers

sectors per track, double-sided diskettes of 8 or 9 sectors per track, and special double-sided (high capacity) diskettes of 15 sectors per track. These five types of diskettes will have five different types of BPBs, varying in media descriptors, number of heads, FAT sectors, and File Directory entries. DOS needs to access this table of BPBs to determine the various sector sizes of each type of disk supported. The steps involved in finding the address of the BPB table are shown in figure 7–7.

The Media Check Command

The Media Check command in table 7–19 is always called before disk reads and writes for other than file I/O operations. When directory or FAT information is accessed, Media Check is called to determine whether the disk has changed. If so, DOS must read in new information on the disk.

DOS passes the media descriptor for the current disk in a particular disk drive, and the device driver can use this to determine if the disk has changed. Normally, as you saw earlier, this is not sufficient information because two similar types of disks (both single-sided, for example) will have the same media descriptor.

The device driver can return an indication of one of three possible conditions. The first condition is the media has not changed. This will be the case for nonremovable hard disks and RAM disks. The second condition is that the device

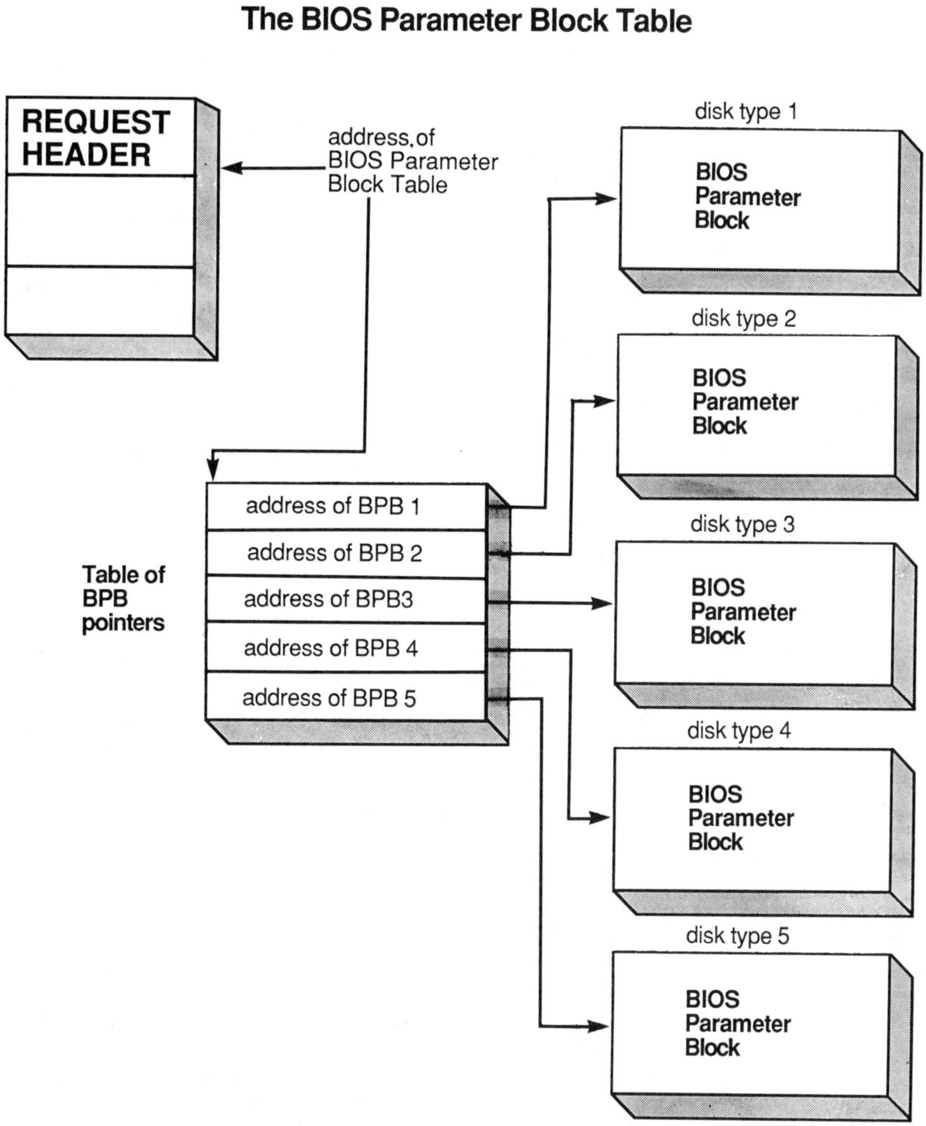

The BIOS Parameter Block Table

Figure 7–7: The Initialization command requirement to return the address of the BIOS Parameter Block Table. This table consists of the addresses for each of the BPBs for the five types of disks the Disk Device Driver supports.

driver has determined that the media has changed. The driver could determine this by checking to see if a disk door open signal has been received from the disk controller or by simply calculating the time since the last access of the drive. If the Media Check command is sent to the driver within a very short time interval since the last access, it is not likely that a disk has been changed.

The last Media Check condition occurs when the device driver does not know if the media has changed. For example, if the time since the last access of the drive has exceeded a short predetermined time interval, the device driver assumes that a disk change could have occurred and returns a "don't know" condition.

The Get BPB Command

The Get BPB command is requested of the device driver whenever a media-is-changed condition is returned to DOS from a Media Check call. Get BPB is called for hard disks only once.

When the Media Check command returns a "don't know" condition, the GET BPB command is called only if DOS has no dirty buffers. Dirty buffers are those buffers that contain modified data for the disk that needs to be written. DOS assumes that if there are dirty buffers (modified data waiting to be written to disk), the disk has not changed.

If the device driver receives a GET BPB command, it will have to read the reserved or boot sector from the disk to access the BPB at offset 11 (decimal) of the boot sector. The BPB will end up in DOS's work area, and the device driver will return a pointer to this BPB to DOS. DOS can then use the BPB to calculate where the FATs and File Directory are on the disk.

The IOCTL Input Command

The IOCTL Input command in table 7–19 tells the device driver to return to DOS an I/O control string. As you have seen, this is usually not data from the device in the normal sense but some information regarding the status of the device. It may be the baud rate for a serial device or the printer control word for a laser printer. For block devices, this does not have much meaning.

The Input Command

The Input command is sent to the device driver whenever DOS needs to read data from the disk. DOS will pass to the driver the number of sectors to read, the starting sector number, and the address of the data-transfer area in which the data is to be placed. DOS will have previously read in the FAT and File Directory and used these to calculate the needed sectors.

The starting sector number is numbered from 0 to the highest sector number for the disk and is relative to the start of the partition if it is a hard disk. For diskettes, the start sector is always the reserved or the boot sector.

It is up to the device driver to translate this starting sector number into the appropriate track, head, and sector for the actual physical disk unit.

The Output Command

The Output command tells the device driver to write one or more sectors onto the disk. As it does for the Input command, DOS passes the starting sector number, the number of sectors to write, and the data-transfer address from which to write. The driver is responsible for translating this logical sector address to a physical disk address.

The Output With Verify Command

The Output With Verify command is the same as the Output command except that after the data is written out, the device driver is responsible for reading the data back in. This insures that the data has been properly written to the disk.

The VERIFY command in COMMAND.COM is used to set VERIFY ON or OFF. If it is set ON, all writes to the disk are passed as Output With Verify commands to the device driver.

The device driver can set a variable to indicate that VERIFY is ON. After writing to the disk, the driver can jump to the Input routine to read back in the previously written data and ensure that it is valid.

The IOCTL Output Command

The IOCTL Output command is similar to the IOCTL Input command, but the direction of data transferred is reversed. This command allows the program to pass an I/O control string to the device driver.

Again, the disk device driver can use this feature to implement just about anything. The I/O control string is not treated as normal data to be written out to the disk but is information that device drivers do not normally get. Without I/O control strings, it would be impossible to communicate with the device driver. The device driver would only get data to be written to the disk or read from the disk.

For instance, we could use I/O control strings to suspend disk operations temporarily and perform some maintenance diagnostics. However, this would involve a large amount of programming.

The Device Open Command

This disk driver command is new for DOS version 3.0 and is designed to signal the device driver that a file open for the disk has occurred. The device driver could keep a count of file opens to ensure that any reads and writes to the disk were preceded by file open commands. If not, we could be writing to the disk when there is no file opened. This would be the situation if a diskette were removed before the file that was opened was properly closed.

In order to be able to receive Device Open and Device Close commands, the device driver must set the Open/Close/Removable bit in the Attribute word of the Device Header. Recall that the Device Header is the table that occupies the first memory locations in the device driver.

The Device Close Command

The Device Close command is sent to the device driver whenever a program has closed the device. For disks, this happens when a file is closed on the disk.

The disk device driver, in conjunction with Device Open commands, could keep a counter of open files. When a Device Open command is sent, the driver would increment a counter. When a Device Close is sent, the device driver would decrement this same counter. Then, whenever a read (Input command) or a write (Output command) is sent to the driver, we could check to see whether a file has been opened for the device. If not, we could disallow any I/O to the disk until files are properly opened or closed.

Unfortunately, this approach to enforcing proper disk usage is not very practical. Let's assume that a user has removed a disk before properly closing the file. The counter is set at 1, because the file was not closed. However, the device driver still thinks that the file is opened, so it will not disallow reads and writes to the disk. In other words, the problem has already occurred and there is no practical way of catching or remedying the situation.

The Removable Media Command

Removable Media is another command that is available for DOS version 3.0. This command is sent to the device driver only if the Open/Close/Removable bit is set in the Attribute word in the Device Header.

With this command, a program could ask the device driver whether the media is removable. This could save time within a program, because if the media is not removable, the program could assume that there would not be any disk changes. When the device driver is sent a Removable Media command, it will return an indication that the media is either removable or nonremovable.

Summary

In this chapter, we have covered just about every aspect of disks within DOS, from what disks are, what information is contained on a disk, and how DOS uses a disk, through the inner workings of DOS and disk device drivers. All disks are treated in a similar manner, and DOS interacts with a disk device driver through a standard set of driver commands. These driver commands allow the device driver to read from, write to, and otherwise control the disk. The device driver can also account for the different types of disks: removable and nonremovable.

You are now ready to tackle the task of writing a disk device driver. In the next chapter, we will use all the information presented in this chapter to build a RAM disk. The RAM disk will be written to handle most of the commands we have just discussed and will work on both DOS 2.0 and 3.0.

Questions

1. What is the proper order on the disk of the following:

   User data area
   File Allocation Table (FAT)
   File Directory
   Boot Record

2. How does the Boot Record get placed on a disk?

3. What is the maximum length of a cluster chain?

4. What is the maximum size of a disk?

5. What is the minimum size of a disk?

6. What is the purpose of the Get BPB driver command?

7. What constitutes an "illegal" file name?

Answers may be found in appendix E.

Chapter 8

A RAM Disk Device Driver

- RAM Disks and How They Work
- What Commands the RAM Disk Device Driver Will Use
- Building the RAM Disk Device Driver
- Modifying the RAM Disk Device Driver

I n this chapter, we present a block-oriented device driver, the RAM Disk Device Driver. Rather than controlling actual hardware, the RAM Disk Device Driver will simulate a floppy disk, so it will use features that we have not presented in the previous device drivers—commands that are applicable to block devices and, more specifically, disk-type block devices. Much of the material about disks from chapter 7 is used here.

The RAM Disk Device Driver simulates a diskette by using random access memory (RAM) to store data normally destined for a hardware disk. Because RAM is a much faster storage medium than magnetic media, a RAM disk has almost instant response to a read or write. The size of the RAM disk will be 100Kb. This 100Kb of storage will all be actual usable space; no overhead is included in this figure. We will also add the ability to change the disk to any desired capacity, limited by the amount of memory in the PC.

Just as hard-disk or floppy diskette units give an audible or visual indication when in use, the RAM Disk Device Driver will have a similar ability. The RAM Disk Device Driver will turn on the PC's internal speaker each time we read or write to the RAM disk. This allows us to hear the RAM disk as we use it.

Using the RAM Disk Device Driver

When you boot DOS with the RAM Disk Device Driver in this chapter, you will see the following message on the screen.:

```
The Waite Group 100k RAM Disk
```

First, you must determine the driver letter that should be associated with the RAM disk. The RAM disk will appear as the first drive letter after the last drive in the PC. For single and dual floppy diskette systems, the RAM disk will be drive C:. If the PC has a single hard disk, the RAM disk will be drive D:.

If you copy a file to the RAM disk, you will notice an audible tone during the transfer. This means the RAM disk is working. If you use a DIR or CHKDSK command, you will hear short clicks from the speaker. Again, you are hearing the RAM disk at work, as DOS reads the RAM disk for information on the files stored on the disk.

RAM Disks and How They Work

Normally, disks are hardware devices that store digital data on sectors, tracks, and cylinders. The disk controller managing a disk unit is responsible for finding, storing, and retrieving the data from the disk itself.

RAM disks simulate the behavior of disk hardware in RAM memory. On a magnetic disk, data is stored in sectors. With a RAM disk, sectors are represented by areas of read/write memory, and the RAM disk data is organized in these ''sectors'' by defining the areas of memory one after the next. Like a hardware disk, the RAM disk defines the storage areas starting with sector 0, followed by sector 1, and so on, creating a one-to-one correspondence between the RAM disk's storage area in memory and the hardware disk storage area. Figure 8–1 shows the similarity of the RAM disk to a disk.

Theoretically, RAM disks can be any size. However, the size is actually limited by the amount of available memory on your PC. On 8086/8088 PC systems without EMS (Expanded Memory System), a maximum of 640Kb of memory is allowed. To use a RAM disk there must be sufficient memory on your PC to run DOS and your largest application program.

Determining the proper amount of memory space is not easy, because you will have to experiment with the particular version of DOS and the size of the application programs you use. The RAM disk driver developed in this chapter is sized at 100Kb, which should not present any problems on most DOS systems.

It should be noted that this capacity problem can be alleviated on 80286/80386 systems. On these systems, it is possible to have ''extended'' memory beyond 640Kb and to define the RAM disk storage area in the extended memory area, leaving the 640Kb of ''normal'' memory for DOS and application programs. An example of a RAM disk device driver that allows this is IBM's standard VDISK.COM driver, which is provided with PC-DOS versions 3.1 and higher. This chapter will not address this concept of extended memory RAM disks.

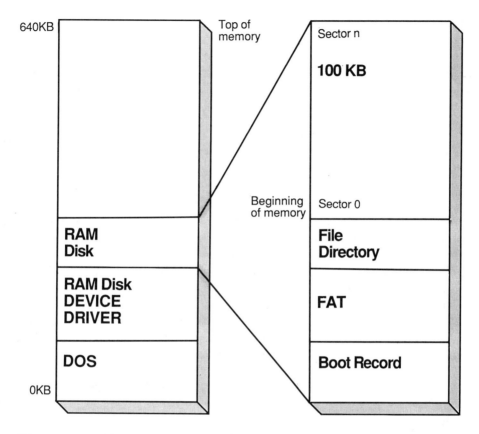

Figure 8–1: How RAM disks use memory to simulate the storage of a diskette. Like the diskette, RAM disks store data in memory in sectors. Exploded view shows the IBM PC's memory space for the RAM disk user area allocated just after the code for the RAM Disk Device Driver.

The RAM Disk Device Driver

The RAM Disk Device Driver will consist of two parts: a device driver written to DOS requirements and the space reserved for the RAM disk data storage.

Within the second part, space is set aside for the Boot Record, the FAT, and the File Directory, just like on magnetic disks. (See figure 8–1.)

The overhead for the RAM disk includes the Boot Record, the FAT, and the

File Directory. Recall from chapter 7 that each has a specific purpose. We will review each of these sections of the RAM disk.

The Boot Record consists of four parts: the *jump* instruction, the vendor identification, the BIOS Parameter Block (BPB), and the optional boot instruction code. For the RAM disk, we will implement only the vendor identification and the BPB. We have no need for the boot-related information, because we cannot boot DOS from the RAM disk.

The BPB defines the disk to DOS. We specify the size of the RAM disk (100Kb), the size of the File Allocation Table (FAT), and the size of the File Directory to DOS through the BPB.

The File Allocation Table (FAT) is used to keep track of where each file stores its data in the RAM disk. Recall that each unit of storage is called a *cluster,* or *allocation unit.* We can define a cluster either as one sector or as a power of two sectors (that is, 2, 4, 8, etc.); the cluster is identified in the FAT through a 1½-byte cluster number. The FAT must be large enough to contain one cluster number for each cluster in the storage space for the RAM disk.

The File Directory is a table of entries that records our use of the RAM disk, including all file names as well as the names of any subdirectories we create in the RAM disk. Because each entry requires 32 bytes, we can store 16 such entries in a 512-byte sector. How large the File Directory will be depends on how many entries we wish the RAM disk to store.

Lastly, we have the actual data-storage area for the RAM disk. If 100Kb is to be allocated for data storage, the actual amount of memory required by the RAM disk will be the amount of overhead for the Boot Record, the FAT, and the File Directory, plus 100Kb.

Specifying the Internal Format of the RAM Disk

To determine what the RAM disk format will be like, we must specify many of the parameters in the BPB, the size of the File Allocation Table, and the number of entries in the File Directory.

In table 8–1, each field of the BPB is specified for the RAM Disk Device Driver as follows. The Sector Size (SS) is 512 bytes per sector. The Allocation Unit (AU) size is 1 sector per cluster, because it is a small disk. The number of Reserved Sectors (RS) is 1 (one and only one is necessary for the boot record). The number of FATs (NF) is one. The Directory Size (DS) is set at 48 entries. The number of Total Sectors (TS) is 205. The Media Descriptor (MD) is feh. The FAT Sectors (FS) is 1. The last three entries in the BPB, the Sectors per Track (ST), the Number of Heads (NH), and the number of Hidden Sectors (HS) are set to 0; they are not meaningful for a RAM disk, because there is no hardware associated with the RAM disk.

Name	Starting Location	Length	Description
SS	0	2	Sector Size in bytes
AU	2	1	Allocation Unit size (sectors per cluster)
RS	3	2	Number of Reserved Sectors
NF	5	1	Number of FATs on this disk
DS	6	2	Directory Size (number of files)
TS	8	2	Number of Total Sectors
MD	10	1	Media Descriptor
FS	11	2	FAT Sectors (each FAT)
ST	13	2	Number of Sectors per Track
NH	15	2	Number of Heads
HS	17	2	Number of Hidden Sectors

Table 8–1: The fields that comprise the BIOS Parameter Block (BPB). The start location for each of the fields is relative to the beginning of the BPB.

Our RAM disk will have only one File Allocation Table. It is unnecessary to have a second FAT because we do not expect media problems with the RAM disk. Also, DOS does not make use of the second copy of the FAT in the event of problems with the first copy, so why bother?

The number of sectors the FAT will require is based on the number of clusters we need for the RAM disk. We have set the number of sectors per cluster (AU) at 1. Thus, for a 100Kb RAM disk at 512 bytes per sector, we have 200 sectors and 200 clusters. Because each cluster will occupy 1½ bytes in the FAT, we need 300 bytes for storing all possible cluster numbers in the FAT. Based on 512-byte sectors, this is well under one sector's worth. Therefore, we set the FAT Sectors (FS) at 1.

The File Directory for the RAM disk will contain up to 48 entries. Because each entry occupies 32 bytes, we need 1,536 bytes, or three sectors. The Total Sectors (TS) is the sum of the overhead sectors plus the space available for data storage. This is calculated as follows:

	1	for the boot record (Reserved Sectors)
+	1	for the first (and only) FAT
+	3	for the file directory
+200		for the 100Kb user data area
205		total sectors in the RAM disk

The format of the RAM disk, the Boot Record and the values for the BPB, are shown in figure 8–2.

Some RAM Disk Driver Design Choices

In the preceding chapters, you have seen that the rules for specific device drivers specify the exact requirements for the Device Header, the command processing, and the setting of the Status word of the Request Header. For a particular device you wish to control, you need to provide functional interfaces to DOS and your specific device for certain standard operations, such as Read, Write, and Ini-

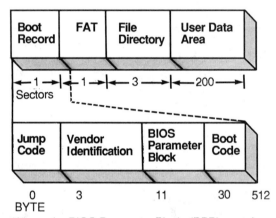

Where the BIOS Parameter Block (BPB) contains:

Name	Start	Value	Description
SS	11	512	Sector size in bytes
AU	13	1	Allocation unit size (sector per cluster)
RS	14	1	Number of reserved sectors
NF	16	1	Number of FATs on this disk
DS	17	48	Directory size (number of files)
TS	19	205	Number of total sectors
MD	21	FEh	Media descriptor
FS	22	1	FAT Sectors (each FAT)
ST	24	0	Number of sectors per track
NH	26	0	Number of heads
HS	28	0	Number of hidden sectors

Figure 8–2: Each of the four parts of the RAM disk, with an exploded view of the specific sections and the values for them within the RAM disk's Boot Record.

tialize. Beyond this, you decide which of the other commands to implement. These include the I/O Control functions, Status and Flush. Not all of these commands are applicable to all device drivers, but you certainly have the choice of whether to implement a particular feature.

The specific design choices made for the RAM Disk Device Driver are to provide only one FAT and to provide an audible indication whenever the RAM disk is being accessed. The RAM Disk Device Driver has been written so that you can alter the size of the RAM disk easily by reassembling the source code. You will see this at the end of the chapter.

What Commands the RAM Disk Device Driver Will Use

Our RAM Disk Device Driver will implement seven standard commands: Initialize (0), Media Check (1), Get BPB (2), Input (3), Output (8), Output With Verify (9), and Removable Media (15). These are the same basic commands required for a disk device driver under DOS.

The RAM Disk Device Driver processes these commands in the same fashion as other disk device drivers do, thus allowing DOS to treat the RAM Disk Device Driver just like a normal disk. In upcoming sections, we will examine each command in depth. However, let's take a quick look at the basic function of each command as it applies to the RAM Disk Device Driver.

The driver's Initialization command will set up memory space to look like a disk, with each sector of the RAM disk represented by a portion of memory. The Media Check command allows DOS to find out whether the RAM disk has been removed. Because the RAM disk uses memory and is not a removable disk, DOS must know that it is not removable. The Get BPB command allows DOS to determine the disk parameters of the RAM disk. DOS will use this information to locate the File Allocation Table and the File Directory, as well as the user data area. The Input command is sent to the RAM Disk Device Driver when DOS requires a sector of data from the RAM disk. The Output command tells the device driver to write data to the RAM disk. The Output With Verify command is similar to the Output command, with the additional task of reading the data back in. This command was built into the device driver strategy because of the possibility of marginal disk media reliability. We verify the write by reading back the data to ensure that the write was successful. Lastly, the Removable Media command allows programs to determine whether to issue messages to change diskettes. Figure 8–3 shows the commands that DOS can send to the RAM Disk Device Driver. Each command causes the RAM Disk Device Driver to perform a function.

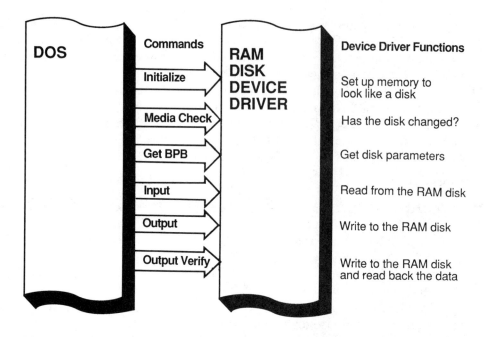

Figure 8–3: The seven commands that the RAM Disk Device Driver will process. Each of the commands requires the RAM Disk Device Driver to perform an action.

The RAM Disk Device Driver Program Listing

We begin our look at the RAM Disk Device Driver with listing 8–1. The format is unchanged from previous device drivers. The first section of code includes a summary of what the RAM Disk Device Driver does. The commands you may implement may not be applicable to all versions of DOS. Note these differences. For example, the Removable Media command is valid only for DOS 3.0.

We have named the main procedure *ramdisk* to distinguish it from others in earlier chapters. In the section called the "Instructions to the Assembler," you will define the *struc*s for each of the commands the driver will process. This allows you to refer to the variables that DOS passes to your device driver, as well as making it easier for it to pass back information to DOS.

Within the main procedure code, you add an assembler pseudo-operation to define the label *start_address,* which will contain the address of the current instruction address. You will use this at the end of the RAM Disk Device Driver to determine where the memory for the RAM disk will begin.

Listing 8–1: The beginning of the RAM Disk Device Driver

```
                page    60,132
                title   A RAM Disk Device Driver

;******************************************************************
;*      This is a RAM Disk Device Driver                          *
;*      Author:  Robert S. Lai                                    *
;*      Date:    29 November 1986                                 *
;*      Purpose: A RAM Disk with audible tones                    *
;*      This is a RAM Disk Device Driver                          *
;******************************************************************

;summary:
;       This RAM disk device driver is built to DOS 3+ requirements
;       but is compatible with DOS 2.
;
;       The command processing allows for 17 commands, numbered from
;       0 thru 16. The specific commands that are allowed in DOS 3
;       are not used to allow the RAM Disk to run under DOS 2.

;******************************************************************
;*      ASSEMBLER DIRECTIVES                                      *
;******************************************************************

cseg            segment para    public  'code'   ;only one segment
ramdisk         proc    far
                assume  cs:cseg,es:cseg,ds:cseg

;structures

rh              struc                   ;request header
rh_len          db      ?               ;len of packet
rh_unit         db      ?               ;unit code
                                        ;(block devices only)
rh_cmd          db      ?               ;device driver command
rh_status       dw      ?               ;returned by device driver
rh_res1         dd      ?               ;reserved
rh_res2         dd      ?               ;reserved
rh              ends                    ;

rh0             struc                   ;Initialization (command 0)
rh0_rh          db      size rh dup (?) ;fixed portion
rh0_nunits      db      ?               ;number of units
                                        ;(block devices only)
rh0_brk_ofs     dw      ?               ;offset address for break
rh0_brk_seg     dw      ?               ;segment address for break
rh0_bpb_tbo     dw      ?               ;offset address of pointer
                                        ;to BPB array
```

Listing 8–1: *(cont.)*

```
rh0_bpb_tbs     dw       ?              ;segment address of pointer
                                        ;to BPB array
rh0_drv_ltr     db       ?              ;first available drive
                                        ;(DOS 3+) (block only)
rh0             ends                    ;

rh1             struc                   ;Media_Check (command 1)
rh1_rh          db       size rh dup (?) ;fixed portion
rh1_media       db       ?              ;media descriptor from DPB
rh1_md_stat     db       ?              ;media status returned by
                                        ;device driver
rh1             ends                    ;

rh2             struc                   ;Get_BPB (command 2)
rh2_rh          db       size rh dup(?)  ;fixed portion
rh2_media       db       ?              ;media descriptor from DPB
rh2_buf_ofs     dw       ?              ;offset address of
                                        ;data transfer area
rh2_buf_seg     dw       ?              ;segment address of
                                        ;data transfer area
rh2_pbpbo       dw       ?              ;offset address of
                                        ;pointer to BPB
rh2_pbpbs       dw       ?              ;segment address of
                                        ;pointer to BPB
rh2             ends                    ;

rh4             struc                   ;INPUT (command 4)
rh4_rh          db       size rh dup(?)  ;fixed portion
rh4_media       db       ?              ;media descriptor from DPB
rh4_buf_ofs     dw       ?              ;offset address of
                                        ;data transfer area
rh4_buf_seg     dw       ?              ;segment address of
                                        ;data transfer area
rh4_count       dw       ?              ;transfer count
                                        ;(sectors for block)
                                        ;(bytes for character)
rh4_start       dw       ?              ;start sector number
                                        ;(block only)
rh4             ends                    ;

rh8             struc                   ;OUTPUT (command 8)
rh8_rh          db       size rh dup(?)  ;fixed portion
rh8_media       db       ?              ;media descriptor from DPB
rh8_buf_ofs     dw       ?              ;offset address of
                                        ;data transfer area
rh8_buf_seg     dw       ?              ;segment address of
                                        ;data transfer area
```

Listing 8–1: (cont.)

```
rh8_count         dw      ?         ;transfer count
                                    ;(sectors for block)
                                    ;(bytes for character)
rh8_start         dw      ?         ;start sector number
                                    ;(block only)
rh8               ends              ;

rh9               struc             ;OUTPUT_VERIFY (command 9)
rh9_rh            db      size rh dup(?)  ;fixed portion
rh9_media         db      ?         ;media descriptor from DPB
rh9_buf_ofs       dw      ?         ;offset address of
                                    ;data transfer area
rh9_buf_seg       dw      ?         ;segment address of
                                    ;data transfer area
rh9_count         dw      ?         ;transfer count
                                    ;(sectors for block)
                                    ;(bytes for character)
rh9_start         dw      ?         ;start sector number (block only)
rh9               ends              ;

rh15              struc             ;Removable (command 15)
rh15_len          db      ?         ;len of packet
rh15_unit         db      ?         ;unit code
                                    ;(block devices only)
rh15_cmd          db      ?         ;device driver command
rh15_status       dw      ?         ;returned by device driver
rh15_res1         dd      ?         ;reserved
rh15_res2         dd      ?         ;reserved
rh15              ends              ;

;commands that do not have unique portions to the request header:
;       INPUT_STATUS    (command 6)
;       INPUT_FLUSH     (command 7)
;       OUTPUT_STATUS   (command 10)
;       OUTPUT_FLUSH    (command 11)
;       OPEN            (command 13)
;       CLOSE           (command 14)
;       REMOVABLE       (command 15)
;

;****************************************************************
;*      MAIN PROCEDURE CODE                                    *
;****************************************************************
;

begin:

start_address           equ     $         ;starting address
```

Listing 8–1: *(cont.)*

```
;*******************************************************************
;*       DEVICE HEADER REQUIRED BY DOS                            *
;*******************************************************************
;
next_dev        dd      -1              ;no device driver after this
attribute       dw      2000h           ;blk dev, non IBM format
strategy        dw      dev_strategy    ;address of strategy routine
interrupt       dw      dev_interrupt   ;address if interrupt routine
dev_name        db      1               ;number of block devices
                db      7 dup(?)        ;7 byte filler
```

In the Device Header section, the RAM disk device is defined in the Attribute word by clearing bit 15 to 0 to indicate that this is a block device. Bit 13 is set to specify that the RAM disk is not IBM format-compatible (which means that DOS will not use the Media Descriptor byte to determine the size of this disk). This Device Header will allow the RAM Disk Device Driver to work under both DOS 2.0 and 3.0. If you are using only version 3.0 of DOS, set bit 11 to tell DOS that the device driver also supports the Open, Close, and Removable Media commands.

Finally, you do not specify a name for the RAM Disk Device Driver, because DOS does not permit block device drivers to have a name. Instead, the value of the first byte equals the number of RAM disk units that the device driver will control. Set this value to 1 to indicate to DOS that there is only one RAM disk.

Work Space for Our Device Driver

In this familiar section, you must define all the variables you will be using in the RAM Disk Device Driver. In listing 8–2, the variables *rh_seg* and *rh_ofs* store the address of the Request Header that DOS passes to the RAM Disk Device Driver during the STRATEGY call.

Next, the Boot Record is defined. Starting with the variable *boot_rec,* we lay out the exact contents of the RAM disk as it will appear in memory using Define Byte (db) and Define Word (dw) directives. You will use this data to build the RAM disk as well as to store the data when DOS requests a copy of the BPB during a Get BPB command (you will see more of this in a later section). Three bytes of zeroes are defined in the *jump* instruction portion of the Boot Record, because the RAM disk is not bootable. Next comes the vendor identification, which identifies the disk as version 1.0 from The Waite Group.

Listing 8–2: The variables used by the RAM Disk Device Driver. The Boot Record contents are declared in this section, as well as the variables that control the transfer of data between DOS and the RAM disk.

```
;****************************************************************
;*          WORK SPACE FOR OUR DEVICE DRIVER                   *
;****************************************************************

rh_ofs          dw      ?           ;offset address of request header
rh_seg          dw      ?           ;segment address of request header

boot_rec        equ     $               ;dummy DOS boot record
                db      3 dup(0)        ;not a jump instruction
                db      'TWG  1.0'      ;vendor id

bpb     equ     $       ;This is the BIOS Parameter Block
bpb_ss  dw      512     ;512 byte sector size
bpb_au  db      1       ;cluster size is 1 sector
bpb_rs  dw      1       ;1 (boot) reserved sector
bpb_nf  db      1       ;1 FAT only
bpb_ds  dw      48      ;#files in the File Directory
bpb_ts  dw      205     ;sects=100KB + 5 overhead
bpb_md  db      0feh    ;media descriptor
bpb_fs  dw      1       ;FAT sectors in each FAT

bpb_ptr dw      bpb     ;bios parameter block pointer array (1 entry)

;current RAM disc information

total           dw      ?           ;transfer sector count
verify          db      0           ;verify 1=yes , 0=no
start           dw      0           ;start sector number
disk            dw      0           ;RAM disk start address
buf_ofs         dw      ?           ;data transfer offset address
buf_seg         dw      ?           ;data transfer segment address

res_cnt         dw      5           ;# reserved sectors
ram_par         dw      6560        ;paragraphs of memory
bell            db      1           ;1= bell on for RAM disk i/o
```

At the label bpb, the BPB is defined. Refer to figure 8–2 to see the definitions of the necessary parameters that will describe the RAM disk to DOS.

The next set of variables includes those that transfer data from the RAM disk to DOS and vice versa when the Read and Write commands are sent to the driver by DOS. The amount of data to be transferred, or the number of sectors, is retrieved from the Request Header and stored in the variable *total*. The *verify* variable is used to determine whether to read the data after processing a Write command. The variable *start* is used to point to the start sector of data to be transferred. The variable *disk* is used to contain the starting memory address of the RAM disk. The variables *buf_ofs* and *buf_seg* are used to store the address of the data area within DOS. This buffer area is used to store data on disk read operations and to write data from write operations.

The last variables defined are used by the driver to control the RAM disk. We use *res_cnt* to indicate the number of sectors reserved for use by the RAM disk (here this number is 5), including the Boot Record, the File Allocation Table, and the File Directory. You can adjust this number for larger or smaller FATs and File Directories. The variable *ram_par* is used to indicate the number of 16-byte memory paragraphs the RAM disk will occupy. Here we use 6560 paragraphs (205Kb times 32 paragraphs per Kb). Lastly, the variable *bell* indicates whether or not to produce a variable-length tone each time the RAM Disk Device Driver processes a command. If you set this variable to 1, you will hear the RAM disk in action.

The RAM Disk STRATEGY and INTERRUPT Sections

The STRATEGY and INTERRUPT routines are the actual entry points from DOS into the RAM Disk Device Driver. The STRATEGY routine saves the Request Header address into the variables *rh_seg* and *rh_ofs*. The INTERRUPT routine processes the command (number) that is stored in the Request Header. These routines are identical to those in earlier chapters (see listing 8–3).

Listing 8–3: The code for the STRATEGY and INTERRUPT routines

---

```
;****************************************************************
;*       THE STRATEGY PROCEDURE                                *
;****************************************************************
;

dev_strategy:   mov  cs:rh_seg,es    ;save the segment address
                mov  cs:rh_ofs,bx    ;save the offset address
                ret                  ;return to DOS


;****************************************************************
;*       THE INTERRUPT PROCEDURE                               *
;****************************************************************
;

;device interrupt handler - 2nd call from DOS
```

Listing 8–3: *(cont.)*

```
dev_interrupt:

        cld                             ;save machine state on entry
        push    ds
        push    es
        push    ax
        push    bx
        push    cx
        push    dx
        push    di
        push    si

        mov     ax,cs:rh_seg    ;restore ES as saved by STRATEGY call
        mov     es,ax           ;
        mov     bx,cs:rh_ofs    ;restore BX as saved by STRATEGY call

;jump to appropriate routine to process command

        mov     al,es:[bx].rh_cmd   ;get request header command
        rol     al,1                ;times 2 for index into word table
        lea     di,cmdtab           ;function (command) table address
        mov     ah,0                ;clear hi order
        add     di,ax               ;add the index to start of table
        jmp     word ptr[di]        ;jump indirect

;CMDTAB is the command table that contains the word address
;for each command. The request header will contain the
;command desired. The INTERRUPT routine will jump through an
;address corresponding to the requested command to get to
;the appropriate command processing routine.

CMDTAB  label   byte            ;* = char devices only
        dw      INITIALIZATION  ; initialization
        dw      MEDIA_CHECK     ; media check (block only)
        dw      GET_BPB         ; build bpb
        dw      IOCTL_INPUT     ; ioctl in
        dw      INPUT           ; input (read)
        dw      ND_INPUT        ;*non destructive input no wait
        dw      INPUT_STATUS    ;*input status
        dw      INPUT_FLUSH     ;*input flush
        dw      OUTPUT          ; output (write)
        dw      OUTPUT_VERIFY   ; output (write) with verify
        dw      OUTPUT_STATUS   ;*output status
        dw      OUTPUT_FLUSH    ;*output flush
        dw      IOCTL_OUT       ; ioctl output
        dw      OPEN            ; device open
        dw      CLOSE           ; device close
        dw      REMOVABLE       ; removable media
        dw      OUTPUT_BUSY     ; output til busy
```

Your Local Procedures

In this section, you must define four procedures for use by the RAM Disk Device Driver. These procedures are *save, cvt2seg, bell1,* and *bell2* (see listing 8–4).

The *save* procedure retrieves information from the Request Header concerning the data transfer between DOS and the RAM Disk Device Driver. Use the Input command *struc rh4* to store the address of the data-transfer buffer into variables *buf_seg* and *buf_ofs.* The starting sector and number of sectors to transfer is stored in variables *start* and *total,* respectively. The driver calls this *save* procedure immediately when it needs to jump to the Input or Output command-processing routines.

The procedure *cvt2seg* is used to calculate the address of a sector in the RAM disk (a starting paragraph). Recall that the sectors of a disk are actually memory locations in the RAM disk, so we need to convert a sector number into an equivalent memory address. Because each sector is 512 bytes in length and there are 16 bytes per paragraph of memory, the sector number should be multiplied by 32 to derive the starting paragraph in the RAM disk's memory. Next, we calculate the number of bytes to transfer by multiplying the number of sectors to transfer by 512 bytes per sector.

Note that a transfer from DOS to the RAM disk cannot exceed 64Kb. This limitation is imposed by the 8086/8088 architecture; each segment is limited to a size of 64Kb. Because a data segment cannot exceed 64Kb, the largest data transfer is likewise limited.

The last two procedures, *bell1* and *bell2,* control the PC's speaker. *Bell1* turns on the speaker and *bell2* turns it off. Both procedures will test the flag variable *bell* before turning on or off the speaker. A value of 1 placed in *bell* allows you to control whether you want to hear an audible tone during reads and writes. The duration of the tone will depend on the length of time between a call to *bell1* and the next call to *bell2.* This way you can hear how long a transfer takes. Short data transfers will make clicks on the speaker, and long transfers will make beeps because the tone is on longer. These two routines are useful for debugging any code. If you place calls to turn on and off the speaker around suspect code, you can determine whether the code is working or looping.

DOS Command Processing

In this section, we will examine the seven DOS commands processed by the RAM Disk Device Driver. These commands are Initialization, Media Check, Get BPB, Input, Output, Output With Verify, and Removable Media. With the exception of the Removable Media command, these commands are the minimum number of commands that a disk device driver must have.

Listing 8–4: The code for four procedures. The *save* procedure stores data from the Request Header. The *cvt2seg* procedure converts a sector information into a RAM disk address. The *bell1* and *bell2* procedures turn the speaker on and off if needed.

```
;*******************************************************************
;*        YOUR LOCAL PROCEDURES                                   *
;*******************************************************************

save     proc    near      ;saves data from Request Header
;
;        called from INPUT, OUTPUT
;
         mov     ax,es:[bx].rh4_buf_seg   ;save data transfer
         mov     cs:buf_seg,ax            ; segment
         mov     ax,es:[bx].rh4_buf_ofs   ;save data transfer
         mov     cs:buf_ofs,ax            ; offset
         mov     ax,es:[bx].rh4_start     ;get start sector number
         mov     cs:start,ax              ; save it
         mov     ax,es:[bx].rh4_count     ;# sectors to transfer
         mov     ah,0                     ;clear hi order
         mov     cs:total,ax              ; save in our area
         ret                              ;return to caller
save     endp

cvt2seg proc    near      ;calculates memory address
;
;        requires cs:start       starting sector
;                 cs:total       total sector count
;                 cs:disk        RAM disk start address
;
;        returns  ds             segment address
;                 cx             count of total bytes
;                 si             = 0 for paragraph boundary
;
;        uses     ax
;                 cx
;                 si
;                 ds
;
         mov     ax,cs:start    ;get starting sector number
         mov     cl,5           ;multiply by 32 paragraphs/sector
         shl     ax,cl          ; by shifting left 5 places
         mov     cx,cs:disk     ;get start segment of RAM disk
         add     cx,ax          ;add to initial segment
         mov     ds,cx          ; DS has start segment
         mov     si,0           ;make it on a paragraph boundary
         mov     ax,cs:total    ;total number of sectors
         mov     cx,512         ;byte per sector
         mul     cx             ;multiply to get xfer length
```

Listing 8–4: *(cont.)*

```
          or    ax,ax               ;too large (carry set)?
          jnz   calc1               ;no (less than 64k)
          mov   ax,0ffffh           ;yes - make it 64k
calc1:    mov   cx,ax               ;move length to cx
          ret                       ;return to caller
cvt2seg endp

bell1     proc  near                ;bell on if needed
          cmp   cs:byte ptr bell,0  ;bell required?
          jz    nobell1             ;no
          mov   al,0b6h             ;magic #
          out   43h,al             ;timer2
          mov   ax,400h             ;cycles
          out   42h,al             ;lsb
          mov   al,ah               ;msb
          out   42h,al
          in    al,61h              ;spkr port
          or    al,3                ;spkr/timer on
          out   61h,al             ;
nobell1:  ret                       ;return
bell1     endp

bell2     proc  near                ;bell off if needed
          cmp   cs:byte ptr bell,0  ;bell off needed?
          jz    nobell2             ;no
          in    al,61h              ;get port
          and   al,0fch             ;spkr/timer2 off
          out   61h,al             ;
nobell2:  ret                       ;return
bell2     endp
```

Command 0—Initialization The Initialization command is an important one for the RAM Disk Device Driver. You build the RAM disk by initializing memory to contain a Boot Record, a File Allocation Table, and a File Directory. This satisfies the requirement that the RAM disk be available for use when it exits from the Initialization command processing. The steps that the RAM Disk Device Driver performs for the Initialization command are shown below:

1. Initialize memory for the RAM disk

2. Build the Boot Record

3. Build the File Allocation Table

4. Build the File Directory

5. Set the Break Address

6. Set the number of RAM Disk units

7. Set the pointer to the BPB array

Listing 8–5 shows that a call to *bell1* will turn on the speaker for an audible tone if the variable *bell* is set to 1. The *initial* procedure is called to display a message indicating the loading of the RAM Disk Device Driver. This *initial* procedure is defined at the end of the RAM Disk Device Driver, in the beginning of what will be the data storage area for the RAM disk. Normally, additional initialization-only code could be placed here. However, because it is the start of the RAM disk storage area, clearing the memory assigned to the disk storage area would erase these instructions before they have a chance to execute. Here the *initial* procedure only displays a message, and the normal initialization code you have seen in the previous chapters is not included in *initial*. The Break Address is now set to point to the end of the RAM disk storage area, not to the *initial* procedure.

To calculate the Break Address, we determine the end address of the RAM Disk Device Driver, add the length of the RAM disk *(ram_par)* to the starting segment of the RAM disk *(disk)*, and then store this segment and offset address in the *struc* variables *rh0_brk_seg* and *rh0_brk_ofs*, respectively.

Next, the number of units that the RAM Disk Device Driver will control is set. This number is part of the Request Header and is set to 1 for this RAM Disk Device Driver.

DOS needs to know what types of disks the device driver can support. The code returns a pointer to an array of BPBs. This lets DOS scan through the table to match a disk type (see chapter 7 for a detailed discussion).

The next couple of steps involve initializing memory to look like a disk. First, we must clear the memory space that will contain the Boot Record, the File Allocation Table, and the File Directory; otherwise, DOS may find random values in the FAT and file-directory areas and think that they are legitimate entries.

The second step is to build the Boot Record. We copy *boot_rec* to the beginning of the RAM disk using the Repeat Move Bytes instruction *(rep movsb)*. This move will copy the *jump* instruction, the vendor identification, and the BPB.

The third step is to build the File Allocation Table. The first two FAT entries, *fefff*h, are placed in the beginning of the FAT. This identifies the RAM disk to DOS whenever DOS inspects the File Allocation Table.

Do not place any information in the File Directory. Instead, leave it initialized to zeroes to indicate to DOS that the File Directory has no entries.

Lastly, we restore the ES and BX registers, turn the speaker off, and exit from the RAM Disk Device Driver.

Listing 8–5: The Initialization command code. The RAM disk is initialized at this point and contains a Boot Record, a File Allocation Table, and a File Directory.

```
;****************************************************************
;*        DOS COMMAND PROCESSING                                *
;****************************************************************
;command 0       Initialization
Initialization:
        call    bell1                   ;optional bell tone
        call    initial                 ;display console message
        push    cs                      ;move cs
        pop     dx                      ; to dx

;calculate end segment of RAM disk
        lea     ax,cs:start_disk        ;start address of RAM disk
        mov     cl,1                    ;hex digit shift count
        ror     ax,cl                   ;divide by 16 = paragraphs
        add     dx,ax                   ;add to current cs value
        mov     cs:disk,dx              ;RAM disk start address
        mov     ax,ram_par              ;add # RAM disk paragraphs
        add     dx,ax                   ;to start segment of RAM disk

;return the break address to DOS
        mov     es:[bx].rh0_brk_ofs,0   ;offset is 0
        mov     es:[bx].rh0_brk_seg,dx  ;segment

;return number of units for a block device
        mov     es:[bx].rh0_nunits,1    ;only one RAM disk

;return address of array of BIOS Parameter Blocks (1 only)
        lea     dx,bpb_ptr              ;address of bpb pointer array
        mov     es:[bx].rh0_bpb_tbo,dx  ;return offset
        mov     es:[bx].rh0_bpb_tbs,cs  ;return segment

;initialize boot, FAT, Directory to zeroes
        push    ds                      ;cvt2seg destroys ds
        mov     cs:start,0              ;start sector = 0
        mov     ax,cs:res_cnt           ;#reserved sectors
        mov     cs:total,ax             ;#sectors
        call    cvt2seg                 ;address and count
        mov     al,0                    ;fill value
        push    ds                      ;save
        pop     es                      ;move to es
        mov     di,si                   ;all offsets = 0
        rep     stosb                   ;clear reserved sectors

;move boot record to sector 0
        pop     ds                      ;restore ds -> RAM disk
        mov     es,cs:disk              ;RAM disk start address
```

Listing 8–5: *(cont.)*

```
        mov     di,0                    ;zero out di (boot record)
        lea     si,cs:boot_rec          ;address of boot record
        mov     cx,24                   ;
        rep     movsb                   ;copy 24 bytes of boot record

;build one and only one FAT
        mov     cs:start,1              ;logical sector 1
        mov     cs:total,1              ;doesn't matter
        call    cvt2seg                 ;get ds:si set quickly
        mov     ds:byte ptr [si],0feh   ;set the first 2 FAT
        mov     ds:byte ptr 1[si],0ffh  ; entries to describe
        mov     ds:byte ptr 2[si],0ffh  ; disc
        call    bell2                   ;optional bell off
;end of initialization - restore es:bx exit
        mov     ax,cs:rh_seg            ;move request header
        mov     es,ax                   ; segment to es
        mov     bx,cs:rh_ofs            ; offset to bx
        jmp     done                    ;set DONE bit & exit
```

Command 1—Media Check DOS uses the Media Check command to determine whether the disk has been removed. DOS makes this check before it reads or writes to the disk to ensure that the disk has not been changed since the last access. The relationship between DOS and the RAM Disk Device Driver for the Media Check command is shown below:

DOS: Has the disk changed?

RAM disk device driver: Return Media Check Status:

- −1   Media has been changed
- 0   Don't know
- +1   Media has not changed

The Media Check Status is set to 1, which indicates to DOS that the media has not changed. This is always true for both RAM disks and fixed disks. Here is the code:

```
        ;command 1    Media_Check
        Media_Check:                    ;block device only
                mov     es:[bx].rh1_media,1   ;media is unchanged
                jmp     done                  ;set DONE bit & exit
```

Command 2—Get BPB DOS uses this command to retrieve the BPB. This command will be issued if the Media Check command returns a status that indicates the disk has changed. If the Media Check command returns a status of "don't know" and DOS has no dirty buffers (data that needs to be written out to the disk), DOS will also issue a Get BPB command. This command allows DOS to determine the locations of the FAT and the File Directory, as well as other key parameters. The Get BPB command requires the RAM Disk Device Driver to return the BPB and the address of the array of BPB to DOS. These steps are shown below:

1. DOS passes a Media Descriptor

2. The RAM Disk Device Driver returns the BPB and the address of the array of BPBs

As shown in listing 8–6, the code for the Get BPB command reads the BPB from the RAM disk into the data buffer specified by DOS. The address of the BPB array is also passed back to DOS in the Request Header.

Command 3—IOCTL Input The RAM Disk Device Driver does not implement IOCTL (I/O Control String) Input, so it is necessary to set the error bit of

---

Listing 8–6: The code for the Get BPB command

```
;command 2      Get_BPB
Get_BPB:                                        ;read Boot record
        push    es                              ;save request header segment
        push    bx                              ;save request header offset
        mov     cs:start,0                      ;boot record = sector 0
        mov     cs:total,1                      ;1 sector
        call    cvt2seg                         ;convert to RAM disk address
        push    cs                              ;set es to
        pop     es                              ;  cs
        lea     di,cs:bpb                       ;address of bios param blk
        add     si,11                           ;add 11 to si
        mov     cx,13                           ;length of bpb
        rep     movsb                           ;move
        pop     bx                              ;restore request header offset
        pop     es                              ;restore request header segment
        mov     dx,cs:bpb_ptr                   ;pointer to BPB array
        mov     es:[bx].rh2_pbpbo,dx            ;  to Request Header
        mov     es:[bx].rh2_pbpbs,cs            ;same for segment
        lea     dx,cs:bpb                       ;address of BPB =
        mov     es:[bx].rh2_buf_ofs,dx          ;  sector buffer offset
        mov     es:[bx].rh2_buf_seg,cs          ;same for segment
        jmp     done                            ;set DONE bit & exit
```

---

the Status word and indicate error 3 to indicate *unknown command*. This is shown as follows:

```
;command 3      IOCTL_Input
IOCTL_Input:

        jmp     unknown             ;set error bit/code & exit
```

Command 4—Input DOS uses the Input command to read data from the RAM disk. This command passes to the RAM Disk Device Driver the starting sector number to read and the number of sectors to transfer. The RAM Disk Device Driver translates this to a RAM disk address and moves the data from the RAM disk to the data buffer specified by DOS. The steps in this process are listed below:

1. DOS passes the starting sector number and the sector count.
2. The RAM Disk Device Driver reads from the RAM Disk.
3. The RAM Disk Device Driver passes data back to DOS.

As listing 8–7 shows, we first turn the speaker on. Then the *cvt2seg* procedure is called to convert the sector starting position and length to a RAM disk

---

Listing 8–7: The code for the Input command. The RAM Disk Device Driver will read from the RAM disk into the buffer specified by DOS.

```
;command 4      Input   Read RAM disk and return data to DOS
Input:
        call    bell1               ;turn on bell if required
        call    save                ;save Request Header data
        call    cvt2seg             ;calc RAM disk start address
        mov     es,cs:buf_seg       ;set destination seg & ofs
        mov     di,cs:buf_ofs       ; to es:di
        mov     ax,di               ;get offset
        add     ax,cx               ;add transfer length
        jnc     input1              ;overflow?
        mov     ax,0ffffh           ;yes - use max transfer
        sub     ax,di               ;subtract offset from max
        mov     cx,ax               ;new transfer count
input1: rep     movsb               ;Read RAM disk to data area
        call    bell2               ;turn off bell if required
        mov     ax,cs:rh_seg        ;move request header
        mov     es,ax               ; segment to es
        mov     bx,cs:rh_ofs        ; offset to bx
        jmp     done                ;set DONE bit & exit
```

---

memory segment address and a count of the number of bytes to transfer. Next, a *mov* instruction is used to transfer the data. Note that you may overflow the segment if the calculation exceeds 64k. If this is the case, you can adjust the maximum transfer to 64k. To exit from the Input command processing, restore the Request Header segment and offset address and then turn the speaker off.

Commands 5, 6, and 7   The RAM Disk Device Driver does not implement the Nondestructive Input (5), Input Status (6), or Input Flush (7) commands. These commands are not applicable to block device drivers. Here is the code for these commands:

```
;command 5      ND_Input
ND_Input:

        jmp     busy            ;set BUSY bit & exit

;command 6      Input_Status
Input_Status:

        jmp     done            ;set DONE bit & exit

;command 7      Input_Flush
Input_Flush:

        jmp     done            ;set DONE bit & exit
```

Command 8—Output   The Output command is used to write data to the RAM disk. DOS passes the address of the data to be written, the sector number in the RAM disk to write to, and the number of sectors of data to be written. The steps involved in processing the Output command are listed below:

1. DOS passes the address of the data, the starting sector, and the sector count.
2. The RAM Disk Device Driver converts the sector number and count to an address.
3. The RAM Disk Device Driver writes the data to the RAM disk.

The Output command processing begins with a call to the *bell1* procedure. This will turn the speaker on if needed. Then the transfer values are saved in the call to the *save* procedure. The procedure *cvt2seg* translates the sector numbers into an address within the RAM disk. Next, the data is moved from the RAM disk to the DOS data buffer. Finally, the *verify* flag is tested; if it contains

Listing 8–8: The code for the Output command. This command reads from the RAM disk into the DOS data buffer. If the *verify* flag is set to 1, jump to the Input command routine to read the data back in to verify that the write was successful.

```
;command 8        Output          Write data to RAM disk
Output:
          call    bell1           ;turn bell on if needed
          call    save            ;save Request Header data
          call    cvt2seg         ;get start address in RAM
          push    ds              ;move to
          pop     es              ; es
          mov     di,si           ;same for di
          mov     ds,cs:buf_seg   ;ds:si points to source
          mov     si,cs:buf_ofs   ; data in DOS
          rep     movsb           ;move ds:si to es:di
          mov     bx,cs:rh_ofs    ;restore es:bx
          mov     es,cs:rh_seg    ;for possible jmp to input
          cmp     cs:verify,0     ;do we verify write?
          jz      out1            ;no
          mov     cs:verify,0     ;reset verify indicator
          jmp     input           ;read those sectors back in
out1:     call    bell2           ;turn bell off if required
          mov     ax,cs:rh_seg    ;move request header
          mov     es,ax           ; segment to es
          mov     bx,cs:rh_ofs    ; offset to bx
          jmp     done            ;set DONE bit & exit
```

a 1, control jumps to the Input routine. Listing 8–8 shows the code for the Output command.

Command 9—Output With Verify This command is similar to the Output command, but it also performs the task of reading the data back in for verification. A read-after-write operation provides an additional assurance that the write was successful. This compensates for media that may be marginal in retaining the data. If the read was not successful, the Write command is reissued. The steps that the Output With Verify command processing performs are listed below:

1. DOS passes the address of the data, the starting sector, and the sector count.

2. The RAM Disk Device Driver converts the sector number and count to an address.

3. The RAM Disk Device Driver writes the data to the RAM disk.

4. The RAM Disk Device Driver reads the data from the RAM disk.

The RAM Disk Device Driver processes the Output With Verify command by setting the *verify* flag to 1; it then passes control to the Output command routine. The Output routine will write the data to the RAM disk and then jump to the Input routine to read the data back in. Here is the code for the Output With Verify command:

```
;command 9      Output_Verify
Output_Verify:                    ;output (write) with verify
         mov    cs:verify,1        ;set the verify flag
         jmp    output             ;go to output routine
```

Commands 10, 11, 12, 13, and 14 These commands have not been implemented in the RAM Disk Device Driver. The Output Status (10) and Output Flush (11) commands are for character-oriented devices and are not valid for block devices. The IOCTL Out (12), Device Open (13), and Device Close (14) commands are applicable to block devices, but we have not implemented them in our RAM Disk Device Driver. The code for these commands is shown below:

```
;command 10     Output_Status
Output_Status:

         jmp    done               ;set DONE bit & exit

;command 11     Output_Flush
Output_Flush:

         jmp    done               ;set DONE bit & exit

;command 12     IOCTL_Output
IOCTL_Out:

         jmp    unknown            ;set error bit/code & exit

;command 13     Open
Open:

         jmp    done               ;set DONE bit & exit

;command 14     Close
Close:

         jmp    done               ;set DONE bit & exit
```

Command 15—Removable Media   This command is available only for DOS versions 3.0 or greater and only for block devices. The Removable Media command returns an indication of whether the disk media is removable. The BUSY bit of the Status word in the Request Header is set if the media is not removable. If the BUSY bit is not set, the media is removable. The steps involved in processing the Removable Media command are listed below:

1. DOS passes the unit number.
2. The RAM Disk Device Driver returns the BUSY bit set if the media is nonremovable; it returns the BUSY bit not set if the media is removable.

DOS will send this command only if a program issues a DOS service request for IOCTL (44h). One of the subfunctions (08h) tests whether the block device is changeable. What is unusual is that this IOCTL function does not appear as an IOCTL Input command but as a Removable Media command. This DOS service is used to determine whether the disk is fixed; if it is not fixed, the program can issue a message to the user requesting a disk change.

We set the BUSY bit on since the RAM disk is not removable:

```
;command 15     Removable
Removable:
        mov     es:[bx].rh_status,0200h ;set busy
        jmp     done                    ;set DONE bit & exit
```

Command 16—Output Til Busy   This command is available to character-oriented devices using versions 3.0 (or higher) of DOS. For the RAM Disk Device Driver, set the ERROR bit and ERROR CODE to 3 *(unknown command)*. Here is the code for the Output Til Busy command:

```
;command 16     Output Til Busy
OUTPUT_BUSY:

        jmp     unknown         ;set error bit/code & exit
```

The Error and Common Exits

In these two sections we process any error exits and common exits by setting the BUSY and DONE bits of the Request Header status word. Listing 8–9 shows the entire two sections.

Listing 8–9: The code for the error and common exits

```
;*******************************************************************
;*        ERROR EXIT                                              *
;*******************************************************************

unknown:
        or      es:[bx].rh_status,8003h  ;set error bit and error code
        jmp     done                     ;set done and exit

;*******************************************************************
;*        COMMON EXIT                                             *
;*******************************************************************

busy:   or      es:[bx].rh_status,0200h  ;set busy bit

done:   or      es:[bx].rh_status,0100h  ;set done

        pop     si                       ;restore all registers
        pop     di
        pop     dx
        pop     cx    .
        pop     bx
        pop     ax
        pop     es
        pop     ds
        ret                              ;return to DOS
```

The End of Program

In the End of Program section of the RAM Disk Device Driver, you will find a rather complex *org* assembler directive. This statement sets the location counter to a multiple of 16 bytes, which forces the RAM disk to start on a paragraph boundary. In doing so, segment addresses are used that assume the offset is 0. This makes it easier for the RAM Disk Device Driver to calculate addresses that correspond to the sector numbers that DOS passes back.

The constant *start_disk* is used by the Initialization command code to store the start address of the RAM disk.

Place the procedure *initial* at the beginning of the RAM disk, because it runs only once during the Initialization command processing and you never need it again. This *initial* procedure displays the RAM Disk Device Driver banner on the screen. Listing 8–10 completes the code for the RAM Disk Device Driver.

Listing 8–10: The last section of the RAM Disk Device Driver shows the code for the End of Program section

```
;****************************************************************
;*          END OF PROGRAM                                     *
;****************************************************************
end_of_program:

;org to paragraph boundary for start of RAM disk

        if      ($-start_address) mod 16
        org     ($-start_address)+16-(($-start_address) mod 16)
        endif

start_disk      equ     $

initial proc    near            ;

        lea     dx,msg1         ;initialization
        mov     ah,9            ; message
        int     21h             ;doscall
        ret                     ;return
initial endp

msg1    db      'The Waite Group 100k RAM Disk',0dh,0ah,'$'

ramdisk endp
cseg    ends
        end     begin

;that's all folks
```

The Whole RAM Disk Device Driver

Listing 8–11 lists the entire RAM Disk Device Driver.

Building the RAM Disk Device Driver

To build the RAM Disk Device Driver, enter the source code from listing 8–11 into a file called *ramdisk.asm,* using a word processor. Next, assemble, link, and convert the code to .COM format. Be sure to add the RAM Disk Device Driver to the CONFIG.SYS file; this specifies to DOS that the driver is a user-installable device driver.

Listing 8–11: The complete RAM Disk Device Driver

```
        page    60,132
        title   A RAM Disk Device Driver

;******************************************************************
;*      This is a RAM Disk Device Driver                          *
;*      Author:   Robert S. Lai                                   *
;*      Date:     29 November 1986                                *
;*      Purpose: A RAM Disk with audible tones                    *
;*      This is a RAM Disk Device Driver                          *
;******************************************************************

;summary:
;       This RAM disk device driver is built to DOS 3+ requirements
;       but is compatible with DOS 2.
;
;       The command processing allows for 17 commands, numbered from
;       0 thru 16. The specific commands that are allowed in DOS 3
;       are not used to allow the RAM Disk to run under DOS 2.

;******************************************************************
;*      ASSEMBLER DIRECTIVES                                      *
;******************************************************************

cseg            segment para    public  'code'   ;only one segment
ramdisk         proc    far
                assume  cs:cseg,es:cseg,ds:cseg

;structures

rh              struc                   ;request header
rh_len          db      ?               ;len of packet
rh_unit         db      ?               ;unit code
                                        ;(block devices only)
rh_cmd          db      ?               ;device driver command
rh_status       dw      ?               ;returned by device driver
rh_res1         dd      ?               ;reserved
rh_res2         dd      ?               ;reserved
rh              ends                    ;

rh0             struc                   ;Initialization (command 0)
rh0_rh          db      size rh dup (?) ;fixed portion
rh0_nunits      db      ?               ;number of units
                                        ;(block devices only)
rh0_brk_ofs     dw      ?               ;offset address for break
rh0_brk_seg     dw      ?               ;segment address for break
rh0_bpb_tbo     dw      ?               ;offset address of pointer
                                        ;to BPB array
rh0_bpb_tbs     dw      ?               ;segment address of pointer
                                        ;to BPB array
```

Listing 8–11: *(cont.)*

```
rh0_drv_ltr    db      ?           ;first available drive
                                   ;(DOS 3+) (block only)
rh0            ends                ;

rh1            struc               ;Media_Check (command 1)
rh1_rh         db      size rh dup (?) ;fixed portion
rh1_media      db      ?           ;media descriptor from DPB
rh1_md_stat    db      ?           ;media status returned by
                                   ;device driver
rh1            ends                ;

rh2            struc               ;Get_BPB (command 2)
rh2_rh         db      size rh dup(?)  ;fixed portion
rh2_media      db      ?           ;media descriptor from DPB
rh2_buf_ofs    dw      ?           ;offset address of
                                   ;data transfer area
rh2_buf_seg    dw      ?           ;segment address of
                                   ;data transfer area
rh2_pbpbo      dw      ?           ;offset address of
                                   ;pointer to BPB
rh2_pbpbs      dw      ?           ;segment address of
                                   ;pointer to BPB
rh2            ends                ;

rh4            struc               ;INPUT (command 4)
rh4_rh         db      size rh dup(?)  ;fixed portion
rh4_media      db      ?           ;media descriptor from DPB
rh4_buf_ofs    dw      ?           ;offset address of
                                   ;data transfer area
rh4_buf_seg    dw      ?           ;segment address of
                                   ;data transfer area
rh4_count      dw      ?           ;transfer count
                                   ;(sectors for block)
                                   ;(bytes for character)
rh4_start      dw      ?           ;start sector number
                                   ;(block only)
rh4            ends                ;

rh8            struc               ;OUTPUT (command 8)
rh8_rh         db      size rh dup(?)  ;fixed portion
rh8_media      db      ?           ;media descriptor from DPB
rh8_buf_ofs    dw      ?           ;offset address of
                                   ;data transfer area
rh8_buf_seg    dw      ?           ;segment address of
                                   ;data transfer area
rh8_count      dw      ?           ;transfer count
                                   ;(sectors for block)
                                   ;(bytes for character)
rh8_start      dw      ?           ;start sector number
                                   ;(block only)
```

Listing 8-11: *(cont.)*

```
rh8             ends            ;

rh9             struc           ;OUTPUT_VERIFY (command 9)
rh9_rh          db      size rh dup(?)  ;fixed portion
rh9_media       db      ?       ;media descriptor from DPB
rh9_buf_ofs     dw      ?       ;offset address of
                                ;data transfer area
rh9_buf_seg     dw      ?       ;segment address of
                                ;data transfer area
rh9_count       dw      ?       ;transfer count
                                ;(sectors for block)
                                ;(bytes for character)
rh9_start       dw      ?       ;start sector number (block only)
rh9             ends            ;

rh15            struc           ;Removable (command 15)
rh15_len        db      ?       ;len of packet
rh15_unit       db      ?       ;unit code
                                ;(block devices only)
rh15_cmd        db      ?       ;device driver command
rh15_status     dw      ?       ;returned by device driver
rh15_res1       dd      ?       ;reserved
rh15_res2       dd      ?       ;reserved
rh15            ends            ;

;commands that do not have unique portions to the request header:
;       INPUT_STATUS    (command 6)
;       INPUT_FLUSH     (command 7)
;       OUTPUT_STATUS   (command 10)
;       OUTPUT_FLUSH    (command 11)
;       OPEN            (command 13)
;       CLOSE           (command 14)
;       REMOVABLE       (command 15)
;

;****************************************************************
;*      MAIN PROCEDURE CODE                                     *
;****************************************************************

begin:

start_address           equ     $          ;starting address

;****************************************************************
;*      DEVICE HEADER REQUIRED BY DOS                           *
;****************************************************************

next_dev        dd      -1              ;no device driver after this
attribute       dw      2000h           ;blk dev, non IBM format
```

Listing 8–11: *(cont.)*

```
strategy        dw      dev_strategy    ;address of strategy routine
interrupt       dw      dev_interrupt   ;address if interrupt routine
dev_name        db      1               ;number of block devices
                db      7 dup(?)        ;7 byte filler

;******************************************************************
;*      WORK SPACE FOR OUR DEVICE DRIVER                          *
;******************************************************************

rh_ofs          dw      ?          ;offset address of request header
rh_seg          dw      ?          ;segment address of request header

boot_rec        equ     $               ;dummy DOS boot record
                db      3 dup(0)        ;not a jump instruction
                db      'TWG  1.0'      ;vendor id

bpb     equ     $       ;This is the BIOS Parameter Block
bpb_ss  dw      512     ;512 byte sector size
bpb_au  db      1       ;cluster size is 1 sector
bpb_rs  dw      1       ;1 (boot) reserved sector
bpb_nf  db      1       ;1 FAT only
bpb_ds  dw      48      ;#files in the File Directory
bpb_ts  dw      205     ;sects=100KB + 5 overhead
bpb_md  db      0feh    ;media descriptor
bpb_fs  dw      1       ;FAT sectors in each FAT

bpb_ptr dw      bpb     ;bios parameter block pointer array (1 entry)

;current RAM disc information

total           dw      ?       ;transfer sector count
verify          db      0       ;verify 1=yes , 0=no
start           dw      0       ;start sector number
disk            dw      0       ;RAM disk start address
buf_ofs         dw      ?       ;data transfer offset address
buf_seg         dw      ?       ;data transfer segment address

res_cnt         dw      5       ;# reserved sectors
ram_par         dw      6560    ;paragraphs of memory
bell            db      1       ;1= bell on for RAM disk i/o

;******************************************************************
;*      THE STRATEGY PROCEDURE                                    *
;******************************************************************

dev_strategy:   mov     cs:rh_seg,es    ;save the segment address
                mov     cs:rh_ofs,bx    ;save the offset address
                ret                     ;return to DOS
```

Listing 8–11: *(cont.)*

```
;**************************************************************
;*        THE INTERRUPT PROCEDURE                             *
;**************************************************************
;

;device interrupt handler - 2nd call from DOS

dev_interrupt:

        cld                     ;save machine state on entry
        push    ds
        push    es
        push    ax
        push    bx
        push    cx
        push    dx
        push    di
        push    si

        mov     ax,cs:rh_seg    ;restore ES as saved by STRATEGY call
        mov     es,ax           ;
        mov     bx,cs:rh_ofs    ;restore BX as saved by STRATEGY call

;jump to appropriate routine to process command

        mov     al,es:[bx].rh_cmd    ;get request header command
        rol     al,1                 ;times 2 for index into word table
        lea     di,cmdtab            ;function (command) table address
        mov     ah,0                 ;clear hi order
        add     di,ax                ;add the index to start of table
        jmp     word ptr[di]         ;jump indirect

;CMDTAB is the command table that contains the word address
;for each command. The request header will contain the
;command desired. The INTERRUPT routine will jump through an
;address corresponding to the requested command to get to
;the appropriate command processing routine.

CMDTAB  label   byte            ;* = char devices only
        dw      INITIALIZATION  ; initialization
        dw      MEDIA_CHECK     ; media check (block only)
        dw      GET_BPB         ; build bpb
        dw      IOCTL_INPUT     ; ioctl in
        dw      INPUT           ; input (read)
        dw      ND_INPUT        ;*non destructive input no wait
        dw      INPUT_STATUS    ;*input status
        dw      INPUT_FLUSH     ;*input flush
        dw      OUTPUT          ; output (write)
        dw      OUTPUT_VERIFY   ; output (write) with verify
```

Listing 8–11: *(cont.)*

```
        dw      OUTPUT_STATUS    ;*output status
        dw      OUTPUT_FLUSH     ;*output flush
        dw      IOCTL_OUT        ; ioctl output
        dw      OPEN             ; device open
        dw      CLOSE            ; device close
        dw      REMOVABLE        ; removable media
        dw      OUTPUT_BUSY      ; output til busy

;*****************************************************************
;*      YOUR LOCAL PROCEDURES                                   *
;*****************************************************************
;
save    proc    near     ;saves data from Request Header
;
;       called from INPUT, OUTPUT
;
        mov     ax,es:[bx].rh4_buf_seg  ;save data transfer
        mov     cs:buf_seg,ax           ; segment
        mov     ax,es:[bx].rh4_buf_ofs  ;save data transfer
        mov     cs:buf_ofs,ax           ; offset
        mov     ax,es:[bx].rh4_start    ;get start sector number
        mov     cs:start,ax             ; save it
        mov     ax,es:[bx].rh4_count    ;# sectors to transfer
        mov     ah,0                    ;clear hi order
        mov     cs:total,ax             ; save in our area
        ret                             ;return to caller
save    endp

cvt2seg proc    near     ;calculates memory address
;
;       requires cs:start       starting sector
;                cs:total       total sector count
;                cs:disk        RAM disk start address
;
;       returns  ds             segment address
;                cx             count of total bytes
;                si             = 0 for paragraph boundary
;
;       uses     ax
;                cx
;                si
;                ds
;
        mov     ax,cs:start     ;get starting sector number
        mov     cl,5            ;multiply by 32 paragraphs/sector
        shl     ax,cl           ; by shifting left 5 places
        mov     cx,cs:disk      ;get start segment of RAM disk
        add     cx,ax           ;add to initial segment
```

Listing 8–11: *(cont.)*

```
          mov     ds,cx              ; DS has start segment
          mov     si,0               ;make it on a paragraph boundary
          mov     ax,cs:total        ;total number of sectors
          mov     cx,512             ;byte per sector
          mul     cx                 ;multiply to get xfer length
          or      ax,ax              ;too large (carry set)?
          jnz     calcl              ;no (less than 64k)
          mov     ax,0ffffh          ;yes - make it 64k
calcl:    mov     cx,ax              ;move length to cx
          ret                        ;return to caller
cvt2seg endp

bell1     proc    near               ;bell on if needed
          cmp     cs:byte ptr bell,0 ;bell required?
          jz      nobell1            ;no
          mov     al,0b6h            ;magic #
          out     43h,al             ;timer2
          mov     ax,400h            ;cycles
          out     42h,al             ;lsb
          mov     al,ah              ;msb
          out     42h,al
          in      al,61h             ;spkr port
          or      al,3               ;spkr/timer on
          out     61h,al             ;
nobell1:  ret                        ;return
bell1   endp

bell2     proc    near               ;bell off if needed
          cmp     cs:byte ptr bell,0 ;bell off needed?
          jz      nobell2            ;no
          in      al,61h             ;get port
          and     al,0fch            ;spkr/timer2 off
          out     61h,al             ;
nobell2:  ret                        ;return
bell2   endp


;****************************************************************
;*        DOS COMMAND PROCESSING                                *
;****************************************************************
;command 0       Initialization
Initialization:
          call    bell1              ;optional bell tone
          call    initial            ;display console message
          push    cs                 ;move cs
          pop     dx                 ; to dx

;calculate end segment of RAM disk
          lea     ax,cs:start_disk   ;start address of RAM disk
          mov     cl,1               ;hex digit shift count
```

Listing 8–11: *(cont.)*

```
        ror     ax,cl                         ;divide by 16 = paragraphs
        add     dx,ax                         ;add to current cs value
        mov     cs:disk,dx                    ;RAM disk start address
        mov     ax,ram_par                    ;add # RAM disk paragraphs
        add     dx,ax                         ;to start segment of RAM disk

;return the break address to DOS
        mov     es:[bx].rh0_brk_ofs,0  ;offset is 0
        mov     es:[bx].rh0_brk_seg,dx ;segment

;return number of units for a block device
        mov     es:[bx].rh0_nunits,1   ;only one RAM disk

;return address of array of BIOS Parameter Blocks (1 only)
        lea     dx,bpb_ptr                    ;address of bpb pointer array
        mov     es:[bx].rh0_bpb_tbo,dx ;return offset
        mov     es:[bx].rh0_bpb_tbs,cs ;return segment

;initialize boot, FAT, Directory to zeroes
        push    ds                            ;cvt2seg destroys ds
        mov     cs:start,0                    ;start sector = 0
        mov     ax,cs:res_cnt                 ;#reserved sectors
        mov     cs:total,ax                   ;#sectors
        call    cvt2seg                       ;address and count
        mov     al,0                          ;fill value
        push    ds                            ;save
        pop     es                            ;move to es
        mov     di,si                         ;all offsets = 0
        rep     stosb                         ;clear reserved sectors

;move boot record to sector 0
        pop     ds                            ;restore ds -> RAM disk
        mov     es,cs:disk                    ;RAM disk start address
        mov     di,0                          ;zero out di (boot record)
        lea     si,cs:boot_rec                ;address of boot record
        mov     cx,24                         ;
        rep     movsb                         ;copy 24 bytes of boot record

;build one and only one FAT
        mov     cs:start,1                    ;logical sector 1
        mov     cs:total,1                    ;doesn't matter
        call    cvt2seg                       ;get ds:si set quickly
        mov     ds:byte ptr [si],0feh         ;set the first 2 FAT
        mov     ds:byte ptr 1[si],0ffh        ; entries to describe
        mov     ds:byte ptr 2[si],0ffh        ; disc
        call    bell2                         ;optional bell off
;end of initialization - restore es:bx exit
        mov     ax,cs:rh_seg                  ;move request header
        mov     es,ax                         ; segment to es
```

313

Listing 8–11: *(cont.)*

```
        mov     bx,cs:rh_ofs            ; offset to bx
        jmp     done                    ;set DONE bit & exit

;command 1       Media_Check
Media_Check:                            ;block device only
        mov     es:[bx].rhl_media,1     ;media is unchanged
        jmp     done                    ;set DONE bit & exit

;command 2       Get_BPB
Get_BPB:                                ;read Boot record
        push    es                      ;save request header segment
        push    bx                      ;save request header offset
        mov     cs:start,0              ;boot record = sector 0
        mov     cs:total,1              ;1 sector
        call    cvt2seg                 ;convert to RAM disk address
        push    cs                      ;set es to
        pop     es                      ; cs
        lea     di,cs:bpb               ;address of bios param blk
        add     si,11                   ;add 11 to si
        mov     cx,13                   ;length of bpb
        rep     movsb                   ;move
        pop     bx                      ;restore request header offset
        pop     es                      ;restore request header segment
        mov     dx,cs:bpb_ptr           ;pointer to BPB array
        mov     es:[bx].rh2_pbpbo,dx    ; to Request Header
        mov     es:[bx].rh2_pbpbs,cs    ;same for segment
        lea     dx,cs:bpb               ;address of BPB =
        mov     es:[bx].rh2_buf_ofs,dx  ; sector buffer offset
        mov     es:[bx].rh2_buf_seg,cs  ;same for segment
        jmp     done                    ;set DONE bit & exit

;command 3       IOCTL_Input
IOCTL_Input:

        jmp     unknown                 ;set error bit/code & exit

;command 4       Input   Read RAM disk and return data to DOS
Input:
        call    bell1                   ;turn on bell if required
        call    save                    ;save Request Header data
        call    cvt2seg                 ;calc RAM disk start address
        mov     es,cs:buf_seg           ;set destination seg & ofs
        mov     di,cs:buf_ofs           ; to es:di
        mov     ax,di                   ;get offset
        add     ax,cx                   ;add transfer length
        jnc     input1                  ;overflow?
        mov     ax,0ffffh               ;yes - use max transfer
        sub     ax,di                   ;subtract offset from max
        mov     cx,ax                   ;new transfer count
```

Listing 8-11: *(cont.)*

```
input1:  rep    movsb                ;Read RAM disk to data area
         call   bell2                ;turn off bell if required
         mov    ax,cs:rh_seg         ;move request header
         mov    es,ax                ; segment to es
         mov    bx,cs:rh_ofs         ; offset to bx
         jmp    done                 ;set DONE bit & exit

;command 5      ND_Input
ND_Input:

         jmp    busy                 ;set BUSY bit & exit

;command 6      Input_Status
Input_Status:

         jmp    done                 ;set DONE bit & exit

;command 7      Input_Flush
Input_Flush:

         jmp    done                 ;set DONE bit & exit

;command 8      Output               Write data to RAM disk
Output:
         call   bell1                ;turn bell on if needed
         call   save                 ;save Request Header data
         call   cvt2seg              ;get start address in RAM
         push   ds                   ;move to
         pop    es                   ; es
         mov    di,si                ;same for di
         mov    ds,cs:buf_seg        ;ds:si points to source
         mov    si,cs:buf_ofs        ; data in DOS
         rep    movsb                ;move ds:si to es:di
         mov    bx,cs:rh_ofs         ;restore es:bx
         mov    es,cs:rh_seg         ;for possible jmp to input
         cmp    cs:verify,0          ;do we verify write?
         jz     out1                 ;no
         mov    cs:verify,0          ;reset verify indicator
         jmp    input                ;read those sectors back in
out1:    call   bell2                ;turn bell off if required
         mov    ax,cs:rh_seg         ;move request header
         mov    es,ax                ; segment to es
         mov    bx,cs:rh_ofs         ; offset to bx
         jmp    done                 ;set DONE bit & exit

;command 9      Output_Verify
Output_Verify:                       ;output (write) with verify
         mov    cs:verify,1          ;set the verify flag
         jmp    output               ;go to output routine
```

Listing 8–11: *(cont.)*

```
;command 10      Output_Status
Output_Status:

        jmp      done            ;set DONE bit & exit

;command 11      Output_Flush
Output_Flush:

        jmp      done            ;set DONE bit & exit

;command 12      IOCTL_Output
IOCTL_Out:

        jmp      unknown         ;set error bit/code & exit

;command 13      Open
Open:

        jmp      done            ;set DONE bit & exit

;command 14      Close
Close:

        jmp      done            ;set DONE bit & exit

;command 15      Removable
Removable:
        mov      es:[bx].rh_status,0200h ;set busy
        jmp      done                    ;set DONE bit & exit

;command 16      Output Til Busy
OUTPUT_BUSY:

        jmp      unknown         ;set error bit/code & exit

;****************************************************************
;*       ERROR EXIT                                            *
;****************************************************************

unknown:
        or       es:[bx].rh_status,8003h ;set error bit and error code
        jmp      done                    ;set done and exit

;****************************************************************
;*       COMMON EXIT                                           *
;****************************************************************

busy:   or       es:[bx].rh_status,0200h ;set busy bit

done:   or       es:[bx].rh_status,0100h ;set done
```

Listing 8–11: *(cont.)*

```
        pop     si                          ;restore all registers
        pop     di
        pop     dx
        pop     cx
        pop     bx
        pop     ax
        pop     es
        pop     ds
        ret                                 ;return to DOS

;****************************************************************
;*      END OF PROGRAM                                         *
;****************************************************************
end_of_program:

;org to paragraph boundary for start of RAM disk

        if      ($-start_address) mod 16
        org     ($-start_address)+16-(($-start_address) mod 16)
        endif

start_disk      equ     $

initial proc    near            ;

        lea     dx,msgl         ;initialization
        mov     ah,9            ; message
        int     21h             ;doscall
        ret                     ;return
initial endp

msgl    db      'The Waite Group 100k RAM Disk',0dh,0ah,'$'

ramdisk endp
cseg    ends
        end     begin

;that's all folks
```

Modifying the RAM Disk Device Driver

The RAM Disk Device Driver, as shown in listing 8–11, is built as a 100Kb RAM disk. You can modify the RAM disk to be any size you want. For example, you can make the size of the user data area larger or smaller, and the File Directory can be made larger to hold more file entries.

The steps in changing the RAM disk are shown below:

1. Decide the size (in Kb) of the user data area for your RAM disk. Multiply this number by 2 to determine the number of sectors in the user data area. (Example: 100Kb = 200 sectors.)

2. Decide the number of sectors per allocation unit. Store this number in the variable *bpb_au*.

3. Determine the number of clusters by dividing the size of the user data area (in sectors) by the sectors per allocation unit.

4. Determine the size of the File Allocation Table by multiplying the number of clusters by 1.5 bytes. Round this number up to the nearest 512 bytes.

5. Divide the FAT size by 512 to determine the number of sectors required for the FAT. Store this number in the variable *bpb_fs*.

6. Decide the number of files the File Directory will contain. Use a multiple of 16. Store this number in the variable *bpb_ds*.

7. Divide the number of File Directory entries by 16 to determine the number of sectors the File Directory will require.

8. Add up the number of reserved sectors in the Boot Record (usually 1), the File Allocation Table, and the File Directory. Store this number in the variable *res_cnt*.

9. Add the reserved-sector count (from step 8) to the size of the user data area from step 1. Store this number in the variable *bpb_ts*.

10. Multiply the number in *bpb_ts* by 32 to determine the number of memory paragraphs the RAM disk will occupy. Store this number in the variable *ram_par*.

11. Lastly, change the text in the variable *msg1* to reflect the new size of the RAM disk.

Summary

In this chapter, we have built a block device driver. The RAM Disk Device Driver builds a simulation of a disk in memory; DOS treats this disk no differently than other disks. You will find that the RAM disk offers much faster access to your files because you do not have to wait for slow mechanical devices to move the data around. Block device drivers are similar to character-oriented devices; the differences are in the commands that each driver supports. Writing drivers for block devices is no different than writing drivers for character-oriented devices.

We have now built device drivers for the console, printer, clock, and disk devices. The format for the device drivers has been standardized to the point that we merely add code for the appropriate commands for each device driver. We have seen that all device drivers share common code for performing common functions and that DOS does not distinguish between the drivers insofar as the command structure is concerned.

You have built enough device drivers that you should now understand what device drivers do and be ready to start writing device drivers on your own. The next chapter deals with that topic.

Questions

1. How does a RAM Disk Device Driver differ from a device driver for a diskette or fixed disk?

2. The BIOS Parameter Block contains which fields:

   a. Sector size
   b. Number of hidden sectors
   c. Number of reserved sectors
   d. Number of heads
   e. Number of files
   f. FAT size
   g. Media descriptor
   h. Number of total sectors
   i. Number of sectors per track
   j. Number of FATs
   k. Size of user data area
   l. Allocation unit size

3. How many FATs does the RAM Disk Device Driver have?

4. What are the basic commands implemented by the RAM Disk Device Driver?

5. What variables are changed if the size of the RAM disk is changed to 200Kb? (Hint: This is tough.)

Answers may be found in appendix E.

Chapter 9

Building a Complete Full-function Device Driver

In this chapter, we will take an in-depth look at writing DOS device drivers. Previous chapters have presented device drivers for standard types of devices. The RAM Disk Device Driver of chapter 8 was a simulation of a real device using memory instead of actual hardware—a virtual device. Each of the device drivers in this book so far contained code for a set of commands unique to that particular driver, and the Device Header defined to DOS specific parameters of each device. This example approach did not cover all the universal aspects of device drivers, however.

This chapter will describe in detail all tasks required to write a device driver, starting with the basics of selecting the tools and establishing the working environment. We will show you how to build a device driver from scratch, starting with the Device Header and going through each of the commands that may be incorporated in your driver.

Required Tools

The tools that you will need to write device drivers are shown in table 9–1. The first is an editor that allows you to enter your assembly language source code (instructions) into a file. The next is an assembler, which translates your source statements into object code. The assembler will also help find certain types of errors in your programs. The linker is a program that converts assembler-generated object code into executable code. Finally, you must use the utility program EXE2BIN to convert the executable file into a special .COM file. Device drivers require .COM-format files in order to load the code into memory as it appears in the file.

Tool	Description
Editor	A word processor or text editor program which allows entering source text into a file. It is also used to modify the text file.
Assembler	A utility program that converts the source assembly language program into relocatable object modules.
LINK	A linker program which combines one or more relocatable object modules into an executable file.
EXE2BIN	A utility program that converts normal executable files into memory image files. Memory image files are known as .COM files and are required for device drivers.

Table 9–1: The programming tools required to write DOS device drivers

The Perfect Editor

We all probably have our favorite word processor or text editor. If we were to write device drivers for a living, however, we would undoubtedly try to find an editor that was designed specially for programmers.

Even the most primitive editors have most of the features you need to write device drivers. These features are the ability to enter and modify text and the ability to Tab to certain columns to line up instructions, operands to the instructions, and comments.

Additional features that make life easier are the ability to have a second *window* that contains the text from another file. This allows you to look at another file while you edit the first file. This second file could be another example of a device driver, a file header your program requires, or a file containing the *struc*s to copy into your device driver file. Having a second file in a window lets you inspect any other file without exiting the current file.

Another useful feature of an editor for programming is the ability to customize function keys to perform a particular function. Although most word processors use the function keys to perform a print command function, such as bold printing of text, such formatting commands are not useful for writing programs. Instead, you will want the ability to replace a function-key command with one more useful to writing programs—for example, a search-and-replace function or a function that repeats a long instruction sequence that is frequently needed.

Assemblers

Many assembler programs are available for the IBM PC. Although each of these has its special features, the device driver programs in this book require only one unusual assembler feature: *struc* pseudo-operation. This assembler feature lets you set up a template to access the data without a lot of unnecessary calculations for relative positions; it also eliminates the need to specify whether the data type is a byte or a word. It is easy to make changes in the structure to reflect a change in the data fields and in the lengths of the entries.

In general, you can use the simplest or the most feature-laden assembler to write a device driver. We used IBM's MASM 1.0, because it was available. Another assembler you can use is Microsoft's MASM.

The Operating Environment

When you write programs, you will want to edit, assemble, and link without having to remember where the program files are on the disk. One useful technique is to use the PATH command to specify a path to the directory in which all your program files reside. Then you can let DOS search your directories for files that do not exist in the current working directory. The PATH command is inserted in the AUTOEXEC.BAT file and could look like this:

```
PATH = C:\util
```

Another aid is a text file, called the *index file,* placed in each directory. This file contains information you create of what each file contains. Start with a directory listing using the DIR command and edit this file to keep notes about each file.

Assembly Language at Its Best and Worst

Source code for programs written in assembly language is either hard or easy to read. Historically, the debate has been between easy-to-read code that is slow and hard-to-read code that is fast. The argument is no different today for assembly language programming on the PC. What is often ignored is that once the code is written, human memory tends to forget the details and nuances behind the procedures.

The examples in the previous chapters have been written with clarity in mind. The code does not have tricky instructions that take advantage of some hidden feature of the 8088/8086 architecture. This approach is always the best for learning what device drivers do.

However, because device drivers control the flow of data between the PC and its devices, you may wish to optimize the code to minimize the time the device drivers execute. This need not make the code obscure or hard to understand; you perform this bit of magic by documenting the code and by understanding what certain instructions do.

Faster Instructions   The first step in speeding up code and keeping it clear is to make sure that all code includes comments. Each instruction deserves a comment explaining its purpose. This is particularly true of instructions whose function is not clear. The second step is to use instructions that are faster in terms of the number of CPU cycles required for execution. Table 9–2 shows some examples of both steps.

The first example in table 9–2 subtracts a register from itself to produce a result of zero. This method of clearing a register is faster than a move of 0 to the AX register. Be sure to comment the instruction to indicate that you need the AX register to be 0. Using the *mov* instruction takes four clock cycles, whereas using the *sub* instruction takes three.

Speed	Code		Description
Normal	mov	ax,0	;make AX = 0
Fast	sub	ax,ax	;make AX = 0 by ;subtracting AX from itself
Normal	mov	ax,offset xx	;get the address of xx
Fast	lea	ax,xx	;get the address of xx
Normal	mov mov	es,cs:rh_seg bx,cs:rh_ofs	;get segment address ;get offset address
Fast	les	bx,cs:rh_ofs	;get segment/offset address
Normal	mov mul	bx,32 bx	;multiply AX ;by 32
Fast	mov shl	cl,5 ax,cl	;multiply AX by 32 ;using a left shift ;of 5 places

Table 9–2: Some coding examples of where using a different instruction results in faster execution times

The next example is the instruction that loads the AX register with the offset address of *xx*. The assembler keyword *offset* is used to generate an offset address. Make this instruction faster by using the Load Effective Address *(lea)* instruction. Using the *lea* instruction typically saves six clock cycles.

The third example is the familiar two-line sequence that restores the ES and BX registers from the INTERRUPT routine of a device driver. Use two instructions for clarity, but a faster method is to use the 8088/8086 instruction *les,* which loads both registers. This saves at least eight clock cycles.

The final example is a specialized one. When you need to multiply a number by some power of 2 (2,4,8,16,32, . . .), make this code sequence faster by shifting left some number of places. Each left shift of 1 position results in a multiplication of 2. As the example shows, instead of multiplying by 32 you left shift 5 positions, yielding the same results in a much quicker period of time. This can save from 61 to 106 cycles.

Know Your Device

Writing device drivers requires several pieces of information. The first and most important piece of information is the device itself. You will need to know a lot about the device: how it is programmed, what it does, and how to use it.

A checklist of necessary information regarding the device for which you are writing a device driver is provided below:

- Description of the device
- I/O port addresses used (also memory addresses used, if any)
- Description of each I/O port address
- Intended use under DOS
- Test programs and diagnostics

First, find out about the device itself. If it is a real device, such as a tape unit, you will need to know how to operate it: the type of media if it is a storage device, how to turn it on and off, etc. This type of information will allow you to integrate this new device into the DOS environment.

The next piece of information involves programming the device. Some devices work with a controller or an adapter card that is plugged into the PC bus. You will need to know how to program the device to transfer data. With many devices, the manufacturer supplies code in a ROM that is part of the controller. Simply use these routines in your device driver in much the same way as you use the BIOS interrupts discussed in previous chapters. If the device adapter does not have ROM-based code, then you will need to know the I/O port addresses that reference registers on the adapter and what functions they perform when you read or write to the port. This establishes how to program the device from within a device driver. Another piece of information you may need is the timing of your device, which may affect how fast you can issue instructions. Lastly, if the device does not come with an adapter, it will generally use the serial or parallel ports that are part of the PC.

In either case, you will need the programming instructions and the sequence of operations for the device. Use these instructions in your device driver to control the device through an appropriate command that DOS requests of your device driver. For example, if the device requires initialization, you will need to add code in the driver's initialization command-processing section.

Appendix A lists the ROM-based BIOS interrupts that you can use in your device drivers.

Another item in the driver checklist is the intended use of the device under DOS. Although many of the devices available for the PC have been derived from older minicomputer technology that is being adapted for PCs, these devices often have hardware features that are not usable by the PC and DOS environment. For example, minicomputer tape drives often have controllers that return diagnostic information on the tape drive. DOS does not know how to make use of such information, so this feature of certain tape drives may not be applicable to your device driver. "Intended use" should make you list what information your intended device will provide.

You will need to match each of the device's operations to a driver command-processing function. At a bare minimum, there is device read or input, device write or output, open and close if it is required by the device, and I/O control for the device.

Finally, you must have test programs and diagnostics for the device. Before you write a device driver you need to see the device in operation and have a method of determining whether the device is functioning properly. These test programs can give you a feel for the device as it should operate under DOS. The practical aspects of the device are also revealed through these test programs. A test program would be a stand-alone, .EXE-type program that could exercise the device in at least some minimum way. Diagnostic programs are also useful in gauging the device reliability and whether you should incorporate more error-handling within your device drivers.

An Overview of the Device Driver

In listing 9–1, we present the device driver skeleton that was first introduced in chapter 3. We will describe, in detail, what you will need to know in order to

Listing 9–1: A skeleton listing from which to develop any device driver

```
        page    60,132
        title   A Device Driver Skeleton

;*****************************************************************
;*      This is a Device Driver                                 *
;*****************************************************************
;
;*****************************************************************
;*          ASSEMBLER DIRECTIVES                                *
;*****************************************************************
;
;*****************************************************************
;*          MAIN PROCEDURE CODE                                 *
;*****************************************************************
;
;*****************************************************************
;*          DEVICE HEADER REQUIRED BY DOS                       *
;*****************************************************************
;
;*****************************************************************
;*          WORK SPACE FOR OUR DEVICE DRIVER                    *
;*****************************************************************
;
;*****************************************************************
;*          THE STRATEGY PROCEDURE                              *
;*****************************************************************
;
;*****************************************************************
;*          THE INTERRUPT PROCEDURE                             *
;*****************************************************************
;
;*****************************************************************
;*          YOUR LOCAL PROCEDURES                               *
;*****************************************************************
;
;*****************************************************************
;*          DOS COMMAND PROCESSING                              *
;*****************************************************************
;
;*****************************************************************
;*          ERROR EXIT                                          *
;*****************************************************************
;
;*****************************************************************
;*          COMMON EXIT                                         *
;*****************************************************************
;
;*****************************************************************
;*          END OF PROGRAM                                      *
;*****************************************************************
;
```

write code for these sections: "Instructing the Assembler," "Device Header Required by DOS," "The STRATEGY Procedure," "the INTERRUPT Procedure," "DOS Command Processing," "Error Exit," and "Common Exit." The rest of the sections will depend on the particular requirements of the device driver being written. In many cases, you can simply lift code from the device drivers already covered in previous chapters.

Instructing the Assembler

This is the section containing the driver's assembler directives that specify the exact requirements for the driver's data structures. Here you set up the segment, the main procedure, and the address generation for the CS, ES, and DS registers. For most device drivers, these directives do not change; you can reference your code and data in all device drivers in the same way.

The most important aspect of this section is the ability to use data structures. Data structures allow you to access the data that DOS passes to the device driver in a consistent fashion. The use of structures minimizes the errors that come with using equates (EQU). Errors are common when using one equate to define another and so on. An error in calculation in the middle of an equate results in errors propagated down the line. The use of structures follows closely the way the data is originally defined; it also allows the assembler to calculate the offset addresses. This important feature of the macro assembler cannot be overrated for its usefulness and utility!

Structures are defined with the keyword *struc* and are given a label. Each entry within a *struc* is given a name, a data-length definition, and a value for initialization. At the end of each *struc* is an *ends* keyword. Structures are not the actual declaration of data space but a definition of how you wish to view the data.

Listing 9–2 shows the *strucs* for the Request Headers for device driver commands 0 through 24 (we will cover each of these *strucs* and commands in detail in later sections of this chapter).

The Device Header

The Device Header is the first piece of data that DOS sees; it defines to DOS how to deal with the device. Figure 9–1 shows the five basic parts of the Device Header.

Three of the five basic components of the Device Header deal with address pointers. The first is a double-word pointer (offset and segment address) to the next device driver in the file. When DOS loads the device driver into memory

---

Listing 9–2: The assembler directives for defining the device driver structures. These data structures define the data that DOS passes to the device driver for each command.

```
;Request Header structures


rh              struc                   ;request header
rh_len          db      ?               ;len of packet
rh_unit         db      ?               ;unit code
                                        ;(block devices only)
rh_cmd          db      ?               ;device driver command
rh_status       dw      ?               ;returned by device driver
rh_resl         dd      ?               ;reserved
rh_res2         dd      ?               ;reserved
rh              ends                    ;

rh0             struc                   ;Initialization (command 0)
rh0_rh          db      size rh dup (?) ;fixed portion
rh0_nunits      db      ?               ;number of units
                                        ;(block devices only)
rh0_brk_ofs     dw      ?               ;offset address for break
rh0_brk_seg     dw      ?               ;segment address for break
rh0_bpb_tbo     dw      ?               ;offset address of pointer
                                        ;to BPB array
rh0_bpb_tbs     dw      ?               ;segment address of pointer
                                        ;to BPB array
rh0_drv_ltr     db      ?               ;first available drive
                                        ;(DOS 3+) (block only)
rh0             ends                    ;

rh1             struc                   ;Media_Check (command 1)
hl_rh           db      size rh dup (?) ;fixed portion
rh1_media       db      ?               ;media descriptor from DPB
rh1_md_stat     db      ?               ;media status returned by
                                        ;device driver
rh1_volid_ofs   dw      ?               ;offset address of
                                        ;volume identification
                                        ;DOS 3+ only
rh1_volid_seg   dw      ?               ;segment address of
                                        ;volume identification
                                        ;DOS 3+ only
rh1             ends                    ;

rh2             struc                   ;Get_BPB (command 2)
rh2_rh          db      size rh dup(?)  ;fixed portion
rh2_media       db      ?               ;media descriptor from DPB
rh2_buf_ofs     dw      ?               ;offset address of
                                        ;data transfer area
```

Listing 9-2 *(cont.)*

```
rh2_buf_seg      dw      ?          ;segment address of
                                    ;data transfer area
rh2_pbpbo        dw      ?          ;offset address of
                                    ;pointer to BPB
rh2_pbpbs        dw      ?          ;segment address of
                                    ;pointer to BPB
rh2              ends               ;

rh3              struc              ;IOCTL_INPUT (command 3)
rh3_rh           db      size rh dup(?)  ;fixed portion
rh3_media        db      ?          ;media descriptor from DPB
rh3_buf_ofs      dw      ?          ;offset address of
                                    ;data transfer area
rh3_buf_seg      dw      ?          ;segment address of
                                    ;data transfer area
rh3_count        dw      ?          ;transfer count
                                    ;(sectors for block)
                                    ;(bytes for character)
rh3_start        dw      ?          ;start sector number
                                    ;(block devices only)
rh3              ends               ;

rh4              struc              ;INPUT (command 4)
rh4_rh           db      size rh dup(?)  ;fixed portion
rh4_media        db      ?          ;media descriptor from DPB
rh4_buf_ofs      dw      ?          ;offset address of
                                    ;data transfer area
rh4_buf_seg      dw      ?          ;segment address of
                                    ;data transfer area
rh4_count        dw      ?          ;transfer count
                                    ;(sectors for block)
                                    ;(bytes for character)
rh4_start        dw      ?          ;start sector number
                                    ;(block devices only)
rh4_volid_ofs    dw      ?          ;offset address of
                                    ;volume identification
                                    ;DOS 3+ only
rh4_volid_seg    dw      ?          ;segment address of
                                    ;volume identification
                                    ;DOS 3+ only
rh4              ends               ;

rh5              struc              ;ND_INPUT (command 5)
rh5_rh           db      size rh dup (?) ;fixed portion
rh5_return       db      ?          ;character returned
rh5              ends               ;

rh6              struc              ;Input_Status (command 6)
```

Listing 9-2 *(cont.)*

```
rh6_len         db      ?       ;len of packet
rh6_unit        db      ?       ;unit code
                                ;(block devices only)
rh6_cmd         db      ?       ;device driver command
rh6_status      dw      ?       ;returned by device driver
rh6_res1        dd      ?       ;reserved
rh6_res2        dd      ?       ;reserved
rh6             ends            ;

rh7             struc           ;Input_Flush (command 7)
rh7_len         db      ?       ;len of packet
rh7_unit        db      ?       ;unit code
                                ;(block devices only)
rh7_cmd         db      ?       ;device driver command
rh7_status      dw      ?       ;returned by device driver
rh7_res1        dd      ?       ;reserved
rh7_res2        dd      ?       ;reserved
rh7             ends            ;

rh8             struc           ;OUTPUT (command 8)
rh8_rh          db   size rh dup(?)   ;fixed portion
rh8_media       db      ?       ;media descriptor from DPB
rh8_buf_ofs     dw      ?       ;offset address of
                                ;data transfer area
rh8_buf_seg     dw      ?       ;segment address of
                                ;data transfer area
rh8_count       dw      ?       ;transfer count
                                ;(sectors for block)
                                ;(bytes for character)
rh8_start       dw      ?       ;start sector number
                                ;(block devices only)
rh8_volid_ofs   dw      ?       ;offset address of
                                ;volume identification
                                ;DOS 3+ only
rh8_volid_seg   dw      ?       ;segment address of
                                ;volume identification
                                ;DOS 3+ only
rh8             ends            ;

rh9             struc           ;OUTPUT_VERIFY (command 9)
rh9_rh          db   size rh dup(?)   ;fixed portion
rh9_media       db      ?       ;media descriptor from DPB
rh9_buf_ofs     dw      ?       ;offset address of
                                ;data transfer area
rh9_buf_seg     dw      ?       ;segment address of
                                ;data transfer area
rh9_count       dw      ?       ;transfer count
                                ;(sectors for block)
                                ;(bytes for character)
```

Listing 9-2 *(cont.)*

```
rh9_start        dw      ?            ;start sector number
                                      ;(block devices only)
rh9_volid_ofs    dw      ?            ;offset address of
                                      ;volume identification
                                      ;DOS 3+ only
rh9_volid_seg    dw      ?            ;segment address of
                                      ;volume identification
                                      ;DOS 3+ only
rh9              ends                 ;

rh10             struc                ;Output_Status (command 10)
rh10_len         db      ?            ;len of packet
rh10_unit        db      ?            ;unit code
                                      ;(block devices only)
rh10_cmd         db      ?            ;device driver command
rh10_status      dw      ?            ;returned by device driver
rh10_resl        dd      ?            ;reserved
rh10_res2        dd      ?            ;reserved
rh10             ends                 ;

rh11             struc                ;Output_Flush (command 0)
rh11_len         db      ?            ;len of packet
rh11_unit        db      ?            ;unit code
                                      ;(block devices only)
rh11_cmd         db      ?            ;device driver command
rh11_status      dw      ?            ;returned by device driver
rh11_resl        dd      ?            ;reserved
rh11_res2        dd      ?            ;reserved
rh11             ends                 ;

rh12             struc                ;IOCTL_OUTPUT (command 12)
rh12_rh          db      size rh dup(?)   ;fixed portion
rh12_media       db      ?            ;media descriptor from DPB
rh12_buf_ofs     dw      ?            ;offset address of
                                      ;data transfer area
rh12_buf_seg     dw      ?            ;segment address of
                                      ;data transfer area
rh12_count       dw      ?            ;transfer count
                                      ;(sectors for block)
                                      ;(bytes for character)
rh12_start       dw      ?            ;start sector number
                                      ;(block devices only)
rh12             ends                 ;

rh13             struc                ;Open (command 13)
rh13_len         db      ?            ;len of packet
rh13_unit        db      ?            ;unit code
                                      ;(block devices only)
```

Listing 9-2 *(cont.)*

```
rh13_cmd        db      ?       ;device driver command
rh13_status     dw      ?       ;returned by device driver
rh13_res1       dd      ?       ;reserved
rh13_res2       dd      ?       ;reserved
rh13            ends            ;

rh14            struc           ;Close command 14)
rh14_len        db      ?       ;len of packet
rh14_unit       db      ?       ;unit code
                                ;(block devices only)
rh14_cmd        db      ?       ;device driver command
rh14_status     dw      ?       ;returned by device driver
rh14_res1       dd      ?       ;reserved
rh14_res2       dd      ?       ;reserved
rh14            ends            ;

rh15            struc           ;Removable (command 15)
rh15_len        db      ?       ;len of packet
rh15_unit       db      ?       ;unit code
                                ;(block devices only)
rh15_cmd        db      ?       ;device driver command
rh15_status     dw      ?       ;returned by device driver
rh15_res1       dd      ?       ;reserved
rh15_res2       dd      ?       ;reserved
rh15            ends            ;

rh16            struc           ;OUTPUT_BUSY (command 16)
rh16_rh         db      size rh dup (?) ;fixed portion
rh16_media      db      ?       ;media descriptor
rh16_buf_ofs    dw      ?       ;offset address of
                                ;data transfer area
rh16_buf_seg    dw      ?       ;segment address of
                                ;data transfer area
rh16_count      dw      ?       ;byte count returned
                                ;from device driver
rh16            ends            ;

rh17            struc           ;(command 17)
rh17_len        db      ?       ;len of packet
rh17_unit       db      ?       ;unit code
                                ;(block devices only)
rh17_cmd        db      ?       ;device driver command
rh17_status     dw      ?       ;returned by device driver
rh17_res1       dd      ?       ;reserved
rh17_res2       dd      ?       ;reserved
rh17            ends            ;

rh18            struc           ;(command 18)
```

Listing 9-2 *(cont.)*

```
rh18_len        db      ?       ;len of packet
rh18_unit       db      ?       ;unit code
                                ;(block devices only)
rh18_cmd        db      ?       ;device driver command
rh18_status     dw      ?       ;returned by device driver
rh18_res1       dd      ?       ;reserved
rh18_res2       dd      ?       ;reserved
rh18            ends            ;

rh19            struc           ;Generic_IOCTL (command 19)
rh19_rh         db      size rh dup (?) ;fixed portion
rh19_major      db      ?       ;major function
rh19_minor      db      ?       ;minor function
rh19_SI         dw      ?       ;contents of SI register
rh19_DI         dw      ?       ;contents of DI register
rh19_pkt_ofs    dw      ?       ;offset address of
                                ;generic IOCTL request
rh19_pkt_seg    dw      ?       ;segment address of
                                ;generic IOCTL request
rh19            ends            ;

rh20            struc           ;(command 20)
rh20_len        db      ?       ;len of packet
rh20_unit       db      ?       ;unit code
                                ;(block devices only)
rh20_cmd        db      ?       ;device driver command
rh20_status     dw      ?       ;returned by device driver
rh20_res1       dd      ?       ;reserved
rh20_res2       dd      ?       ;reserved
rh20            ends            ;

rh21            struc           ;(command 21)
rh21_len        db      ?       ;len of packet
rh21_unit       db      ?       ;unit code
                                ;(block devices only)
rh21_cmd        db      ?       ;device driver command
rh21_status     dw      ?       ;returned by device driver
rh21_res1       dd      ?       ;reserved
rh21_res2       dd      ?       ;reserved
rh21            ends            ;

rh22            struc           ;(command 22)
rh22_len        db      ?       ;len of packet
rh22_unit       db      ?       ;unit code
                                ;(block devices only)
rh22_cmd        db      ?       ;device driver command
rh22_status     dw      ?       ;returned by device driver
rh22_res1       dd      ?       ;reserved
```

Listing 9-2 *(cont.)*

```
rh22_res2      dd       ?        ;reserved
rh22           ends              ;

rh23           struc             ;Get_Device (command 23)
rh23_rh        db       size rh dup (?) ;fixed portion
rh23_IO        db       ?        ;Input (unit code)
                                 ;Output (last device)
rh23_dev_cmd   db       ?        ;command code
rh23_dev_stat  dw       ?        ;status
rh23_reserved  dd       ?        ;reserved
rh23           ends              ;

rh24           struc             ;Set_Device (command 24)
rh24_rh        db       size rh dup (?) ;fixed portion
rh24_IO        db       ?        ;Input (unit code)
                                 ;Output (last device)
rh24_dev_cmd   db       ?        ;command code
rh24_dev_stat  dw       ?        ;status
rh24_reserved  dd       ?        ;reserved
rh24           ends              ;

;commands that do not have unique portions to the request header:
;      INPUT_STATUS    (command 6)
;      INPUT_FLUSH     (command 7)
;      OUTPUT_STATUS   (command 10)
;      OUTPUT_FLUSH    (command 11)
;      OPEN            (command 13)
;      CLOSE           (command 14)
;      REMOVABLE       (command 15)
;
```

---

from a file, other device drivers can be added to the same file. In fact, the PC-DOS standard device drivers for the console, floppy disk, printer, communications port, and clock are contained in a single file named IBMBIO.COM. DOS uses the pointer to index past the current device driver for the next device driver, if there is one. To signal to DOS that there is not another device driver, place −1s in both words of this first field.

The second and third pointers of the Device Header·are used by DOS to locate the driver's STRATEGY and INTERRUPT procedures. These fields contain the offset addresses of these procedures; they are simply the labels that locate the procedures.

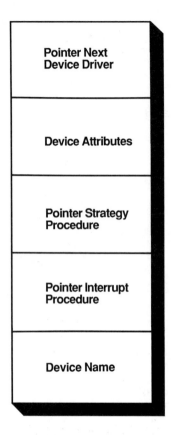

Figure 9–1: The five components of the Device Header

The Device Attribute Field   The second field of the Device Header is important for DOS. This field describes to DOS the type of device your device driver is controlling, and, more importantly, it defines the types of commands that must be implemented in the device driver. In earlier versions of DOS, this field used bits to define the type of device. In later versions, some of the bits were used to indicate for what types of commands the device driver provided processing. Table 9–3 completely describes the Attribute word of the Device Header.

Let's look at the purpose of each bit in detail.

Bits 15 and 14   Bit 15 defines to DOS whether the device driver controls a block-oriented device (0) or a character-oriented device (1). This bit is crucial

Bit	Value	Description	DOS Version
15	0	Device is block-oriented	2+
	1	Device is character-oriented	
14	0	I/O control is not supported	2+
	1	I/O control is supported	
13	0	IBM format block device	2+
	1	Non-IBM format block device	
	1	Output Til Busy command	3+
		Available for character devices	
12	0	Undefined (value should be 0)	
11	0	Open/Close/Removable Media not supported	3+
	1	Open/Close/Removable Media supported	
10	0	Undefined (value should be 0)	
9	0	Undefined (value should be 0)	
8	0	Undefined (value should be 0)	
7	0	Undefined (value should be 0)	
6	0	Get/Set Logical Device (block device)	3.2+
5	0	Undefined (value should be 0)	
4	1	Special bit for fast console I/O	2
3	1	Current clock device	2+
2	1	Current NUL device	2+
1	1	Current standard output device	2+
0	1	Current standard input device (character device)	2+
	1	Supports generic I/O Control (block device)	3.2+

Table 9–3: The bit settings of the Attribute word

because several of the following bits (13 and 0) have different meanings depending on whether the device is a block or a character device. Also, the name field of the Device Header (described later) will have different meanings depending on the type of device.

Bit 14 is used to tell DOS whether the device driver supports the I/O control commands (IOCTL Input and IOCTL Output). Recall that I/O control is used to pass control information to and from the driver. If this bit is set, you need to implement the two IOCTL commands.

The Evolving Bit 13 Bit 13 has several meanings, depending on the device type. If the device is block-oriented, setting this bit will indicate to DOS that the device is a disk that contains a non–IBM-compatible format; leaving this bit off will tell DOS that the device contains an IBM-compatible format. If the device is character-oriented and the DOS version is 3.0 or greater, setting this bit indicates that the device driver can handle Output Til Busy commands.

The issue of whether a disk uses an IBM-compatible format has evolved from a simple concept to a complex one. Recall from chapter 7 that the File Allocation Table follows the Boot Record (also known as the reserved area). On all IBM PC-DOS formatted diskettes, the FAT is always the second sector of the diskette. This was the initial definition for bit 13 set to 0. This also meant that DOS used the Media Descriptor to identify diskettes. Instead of using the Media Descriptor byte from the BIOS Parameter Block, however, DOS used the Media Descriptor byte from the first FAT entry. Thus, to identify the type of diskette in use, DOS would have to read the FAT into memory and pick off the first FAT entry. DOS could not do this unless it could presume that the FAT was always in the same place on all diskettes. The inner workings of DOS to accomplish this task are even more complicated. As we shall show you later, in the section on the Get BPB command, the contents of the data-transfer area will depend on whether or not bit 13 is set.

To make matters worse, the definition of bit 13 in later versions of DOS has changed subtly. You may recall that if bit 13 is set to 1, the format of the disk need not be IBM-compatible. This means that the FAT need not start at the second sector. What DOS will do at this point is to use the BPB to locate the FAT, the File Directory, and the user data area. This is the current definition of bit 13 as found in the manuals. If bit 13 is not set, the device driver uses the Media Descriptor from the FAT to determine the media type. If bit 13 is set, the device driver uses the BPB to determine the media type.

To try to make some sense of all this, keep in mind that, as we showed in the chapter on disk fundamentals, the media descriptor is not a good mechanism to determine the media type. Disks come in all different sizes and have different physical characteristics, such as the number of tracks, cylinders, and heads. With different sizes for the FAT, the number of FATs, and File Directory, it is impossible to fit all these different combinations into a single media descriptor, particularly one that is limited to eight combinations (F8h to FFh). This is made worse by the fact that disks can have almost any media descriptor; there is nothing sacred about a given media descriptor value.

In order to allow for all of these possibilities, you can set bit 13 on, allowing DOS to use the BPB to determine where things are.

Bits 12 to 0   Bit 12 is undefined and should contain a value of 0.

Bit 11 is used to indicate whether the device driver supports the Device Open, the Device Close, and the Removable Media commands. Note that all three commands are applicable to block-oriented devices, such as disk drives, and only the first two are applicable to character-oriented devices such as screens.

Bits 10 through 7 are undefined and should be set to 0.

Bit 6 is used only with device drivers written for DOS version 3.2 and indicates whether the device driver supports the Get Logical Device command (23) and the Set Logical Device Command (24).

Bit 5 is undefined and should be set to 0.

Bit 4 is the Special bit that is set if the device driver supports fast console I/O by implementing interrupt 29h code. The use of this feature is discussed in chapter 10, "Tips and Techniques."

Bit 3 is set if the device driver implements a clock device. If this bit is set, DOS replaces the standard clock device driver with the current clock device driver.

Bit 2 is set if the device driver is the NUL: device. You cannot replace the NUL: device driver, so this bit is not available for use. This bit is set for the standard NUL: device driver and allows DOS to identify when it is being used.

Bit 1 is set if the current device driver is to be the standard output device (also known as the screen or video output device). Set this bit to indicate that you are replacing the standard console output device. If this is the case, then bit 0 should also be set.

Bit 0 has several meanings. For character-oriented devices, setting this bit indicates that the DOS standard console input device is being replaced by the current device driver. For DOS version 3.2 or greater, if the device is a block-oriented device, setting this bit indicates to DOS that the device driver supports Generic I/O Control through command 19.

Bottom-line Necessary Settings   As we mentioned earlier, setting some of the Attribute bits will trigger the possibility of DOS sending certain types of commands to the device driver for processing. This is because some of the bits are used not just for device definition but for command definition. Table 9–4

Commands Triggered	Bits Set															
	15	14	13	12	11	10	9	8	7	6	5	4	3	2	1	0
Initialize																
Media Check																
Get BPB																
IOCTL Input			R													
Input																
ND Input																
Input Status																
Input Flush																
Output																
Output Verify																
Output Status																
Output Flush																
IOCTL Output			R													
Device Open					R											
Device Close					R											
Removable					B											
Output til Busy				C												
Undefined																
Undefined																
Generic IOCTL																B
Undefined																
Undefined																
Undefined																
Get Logical Device										B						
Set Logical Device										B						

R = Required for both character and block devices
C = Character devices only
B = Block devices only

Table 9–4: Which Attribute bits, when set, will trigger device driver commands. Note that many of the commands will be sent by DOS to the device driver as part of normal processing.

shows a cross index of Attribute bits and commands that the device driver may encounter. Not shown in this table are the commands that the device driver normally processes that are not triggered by an Attribute bit being set.

In summary, the Attribute word is a powerful feature that allows each driver to identify itself to DOS. You can control the commands that DOS is allowed to send to the device driver as well as replace the DOS standard devices. Table 9–5 summarizes the Attribute words for various versions of DOS for the DOS standard devices.

The Device Header Name Field   The Device Name field is 8 bytes in length and has two meanings. For character-oriented devices, this field contains the actual text name of the device. If you replace any of the DOS standard devices, you must supply the name of the device you replace: con:, prn:, etc. If you are not replacing a standard device, supply the name you wish to use to identify the device. Be sure to choose a name that does not normally interfere with file names that are in use. For example, if you use the name *basic* for your driver, you can no longer refer to files named *basic*. Indeed, the name that you supply for a driver's name becomes a reserved name and is no longer available for use as a file name. If the device name is less than 8 bytes in length, you have to fill the rest of the field with blanks.

   For block-oriented devices, this field does not specify the device name; instead, the first byte of the field is used to specify the number of devices the device driver controls. Because block devices are assumed to be disks, the number of disks already installed by DOS will determine the drive letters with which a particular device driver will start. If another disk-type device driver follows the current one, the sum of the disks already installed by DOS and the current number of units will determine the drive letter for the following disk device driver.

   Now that we have covered the Device Header in great detail, you should be ready for the guts of the device driver. We will cover the STRATEGY and INTERRUPT procedures briefly before going onto the DOS command processing.

The STRATEGY and INTERRUPT Procedures

For the purposes of completeness we show the STRATEGY and INTERRUPT procedure code in listing 9–3. Details on how these routines work are found in chapter 2. The INTERRUPT procedure will allow you to write device drivers for DOS versions 2.0 through 3.2; the table of command-processing procedure addresses covers the commands 0 through 24.

DOS Command Processing

When DOS makes a request of the device driver, a command is sent to the device driver in the form of a Request Header. DOS expects the device driver to perform a function based on the command. There are 25 different commands available to device drivers for processing.

Device Name	DOS Version	Vendor	Attribute Word	Bits Set and Description
NUL:	All	All	8004h	15 character device 2 NUL: device
CON:	All	Most	8013h	15 character device 4 Fast I/O 1 Standard Output 0 Standard Output
	2.11	Victor	C013h	15 character device 14 IOCTL support 4 Fast I/O 1 Standard Output 0 Standard Output
AUX:	All	Most	8000h	15 character device
	2.11	Victor	C000h	15 character device 14 IOCTL support
PRN: LPTx:	2	IBM	8000h	15 character device
	2.11	Others	8000h	15 character device
	2.11	Victor	C000h	15 character device 14 IOCTL support
	3.0	IBM	8800h	15 character device 11 Open/Close
	3.1	IBM	A000h	15 character device 13 Output Til Busy
	3.2	IBM	A040h	15 character device 13 Output Til Busy 6 Get/Set Logical Device
COMx:	All	Most	8000h	15 character device
	2.11	Victor	C000h	15 character device 14 IOCTL support
CLOCK$	All	Most	8008h	15 character device 3 Clock device

Device Name	DOS Version	Vendor	Attribute Word	Bits Set and Description
	2.11	Victor	C008h	15 character device 14 IOCTL support 3 Clock device
Disk	2	IBM	0000h	— block device
	All	Victor	6000h	— block device 14 IOCTL support 13 Non-IBM format
	3.0,3.1	IBM	0800h	— block device 11 Open/Close/ Removable
	3.2	IBM	0840h	— block device 11 Open/Close/ Removable 6 Get/Set Logical Device

Table 9–5: The various Attribute words found in various versions of DOS. Note that various vendors will implement each device driver with different Attribute bits set.

No single device driver will have to process all 25 of these commands. Some of the commands are not defined and are reserved for use by future versions of DOS; some commands are only applicable for certain types of devices. The version of DOS for which you write a device driver will determine the number of commands that are applicable. Finally, you can simply choose not to implement some commands.

Table 9–6 shows the list of DOS device driver commands with device-type and DOS-version applicability.

The number of commands that a device driver needs to process will depend on four factors: the operations permitted by a device, the type of device being controlled, the Attribute bits set, and the DOS version for which it is intended. Drivers for output-only devices, such as printers, need only implement the Output commands (Output, Output Verify, Output Status, Output Flush, Output Til Busy). Character-oriented devices will have a maximum of 14 applicable com-

---

Listing 9–3: The code for the STRATEGY and INTERRUPT procedures. These procedures are intended to be used for device drivers written for any DOS version from 2.0 through 3.2.

```
;****************************************************************
;*      THE STRATEGY PROCEDURE                                 *
;****************************************************************

dev_strategy:   mov   cs:rh_seg,es    ;save the segment address
                mov   cs:rh_ofs,bx    ;save the offset address
                ret                   ;return to DOS


;****************************************************************
;*      THE INTERRUPT PROCEDURE                                *
;****************************************************************

;device interrupt handler — 2nd call from DOS

dev_interrupt:

        cld                       ;save machine state on entry
        push    ds
        push    es
        push    ax
        push    bx
        push    cx
        push    dx
        push    di
        push    si

        mov     ax,cs:rh_seg      ;restore ES as saved by STRATEGY call
        mov     es,ax             ;
        mov     bx,cs:rh_ofs      ;restore BX as saved by STRATEGY call

;jump to appropriate routine to process command

        mov     al,es:[bx].rh_cmd ;get request header command
        rol     al,1              ;times 2 for index into word table
        lea     di,cmdtab         ;function (command) table address
        mov     ah,0              ;clear hi order
        add     di,ax             ;add the index to start of table
        jmp     word ptr[di]      ;jump indirect

;CMDTAB is the command table that contains the word address
;for each command. The request header will contain the
;command desired. The INTERRUPT routine will jump through an
;address corresponding to the requested command to get to
;the appropriate command processing routine.

CMDTAB  label   byte              ;* = char devices only
        dw      INITIALIZATION    ; initialization
```

Listing 9-3 *(cont.)*

```
dw      MEDIA_CHECK       ; media check (block only)
dw      GET_BPB           ; build bpb
dw      IOCTL_INPUT       ; ioctl in
dw      INPUT             ; input (read)
dw      ND_INPUT          ;*non destructive input no wait
dw      INPUT_STATUS      ;*input status
dw      INPUT_FLUSH       ;*input flush
dw      OUTPUT            ; output (write)
dw      OUTPUT_VERIFY     ; output (write) with verify
dw      OUTPUT_STATUS     ;*output status
dw      OUTPUT_FLUSH      ;*output flush
dw      IOCTL_OUT         ; ioctl output
dw      OPEN              ; device open
dw      CLOSE             ; device close
dw      REMOVABLE         ; removable media
dw      OUTPUT_BUSY       ; output til busy
dw      COMMAND17         ; undefined
dw      COMMAND18         ; undefined
dw      GENERIC_IOCTL     ; generic ioctl
dw      COMMAND20         ; undefined
dw      COMMAND21         ; undefined
dw      COMMAND22         ; undefined
dw      GET_DEVICE        ; get logical device
dw      SET_DEVICE        ; set logical device
```

---

mands. In addition, by not setting certain bits in the Attribute word, you can avoid having to implement associated commands. For example, if bits 14 (I/O Control) and 11 (Device Open/Device Close/Removable Media) are not set, up to five of the commands need not be implemented. Lastly, if you write device drivers for DOS version 2.0, you will be dealing with only 13 commands.

In the following sections we will describe each of the commands and what they do. We will use the corresponding Request Header structures as an aid to developing the required responses for each command.

A Quick Note on Request Headers   Throughout this book we have made every effort to make device drivers less of a mystery and more of a programming challenge. Part of the mystique of device drivers has been in the obscure definitions that device drivers use. In the case of Request Headers, there are differences between the descriptions in this book and those found in other documents, such as the *MS-DOS Programmer's Guide*.

Each request that DOS makes of the device driver is contained in a packet of data that is passed between DOS and the device driver. We have called this packet the *Request Header*. The actual size of the packet varies in size depending

Command Number	DOS Version	Device Type	Description
0	2+	Both	Initialization
1	2+	Block	Media Check
2	2+	Block	Get BIOS Parameter Block
3	2+	Both	I/O Control Input
4	2+	Both	Input (from device)
5	2+	Character	Non-Destructive Input
6	2+	Character	Input Status
7	2+	Character	Input Flush
8	2+	Both	Output (to device)
9	2+	Both	Output With Verify
10	2+	Character	Output Status
11	2+	Character	Output Flush
12	2+	Both	I/O Control Output
13	3+	Both	Device Open
14	3+	Both	Device Close
15	3+	Block	Removable Media
16	3+	Character	Output Til Busy
17–18	3.2+	—	Undefined
19	3.2+	Block	Generic I/O Control
20–22	3.2+	—	Undefined
23	3.2+	Block	Get Logical Device
24	3.2+	Block	Set Logical Device

Table 9–6: The DOS device driver commands, the DOS versions and the device types with which they work. Note that several of the commands are undefined; they are reserved for future use.

on the command. All of these packets share a common portion, often called the *static portion* because it does not change in size or number of fields. Other packets have data beyond the fixed or static part of the Request Header. In order to determine the size of the packet, you must use a field that is part of the Request Header that contains the length of the Request Header. As you read through each of the commands, you will see both the static and the dynamic portions of the Request Headers in each structure. Within the static and dynamic portions of the Request Header, we will use *strucs* to define each of the various fields.

We will now examine each of the 24 driver commands in detail.

Command 0—Initialization This is the first command that the device driver will process. DOS passes an Initialization command to the device driver immediately after loading the device driver into memory. Once the command is processed, the device driver never sees another Initialization command again.

The purpose of this command is to allow the device driver to prepare the device for use by setting up values in various registers, data buffers, pointers, and counters. Once the device driver has been initialized, DOS assumes that it is ready to process other commands.

Listing 9–4 shows the *struc* for the Initialization command. The steps required to process the Initialization command are listed below:

1. Initialize the device, data buffers, and counters

2. Display optional Initialization message

3. Set the number of units for block devices

4. Set the Break Address

5. Set the pointer to the table of BPB addresses for block devices

6. Set the Status word

It is critical to understand that although DOS service calls are allowed in processing the Initialization command, they are not allowed in any other command in a driver. Even this feature, being allowed in driver initialization, is limited to DOS services 01h through 0Ch and 30h. Other services are not permitted, for DOS is still in the process of initializing itself. You can use these services to determine the DOS version and to display messages on the screen only during initialization. Table 9–7 lists the allowable DOS services.

Listing 9–4: The Request Header for the Initialization command

```
rh0          struc              ;Initialization (command 0)
rh0_rh       db     size rh dup (?) ;fixed portion
rh0_nunits   db     ?           ;number of units
                                ;(block devices only)
rh0_brk_ofs  dw     ?           ;offset address for break
rh0_brk_seg  dw     ?           ;segment address for break
rh0_bpb_tbo  dw     ?           ;offset address of pointer
                                ;to BPB array
rh0_bpb_tbs  dw     ?           ;segment address of pointer
                                ;to BPB array
rh0_drv_ltr  db     ?           ;first available drive
                                ;(DOS 3+) (block only)
rh0          ends               ;
```

Service	Description
1h	Keyboard Input
2h	Display Output
3h	Auxiliary Input
4h	Auxiliary Output
5h	Printer Output
6h	Direct Console I/O
7h	Direct Console Input Without Echo
8h	Console Input Without Echo
9h	Print String
Ah	Buffered Keyboard Input
Bh	Check Standard Input Status
Ch	Clear Keyboard buffer
30h	Get DOS Version Number

Table 9–7: The DOS services that device drivers may use when processing the Initialization command

Let's look at the structure used to define the dynamic part of the Request Header (refer to listing 9–4). The byte variable, *rh0_nunits,* set by block device drivers, indicates the number of units controlled. The device driver must return the number of units. This number overrides the first byte of the Device Name field of the Device Header.

The variables *rh0_brk_ofs* and *rh0_brk_seg* contain the Break Address, which signals the end location in memory of the device driver. This address tells DOS where the next available memory location is for loading other drivers. You can use this feature to your advantage. Because the initialization code is used only once, you can place this code at the end of your device driver and specify the beginning of this code as the Break Address. This address is required for all device drivers.

If you detect a problem during initialization of the device driver, you can abort the loading of the device driver by simply specifying the Break Address as the beginning of the device driver. For block devices, you must set the variable *rh0_nunits* to 0.

The variables *rh0_bpb_tbo* and *rh0_bpb_tbs* are the addresses (offset and segment, respectively) of the BPB table that must be returned to DOS by block device drivers that control a disk. DOS needs to know the types of disks the device driver can handle. You can satisfy this requirement by building a BPB for each type of disk the device driver can handle. A table is created that contains the addresses of each of these BPBs, and it is the address of this table that is returned to DOS. With this information, DOS and the device driver can determine if disks have been removed or changed and where the information is on each disk.

The address used by the BPB table pointer is also used by DOS to pass to the device driver a pointer to the command line in the CONFIG.SYS file. Recall that a DEVICE = command specifies to DOS that a device driver is to be loaded. You can use this pointer in both character and block device drivers to access the entire string beyond the " = " character. Note that you cannot change the command line but you can use this feature to specify run-time parameters that the device driver can use for special configuration. For example, you can specify arguments to a serial printer device driver to set the baud rate using DEVICE = . This is a once-only alternative to the use of the I/O Control strings shown in chapter 5's Printer Device Driver.

Note that the DEVICE = command string is terminated by an Ah when there are no arguments. When there are arguments, the string is terminated with the following sequence: Oh, Dh, Ah.

The variable *rh0_drv_ltr* contains the next available driver letter. This variable is available for device drivers running under DOS versions 3.0 and greater. Block device drivers can use this information to display the drive letters that are controlled by the device driver. The drive letter is actually a number that corresponds to the drive letter (0 means A:, 1 means B:, etc).

Lastly, the Status word, *rh_status,* must be set before exiting from the device driver.

Command 1—Media Check   The Media Check command is valid only for block devices. This command is sent by DOS to determine whether the disk has changed. Among the three types of disks (diskette, hard disk, and RAM disk) discussed so far, only the diskette is capable of being changed. However, DOS plays it safe by always issuing a Media Check command before performing any reads or writes to any disk.

The *struc* for the Media Check command is shown in listing 9–5. The sequence of events for determining whether the media has changed is shown below:

1. Retrieve the Media Descriptor byte.

2. Determine whether the disk has changed by checking the amount of time elapsed since the last access, using hardware detection methods, or comparing disk information.

3. Set Media Status.

4. Set the Status word of the Request Header.

Hard disks and RAM disks do not change, so you can simply indicate this. However, for diskettes, determining whether the media has changed is a difficult task. As shown above, three basic methods can be used to determine whether the media has changed: a check for elapsed time, a check for hardware-detected disk change, and a check of disk information.

The first method involves keeping track of the time of the last disk access compared with the current time. From a practical point of view, changing diskettes takes a certain amount of time, at least two seconds. If you calculate that less than two seconds have elapsed since the last access, you can assume that the media has not changed. If the last access was more than two seconds ago, however, you cannot be sure whether the disk has changed.

The second method is the best of the three. High-capacity (1.2MB) diskette drives send a signal when the drive door is opened; we can detect this and set the media status accordingly. This signal is often called the *changeline signal* and is active if the door has been opened. Unfortunately, this signal is not available from most other diskette drives.

The last method is the most complex, requiring the disk device driver to save information on the disk with each access. The information saved includes the media descriptor byte, the volume ID, and the BPB. If any of these parameters changes between the last disk access and the current one, we can assume that the disk has changed. However, this method is not always reliable. For example, comparing the media descriptor byte from the Request Header with the media descriptor of the current disk does not reliably indicate a disk change. If they are different, the disk has changed. If we changed disks using two similarly formatted diskettes whose media descriptor bytes would be identical, this

Listing 9–5: The Request Header for the Media Check command

```
rhl             struc           ;Media_Check (command 1)
rhl_rh          db      size rh dup (?) ;fixed portion
rhl_media       db      ?       ;media descriptor from DPB
rhl_md_stat     db      ?       ;media status returned by
                                ;device driver
rhl_volid_ofs   dw      ?       ;offset address of
                                ;volume id
                                ;DOS 3+ only
rhl_volid_seg   dw      ?       ;segment address of
                                ;volume id
                                ;DOS 3+ only
rhl             ends            ;
```

method could erroneously assume that the disk has not changed. This would also be the case if we compared the BPBs or the volume IDs.

However, there is a way around the problem of determining disk changes. As shown in table 9–8, the media change status allows for three conditions: "media has changed," "media has not changed," and "don't know whether media has changed." If we cannot determine whether the disk has changed, then we set the media status word, *rh1_md_stat,* to 0, which indicates "do not know if the media has changed."

The media status word should be set to − 1 (media has changed) for all disk types on the first Media Check command. This is true for the very first access of RAM disks and hard disks as well as floppy disks, because DOS does not have accurate information on the disk. Subsequent Media Check commands for hard disks and RAM disks should have the media status word set to 1 (media has not been changed).

If the disk device driver has set bit 11 (Open/Close/Removable Media) of the Attribute word in the Device Header, there is an additional programming consideration. If the disk device driver sets the variable *rh1_md_stat* to − 1 (media has changed), then the variables *rh1_volid_ofs* and *rh1_volid_sig* must be set to the offset and segment address of the previous volume ID. This presumes that the device driver has saved the volume ID of the previous disk. If the device driver has not been programmed to save the volume ID, these variables should point to a field containing a volume ID of NO NAME, followed by four spaces and a 0h. This is the signal that tells DOS that there should be no checking of the volume ID.

DOS uses the volume ID information on a disk change to determine if the previous disk needs to be reinserted. This allows DOS to update the disk that was prematurely removed.

Lastly, the Status word of the Request Header must be set before exiting

Value	Description
− 1	Media has changed
0	Don't know if media has changed
+ 1	Media has not changed

Table 9–8: The three values for the media change status word

the device driver. If there is an error in reading the disk for media information, the Error bit and Error code should be set with the number of the error that was encountered.

Command 2—Get BPB The Get BIOS Parameter Block (BPB) command is valid for block device drivers only. DOS sends this command to the device driver when it needs to know more about the current disk. This occurs under two conditions: if the Media Check command returns a status of -1 (media has changed) or if the Media Check command returns a status of 0 (don't know) and there are no dirty buffers for the disk.

Recall from the previous section that DOS needs to check that the disk has not changed before any reads or writes. DOS assumes that the disk will not change as long as there is data to be written to the disk. These are buffers within DOS that contain modified data for a particular disk. If DOS determines that there are no dirty buffers, and if the Media Check returns a status of 0 (don't know), DOS will assume that the disk has changed. This neatly solves the dilemma of determining disk changes that was discussed in the previous section. The reason this works is simple: If there are any buffers to be written out, DOS will do so at the earliest possible time. This ensures that disks can be changed at any time without having to perform an action to write out data. Thus, if a time period has been exceeded or if the device driver cannot determine a disk change, DOS assumes that the disk has been changed. This causes DOS to assume that the disk is new and that new disk information will be received.

The Get BPB command accesses the disk and returns to DOS the BPB. This information allows DOS to locate the File Allocation Table, the File Directory, and the user data area for the new disk. The steps needed to process the Get BPB command are shown below:

1. Determine where the Boot Record is on the new disk.

2. Read the Boot Record into memory.

3. Retrieve the BPB from the Boot Record.

4. Return a pointer to the new BPB.

5. If Attribute word bit 11 is set, determine where the File Directory begins, search the File Directory for the volume ID, save the old volume ID, and save the new volume ID.

6. Set the Status word of the Request Header.

The device driver is responsible for reading the BPB from the disk. A pointer to the new BPB is then returned to DOS through the Request Header variables *rh2_pbpbo* and *rh2_pbpbs*. The Get BPB *struc* is shown in Listing 9–6.

Listing 9–6: The Request Header for the Get BPB command

```
rh2             struc                ;Get_BPB (command 2)
rh2_rh          db      size rh dup(?)  ;fixed portion
rh2_media       db      ?            ;media descriptor from DPB
rh2_buf_ofs     dw      ?            ;offset address of
                                     ;data transfer area
rh2_buf_seg     dw      ?            ;segment address of
                                     ;data transfer area
rh2_pbpbo       dw      ?            ;offset address of
                                     ;pointer to BPB
rh2_pbpbs       dw      ?            ;segment address of
                                     ;pointer to BPB
rh2             ends                 ;
```

The BPB is located in the Boot Record (also known as the reserved area). For diskettes, this is the first sector of the disk; for hard disks, this is the first sector of the logical disk drive. Recall that a hard disk may be partitioned into several logical drives. It is up to the device driver to determine the start of the logical drive (partition) relative to the first physical sector of the hard disk. Obviously, many calculations are necessary to find the hard disk BPB. Table 9–9 describes the BPB.

Name	Starting Location	Length	Description
SS	0	2	Sector Size in bytes
AU	2	1	Allocation Unit size (sectors per cluster)
RS	3	2	Number of Reserved Sectors
NF	5	1	Number of FATs on this disk
DS	6	2	Directory Size (number of files)
TS	8	2	Number of Total Sectors
MD	10	1	Media Descriptor
FS	11	2	FAT Sectors (each FAT)
ST	13	2	Number of Sectors per Track
NH	15	2	Number of Heads
HS	17	2	Number of Hidden Sectors

Table 9–9: The fields that comprise the BPB. The BPB is located at byte 11 from the beginning of the boot area.

The buffer address specified by the variables *rh2_buf_ofs* and *rh2_buf_seg* has different meanings depending on the DOS version and the setting of bit 13 of the Attribute word of the Device Header. Bit 13 is set to indicate that the disk format is not IBM-compatible. This specifies to the device driver that the buffer can be used for anything. Otherwise, the buffer contains the initial FAT sector (with the first entry being the media descriptor byte) and must not be altered for DOS version 2.0. For DOS version 3.2, you can use this buffer even if bit 13 is not set. You need not concern yourself with this, for the BPB contains all the information that DOS needs about the new disk.

Lastly, because DOS assumes that there is a new disk, the device driver can read the new volume ID off the new disk and save the old volume ID. This involves determining where the File Directory is on the new disk and searching through it for the volume ID entry. Once the volume ID is found and stored in a variable, the other command processing sections can return the old volume ID in the event of an illegal disk change. For example, the Media Check command returns this old volume ID if the disk has changed. You will see more of this volume ID in other command processing.

Command 3—I/O Control Input   Command 3, I/O Control Input, is valid for block and character device drivers if the I/O Control Support bit (14) of the Attribute word is set. Recall that the Attribute word of the Device Header allows DOS to pass I/O control strings to and from the device driver. I/O control strings are data passed between a program and the device driver. The data is not intended to be sent to the device; these strings are merely a means of communicating with the device driver.

As you saw in chapter 5's Printer Device Driver, you can use I/O control strings in two ways. The DOS service IOCTL Output is used to send control information to the device driver. When control information from the device driver is required, the IOCTL Input DOS service is used. The DOS 44h services call provides IOCTL functions.

Listing 9–7 shows the IOCTL Input *struc*. The steps required to process the IOCTL Input command are listed below:

1. Retrieve the address of the data-transfer area.

2. Retrieve the transfer count from the Request Header.

3. Store the I/O control string in the data-transfer area.

4. Return the transfer count.

5. Set the Status word of the Request Header.

Listing 9–7: The Request Header for the IOCTL Input command

```
rh3             struc           ;IOCTL_INPUT (command 3)
rh3_rh          db      size rh dup(?)   ;fixed portion
rh3_media       db      ?       ;media descriptor from DPB
rh3_buf_ofs     dw      ?       ;offset address of
                                ;data transfer area
rh3_buf_seg     dw      ?       ;segment address of
                                ;data transfer area
rh3_count       dw      ?       ;transfer count
                                ;(sectors for block)
                                ;(bytes for character)
rh3_start       dw      ?       ;start sector number
                                ;(block devices only)
rh3             ends            ;
```

The I/O control string data that is passed to the device driver in the data transfer area need not be moved into a buffer inside the device driver. The device driver can simply use a pointer to access the data.

The format for the I/O control string information must be agreed upon between the program and the device driver. Otherwise, the program sends data that the device driver does not understand. This data can be binary, ASCII, or a combination of both. Set up a command code, one for each function desired. Then, within the application program using the IOCTL functions, decide how to interact with the user to determine which of the command codes to send to the device driver. This may be a series of prompts, such as those you saw in chapter 5's IOCTL program. Within the device driver, you must add code to recognize these command codes and process them accordingly.

The transfer-count variable *rh3_count* is an important part of the common I/O control string format. This transfer count determines if the data transferred is correct. Because both sides must agree on the format, the number of bytes to be transferred can also be confirmed.

Using the variables *rh3_buf_ofs* and *rh3_buf_seg* as a pointer, the device driver can read or write an I/O control string in the data-transfer area. For the IOCTL Input command, the device driver is instructed to return an I/O control string to DOS. DOS, in turn, returns it to the program requesting I/O control information.

Once an I/O control string is stored in the data-transfer area, the device driver sets the variable *rh3_count* to indicate the number of bytes in the data-transfer area. Next, the Status word of the Request Header is set to indicate the appropriate status; the device driver then exits back to DOS.

Command 4—Input The listing for the *struc* is shown in listing 9–8. The Input command is used by all device drivers to send data from the device back to DOS. The steps for processing this command are shown below:

1. Retrieve the address of the data-transfer area.
2. Retrieve the transfer count from the Request Header.
3. Read the requested amount of information from the device.
4. Return the transfer count.
5. Set Status word of the Request Header.

The Input command reads data from the device into the data-transfer address specified by the variables *rh4_buf_ofs* and *rh4_buf_seg*. The count is contained in the variable *rh4_count*. For character devices the count is the number of bytes to be transferred. For block devices the count is the number of sectors to be transferred. In addition, the variable *rh4_start* indicates the starting sector for the block device.

Listing 9–8: The Request Header for the Input command

```
rh4            struc              ;INPUT (command 4)
rh4_rh         db      size rh dup(?)   ;fixed portion
rh4_media      db      ?          ;media descriptor from DPB
rh4_buf_ofs    dw      ?          ;offset address of
                                  ;data transfer area
rh4_buf_seg    dw      ?          ;segment address of
                                  ;data transfer area
rh4_count      dw      ?          ;transfer count
                                  ;(sectors for block)
                                  ;(bytes for character)
rh4_start      dw      ?          ;start sector number
                                  ;(block devices only)
rh4_volid_ofs  dw      ?          ;offset address of
                                  ;volume identification
                                  ;DOS 3+ only
rh4_volid_seg  dw      ?          ;segment address of
                                  ;volume identification
                                  ;DOS 3+ only
rh4            ends               ;
```

Once the transfer is complete, the device driver specifies the number of bytes or sectors transferred in the same variable, *rh4_count*. This variable does not have to be updated if the transfer was successful, because the original number is still correct. If the transfer was not successful, this variable must be changed to indicate the number of bytes or sectors transferred. This tells DOS that the data was only partially transferred.

For block device drivers that implement the Open/Close/Removable Media bit (11) of the Device Header Attribute word, there is an additional programming consideration. You may recall from the Get_BPB command section that disks can be changed even though DOS still has data for the disk. If the device driver receives an Input command and determines that the wrong disk is in the unit, the device driver aborts the Input command and returns an error to DOS. This type of error is detected by timing the last disk accessor or by monitoring a diskette-changed signal from the hardware. If it is determined that the Input command is for the wrong disk, the device driver returns an error (0Fh—illegal disk change) and the old volume ID. This allows DOS to ask the user to reinsert the disk that has the old volume ID. Note that this feature is for DOS versions 3.0 or greater.

The Status word in the Request Header is set to indicate DONE and any errors before the device driver exits back to DOS. This is particularly important if we have encountered an error.

Command 5—Nondestructive Input The Nondestructive Input command is valid for character devices only. The applications program using the DOS service Get Input Status (0Bh) causes DOS to send this command to the device driver, asking it to look ahead one character. DOS assumes that character devices have an input buffer in which characters are stored. The device driver requests the next character in this buffer. Some devices have the ability to retrieve a character from the buffer without removing the character. Other devices require the character to be removed from the buffer. The term nondestructive means that the character will still be available for the next Input command.

Not all devices have a data buffer. For devices that do not, the device driver must actually do a read of one character. This character is saved for the next Input command as well as being passed back to DOS to satisfy the Nondestructive Input command. Device drivers also store characters for keyboard devices. Recall from chapter 4 that keyboard input using the ROM BIOS interrupt 16h returns two bytes. The device driver returns one byte and saves the other. The Nondestructive Input command would simply retrieve the stored character. If the device driver did not have a character saved, the device driver would request the next character.

The steps required to process the Nondestructive Input command are listed below:

1. Retrieve a byte from the device.

2. Set the Status word of the Request Header.

The device driver retrieves a byte from the device and stores it in the variable *rh5_return*. If there is no character in the device buffer, the device driver sets the BUSY bit of the Status word to indicate that the device buffer is empty. The Status word of the Request Header is set before exiting from the device driver. The listing for the Nondestructive Input *struc* is shown in listing 9–9.

Command 6—Input Status   The Input Status command is valid for character devices only. This command returns the status of the character-device input buffer, telling DOS whether there are any characters in the device buffer ready to be input. Listing 9–10 shows the *struc* for the Input Status command. The steps involved in processing the Input Status command are shown below:

1. Retrieve the status from the device.

2. Set the BUSY bit of the Status word:

    0   If there are characters in the device buffer or if the device does not have a buffer

    1   If there are no characters in the buffer

3. Set Status word of the Request Header.

The device driver processes this command by retrieving the status from the device. If the device has characters in the buffer, the BUSY bit is not set. If the device does not have characters in the buffer, the BUSY bit is set.

Listing 9–9: The Request Header for the Nondestructive Input command

```
rh5            struc              ;ND_INPUT (command 5)
rh5_rh         db      size rh dup (?) ;fixed portion
rh5_return     db      ?          ;character returned
rh5            ends               ;
```

Listing 9–10: The Request Header for the Input Status command

---

```
rh6            struc              ;Input_Status (command 6)
rh6_len        db       ?         ;len of packet
rh6_unit       db       ?         ;unit code
                                  ;(block devices only)
rh6_cmd        db       ?         ;device driver command
rh6_status     dw       ?         ;returned by device driver
rh6_res1       dd       ?         ;reserved
rh6_res2       dd       ?         ;reserved
rh6            ends               ;
```

For devices that do not have a data buffer, the BUSY bit is not set. This is contrary to what you might expect based on the preceding descriptions. The logic behind this is that DOS will wait for the device buffer to fill if the BUSY bit is set. On the other hand, if the BUSY bit is not set, DOS will issue an Input command immediately. This will result in an actual read, and DOS will not have to wait for a nonexistent buffer to fill.

Command 7—Input Flush   The Input Flush command is valid for character devices only. This command empties the character device buffer. Listing 9–11 shows the listing for the Input Flush *struc*. The steps required to process the Input Flush command are listed below:

1. Flush the character device buffer.
2. Set Status word of the Request Header.

Listing 9–11: The Request Header for the Input Flush command

```
rh7            struc              ;Input_Flush (command 7)
rh7_len        db       ?         ;len of packet
rh7_unit       db       ?         ;unit code
                                  ;(block devices only)
rh7_cmd        db       ?         ;device driver command
rh7_status     dw       ?         ;returned by device driver
rh7_res1       dd       ?         ;reserved
rh7_res2       dd       ?         ;reserved
rh7            ends               ;
```

To process this command, execute instructions that cause the device buffer to empty. Most devices do not accept control information that causes the buffer to drain. Instead, the device driver simply reads characters from the device until the device status indicates that there are no more characters in the buffer. The device driver sets the Status word in the Request Header before exiting.

Command—8 Output Command 8, Output, is used by all device drivers to send data to the device. Listing 9–12 shows the *struc* to use to process the Output command. The steps taken to process the Output command are listed below:

1. Retrieve the address of the data transfer area.

2. Retrieve the transfer count from the Request Header.

3. Write the requested amount of information in the data transfer area to the device.

4. Return the transfer count.

5. Set Status word of the Request Header.

The device driver processes this command by first retrieving the pointer to the data-transfer area. The variables *rh8_buf_ofs* and *rh8_buf_seg* contain the

---

Listing 9–12: The Request Header for the Output command

```
rh8             struc            ;OUTPUT (command 8)
rh8_rh          db      size rh dup(?)   ;fixed portion
rh8_media       db      ?        ;media descriptor from DPB
rh8_buf_ofs     dw      ?        ;offset address of
                                 ;data transfer area
rh8_buf_seg     dw      ?        ;segment address of
                                 ;data transfer area
rh8_count       dw      ?        ;transfer count
                                 ;(sectors for block)
                                 ;(bytes for character)
rh8_start       dw      ?        ;start sector number
                                 ;(block devices only)
rh8_volid_ofs   dw      ?        ;offset address of
                                 ;volume identification
                                 ;DOS 3+ only
rh8_volid_seg   dw      ?        ;segment address of
                                 ;volume identification
                                 ;DOS 3+ only
rh8             ends             ;
```

---

offset and segment address in which the data resides. Next, the device driver retrieves the transfer count in the variable *rh8_count*. For character devices, this is the number of bytes to write; for block devices, this is the number of sectors to write. The variable *rh8_start* is for block devices and indicates the starting sector number for the write operation.

For block devices, the device driver must translate the relative sector number into a set of physical parameters (track, head, sector). The sector numbers that are passed in the Request Header are those numbers relative to the start of the logical drive. Hard disks are often partitioned into one or more logical drives. For both floppy and hard disks, the device driver must convert this relative sector number into a track number, a head number, and a sector number.

If the write operation is successful, the device driver sets the Status word and exits. If the write operation fails, the device driver must set the ERROR bit and indicate the error number; both the ERROR bit and number are defined in the Status word of the Request Header. In addition, the device driver must return, in the variable *rh8_count,* the transfer count up to the point of failure. This indicates to DOS how much data there is in the data-transfer area.

In addition, if the Device Header Attribute bit 11 (Open/Close/Removable Media) is set, block device drivers need to process another type of error. If the block device driver has determined that there has been an illegal disk change, it must abort the write operation. The driver then sets the ERROR bit and indicates an error code of 0Fh (illegal disk change). Then the pointer variables *rh8_volid_ofs* and *rh8_volid_seg* are set to point to the old volume ID. When DOS receives the 0Fh error, DOS will prompt the user with the old volume ID, requesting a reinsertion of the old disk.

Command 9—Output With Verify   The Output With Verify command is valid for both character and block devices. This command is used much as the Output command is, except that, if possible, you should build your driver to read back the data after it is written to the device. Use this command to ensure that the data has been written to the device correctly. The *struc* for the Output With Verify command is shown in listing 9–13. The steps required to process this command are shown below:

1. For devices that cannot read data just written, jump to the Output routine.

2. For devices that can read data just written, set a flag to indicate a read. Next, jump to the Output routine and modify it to read the data back in if the flag is set.

Listing 9–13: The Request Header for the Output With Verify command

```
rh9             struc                   ;OUTPUT_VERIFY (command 9)
rh9_rh          db      size rh dup(?)  ;fixed portion
rh9_media       db      ?               ;media descriptor from DPB
rh9_buf_ofs     dw      ?               ;offset address of
                                        ;data transfer area
rh9_buf_seg     dw      ?               ;segment address of
                                        ;data transfer area
rh9_count       dw      ?               ;transfer count
                                        ;(sectors for block)
                                        ;(bytes for character)
rh9_start       dw      ?               ;start sector number
                                        ;(block devices only)
rh9_volid_ofs   dw      ?               ;offset address of
                                        ;volume identification
                                        ;DOS 3+ only
rh9_volid_seg   dw      ?               ;segment address of
                                        ;volume identification
                                        ;DOS 3+ only
rh9             ends                    ;
```

The VERIFY command is used to set the verify flag within DOS. If this flag is set, all writes to the device will appear in the device driver as Output With Verify commands instead of Output commands.

For devices that cannot read data just written, process this command by including a *jump* instruction to the Output routine. If the device can read data just written (as disks can), set a flag to indicate that you want to validate the data by reading it back in. Then jump to a modified Output routine. The Output routine will write the data to the device and, if the flag is set, will read the data back in. This method uses both the Output and the Input routines to process the Output With Verify command.

Command 10—Output Status   The Output Status command is valid for character devices only. Use this command to return the status of the device output to DOS. Devices that are output only, such as printers, have buffers that contain characters waiting to be output. Check the status of this buffer with this command. The *struc* for the Output Status command is shown in listing 9–14. The steps for processing this command are shown below:

1. Retrieve the status from the device.

Listing 9–14: The Request Header for the Output Status command

```
rh10          struc          ;Output_Status (command 10)
rh10_len      db     ?       ;len of packet
rh10_unit     db     ?       ;unit code
                             ;(block devices only)
rh10_cmd      db     ?       ;device driver command
rh10_status   dw     ?       ;returned by device driver
rh10_res1     dd     ?       ;reserved
rh10_res2     dd     ?       ;reserved
rh10          ends           ;
```

---

2. Set the BUSY bit of the Status word:

0   If the device is idle or the buffer is not full

1   If the device is busy or the buffer is full

3. Set the Status word of the Request Header.

When DOS needs to write to a device, an Output Status command is first issued to the device driver. This tells DOS whether to send the Output command immediately or to wait and issue another Output Status command.

To process this command, set the BUSY bit of the Request Header Status word. If the device is ready for output, the device driver does not set the BUSY bit. If the device is not ready, the driver sets the BUSY bit.

Command 11—Output Flush The Output Flush command is valid for character devices only. Use this command to empty the output device's buffer. The *struc* for the Output Flush command is shown in listing 9–15. The steps for processing this command are listed below:

1. For devices that have an output buffer, execute instructions to empty the buffer.

2. Set the Status word of the Request Header.

To process the Output Flush command, the device driver executes instructions that empty the output device's data buffer. If the output device does not have a buffer, the device driver simply does nothing. Before the device driver exits, set the Status word in the Request Header.

Listing 9–15: The Request Header for the Output Flush command

---

```
rh11            struc              ;Output_Flush (command 11)
rh11_len        db      ?          ;len of packet
rh11_unit       db      ?          ;unit code
                                   ;(block devices only)
rh11_cmd        db      ?          ;device driver command
rh11_status     dw      ?          ;returned by device driver
rh11_res1       dd      ?          ;reserved
rh11_res2       dd      ?          ;reserved
rh11            ends               ;
```

Command 12—I/O Control Output   The I/O Control Output command is valid for character and block devices if the Device Header Attribute bit 14 is set, indicating that I/O Control is supported. Use this command to send control information from a program directly to the device driver. Data that is passed to the device driver is not meant for the device but for controlling the device. The device driver may use this information in any fashion. The format of the control information must be agreed upon by both the program issuing IOCTL service calls and the device driver. The *struc* for the IOCTL command is shown in listing 9–16. The steps required to process the IOCTL Output command are listed below:

1. Retrieve the address of the data-transfer area.

2. Retrieve the transfer count from the Request Header.

3. Decode the I/O control string contained in the data-transfer area.

4. Set the Status word of the Request Header.

The device driver processes this command by retrieving the address of the data-transfer area in the variables *rh12_buf_ofs* and *rh12_buf_seg*. The length of the I/O control string to process is contained in the variable *rh12_count*. This count allows the device driver to determine if the I/O control string has been properly constructed. As we discussed in the IOCTL Input section, the length of the transfer is important in ensuring that the format of the I/O control string is correct.

The device driver then processes the I/O control string by performing the functions requested. These functions will vary depending on the type of device being controlled and the actions desired. In chapter 5, you saw that the Printer

---

Listing 9–16: The Request Header for the IOCTL Output command

```
rh12            struc                    ;IOCTL_OUTPUT (command 12)
rh12_rh         db      size rh dup(?)   ;fixed portion
rh12_media      db      ?                ;media descriptor from DPB
rh12_buf_ofs    dw      ?                ;offset address of
                                         ;data transfer area
rh12_buf_seg    dw      ?                ;segment address of
                                         ;data transfer area
rh12_count      dw      ?                ;transfer count
                                         ;(sectors for block)
                                         ;(bytes for character)
rh12_start      dw      ?                ;start sector number
                                         ;(block devices only)
rh12            ends                     ;
```

Device Driver used I/O control strings to switch printers. You could have easily used I/O control strings to change the baud rate of your devices or to issue a forms control for a printer.

If there are any errors, the device driver sets the Request Header Status word accordingly.

Command 13—Device Open   The Device Open command is available to both character and block devices under DOS version 3.0 or greater if the Device Header Attribute bit 11 (Open/Close/Removable Media) is set. This command is sent by DOS each time the device is opened by a program. Use this command to track the number of times a device has been opened. Used in conjunction with the Device Close command, this command can enable you to determine if devices are being accessed properly. For example, if you want the device to be accessed by only one user at a time, you can reject new opens of your device if you have not received a close command for the previous open. The *struc* for the Device Open command is shown in listing 9–17. The steps required to process this command are listed below:

1. Increment a (device open) counter.

2. For character devices, send out an initialization string.

3. Set the Status word of the Request Header.

To process this command, increment a counter within your device driver. The count is incremented when the device driver receives Device Open com-

---

Listing 9–17: The Request Header for the Device Open command

```
rh13            struc                ;Open (command 13)
rh13_len        db       ?           ;len of packet
rh13_unit       db       ?           ;unit code
                                     ;(block devices only)
rh13_cmd        db       ?           ;device driver command
rh13_status     dw       ?           ;returned by device driver
rh13_res1       dd       ?           ;reserved
rh13_res2       dd       ?           ;reserved
rh13            ends                 ;
```

---

mands and is decremented when the driver receives Device Close commands. This allows the device driver to determine when the device is free.

For character devices, use the Device Open command to initialize the device. For example, you can initialize printers by sending a command that sets the top of form or loads a standard font.

For block devices, you can use the device open counter in a different manner. Recall that setting the Attribute bit 11 requires the block device driver to determine whether there is an illegal disk change. You can use the device open counter for this purpose. Disks can be changed when the device open counter is 0 (which means that there are no open files for the disk). As long as the counter is not 0, disks cannot be changed, for there are files opened for the disk.

Command 14—Device Close   The Device Close command is available to character and block devices running under DOS version 3.0 or greater if the Device Header Attribute bit 11 (Open/Close/Removable Media) is set. This command is sent by DOS each time the device is closed by a program. Use this command to track the number of times a device has been opened. Used with the Device Open command just described, this command can enable you to determine if devices are being accessed properly. The *struc* for the Device Close command is shown in listing 9–18. The steps required to process this command are listed below:

1. Decrement a (Device Open) counter.

2. Set the Status word of the Request Header.

To process this command, decrement the counter within your device driver that was incremented by a Device Open command. When the count is 0, you will know that there are no outstanding opens for this device: the device is free.

Listing 9–18: The Request Header for the Device Close command

```
rh14            struc               ;Close command 14)
rh14_len        db      ?           ;len of packet
rh14_unit       db      ?           ;unit code
                                    ;(block devices only)
rh14_cmd        db      ?           ;device driver command
rh14_status     dw      ?           ;returned by device driver
rh14_res1       dd      ?           ;reserved
rh14_res2       dd      ?           ;reserved
rh14            ends                ;
```

For character devices, use the Device Close command to send an optional string to the device. For example, you can send a form feed command to finish a print job. Note that the con:, aux:, and prn: devices are never closed.

As you have just seen for the Device Open command, you can use this device open counter differently for block devices. If the device open counter is 0, the disk may be changed. Therefore, if a GET BPB command is received by the device driver, the disk change is legal. However, if the device open counter is not 0 and the device driver receives a GET BPB command, the disk change is in error.

Command 15—Removable Media   The Removable Media command is valid for block devices running under DOS version 3.0 or greater that have the Device Header Attribute bit 11 (Open/Close/Removable Media) set. This command is sent by DOS when a program issues an IOCTL service call (44h) asking whether the media is removable (08h). Programs use this command to determine whether the disk is changeable. The *struc* for the Removable Media command is shown in listing 9–19. The steps required to process this command are shown below:

1. Set the BUSY bit of the Status word:

   0   Media is removable

   1   Media is not removable

2. Set the Status word of the Request Header.

To process this command, return the BUSY bit in the Request Header Status word, indicating the media status. Set the BUSY bit if the media is not removable; do not set it if the media is removable.

Programs that request this information through the IOCTL service call can

---

Listing 9–19: The Request Header for the Removable Media command

```
rh15            struc               ;Removable (command 15)
rh15_len        db      ?           ;len of packet
rh15_unit       db      ?           ;unit code
                                    ;(block devices only)
rh15_cmd        db      ?           ;device driver command
rh15_status     dw      ?           ;returned by device driver
rh15_res1       dd      ?           ;reserved
rh15_res2       dd      ?           ;reserved
rh15            ends                ;
```

---

decide whether to prompt the user to change disks. For example, the FORMAT program uses this information to prompt the user for diskettes but not for hard disks.

Command 16—Output Til Busy The Output Til Busy command is valid for character devices running under DOS version 3.0 or greater that have the Device Header Attribute bit 13 set (Output Til Busy supported). This command is used by print spoolers to output data to a character device until the device signals busy. The *struc* for the Output Til Busy command is shown in listing 9–20. The steps required to process this command are listed below:

1. Retrieve the address of the data-transfer area.

2. Retrieve the transfer count from the Request Header.

3. Write the requested amount of information in the data-transfer area to the device until the device signals busy.

4. Return the transfer count.

5. Set the Status word of the Request Header.

To process this command, first retrieve the pointer to the data-transfer area. The variables *rh16_buf_ofs* and *rh16_buf_seg* contain the offset and segment address at which the data resides. Then retrieve the transfer count in the variable *rh16_count,* which is the number of bytes to write.

The device driver writes characters from the data-transfer area to the device until all the characters are written or until the device signals busy. If all the characters were not written, the number actually written is returned in the

---

Listing 9–20: The Request Header for the Output Til Busy command

---

```
rh16              struc              ;OUTPUT_BUSY (command 16)
rh16_rh           db       size rh dup (?)  ;fixed portion
rh16_media        db       ?         ;media descriptor
rh16_buf_ofs      dw       ?         ;offset address of
                                     ;data transfer area
rh16_buf_seg      dw       ?         ;segment address of
                                     ;data transfer area
rh16_count        dw       ?         ;byte count returned
                                     ;from device driver
rh16              ends               ;
```

---

variable *rh16_count*. The device driver sets the Request Header Status word upon exit.

Commands 17 and 18   Commands 17 and 18 are undefined; they are reserved for use by future versions of DOS. For the sake of completeness, the Request Header *struc*s for both commands are shown in listing 9–21.

Listing 9–21: The Request Header for commands 17 and 18

```
rh17              struc              ;(command 17)
rh17_len          db       ?         ;len of packet
rh17_unit         db       ?         ;unit code
                                     ;(block devices only)
rh17_cmd          db       ?         ;device driver command
rh17_status       dw       ?         ;returned by device driver
rh17_res1         dd       ?         ;reserved
rh17_res2         dd       ?         ;reserved
rh17              ends               ;

rh18              struc              ;(command 18)
rh18_len          db       ?         ;len of packet
rh18_unit         db       ?         ;unit code
                                     ;(block devices only)
rh18_cmd          db       ?         ;device driver command
rh18_status       dw       ?         ;returned by device driver
rh18_res1         dd       ?         ;reserved
rh18_res2         dd       ?         ;reserved
rh18              ends               ;
```

Command 19—Generic I/O Control The Generic I/O Control command is valid for block devices running under DOS version 3.2 or greater that have the Device Header Attribute bit 0 set (Generic I/O Control supported). This command is used by programs that issue an IOCTL service call (44h) specifying Generic I/O Control functions (0Dh). The *struc* for the Generic I/O Control command is shown in listing 9–22. The steps required to process this command are listed below:

1. Retrieve the Major and Minor function codes.

2. Process the Minor function request.

3. Return the transfer count.

4. Set the Status word of the Request Header.

The purpose of this command is to provide a standard I/O control service for block-oriented devices. Beginning with version 3.2, DOS defines a more standard approach to controlling block devices. The Minor function codes define operations that were not truly a part of DOS. For example, formatting a disk was an operation performed by utility programs.

To process this command, first retrieve the Major and Minor function codes that are contained in the variables *rh19_major* and *rh19_minor*. Next, verify that the Major function code is correct. For DOS version 3.2, the only Major code defined is 08h. The Minor codes and their meanings are shown in table 9–10.

The Request Header contains additional information that assists the device

---

Listing 9–22: The Request Header for the Generic IOCTL command

```
rh19            struc                  ;Generic_IOCTL (command 19)
rh19_rh         db      size rh dup (?) ;fixed portion
rh19_major      db      ?              ;major function
rh19_minor      db      ?              ;minor function
rh19_SI         dw      ?              ;contents of SI register
rh19_DI         dw      ?              ;contents of DI register
rh19_pkt_ofs    dw      ?              ;offset address of
                                       ;generic IOCTL request
rh19_pkt_seg    dw      ?              ;segment address of
                                       ;generic IOCTL request
rh19            ends                   ;
```

Value	Description
40h	Set Device Parameters
60h	Get Device Parameters
41h	Write logical drive track
61h	Read logical drive track
42h	Format and verify logical drive track
62h	Verify logical drive track

Table 9–10: The Minor function codes for the Major function 08h. These codes are defined for the DOS IOCTL service (44h) request for Generic I/O Control (0Dh).

driver in processing the Generic I/O Control command. Refer to the *DOS Technical Reference* manual for details in implementing this command.

Commands 20, 21, and 22   Commands 20, 21, and 22 are undefined; they are reserved for future DOS versions. The Request Header strucs for these commands are shown in listing 9–23.

Command 23—Get Logical Device   The Get Logical Device command is available for block devices running under DOS version 3.2 or greater that have the Device Header Attribute bit 6 set (Get/Set Logical Device supported). DOS 3.2 allows the user to specify multiple drive letters for a device unit. For example, the second diskette unit, normally accessed as logical drive letter B:, can also be accessed with the logical drive letter E:. Listing 9–24 shows the *struc* for the Get Logical Device command. The steps required to process this command are listed below:

1. Retrieve the input unit code.

2. Return the last device referenced.

3. Set the Status word of the Request Header.

This command is processed by retrieving the logical unit specified in the variable *rh23_io*. The device driver will determine if there is another logical drive assigned to the same logical unit. If there is no other logical drive assigned,

---

Listing 9–23: The Request Header for the commands 20, 21, 22

```
rh20            struc           ;(command 20)
rh20_len        db      ?       ;len of packet
rh20_unit       db      ?       ;unit code
                                ;(block devices only)
rh20_cmd        db      ?       ;device driver command
rh20_status     dw      ?       ;returned by device driver
rh20_res1       dd      ?       ;reserved
rh20_res2       dd      ?       ;reserved
rh20            ends            ;

rh21            struc           ;(command 21)
rh21_len        db      ?       ;len of packet
rh21_unit       db      ?       ;unit code
                                ;(block devices only)
rh21_cmd        db      ?       ;device driver command
rh21_status     dw      ?       ;returned by device driver
rh21_res1       dd      ?       ;reserved
rh21_res2       dd      ?       ;reserved
rh21            ends            ;

rh22            struc           ;(command 22)
rh22_len        db      ?       ;len of packet
rh22_unit       db      ?       ;unit code
                                ;(block devices only)
rh22_cmd        db      ?       ;device driver command
rh22_status     dw      ?       ;returned by device driver
rh22_res1       dd      ?       ;reserved
rh22_res2       dd      ?       ;reserved
rh22            ends            ;
```

Listing 9–24: The Request Header for the Get Logical Device command

```
rh23            struc                   ;Get_Device (command 23)
rh23_rh         db      size rh dup (?) ;fixed portion
rh23_IO         db      ?               ;Input (unit code)
                                        ;Output (last device)
rh23_dev_cmd    db      ?               ;command code
rh23_dev_stat   dw      ?               ;status
rh23_reserved   dd      ?               ;reserved
rh23            ends                    ;
```

the device driver returns a 0 in *rh23_io*. Otherwise, the device driver returns the logical drive that was last referenced. The values contained in *rh23_io* are 1 for drive A:, 2 for drive B:, etc. Confusing as this sounds, this command is asking the device driver what other drive letter was used to access the same physical device unit.

Command 24—Set Logical Device   The Set Logical Device command is available for block devices running under DOS version 3.2 or greater that have the Device Header Attribute bit 6 set (Get/Set Logical Device supported). This command allows DOS 3.2 users to specify multiple drive letters for a logical drive. Listing 9–25 shows the *struc* for the Set Logical Device command. The steps required to process this command are listed below:

1. Retrieve the input unit code.

2. Save this unit code.

3. Set the Status word of the Request Header.

This command is processed by retrieving and saving the logical unit specified in the variable *rh23_io*. If the device driver does not recognize this drive letter as an alternate drive letter for the units controlled, a 0 is returned in *rh24_io*. The drive letters are numbered starting with 1, where 1 represents A:, 2 represents B:, etc.

Assigning alternate drive letters is accomplished through the use of the DRIVER.SYS device driver supplied with DOS version 3.2. Arguments on the DEVICE command for this device driver specify additional drive letters for the unit specified. Refer to the *DOS Technical Reference* manual for more information.

Listing 9–25: The Request Header for the Set Logical Device command

```
rh24            struc               ;Set_Device (command 24)
rh24_rh         db      size rh dup (?) ;fixed portion
rh24_IO         db      ?           ;Input (unit code)
                                    ;Output (last device)
rh24_dev_cmd    db      ?           ;command code
rh24_dev_stat   dw      ?           ;status
rh24_reserved   dd      ?           ;reserved
rh24            ends                ;
```

Programs make use of this feature by using the DOS IOCTL service call (44h) to get and set logical drives.

This concludes the description of the DOS command-processing sections.

Exiting from the Device Driver

When device drivers exit to DOS, the Status word in the Request Header must be set. There are four items about which you need to be concerned. The DONE bit is always set upon exit from the device driver. This indicates to DOS that the command was properly processed. Next, certain commands (Input Status, Output Status, Removable Media, and Output Til Busy) will set the BUSY bit. The ERROR bit is set if the device driver determines that an error has occurred; in addition, the ERROR_CODE field must contain a code indicating the error. Table 9–11 lists the appropriate error codes for use by the device driver.

The code that executes when exiting from a device driver sets the Request Header Status word and restores the registers that were saved on entry. Listing 9–26 illustrates the code necessary to exit the device driver properly.

Hex Code	Description of ERROR_CODE
0	Write protect violation
1	Unknown unit
2	Drive not ready
3	Unknown command
4	CRC error
5	Bad drive request structure length
6	Seek error
7	Unknown media
8	Sector not found
9	Printer out of paper
A	Write fault
B	Read fault
C	General failure
D	Reserved (DOS 3 +)
E	Reserved (DOS 3 +)
F	Invalid disk change (DOS 3 +)

Table 9–11: The standard error codes for DOS device drivers. Note that error codes 0Dh through 0Fh are valid only for DOS versions 3.0 or greater.

Listing 9–26: The code for exiting the device driver

```
;***************************************************************
;*      ERROR EXIT                                            *
;***************************************************************

unknown:
        or      es:[bx].rh_status,8003h ;set error bit and error code
        jmp     done                    ;set done and exit

;***************************************************************
;*      COMMON EXIT                                           *
;***************************************************************

busy:   or      es:[bx].rh_status,0200h ;set busy bit

done:   or      es:[bx].rh_status,0100h ;set done

        pop     si                      ;restore all registers
        pop     di
        pop     dx
        pop     cx
        pop     bx
        pop     ax
        pop     es
        pop     ds
        ret                             ;return to DOS
```

The Status Word for Unimplemented Commands

When you write device drivers for new devices, you may often be puzzled by what bits in the Request Header Status word to set. We have found that there is no easy formula. Based on the experience of writing many device drivers, we have put together a table that shows bits that should be set for each command upon exit (see Table 9–12).

Summary

We have discussed at length what writing a device driver entails. The Device Header, the commands, and the Request Headers have all been discussed in great detail. With this information and the five working device drivers presented in previous chapters, you should be ready to write your own device driver.

Command	Status Word
Initialization	DONE
Media Check	DONE
Get BPB	DONE
IOCTL Input	DONE, ERROR, ERROR_CODE = 3
Input	DONE
Non-destructive Input	DONE, BUSY
Input Status	DONE
Input Flush	DONE
Output	DONE
Output With Verify	DONE
Output Status	DONE
Output Flush	DONE
IOCTL Output	DONE, ERROR, ERROR_CODE = 3
Device Open	DONE
Device Close	DONE
Removable Media	DONE, ERROR, ERROR_CODE = 3
Output Til Busy	DONE, ERROR, ERROR_CODE = 3
Generic IOCTL	DONE, ERROR, ERROR_CODE = 3
Get Logical Device	DONE, ERROR, ERROR_CODE = 3
Set Logical Device	DONE, ERROR, ERROR_CODE = 3

Table 9–12: The Request Header Status word for commands that are not implemented in device drivers

Questions

1. What is the Generic I/O Control command used for?

2. If an argument is passed in the *DEVICE* = command, is it necessary to process it in the driver?

3. In table 9–4, the Get/Set Logical Device Attribute bit (6) is set for *prn:/lptx:*. In table 9–5, the Get/Set Logical Device commands are applicable to block device drivers only. Isn't this a contradiction?

4. What is the purpose of the Output Til Busy command?

Answers may be found in appendix E.

Chapter 10

Tips and Techniques

- A Checklist for Writing Device Drivers
- The Art of Debugging Device Drivers
- Prototyping Device Drivers
- Where Is My Device Driver?
- Adding Debugging Routines
- A New Stack
- The Special Bit
- Machine Incompatibilities

I n this chapter, we will focus on the tips and techniques that make it easier to write device drivers. The ideas presented here are based on practical experience with device driver programs. We will look at coding notes, checklists, and procedures to use when implementing and debugging device drivers.

A Checklist for Writing Device Drivers

In the past chapters, we concentrated on what device drivers require in terms of code, but we neglected some of the practical aspects of writing programs— aspects that are equally applicable to device drivers. Now we will cover this background information in detail.

Table 10–1 is a checklist for writing device drivers. These are notes that you should keep foremost in your mind as you write the code for a device driver.

Item 1 on this checklist is often overlooked. For ease of testing, build a test disk to use when you are booting DOS with your device drivers. This isolates testing and does not affect the normal working environment. We have used several test disks, one for each version of DOS. This has proven beneficial, because it provides a verification that DOS does indeed behave identically across versions. Another benefit of using test disks is that you can take the test disk to another machine to try out the device driver.

Item 2 in Table 10–1 has to do with the differences between normal assembly language programs and device driver programs. Normal programs that work under DOS require the start of the program to be at location 100h; to accomplish this, you use an *org* statement specifying 100h as the start address. Device drivers cannot start at location 100h, so you must leave out this statement.

Item 3 is a reminder that device driver programs must be in .COM format. There are two formats for executable programs in DOS: .EXE and .COM files. The LINK program automatically produces files that are in .EXE format. You

1. Always use a test disk for testing device drivers.
2. Does the device driver start at location 0?
3. Is the device driver in .COM format?
4. Are the Request Header data structures correct?
5. Is the Device Header Link field set to −1?
6. Are the Device Header Attribute bits set correctly?
7. Is the main procedure a FAR procedure?
8. Are the ASSUME statements correct?
9. Do the variables have a CS segment override?
10. Are the ES and BX registers correct when you set the Status word?
11. Are local procedures saving the registers used?
12. Did you assume that a local register has been preserved after returning from a procedure or an interrupt routine?
13. Have you Popped all your Pushes?

Table 10–1: A checklist for writing device drivers

must convert the .EXE file to a .COM file using the EXE2BIN utility. DOS does not allow device drivers to be in .EXE format, because programs in .EXE format have relocation information for each of the defined segments that must be loaded into memory by COMMAND.COM. Because DOS has not loaded COMMAND.COM into memory at the time a device driver is being loaded, the device driver must be in memory-image .COM format.

Item 4 in this table is a check to ensure that the device driver processes the data that DOS sends properly. You can eliminate many of the possible errors in retrieving data if you use *strucs*. Chapter 9 defines the *strucs* for each command you need to process.

Item 5 makes sure that DOS can link to the next device driver after yours. You need to specify a −1 in both words of the Next Device field in the Device Header. DOS overrides these fields after loading the next device driver. If you do not set these fields to −1, DOS will assume that there is another device driver following. If there is no other device driver, a crash will occur.

Item 6 is often overlooked, particularly in modifying an existing device driver. A number of the bits are important in specifying the type of device you are installing into DOS. If you write a replacement for the con: device, you must set bits 0 and 1 of the Device Header Attribute word. Also, if you forget to set some bits, you may find that certain functions do not work. For example, if bit 14 (IOCTL supported) is not set, programs using the DOS I/O Control services (44h) will not work.

Item 7 is a reminder that the main procedure of the device driver must have the FAR operator specified. The 8088/8086 instruction set provides for a short return and a far return. The call to your device driver is a FAR call, and the device driver must exit with a FAR return. If you do not specify the FAR option, you will find all sorts of problems with your device driver, especially with the stack and the instruction pointer.

Items 8 and 9 can be really nasty if you forget what device drivers can assume. Normal programs reference data variables through the DS register, so you must set up an assembler segment directive to indicate this. Device drivers use only one segment, which is one of the requirements for .COM format files. The segment registers CS, DS, and ES all reference this one segment through the ASSUME directive, which you have seen in all of this book's device drivers. This directive instructs the assembler to generate address offsets relative to the one defined segment. Other segments are not allowed in device drivers.

There is another consideration when DOS passes control to device drivers. The device driver cannot assume that the DS and ES registers are properly set up to point to your data variables. The only register you can assume is correct is the CS register. Therefore, when the device driver references data variables in your device drivers, you must specify a CS segment override. The instruction would look like this:

```
mov     es, CS:rh_seg
```

Because we are all human and tend to forget even the most important items, there is a way around all of the segment overriding code, which incidentally, does require more memory. You can add code to the INTERRUPT routine to set up the DS segment register correctly. The code would look like this:

```
push     cs        ;save value of CS
pop      ds        ;make DS the same as CS
```

Item 10 deals with the only registers that you need at the end of the device driver command processing. Because the Request Header data is pointed to by the ES and BX registers, the device drivers have used these two registers to set the Status word. You need not use the ES and BX registers to do so. However, you do need to have the Request Header's segment and offset addresses available to set the Status word properly. The 8088/8086 instruction set requires the use of the ES register in string moves, such as the REP MOVSB instruction. If you use the ES register in this manner, you must restore it for setting the Status word when the device driver exits.

Note that once the INTERRUPT routine saves all the registers on the stack, you can use all the registers in your device driver. You do need to save them when you call procedures or when you use the ROM BIOS interrupts.

Item 11 is a reminder that local procedures you build for device drivers will use registers that should be preserved. The best way to catch these types of mistakes is to document the local procedure in terms of registers required, used, and returned. The local procedures should initially PUSH all registers that are used and should POP them when returning to the caller.

Item 12 is a corollary to item 11. Within your command-processing routines, you may often call local procedures or use ROM BIOS interrupts. In doing so, you may sometimes forget to save registers on the stack if the called procedure will destroy them. This is particularly true for BIOS interrupts. For example, the Video BIOS interrupt (10h) destroys the BP, SI, and DI registers. Therefore, if the device driver uses these registers, save them before you call the Video BIOS interrupt, and you will save a lot of grief.

Item 13 has trapped us many times. Watch out when you write local procedures. Start by defining the procedure using the PROC and ENDP assembler directives. Then write the code. When you use a register to perform a calculation, save it on the stack with a PUSH. Do not forget the POP at the end of the procedure, and do not forget to reverse the order if more than one item is pushed on the stack. Don't let this one get you!

The Art of Debugging Device Drivers

The best way to build a device driver is to implement the code for all the commands in a normal assembly language program. This is called *prototyping,* and details on this approach will be covered in the next section. This method allows you to test each command function before you incorporate it into a device driver.

There are many good reasons for prototyping the device driver in a normal program. The first is that you cannot use the DOS DEBUG to load the device driver into memory and trace through the code execution. As you may recall, device drivers are part of DOS and are loaded into memory before you can execute the DEBUG utility. Because you cannot load the DEBUG program into memory before the device driver, you cannot use DEBUG. Even after DOS loads the device driver into memory, DEBUG cannot be used, because it interferes with the device driver. DEBUG uses the same DOS resources that the device driver uses, thus destroying and invalidating those resources. Another point to mention here is that the DEBUG utility was not designed to debug device drivers. Debuggers for device drivers provide their own routines to access the keyboard and the screen to allow the device driver to use BIOS routines without interference.

There are third-party debuggers designed for use on device drivers. Such debuggers do not use DOS resources for console I/O; they provide their own resources. These programs are useful for tracing through command functions. For example, Data Base Decisions' Periscope product was used for debugging the Clock Device Driver in this book.

Another reason for prototyping is that you can implement each of the commands into a device driver once they have been debugged in a normal program. You can use the DEBUG utility in a normal program to ensure that the code for the command works as designed. This method allows you to build a device driver step by step, knowing that the device driver will work with the code previously added.

The major barrier is the Initialization command code. You do not have control over when this code executes. DOS will call the device driver with this command immediately after loading the device driver into memory. All of the other commands are triggered by program access of the device through DOS Read, Write, or I/O Control services, which you can control.

The Initialization command is used to set up the device driver for access by programs. You can display console messages, initialize the device, set up interrupt vectors, and add resident code from this command. If the Initialization command contains too much complicated code, it is better to perform the same function through an I/O Control sequence. For example, the screen time display from chapter 6's Clock Device Driver was a result of pointing the timer interrupt to a routine of our own. You can easily place this code in a I/O Control function instead of in the Initialization command.

Prototyping Device Drivers

Prototyping the device driver in a normal assembly language program provides many benefits. You can use the DOS DEBUG utility to debug the program as well as to build the device driver command by command.

All of the data structures from device drivers can be placed into this program. You can also include the data variables that store the Request Header and local variable storage.

Listing 10–1 shows the prototype that was used to build the Clock Device Driver for chapter 6.

Listing 10-1: The prototyping program for the Clock Device Driver

```
title    The CLock Device Driver Prototype
page     60,132
;program         proto.asm
;date            15 November 1986
;

code     segment                         ;define segment as code
         assume  cs:code, ds:code        ;COM file DS=CS
         org     100h                    ;COM file start

main     proc                    ;main procedure
start:                           ; start
loop:    call    select          ;prompt for selection

         cmp     al,'F'          ;find clock address?
         jne     lread           ;no
         call    find            ;find clock chip base address
         jmp     loop            ;

lread:   cmp     al,'R'          ;read?
         jne     ltime           ;no
         call    isetup          ;setup for INPUT
         call    read            ;INPUT — read chip
         jmp     loop            ;

ltime:   cmp     al,'T'          ;display time?
         jne     lwrite          ;no
         call    time            ;
         jmp     loop            ;

lwrite:  cmp     al,'W'          ;write?
         jne     exit            ;no
         call    osetup          ;setup for OUTPUT
         call    write           ;OUTPUT — DOS date to chip
         jmp     loop            ;

exit:    cmp     al,'E'          ;exit?
         jne     loop            ;no
         int     20h             ;exit back to DOS

;structures for the Device Driver

dosdate struc                    ;DOS DATE structure
dos_day dw      ?                ;days since 1/1/80
dos_min db      ?                ;minutes
dos_hr  db      ?                ;hours
dos_hun db      ?                ;hundredths of a second
```

Listing 10–1: *(cont.)*

```
dos_sec db      ?           ;seconds
dosdate ends                ;end of struc

;structures

rh          struc           ;request header
rh_len      db      ?       ;len of packet
rh_unit     db      ?       ;unit code
                            ;(block devices only)
rh_cmd      db      ?       ;device driver command
rh_status   dw      ?       ;returned by device driver
rh_res1     dd      ?       ;reserved
rh_res2     dd      ?       ;reserved
rh          ends            ;

rh0         struc           ;Initialization (command 0)
rh0_rh      db      size rh dup (?) ;fixed portion
rh0_nunits  db      ?       ;number of units
                            ;(block devices only)
rh0_brk_ofs dw      ?       ;offset address for break
rh0_brk_seg dw      ?       ;segment address for break
rh0_bpb_tbo dw      ?       ;offset address of pointer
                            ;to BPB array
rh0_bpb_tbs dw      ?       ;segment address of pointer
                            ;to BPB array
rh0_drv_ltr db      ?       ;first available drive
                            ;(DOS 3+) (block only)
rh0         ends            ;

rh4         struc           ;INPUT (command 4)
rh4_rh      db      size rh dup(?)  ;fixed portion
rh4_media   db      ?       ;media descriptor from DPB
rh4_buf_ofs dw      ?       ;offset address of
                            ;data transfer area
rh4_buf_seg dw      ?       ;segment address of
                            ;data transfer area
rh4_count   dw      ?       ;transfer count
                            ;(sectors for block)
                            ;(bytes for character)
rh4_start   dw      ?       ;start sector number
                            ;(block only)
rh4         ends            ;

rh8         struc           ;OUTPUT (command 8)
rh8_rh      db      size rh dup(?)  ;fixed portion
rh8_media   db      ?       ;media descriptor from DPB
rh8_buf_ofs dw      ?       ;offset address of
                            ;data transfer area
```

Listing 10–1: *(cont.)*

```
rh8_buf_seg    dw      ?       ;segment address of
                               ;data transfer area
rh8_count      dw      ?       ;transfer count
                               ;(sectors for block)
                               ;(bytes for character)
rh8_start      dw      ?       ;start sector number
                               ;(block only)
rh8            ends           ;

rh9            struc           ;OUTPUT_VERIFY (command 9)
rh9_rh         db      size rh dup(?)  ;fixed portion
rh9_media      db      ?       ;media descriptor from DPB
rh9_buf_ofs    dw      ?       ;offset address of
                               ;data transfer area
rh9_buf_seg    dw      ?       ;segment address of
                               ;data transfer area
rh9_count      dw      ?       ;transfer count
                               ;(sectors for block)
                               ;(bytes for character)
rh9_start      dw      ?       ;start sector number (block only)
rh9            ends           ;

;local storage

dosdays        dw      0       ;DOS date (days since 1/1/80)
clock_port     dw      340h    ;clock chip base address

table   label  byte
jan     db     31
feb     db     28
mar     db     31
apr     db     30
may     db     31
jun     db     30
jul     db     31
aug     db     31
sep     db     30
oct     db     31
nov     db     30
decm    db     31

;local procedures

hex2bcd proc   near    ;convert AL from Hex to BCD
;uses   ax,cx
        push   cx
        mov    cl,10   ;divide by 10
        mov    ah,0    ;setup for divide
        div    cl      ;get 10's digits
```

Listing 10–1: *(cont.)*

```
        mov     cl,4        ;shift count
        shl     al,cl       ;place 10's in left half
        or      al,ah       ;add back 1's
        pop     cx
        ret                 ;return to caller
hex2bcd endp

bcd2hex proc    near        ;convert AL from BCD to hex
;uses ax,cx
        push    cx
        mov     ah,0        ;setup for divide
        push    ax          ;save for 1's processing
        mov     cl,16       ;divide for left half of byte
        div     cl          ; to get 10's digits
        mov     ah,0        ;have 10's digits
        mov     cl,10       ;convert to base 10
        mul     cl          ; by multiplying by 10
        pop     cx          ;process 1's digits
        and     cl,0fh      ;keep 1's only
        add     al,cl       ;add 1's to 10's
        pop     cx
        ret                 ;return to caller
bcd2hex endp

;chip parameters
;       base address for the clock chip is hardware selcted
;       each port referenced to this base address contains
;       either a chip-maintained counter or a RAM location
;       for use by a program.
;
;base port address                     base port address
;
;+0     1/10,000ths counter     +c     not used - RAM
;+1     1/100 +1/10 counter     +d     not used - RAM
;+2     seconds     counter     +e     not used - RAM
;+3     minutes     counter     +f     not used - RAM
;+4     hours       counter     +10    interrupt status register
;+5     day of week counter     +11    interrupt control register
;+6     day of monthcounter     +12    counter reset
;+7     month       counter     +13    ram reset
;+8     not used        RAM     +14    status bit
;+9     not used        RAM     +15    GO command
;+a     not used        RAM     +16    standby interrupt
;+b     not used        RAM     +1f    test mode

;data declarations for the prototype program

input_data      label   byte
        db      16h         ;length of request header
```

Listing 10–1: *(cont.)*

```
          db      0           ;units
          db      4           ;command = input
          dw      ?           ;status
          dd      ?           ;reserved
          dd      ?           ;reserved
          db      ?           ;media descriptor
          dw      clkdata     ;offset address of data transfer area
inseg     dw      ?           ;segment address of same
          dw      6           ;6 bytes in DOS date format
          dw      ?           ;start sector

output_data     label   byte
          db      16h         ;length of request header
          db      0           ;units
          db      8           ;command = input
          dw      ?           ;status
          dd      ?           ;reserved
          dd      ?           ;reserved
          db      ?           ;media descriptor
          dw      clkdata     ;offset address of data transfer area
outseg    dw      ?           ;segment address of same
          dw      6           ;6 bytes in DOS date format
          dw      ?           ;start sector

clkdata   db      6           dup(?)

rh_ofs    dw      ?           ;request header offset address
rh_seg    dw      ?           ;request header segment address

pmsg1     db      '[F]indAddress,[R]ead,[T]imeDisplay,',
          db      '[W]rite,[E]xit : ',
pmsg1a    db      0dh,0ah,'$'
pmsg2     db      'no chip found!',0dh,0ah,'$'
pmsg3     db      'Clock chip found at address ',
pmsg3a    db      '0000h!',0dh,0ah,'$'
pmsg4     db      'Chip Time is ',
pmsg4m    db      '00/',
pmsg4d    db      '00/',
pmsg4y    db      '0000 ',
pmsg4h    db      '00:',
pmsg4mn   db      '00:',
pmsg4s    db      '00',0dh,0ah,'$'

select    proc    near        ;prompt and select function
          lea     dx,pmsg1        ;address of display string
          call    Dos9            ;display
          mov     ah,1            ;keyboard input
          int     21h             ;DOS call
          push    ax              ;save for return
```

Listing 10–1: *(cont.)*

```
        lea     dx,pmsgla           ;CR/LF
        call    dos9                ;display
        pop     ax                  ;restore input character
        ret                         ;return to caller
select  endp                ;

isetup  proc    near        ;set up ESBX for prototype use
        mov     ax,cs                   ;get code segment address
        mov     cs:rh_seg,ax            ;save it
        mov     cs:inseg,ax             ;set segment address
        mov     es,ax                   ;setup ES
        lea     bx,cs:input_data        ;get offset address
        mov     cs:rh_ofs,bx            ;save it
        ret                             ;return to caller
isetup  endp

osetup  proc    near        ;set up ESBX for prototype use
        mov     ax,cs                   ;get code segment address
        mov     cs:rh_seg,ax            ;save it
        mov     cs:outseg,ax            ;set segment address
        mov     es,ax                   ;setup ES
        lea     bx,cs:output_data       ;get offset address
        mov     cs:rh_ofs,bx            ;save it
        ret                             ;return to caller
osetup  endp

clock_table     label   byte    ;table of possible clock addresses
        dw      0240h               ;first address
        dw      02c0h               ;second address
        dw      0340h               ;third address

find    proc    near        ;find clock chip base address
        lea     si,cs:clock_table       ;get address of table
        mov     cx,3                    ;three addressess
find1:  mov     dx,cs:[si]              ;get 1st address
        add     dx,2                    ;base+2 = seconds
        in      al,dx                   ;get seconds
        test    al,80h                  ;high order bit set?
        jz      find2                   ;no - not empty port
        add     si,2                    ;next address
        loop    find1                   ;search thru clock table
;no port found
        lea     dx,pmsg2                ;no port found
        call    dos9                    ;DOS call
        jmp     find3                   ;exit
;cx     3       2       1
;port   1st     2nd     3rd
find2:  mov     dx,3                    ;convert back to port #
        sub     dx,cx                   ;port position
```

Listing 10-1: *(cont.)*

```
          shl     dx,1                  ;double it
          lea     di,cs:clock_table     ;address of chip table
          add     di,dx                 ;word index
          mov     dx,cs:[di]            ;get port
          lea     di,cs:pmsg3a          ;string address
          call    hex2asc               ;convert to ASCII
          lea     dx,pmsg3              ;string to display
          call    dos9                  ;console display
find3:    ret           \               ;return to caller
find      endp                          ;

hex2dec proc    near      ;convert hex to decimal ASCII
;                         AX - input
;                         DI - destination string
;                         CX - number of places
          push    ax                    ;save ax
          push    cx                    ;save cx
          push    dx                    ;save dx
          cmp     cx,2                  ;2 or 4 place conversion
          je      d10                   ;2!
          mov     cx,1000               ;four places
          mov     dx,0                  ;clear hi order
          div     cx                    ;q=ax, rem=dx
          add     al,30h                ;make it ASCII
          mov     cs:[di],al            ;store it
          inc     di                    ;next
          mov     ax,dx                 ;remainder back in ax
          mov     cx,100                ;three places
          mov     dx,0                  ;clear hi order
          div     cx                    ;q=ax, rem=dx
          add     al,30h                ;make it ASCII
          mov     cs:[di],al            ;store it
          inc     di                    ;next
          mov     ax,dx                 ;remainder back in ax
d10:      mov     cx,10                 ;two places
          mov     dx,0                  ;clear hi order
          div     cx                    ;q=ax, rem=dx
          add     al,30h                ;make it ASCII
          mov     cs:[di],al            ;store it
          inc     di                    ;next
          mov     ax,dx                 ;remainder back in ax
          add     al,30h                ;make it ASCII
          mov     cs:[di],al            ;store it
          inc     di                    ;next
          pop     dx                    ;
          pop     cx                    ;
          pop     ax                    ;
          ret
hex2dec endp
```

Listing 10–1: *(cont.)*

```
time    proc    near                    ;display clock chip contents

        mov     dx,cs:clock_port        ;get chip base address
        add     dx,2                    ;base+2 (seconds)
        in      al,dx                   ;get it
        call    bcd2hex                 ;convert to hex
        mov     ah,0                    ;clear hi order
        mov     cx,2                    ;2 places
        lea     di,cs:pmsg4s            ;
        call    hex2dec                 ;convert to decimal ASCII
        inc     dx                      ;base+3 (minutes)
        in      al,dx                   ;get it
        call    bcd2hex                 ;
        mov     ah,0                    ;clear hi-order
        lea     di,cs:pmsg4mn           ;
        call    hex2dec
        inc     dx                      ;base+4 (hours)
        in      al,dx                   ;get it
        call    bcd2hex                 ;
        mov     ah,0                    ;clear hi-order
        lea     di,cs:pmsg4h            ;
        call    hex2dec
        add     dx,2                    ;base+6 (day)
        in      al,dx                   ;get it
        call    bcd2hex                 ;
        mov     ah,0                    ;
        lea     di,cs:pmsg4d            ;
        call    hex2dec                 ;
        inc     dx                      ;base+7 (month)
        in      al,dx                   ;
        call    bcd2hex                 ;
        mov     ah,0                    ;
        lea     di,cs:pmsg4m            ;
        call    hex2dec                 ;
        add     dx,3                    ;base+10
        in      al,dx                   ;get year in hex
        mov     ah,0                    ;
        lea     di,cs:pmsg4y            ;
        add     ax,1980                 ;make it readable
        mov     cx,4                    ;
        call    hex2dec                 ;convert year
        lea     dx,pmsg4                ;
        call    dos9                    ;
        ret                             ;return to caller
time    endp            ;

write   proc    near
;This procedure takes the date in DOS date format and
;converts to clock chip format for writing to the clock chip
;
```

Listing 10–1: *(cont.)*

```
;es:bx points to the request header
; point to DOS date and let ES:BX point to beginning
        mov     si,es:[bx].rh8_buf_ofs   ;get data offset
        mov     ax,es:[bx].rh8_buf_seg   ;get data segment
        mov     ds,ax                    ;to DS for (DS:SI use)
        push    si                       ;save offset
        push    ds                       ;save segment
        push    cs                       ;
        pop     es                       ;ES points to here
        lea     di,cs:dosdays            ;destination address
        mov     cx,2                     ;move count = 2
        cld                              ;direction is forward
        rep     movsb                    ; from DOS to us
        push    cs                       ;restore DS
        pop     ds                       ; by using CS
;update clock chip with time from DOS date data
outchip:
        pop     es                       ;restore DOS date segment
        pop     bx                       ;restore DOS date offset
        mov     dx,cs:clock_port         ;get clock port
        inc     dx                       ;base+1
        mov     al,es:[bx].dos_hun       ;get hundredths
        call    hex2bcd                  ;convert for clock use
        out     dx,al                    ;send to clock chip
        inc     dx                       ;base+2
        mov     al,es:[bx].dos_sec       ;get seconds
        call    hex2bcd                  ;convert for clock use
        out     dx,al                    ;send to clock chip
        inc     dx                       ;base+3
        mov     al,es:[bx].dos_min       ;get minutes
        call    hex2bcd                  ;convert for clock use
        out     dx,al                    ;send to clock chip
        inc     dx                       ;base+4
        mov     al,es:[bx].dos_hr        ;get hours
        call    hex2bcd                  ;convert for clock use
        out     dx,al                    ;send to clock chip

;chip loaded with time - now calc chip date from DOS date
out_years:
        mov     ax,cs:dosdays            ;get days since 1/1/80
        cmp     ax,0                     ;date not set?
        je      out8                     ;skip everything
        mov     bx,0                     ;BX = year count
out1:   cmp     ax,365                   ;day count within a year?
        jle     out2                     ;yes
        sub     ax,365                   ;no - subtract 365
        inc     bx                       ;increment year count
        jmp     out1                     ;continue until w/i 1 yr
```

Listing 10–1: *(cont.)*

```
;BX has years since 1980 - now adjust for leap years
out2:    push    ax                  ;save leftover days
         mov     ax,bx               ;AX now has years
         mov     cl,4                ;divisor for leap years
         div     cl                  ;al=leaps, ah=remainder
         mov     cl,ah               ;remainder=0 is leap itself
         mov     ah,0                ;set up for subtract
         inc     ax                  ;add 1 to leap year count
         mov     dx,ax               ;DX has 1 day/leap yr passed
         pop     ax                  ;restore days remaining
         sub     ax,dx               ;subtract 1 day for each leap yr
         cmp     ax,0                ;are we negative?
         jg      out3                ;no - we are ok
         add     ax,365              ;add back 365 days
         dec     bx                  ;subtract 1 year
out3:    push    bx                  ;save year count
         cmp     cl,0                ;leap year if 0
         jne     out5                ;not a leap year
         cmp     ax,59               ;Feb 29?
         je      out4                ;yes - set and exit
         jg      out5                ;past Feb 29
         inc     ax                  ;before - reverse subtraction
         jmp     out5                ;
out4:    mov     cx,2                ;Feb
         mov     ax,29               ; 29
         jmp     out7                ;exit
;AX has days left in current year - now find month and day
out5:    mov     cx,1                ;month count
         lea     di,cs:table         ;days per month
         mov     bh,0                ;clear hi-order
out6:    mov     bl,es:[di]          ;get days in each month
         inc     di                  ;increment to next month
         cmp     ax,bx               ;less than last day?
         jle     out7                ;yes (in current month)
         sub     ax,bx               ;no subtract days in month
         inc     cx                  ;increment month count
         jmp     out6                ;continue until month found
;AX has days, CX has month - now get years since 1980
out7:    pop     bx                  ;restore year count
         jmp     out9                ;go load chip
;no date set (special case)
out8:    mov     bx,0                ;1980
         mov     cx,1                ;Jan
         mov     ax,1                ; 1st
;BX = years since 1980, CX = month, AX = days - now load clock chip
out9:    mov     dx,cs:clock_port    ;get chip base address
         add     dx,6                ;base+6
         push    cx                  ;Hex2bcd destroys cx
```

Listing 10-1: *(cont.)*

```
        call    hex2bcd              ;convert for chip use
        out     dx,al                ;set days counter
        inc     dx                   ;base+7
        pop     ax                   ;restore month count
        call    hex2bcd              ;convert for chip use
        out     dx,al                ;set months counter
        add     dx,2                 ;base+9
        out     dx,al                ;set months RAM
        inc     dx                   ;base+10
        xchg    al,bl                ;move years to al
        out     dx,al                ;set years since 1980 RAM
        ret                          ;back to caller

write   endp

read    proc    near    ;convert clock chip data to DOS format
;This procedure takes the clock chip date and time
;and converts to DOS date format
        mov     dx,es:[bx].rh4_buf_ofs  ;get dos date data area
        mov     ax,es:[bx].rh4_buf_seg  ;
        mov     es,ax                ;set up es
        mov     bx,dx                ;set up bx
;es:bx now points to the data area where DOS
;expects the DOS date format returned
        push    es                   ;save segment for later
        push    bx                   ;save offset for later
;first read the clock chip for time
        mov     dx,cs:clock_port     ;get the clock base address
        inc     dx                   ;base+1
        in      al,dx                ;get hundredths
        call    bcd2hex              ;convert data
        mov     es:[bx].dos_hun,al   ;store hundredths
        inc     dx                   ;base+2
        in      al,dx                ;get seconds
        call    bcd2hex              ;convert data
        mov     es:[bx].dos_sec,al   ;store seconds
        inc     dx                   ;base+3
        in      al,dx                ;get minutes
        call    bcd2hex              ;convert data
        mov     es:[bx].dos_min,al   ;store minutes
        inc     dx                   ;base+4
        in      al,dx                ;get hours
        call    bcd2hex              ;convert data
        mov     es:[bx].dos_hr,al    ;store hours
;now convert chip date (BCD format) to DOS date format (hex)

;first check to see if month (and therefore year) has changed
;by comparing the months COUNTER against the month RAM location
```

Listing 10–1: *(cont.)*

```
incheck:
        mov     dx,cs:clock_port         ;get base clock address
        add     dx,7                     ;base+7
        in      al,dx                    ;get chip's month counter
        call    bcd2hex                  ;convert to hex
        mov     bl,al                    ;save in bl
        add     dx,2                     ;base+9
        in      al,dx                    ;get RAM version of month
        call    bcd2hex                  ;convert to hex
        cmp     al,bl                    ;is RAM & counter same?
        jg      newyear                  ;last month > current ( 12>1 )
        jl      updatemonth              ;last month < current
        jmp     prev_days                ;same month
;December rolled over to January - update the Year count in RAM
newyear:
        inc     dx                       ;base+10
        in      al,dx                    ;get year (stored in RAM)
        inc     al                       ;add 1 year
        out     dx,al                    ;store in RAM year
        dec     dx                       ;make it base+9
;now update month in RAM
updatemonth:
        mov     al,bl                    ;set current month
        call    hex2bcd                  ;convert for clock chip
        out     dx,al                    ;update month RAM

;determine days in previous years
prev_days:
        inc     dx                       ;base+10 (RAM)
        in      al,dx                    ;get years since 1980
        mov     ah,0                     ;set up for multiply
        push    ax                       ;save for leap year processing
        mov     bx,365                   ;days per year
        mul     bx                       ;times years - AX has days
        xchg    bx,ax                    ;save days in BX
        mov     cl,4                     ;leap divisor
        pop     ax                       ;get year count again
        div     cl                       ;divide for leap years elapsed
        mov     cl,ah                    ;save leap year indicator
;BX has total days and cl has leap year indicator
        mov     ah,0                     ;set up for add
        add     bx,ax                    ;add leap days to total

;we have days since 1/1/80 for all previous years including
; the extra days in leap years past
;now figure out the days in the current year
;note:           1-31, 1-28
;                1 31 32 59 60
```

Listing 10–1: *(cont.)*

```
curr_days:
        push    bx                          ;save total days past
        mov     dx,cs:clock_port            ;get base clock chip address
        add     dx,7                        ;base+7
        in      al,dx                       ;get month counter
        call    bcd2hex                     ;convert to hex
        mov     ah,0                        ;set up for index
        push    cs                          ;days per month table
        pop     es                          ;  addressed by ES
        lea     di,cs:table                 ;  and DI
        mov     cx,0                        ;clear current year day count
        xchg    ax,cx                       ;month loop count in cx
        push    cx                          ;save for leap year check
        mov     bh,0                        ;clear hi-order
cvt2days:
        mov     bl,es:[di]                  ;days in this month
        inc     di                          ;increment for next month
        add     ax,bx                       ;add to total days
        loop    cvt2days                    ;until month count exhausted
        pop     cx                          ;restore months
        pop     bx                          ;total days past
        add     ax,bx                       ;add to dyas in current year
        cmp     cl,3                        ;past March?
        jl      leapyr                      ;no
        inc     ax                          ;yes - add 1 for 2/29
leapyr: pop     bx                          ;restore DOS date offset
        pop     es                          ;restore DOS date segment
        mov     es:[bx].dos_day,ax          ;return days since 1/1/80
        ret                                 ;return to caller
read    endp

dos9    proc    near
        mov     ah,9    ;display service
        int     21h     ;DOS Call
        ret             ;return to caller
dos9    endp

hex2asc proc

;requires:
;               dx = binary number
;               di = address of ASCII string
;uses:
;               ax - for character conversion
;               cx - loop control
;returns:
;               nothing
```

Listing 10–1: *(cont.)*

```
          push    cx          ;save cx
          push    ax          ;save ax
          mov     cx,4        ;number of hex digits
h1:       push    cx          ;save cx inside this loop
          mov     cl,4        ;shift count (bits/hex digit)
          rol     dx,cl       ;rotate left 1 hex digit
          mov     al,dl       ;move hex digit to al
          and     al,0fh      ;mask off desired hex digit
          cmp     al,0ah      ;is it above 9h?
          jge     h2          ;yes
          add     al,30h      ;numeric hex digit
          jmp     h3          ;skip
h2:       add     al,37h      ;alpha hex digit
h3:       mov     cs:[di],al        ;store hex digit in string
          inc     di          ;next string address
          pop     cx          ;get saved loop count
          loop    h1          ;loop start
          pop     ax          ;restore ax
          pop     cx          ;restore cx
          ret                 ;return to caller
hex2asc   endp

main      endp                      ;end of main procedure
code      ends                      ;end of code segment
          end     start             ;
```

Where Is My Device Driver?

Another method of debugging device drivers is to store values as they change within the device driver. This method is very tedious, for the device driver must be modified to contain a lot of data variables. Any change to critical values is stored into these variables. You can use the DEBUG utility to get into the device driver to inspect these variables. Although you cannot change the execution sequence or set a breakpoint at certain instructions, you can see whether the variables have correct values.

To find where in memory your device driver is loaded, you will have to display the address of the device driver during the Initialization command. You can do so with the code shown in listing 10–2. This code displays the segment address of the device driver using a DOS service call to display a message on the console. In addition, use the procedure HEX2ASC to convert a hex segment address to an ASCII string. This procedure is shown in listing 10–3.

Listing 10–2: The code placed in the Initialization command to display the address at which the device driver is loaded. Use the address displayed with the DEBUG program to inspect the variables you have set up in a device driver.

```
;
;display the segment address of the device driver
;
        push    cs                  ;save the segment address
        pop     dx                  ; in dx
        lea     di,pmsgla           ;address of ASCII string
        call    hex2asc             ;convert DX to ASCII string
        mov     ah,9                ;service = console display
        lea     dx,pmsgl            ;string to be displayed
        int     21h                 ;DOS service call

pmsgl   db      'Device driver loaded at '
pmsgla  db      '0000:0000h',0Dh,0Ah,'$'
```

Adding Debugging Routines

You may be curious about the interactions between DOS and the device driver: what commands are being passed, what the Request Headers contain, etc. Would you like the ability to have the device driver display this and other information? You want a routine to perform some of the display functions of a debugger.

The problem with this type of facility is that you must devise a means of displaying the information. You cannot use DOS calls in a device driver, nor can you call upon the services of a device driver. If you are writing a device driver for an output device, you could use the device driver itself, but this gets complicated quickly: it is difficult to use a device to output information as it is outputting data using same the device!

The solution to this problem comes with the realization that the PC's ROM BIOS contains routines to output to several devices. Recall that the ROM BIOS contains interrupt procedures for the console display (con:), the printer (prn: and lptx:), and the communications ports (comx:). These interrupts are always available for your use, so why not take advantage of them in displaying device driver information? This also solves the problem of building a display routine that will work with most device drivers you may be writing.

We have built a dump routine that displays the Request Header information to the printer. The display device used is the printer connected to the first parallel port. We chose to use the printer because using the console display would

---

Listing 10–3: The HEX2ASC procedure, which converts a hex number into ASCII

```
hex2asc proc

;requires:
;                       dx = binary number
;                       di = address of ASCII string
;uses:
;                       ax - for character conversion
;                       cx - loop control
;returns:
;                       nothing

        push    cx      ;save cx
        push    ax      ;save ax
        mov     cx,4    ;number of hex digits
h1:     push    cx      ;save cx inside this loop
        mov     cl,4    ;shift count (bits/hex digit)
        rol     dx,cl   ;rotate left 1 hex digit
        mov     al,dl   ;move hex digit to al
        and     al,0fh  ;mask off desired hex digit
        cmp     al,0ah  ;is it above 9h?
        jge     h2      ;yes
        add     al,30h  ;numeric hex digit
        jmp     h3      ;skip
h2:     add     al,37h  ;alpha hex digit
h3:     mov     cs:[di],al      ;store hex digit in string
        inc     di      ;next string address
        pop     cx      ;get saved loop count
        loop    h1      ;loop start
        pop     ax      ;restore ax
        pop     cx      ;restore cx
        ret             ;return to caller
hex2asc endp
```

---

have meant that there would not be a hard copy, and rewriting the information was not a good use of time. Using the communications ports would have meant that the printer connected to the serial port would have to be initialized to the correct baud rates, parity, and stop bits before use. In the final analysis, the parallel printer seemed the best choice.

The procedures shown in listing 10–4 dump the Request Header information for each command. A call to the *dump* procedure may be placed anywhere in the device driver. If placed in the INTERRUPT procedure, it should be after the registers are saved on the stack. This allows all the commands that enter

---

Listing 10–4: The *dump* procedure used to display device driver command information to the parallel printer. The *dump* procedure uses the HEX2ASC routine to convert hex numbers to ASCII. The *prtmsg* procedure is used to print messages to the printer using the BIOS printer interrupt (17h).

```
dump      proc                    ;dumps device driver information
                                  ;to lptl via int 17h BIOS routine

;requires:
;                   nothing (user must preserve required registers)
;uses:
;
;returns:
;                   nothing


;get command descriptor

          mov       ax,cs:rh_seg      ;get the ES register
          mov       es,ax             ;
          mov       bx,cs:rh_ofs      ;get the BX register
          mov       al,es:[BX]+2      ;get command code
          mov       ah,0              ;clear high-order of AX
          rol       al,1              ;left shift 1 to multiply by 2
          lea       di,cmtab          ;get address of command msg table
          add       di,ax             ;index to address of command msg
          mov       ax,[di]           ;get address
          call      prtmsg            ;print command message

;display the request header

          mov       dl,es:[bx]        ;LEN of request header
          mov       dh,0              ;clear high-order DX
          lea       di,cs:crhl        ;address of display message
          call      hex2asc           ;convert to ASCII
          mov       dl,es:[bx]+1      ;UNIT of request header
          mov       dh,0              ;clear high-order DX
          lea       di,cs:crh2        ;address of display message
          call      hex2asc           ;convert to ASCII
          mov       dl,es:[bx]+2      ;CMD of request header
          mov       dh,0              ;clear high-order DX
          lea       di,cs:crh3        ;address of display message
          call      hex2asc           ;convert to ASCII
          mov       dx,es:word ptr [bx]+3   ;STATUS of request header
          lea       di,cs:crh4        ;address of display message
          call      hex2asc           ;convert to ASCII
          lea       ax,cs:crh         ;print the request header
          call      prtmsg            ;
```

Listing 10–4: *(cont.)*

```
;display request header unique to each command

        mov     al,es:[BX]+2      ;get command code
d0:     cmp     al,0              ;initialization?
        jne     dl                ;no

dl:     cmp     al,1              ;media_check?
        jne     d2                ;no
        mov     dl,es:[bx]+14     ;media status
        mov     dh,0              ;clear hi-order DX
        lea     di,cs:cpla        ;
        call    hex2asc           ;
        lea     ax,cs:cpl         ;
        call    prtmsg            ;
        jmp     dexit             ;
d2:     cmp     al,2              ;get_bpb?
        jne     d3                ;no

d3:     cmp     al,3              ;ioctl_input?
        jne     d4                ;no

d4:     cmp     al,4              ;input?
        jne     d5                ;no
        mov     dx,es:word ptr [bx]+18   ;count
        lea     di,cs:cp4a        ;
        call    hex2asc           ;
        mov     dx,es:word ptr [bx]+20   ;start sector
        lea     di,cs:cp4b        ;
        call    hex2asc           ;
        lea     ax,cs:cp4         ;
        call    prtmsg            ;
        jmp     dexit             ;
d5:     cmp     al,5              ;nd_input?
        jne     d6                ;no

d6:     cmp     al,6              ;input_status?
        jne     d7                ;no

d7:     cmp     al,7              ;input_flush?
        jne     d8                ;no

d8:     cmp     al,8              ;output?
        jne     d9                ;no
        mov     dx,es:word ptr [bx]+18   ;count
        lea     di,cs:cp4a        ;
        call    hex2asc           ;
        mov     dx,es:word ptr [bx]+20   ;start sector
        lea     di,cs:cp4b        ;
```

Listing 10-4: *(cont.)*

```
            call    hex2asc             ;
            lea     ax,cs:cp4           ;
            call    prtmsg              ;
            jmp     dexit               ;
d9:         cmp     al,9                ;output_verify?
            jne     da                  ;no
            mov     dx,es:word ptr [bx]+18    ;count
            lea     di,cs:cp4a                ;
            call    hex2asc             ;
            mov     dx,es:word ptr [bx]+20    ;start sector
            lea     di,cs:cp4b          ;
            call    hex2asc             ;
            lea     ax,cs:cp4           ;
            call    prtmsg              ;
            jmp     dexit               ;
da:         cmp     al,0ah              ;output_status?
            jne     dbb                 ;no

dbb:        cmp     al,0bh              ;output_flush?
            jne     dc                  ;no

dc:         cmp     al,0ch              ;ioctl_out?
            jne     ddd                 ;no

ddd:        cmp     al,0dh              ;open?
            jne     de                  ;no

de:         cmp     al,0eh              ;close?
            jne     df                  ;no

df:         cmp     al,0fh              ;removable?
            jne     d10                 ;no

d10:        cmp     al,10h              ;output_busy?
            jne     dexit               ;no

dexit:      ret
dump        endp

crh         db      ' len '
crh1        db      '0000',0dh,0ah
            db      ' unit '
crh2        db      '0000',0dh,0ah
            db      ' cmd '
crh3        db      '0000',0dh,0ah
            db      ' status '
crh4        db      '0000',0dh,0ah,'$'

cp1         db      ' media status '        ;command 1
cp1a        db      '0000',0dh,0ah,'$'
```

Listing 10–4: *(cont.)*

```
cp4     db      ' count '                       ;commands 4,8,9
cp4a    db      '0000',0dh,0ah
        db      ' start '
cp4b    db      '0000',0dh,0ah,'$'

cm0     db      'initialization',0dh,0ah,'$'
cml     db      'media_check  ',0dh,0ah,'$'
cm2     db      'get_bpb      ',0dh,0ah,'$'
cm3     db      'ioctl_in     ',0dh,0ah,'$'
cm4     db      'input        ',0dh,0ah,'$'
cm5     db      'nd_input     ',0dh,0ah,'$'
cm6     db      'input_status ',0dh,0ah,'$'
cm7     db      'input_flush  ',0dh,0ah,'$'
cm8     db      'output       ',0dh,0ah,'$'
cm9     db      'output_verify ',0dh,0ah,'$'
cma     db      'output_status ',0dh,0ah,'$'
cmb     db      'output_flush  ',0dh,0ah,'$'
cmc     db      'ioctl_out    ',0dh,0ah,'$'
cmd     db      'open         ',0dh,0ah,'$'
cme     db      'close        ',0dh,0ah,'$'
cmf     db      'removable    ',0dh,0ah,'$'
cm10    db      'output_busy  ',0dh,0ah,'$'

cmtab   label   word
        dw      cm0
        dw      cml
        dw      cm2
        dw      cm3
        dw      cm4
        dw      cm5
        dw      cm6
        dw      cm7
        dw      cm8
        dw      cm9
        dw      cma
        dw      cmb
        dw      cmc
        dw      cmd
        dw      cme
        dw      cmf
        dw      cm10

hex2asc proc

;requires:
;               dx = binary number
;               di = address of ASCII string
;uses:
;               ax - for character conversion
;               cx - loop control
```

Listing 10–4: *(cont.)*

```
;returns:
;                nothing

        push     cx        ;save cx
        push     ax        ;save ax
        mov      cx,4      ;number of hex digits
h1:     push     cx        ;save cx inside this loop
        mov      cl,4      ;shift count (bits/hex digit)
        rol      dx,cl     ;rotate left 1 hex digit
        mov      al,dl     ;move hex digit to al
        and      al,0fh    ;mask off desired hex digit
        cmp      al,0ah    ;is it above 9h?
        jge      h2        ;yes
        add      al,30h    ;numeric hex digit
        jmp      h3        ;skip
h2:     add      al,37h    ;alpha hex digit
h3:     mov      cs:[di],al       ;store hex digit in string
        inc      di        ;next string address
        pop      cx        ;get saved loop count
        loop     h1        ;loop start
        pop      ax        ;restore ax
        pop      cx        ;restore cx
        ret                ;return to caller
hex2asc endp

prtmsg  proc

;requires:
;                ax = address of string to be printed
;uses:
;                dx - printer number (0 = lptl:)
;                si - source string address
;returns:
;                nothing

        push     dx                ;save dx
        push     si                ;save si
        mov      dx,0              ;printer 0
        mov      si,ax             ;use si as pointer
prtl:   mov      ah,0              ;print a character
        mov      al,[si]           ;get a character
        cmp      al,'$'            ;end of string?
        je       prt2              ;yes - exit
        int      17h               ;print BIOS call
        inc      si                ;next
        jmp      prtl              ;loop back
prt2:   pop      si                ;restore si
        pop      dx                ;restore dx
        ret                        ;return to caller
prtmsg  endp
```

---

the device driver to be displayed on the printer. If the call to *dump* is placed in the command-processing sections, only the Request Header for that command will be displayed on the printer. Note that there are three requirements for using this *dump* procedure. First, a parallel printer is required. Second, the *dump* procedure does not save any registers on the stack. Any registers that need to be preserved after a call to *dump* must be added to the device driver. Lastly, the *dump* procedure does not check for any errors resulting from the use of the BIOS printer interrupt (17h). This means that the printer should have paper in the unit and should be on-line.

As a final note, the *dump* procedure may be modified to display any information you want.

A New Stack

The stack that is normally used within device drivers is limited to about 20 PUSHES. This may not be enough if the device drivers you write contain a lot of nested procedure calls. The use of the stack is important for two reasons: first, to preserve the registers upon entry to the device driver, and second, to allow you to call other procedures from within the device driver. Both of these reasons may cause your device drivers to run out of stack space, in which case you will need a larger stack.

Defining a new stack is easy. First, save the Stack Segment register SS and the Stack Pointer SP in variables defined in the device driver. Then set the Stack Segment and Pointer to a stack within the device driver. You can define an array of bytes to accomplish this.

Define this new stack on entry to your device driver by placing a call to *switch2new* just after saving the registers on the old stack in the INTERRUPT routine. Then, when the device driver is about to exit, restore the old stack. A call to *switch2old* is placed after setting the DONE bit of the Request Header Status word in the Common Exit section and before restoring the registers from the old stack. Listing 10–5 shows the two procedures *switch2new* and *switch2old*.

In listing 10–5 you will see that interrupts are disabled when you switch stacks. This prevents an interrupt from interfering with your stack-changing operation. The new stack is 256 bytes in length, but this can be smaller depending on the device driver requirements.

The Special Bit

The Special bit (4) of the Device Header Attribute word is indeed special. This bit signifies that the console device driver provides a fast way to output char-

---

Listing 10–5: The two procedures that allow a device driver to switch from the DOS stack to one of its own. The *switch2new* procedure switches from the DOS stack to a new one, and the *switch2old* procedure switches the stack back to the DOS stack.

```
;
;Define save area for old stack and new stack
;
stack_ptr        dw      ?          ;old stack pointer
stack_seg        dw      ?          ;old stack segment

newstack         db 100h dup (?) ;256 bytes for new stack
newstacktop      equ     $-2        ;top of new stack


;
;switch to new stack
;
switch2new       proc    near             ;switch to new stack
                 cli                       ;turn interrupts off
                 mov     cs:stack_ptr,sp  ;save old SP
                 mov     cs:stack_seg,ss  ;save old SS
                 mov     ax,cs            ;get current segment
                 mov     ss,ax            ;set stack segment
                 mov     sp,newstacktop   ;set stack pointer
                 sti                      ;re-enable interrupts
                 ret                      ;return to caller
switch2new       endp                     ;


;
;switch back to old stack
;
switch2old       proc    near             ;switch back to old stack
                 cli                       ;turn interrupts off
                 mov     ss,cs:stack_seg  ;restore old SS
                 mov     sp,cs:stack_ptr  ;restore old SP
                 sti                      ;re-enable interrupts
                 ret                      ;return to caller
switch2old       endp                     ;
```

---

acters. There is little information on the use of this bit—in fact, it has been noted that the use of this feature will not be supported in future versions of DOS.

This bit is significant only for console device drivers. If it is set, the device driver must set up interrupt 29h to point to a routine to output characters quickly. Normally, DOS inspects each character input from the keyboard for a CON-

TROL-C (this is often called *cooked mode;* when fast console output is desired, the character stream is not checked, which is known as *raw mode*). Programs use this raw-mode output by calling the DOS I/O Control service (44h) with bit 5 of the DX register set.

Because the device driver is responsible for setting up interrupt 29h, it is clear that there should only be one such Special bit set in any device driver.

Listing 10–6 shows the code for implementing interrupt 29h. This is necessary only if the Special bit (4) is set in the Device Header Attribute word. The code to initialize the 29h interrupt is added to the Initialization command.

Machine Incompatibilities

Most PCs available today are IBM PCs or compatibles. What this means is that the ROM BIOS routines work in a standard way. The device drivers presented in this book will work on this class of machines.

However, you may have an older machine that is not compatible with the IBM PC. These machines have ROM-based BIOS routines that are different from

---

Listing 10–6: The code for interrupt 29h. The code initializing the interrupt 29h is added to the Initialization command.

```
;
;code to perform fast console I/O
;
int29h: sti                 ;re-enable interrupts
        push    ax          ;save ax
        push    bx          ;save bx
        mov     bl,07h      ;white on black attribute
        mov     ah,0Eh      ;Write character as TTY
        int     10h         ;Video BIOS interrupt
        pop     bx          ;restore bx
        pop     ax          ;restore ax
        iret                ;interrupt return


;
;initialize the interrupt vector for 29h
;points to the routine labelled int29h
;
set29h: mov     bx,0A4h     ;address of int 29h
        lea     ax,int29h   ;offset address (int29h)
        mov     [bx],ax     ;set int 29h offset
        mov     [bx+2],cs   ;set int 29h segment
```

---

those found in IBM-PC compatibles. In general, these machines have the same ROM-based routines, but the interrupts are numbered differently.

For the device drivers presented in this book to work properly on these machines, the BIOS interrupts have to be changed. This is a matter of getting a copy of the *Technical Reference* manual for your particular machine and finding the BIOS interrupts that are equivalent to those that were used in this book.

DOS Differences

There is little difference between PC-DOS and MS-DOS. Provided that there are no BIOS differences, the device drivers written for one will work on the other. Device drivers written for one version of MS-DOS or PC-DOS will work on a higher-numbered version. This confirms the universality of DOS for device drivers.

DOS Version Differences

Writing device drivers that work across a range of DOS versions is an interesting topic to which we could devote another dozen chapters. In chapter 9, you saw that there are different numbers of commands for each version of DOS. If you write a device driver for one version, you can be reasonably sure that it will work in the next version of DOS.

But what about writing device drivers that work across all the versions? A trade-off is involved in doing so. We write device drivers to provide a standard interface between DOS and the device we are controlling. This allows our device to be used by any program, provided the device has been opened. Therein lies the problem: certain features from one version of DOS that are built into the device driver as part of our design may not work in another version. We should also consider building the device so that it works on all versions of DOS.

Making the device driver work under all versions of DOS is well worth the effort. To accomplish this, there are two considerations.

First, each version of DOS supports a different number of commands. Each DOS version since 2.0 has added device driver commands. You need to check that the device driver receives only the commands allowed under a particular version of DOS. This is shown in table 10–2. Listing 10–7 shows the procedure to be called from the Initialization command to check for the highest-numbered command allowed. Listing 10–8 shows the code for the INTERRUPT routine to check each command to ensure that it does not exceed the highest-numbered command allowed for the DOS version running.

DOS Version	Highest Command Number
2	12
3.0	16
3.20	24

Table 10–2: The highest command number for each version of DOS

Listing 10–7: This procedure, which is called from the Initialization command, checks for the highest-numbered command for the DOS version being used.

```
dosver  proc    near                    ;set command limit
;
;This procedure is called from the Initialization
;command processing code. The DOS version is retrieved
;and the maximum command number is set in variable
;cs:max_cmd. The INTERRUPT code uses the number contained
;in cs:max_cmd to determine if an invalid command number
;has been passed to the device driver.
;
        push    ax                      ;save ax
        push    cx                      ;save cx
        mov     ah,30h                  ;Get DOS version
        int     21h                     ;DOS service call
;DOS returns    major version (2,3) in al and
;               minor version (10,11,20) in ah
        cmp     al,2                    ;Version 2?
        jne     ver3                    ;no - assume three
        mov     cl,12                   ;13 commands for DOS 2
        jmp     ver4                    ;store it
ver3:   cmp     ah,20                   ;Version 3.20?
        je      ver320                  ;yes
        mov     cl,16                   ;17 commands for DOS 3, 3.1
        jmp     ver4                    ;store it
ver320: mov     cl,24                   ;25 commands for DOS 3.20
ver4:   mov     cs:max_cmd,cl           ;save command limit
        pop     cx                      ;restore cx
        pop     ax                      ;restore ax
        ret                             ;return to caller
dosver  endp                            ;end of dosver
```

Listing 10–8: The two lines that are added to the INTERRUPT procedure when command-checking is required are shown in bold face. The variable *cs:max_cmd* is set by the procedure *dosver*, which is called from the Initialization command.

```
;********************************************************************
;*        THE INTERRUPT PROCEDURE                                  *
;********************************************************************

;device interrupt handler - 2nd call from DOS

dev_interrupt:

        cld                         ;save machine state on entry
        push    ds
        push    es
        push    ax
        push    bx
        push    cx
        push    dx
        push    di
        push    si

        mov     ax,cs:rh_seg        ;restore ES as saved by STRATEGY call
        mov     es,ax               ;
        mov     bx,cs:rh_ofs        ;restore BX as saved by STRATEGY call

;jump to appropriate routine to process command

        mov     al,es:[bx].rh_cmd   ;get request header command
        cmp     al,cs:max_cmd       ;is command number too large?
        ja      unknown             ;yes - set error and exit
        rol     al,1                ;times 2 for index into word table
        lea     di,cmdtab           ;function (command) table address
        mov     ah,0                ;clear hi order
        add     di,ax               ;add the index to start of table
        jmp     word ptr[di]        ;jump indirect
```

We come now to the second consideration in making device drivers work on all versions of DOS. How do we notify DOS that our device driver is capable of handling the extra commands that are available with later versions of DOS?

We take an unorthodox approach. Recall that chapter 5's Printer Device Driver had two Device Headers: one for version 2.0 and one for version 3.0. The only difference was that the Attribute bit (13) for Output Til Busy was set for version 3.0. You can build a device driver with code for all the commands but leave the Device Header Attribute word set for version 2.0. Then, when your driver is running under version 3.0 or greater, set the appropriate Device Header

---

Listing 10–9: The procedure *setatt*, which sets the Device Header Attribute bits. This procedure will set certain Attribute bits if they are available for the particular version of DOS. This procedure is called from the Initialization command.

```
setatt  proc    near            ;set Attribute word
;
;This procedure is called from the Initialization
;command processing code. The Device Header Attribute
;bits are set depending on the DOS version. Bits which
;are version dependent:
;
;type    bit     Description             DOS
;
;char    13      Output Til Busy         3+
;both    11      Open/Close/Removable Media  3+
;block   6       Get/Set Logical Device  3.20
;block   0       Generic I/O Control     3.20
;
        push    ax              ;save ax
        push    cx              ;save cx
        mov     ah,30h          ;Get DOS version
        int     21h             ;DOS service call
;DOS returns     major version (2,3) in al and
;                minor version (10,11,20) in ah
        cmp     al,2            ;Version 2?
        je      att8            ;yes - exit with no bits set
        mov     cx,cs:attribute ;get Attribute word
        cmp     ah,20           ;version 3.20?
        jb      att3            ;less than 3.20
        test    cx,8000h        ;test for char device (bit 15)
        jnz     att3            ;yes - don't set 6 or 0
        or      cx,0040h        ;set bit 6 (Get/Set Logical Device)
        or      cx,0001h        ;set bit 0 (Generic I/O Control)
att3:   or      cx,0800h        ;set bit 11 (Open/Close/Removable)
        test    cx,8000h        ;test for char device (bit 15)
        jz      att4            ;no - don't set bit 13
        or      cx,2000h        ;set bit 13 (Output Til Busy)
att4:   mov     cs:attribute,cx ;save new Attribute word
att8:   pop     cx              ;restore cx
        pop     ax              ;restore ax
        ret                     ;return to caller
setatt  endp                    ;end of setatt
```

Attribute bits in the Initialization command to allow DOS to access the extra commands.

You can accomplish this with the procedure *setatt* shown in listing 10–9. This procedure will set the Device Header Attribute bits for the appropriate version of DOS. Note that those commands that are not applicable to a given device driver need not have the corresponding Attribute bits set; simply remove the OR instruction that sets the bit in the Device Header Attribute word.

Summary

In this book, we have covered much information on device drivers. We have presented what it takes to build a console, a printer, a clock, and a RAM Disk Device Driver. We have covered, in detail, all of the parts of a device driver. In this last chapter, we have discussed the practical aspects of building device drivers. You have seen how to build working device drivers, from simple ones to complex ones. Now you can go on to building custom device drivers of your own!

Questions

1. In listing 10–2, why is there only one call to *hex2asc* to convert the segment address? Shouldn't there be another call to convert the offset address?

2. If a device driver is not loaded by DOS, what should be done?

3. Is it necessary to implement the Special bit of the Device Header Attribute word in a console device driver?

4. If a device driver is loaded into memory but does not seem to work, what should be done?

Answers may be found in appendix E.

Appendix A

An Overview of the 8086/8088 Architecture

T

his appendix provides a "refresher course" on the architecture of Intel 8086/8088 systems. The following sections review the memory structure and segmentation techniques, the I/O structure, and the register structure of the 8086/8088 system. Reviewing the contents of this appendix will enable you to acquire a basic level of knowledge to aid you in better understanding the information presented in the main body of this book.

As an introduction, let's start by reviewing the basic characteristics of the 8086 and 8088 CPU chips.

The Intel 8086/8088 Microprocessor Chips

The Intel 8086 is a 16-bit microprocessor chip available in speeds of 8MHz, 10MHz, and 12MHz. The 8086 was the first successful microprocessor chip to include memory segmentation, a feature that provided freedom from the design limitations of earlier chips. Before the introduction of the 8086, 8-bit chips could address only 64 Kb via 8-bit addresses. The 8086 can address 1 Mb of data with only 16-bit addresses. This is accomplished by segmenting memory into separate 64Kb groups of data. Each 64Kb group is controlled by hardware and instructions integral to the 8086.

There are few differences between the 8086 and 8088 CPU chips. The primary distinction is in the external data bus, which is the mechanism used to transfer data between external devices and the CPU. The popular 8088 chip is an 8-bit bus version of the 8086. Its instruction set and basic architecture are identical to those of the 8086. Instead of the 16-bit external data bus found on the 8086, however, the 8088 has an 8-bit external data bus. This difference is not significant for consideration in this book. However, it should be noted that the 8088's 8-bit data bus makes it easier to interface the many 8-bit devices used on older 8-bit microprocessor systems.

CPU speed is another aspect in which the 8086 and 8088 differ. Typically, 8088-based systems run with a 4.77-MHz clock speed, much slower than the 8-MHz speed of the 8086. However, there are now versions of the 8088 that run at faster speeds, thereby reducing the distinction between the two chips.

The 8086/8088 Memory Structure

The 8086/8088 system manages memory in 8-bit quantities called *bytes*. Up to approximately 1 million bytes (1 Mb) can comprise memory, with each byte having its own unique *address*. The possible range of addresses for 1 Mb of data is expressed in hexadecimal form as the numbers 00000 to FFFFF. In binary form, these addresses are represented as 0000 0000 0000 0000 0000 to 1111 1111 1111 1111 1111.

Two consecutive bytes form one *word*. Each byte within a word has its own *byte address:* the smaller of the two byte addresses within a word is used as the *word address*. Figure A–1 illustrates how memory is viewed as a series of bytes, with pairs of bytes being viewed as words. Note that when the lower byte address is an even number, the word is said to start at an *even address*. If the lower address is an odd number, the word is said to start at an *odd address*. The important concept to understand here is that the 8086/8088 memory is always viewed as a series of 8-bit bytes. Even when it is necessary to access (and manipulate) the contents of memory in the 16-bit quantities called *words,* the CPU treats each word as two bytes.

Data Storage in 8086/8088 Memory

One important aspect of the memory structure of an 8086/8088 is the method of data storage in memory. We have defined a word as 16 bits. These bits are numbered from 0 (least-significant, or low-order, bit) to 15 (most-significant, or high-order, bit). Bits 0 through 7 are referred to as the *low-order* (least-significant) *byte*. Bits 8 through 15 are referred to as the *high-order* (most-significant) *byte*. Example 2 from figure A–1 illustrates how a 16-bit word in memory might be viewed.

As noted earlier, the address of the word is the lower of the two addresses of the bytes comprising the word. Therefore, the low-order byte has the lower memory address, and the high-order byte has the higher memory address.

This is an important concept to understand. The technique by which 16-bit quantities are stored in the byte-oriented 8086/8088 memory structure makes it appear that data is stored backwards in memory. To illustrate this point, let's take a look at some examples.

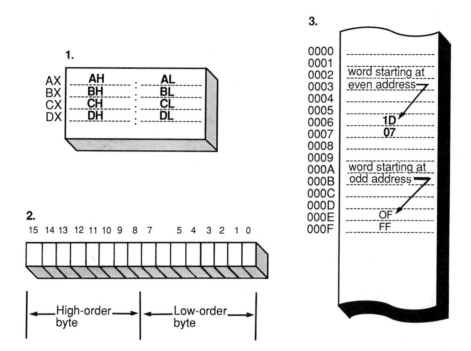

Figure A–1: The Intel 8086/8088 memory structure: a) the sixteen-bit general purpose registers; b) a single sixteen-bit memory register comprised of two eight-bit bytes; c) Intel memory showing a word 071Dh at address location 00006.

Looking first at numeric data, the numeric value 1,821 (decimal) is represented as the hexadecimal value 071Dh (the *h* indicates *hexadecimal*). If the value 071Dh is stored in the word beginning at address 00006, byte 00006 would contain the value 1Dh, and byte 00007 would contain the value 07h. Figure A–1 illustrates how the value 071Dh would be stored (example 3).

Paragraphs

Another important aspect of the 8086/8088 memory structure is that of *paragraphs*. A paragraph is defined to have 16 bytes. The *paragraph address* is the address of the lowest byte contained in the paragraph. It follows that one million bytes (1 Mb) of memory can also be viewed as illustrated by table A–1.

Paragraph address (in hex)	Bytes in paragraph (in hex)
00000	00000 – 0000F
00010	00010 – 0001F
00020	00020 – 0002F
...	.....
FFFF0	FFFF0 – FFFFF

Table A–1: 1 Mb of Memory as Viewed in Paragraphs

Notice that there are FFFFh (or 65,536) paragraphs for a total of FFFFFh (1 million) bytes. All paragraph address are *fixed* (that is, automatically defined) by the memory structure. The effect of this fixed definition is that all paragraph addresses (when expressed in hexadecimal) *end with 0*. Each paragraph consists of 16 bytes, numbered from 0 to 15 (decimal) or from 0 to F (hexadecimal). The byte addresses of the bytes within a paragraph are then determined by taking the paragraph address and adding 0h to Fh (0 to 15 decimal) (see table A–1). The significance of this method of viewing memory as paragraphs will be seen in the upcoming discussion. Let's continue by looking at how the 8086/8088 segments its memory.

Memory Segmentation

The 8086/8088 supports a maximum of 1 Mb of memory, with the highest byte address being FFFFFh. Representing the location of each byte in its absolute form (called the *absolute address*) requires 20 bits. However, the 8086/8088 system is a 16-bit system. How do we represent a 20-bit address in 16 bits? Intel's answer was to organize memory into *segments*.

One segment is defined as any number of bytes up to a maximum of 64K bytes. A segment may start any place in memory, as long it is on a *paragraph boundary*. This means that the absolute address of the start of a segment would always end in 0 (for example, 034F0h). Thus, we can "throw away" the last 4 bits of the segment's starting absolute address, leaving a 16-bit *segment address*. Therefore, the segment starting at absolute location 034F0h can be represented by the 16-bit segment address of 034Fh. Remember this concept of a 16-bit segment address; it will quickly become more significant.

Now, if each segment contains a maximum of 64Kb, the bytes are numbered within the segment as 0 to 65,535 (decimal) or 0000 to FFFF (hexadecimal). To reference a byte within a segment in this manner is to use the *byte offset* within the segment. Notice that the byte offset can be represented with a 16-bit value.

To illustrate this, we can look at the earlier example of the segment that started at location 034F0h. We saw that this segment is more conveniently referenced as segment 034Fh. Now, let's consider location 034F6h as being within the segment. This byte location is located 6 bytes from the start (034F0h) of the segment. We therefore say that byte 034F6h is at offset 6 within the segment 034Fh. Now, let's review everything and tie it together.

We said before that the 8086/8088 system is a 16-bit system. This implies that the largest address that can be formed must be represented as a 16-bit value. We also saw, however, that if we want to address up to 1 Mb of memory, we need to have 20-bit addresses. By splitting memory into paragraphs of 16 bytes each, any paragraph in memory can be referenced by a 16-bit address.

Earlier, we saw that a segment is defined to start on a paragraph boundary. It follows that a segment can start at any paragraph in memory and be referenced by the 16-bit address of that paragraph. Finally, if each segment contains up to 64K bytes within it, each byte can be referenced by a 16-bit address. It becomes quickly obvious that, to the user, it is often convenient to refer to a specific location in memory as:

```
segment:offset
```

where the offset is the byte offset within the segment. The next section will show how this fits into the architecture of the 8086/8088 system as designed by Intel.

Memory Segmentation and Segment Registers

Any given program can address all of the 1 Mb of memory. However, at any one time, only 256 Kb is available for access by the program. Why?

Any program running under MS-DOS on the 8086/8088 is allowed to specify up to four distinct segments for simultaneous use within the program. Because each segment is a maximum of 64Kb, the program is limited to referencing only 256Kb at any one time.

We will explain the reasons for this restriction later in this section. However, it should be noted here that the restriction is only for simultaneous access to multiple segments at any one time. Essentially, all of memory is available to the program, if necessary.

Each of the four segments that may be declared by a program has a specific use within the program. The intended purpose of each segment is identified by its name. The four segment names are: *Code Segment, Data Segment, Extra Segment,* and *Stack Segment.*

The *Code Segment* is the segment that contains the program instructions, and the *Data Segment* contains the program's data. The *Extra Segment* may be used for storing additional data and is usually used to hold and manipulate string data. The *Stack Segment* may be specified for the dedicated purpose of containing the program's run-time stack (used for calling subroutines and passing data arguments between routines).

To allow the program to reference these four segments, the 8086/8088 defines four 16-bit hardware *segment registers* to hold the starting addresses of the segments. These registers are named CS (Code Segment register), DS (Data Segment register), ES (Extra Segment register), and SS (Stack Segment register). As noted in the introduction to memory segments, a segment may start anywhere in memory, as long as it is on a paragraph boundary. The segment registers are used to hold the 16-bit starting paragraph addresses of their respective segments.

A program will always use at least one register, the CS register, to hold its code and sometimes its data. The .COM files that are so familiar to you in MS-DOS are examples of programs that use a single 64Kb segment to hold program code, data, and the stack. These programs are characterized by their compact size and the high speed at which they can be loaded into memory (from disk).

More commonly a program will declare at least the Data Segment (DS) in addition to its code segment. The use of a data segment allows the program code to grow to a larger size, while also providing the capability of handling more data in memory. In the case of very large programs, the additional ES and SS registers may also be declared.

Earlier it was noted that all 1 Mb of memory is available to the program if required. How is this done? The easiest way to understand this is to consider a program that requires 256Kb of data space (code not included).

Storing 256Kb of data requires the use of four segments at 64Kb each. However, the program may declare only one data segment. This data segment is pointed to by the DS register. If the program loads all 256Kb of data into four different segments of memory, it can change the contents of the DS register to point to each data segment as it is needed. Doing so allows it to handle its required 256Kb of data properly.

Although this is a nifty technique for managing large amounts of data, it is not often done in assembly language programs. However, it is frequently set up and performed automatically within programs written in higher-level languages, such as Pascal and C. In such programs, this type of segment-register manipulation might be done for the Code and Extra segments, as well as for the Data Segment.

Hardware Registers in the 8086/8088 Architecture

In the previous discussion of memory segments, it was noted that the 8086/8088 has four hardware registers dedicated to controlling the four segments that may be declared by a program. There are nine additional hardware registers in the 8086/8088 architecture, for a total of thirteen 16-bit hardware registers.

The thirteen 16-bit hardware registers of the 8086/8088 architecture are divided into four groups. These four groups and their respective registers are listed in table A–2.

General Registers

AX, BX, CX, DX are the general purpose 16-bit registers. Each of these 16-bit registers can also be considered as two 8-bit registers, distinguished as the high- and low-order bytes of the respective 16-bit register and referenced, respectively, as AH, AL, BH, BL, CH, CL, DH, and DL. A reference to an 8-bit register is the same as a reference to the high- or low-order byte of the respective 16-bit register. These 8-bit register designations have been carried over from the 8080/8085 8-bit microprocessors for compatibility.

Each of the 16-bit registers (and some of the 8-bit half-registers) have specialized uses in certain 8086/8088 instructions. Figure A–1 illustrates how the 16-bit registers (and their 8-bit half-registers) are viewed (example 1).

Pointer and Index Registers

The four *Pointer* and *Index registers* are SP (Stack Pointer), BP (Base Pointer), SI (Source Index), and DI (Destination Index).

Register Group	Registers Contained in Group
General registers	AX, BX, CX and DX
Pointer and Index registers	SP, BP, SI and DI
Segment registers	CS, DS, ES and SS
Instruction Pointer register	IP

Table A–2: 8086/8088 16-bit Hardware Registers

The SP (Stack Pointer) register points to the current "top of stack" within the Stack Segment. When the stack is used, it "grows" from the top of memory (high-address locations) in the Stack Segment down to the bottom of memory (lower-addressed locations) in the Stack Segment. This current "bottom-of-stack" memory is called the *top of the stack*. The SP register points to this location. In other words, the SP register is always pointing to the location at which the stack will be expanded downward. The SP is also described as the pointer to the next available location on the stack.

The BP (Base Pointer) is used with the Stack Pointer. It is an offset from the Stack Pointer, and is used to retrieve data from the Stack.

The SI and DI registers primarily function as the *Source Index* and *Destination Index* for string instructions. Both may also function as general-purpose index registers, if the need arises. The *string instructions* are a special-purpose subset of the 8086/8088 instruction set. They provide extensive string-manipulation capabilities that were relatively unknown in previous assembly language instruction sets.

Segment Registers

As discussed earlier, four segment registers are available to a program: CS, DS, ES, and SS. The CS (Code Segment) register points to the current code segment. The DS (Data Segment) register points to the current data segment.

The ES (Extra Segment) register points to the current extra segment. The use of this extra segment is optional. Its primary use is by string instructions for the manipulation of string (character) data.

The SS (Stack Segment) register points to the current stack segment. Although its use is optional, most programs will have one allocated.

Instruction Pointer Register

The last of the thirteen 16-bit registers in the 8086/8088 architecture is the *Instruction Pointer (IP)* register, which contains the address of the next instruction to be executed. The IP register is used with the CS register to fetch the next instruction from memory.

Flags

The final aspect of our discussion of the 8086/8088 registers concerns the group of nine 1-bit flags that record information concerning processor activity. Instructions within a program set or reset these flags to indicate the state of the CPU after the execution of one or more instructions. The 8086/8088 instruction set includes special assembler instructions that will test these flags for their current setting. These *test instructions* are often used after other instructions that may affect the status of one or more flags. Table A–3 lists the nine flags and describes their functions.

The 8086/8088 Input/Output (I/O) Structure

All input or output (I/O) is accomplished through one of two mechanisms, *I/O ports* and *interrupts*. The I/O ports are essentially the points of interface between the 8086/8088 processor and the device controllers. There are 65,536 (64K) I/O ports defined for an 8086/8088 system. Each I/O port is attached to the address and data busses in the same manner as memory. When the CPU wishes to transfer data to/from a device via its assigned port, it sends out the "address" of the port to the address bus. The CPU then transfers data to/from the port via

Flag Mnemonic	Flag Name	Function
OF	Overflow Flag	Set if a result has overflowed a range.
DF	Direction Flag	Determines the direction of string instructions.
IF	Interrupt Enable Flag	Allows/disallows interrupts to be processed.*
TF	Trap Flag	If set, tells the 8086/8088 to single-step instruction execution for program debugging.
SF	Sign Flag	Set when an arithmetic instruction generates a negative result.
ZF	Zero Flag	Set when an arithmetic instruction produces a zero result.
AF	Auxiliary Flag	Indicates carry generated from the least-significant four bits of the last instruction's result.
PF	Parity Flag	Set when a result has even parity.
CF	Carry Flag	Set if the result of an operation has generated a carry.

*When IF is clear, all interrupts are disabled, with the exception of the Non-Maskable Interrupt (NMI).

Table A–3: 8086/8088 1-bit flags

special-purpose I/O assembler instructions. Each port is used to transfer 8 bits of data. When necessary, two consecutive ports are joined to form a 16-bit port. I/O ports can be used for input, output, or both. A program may transfer data to or from a device by directly referencing these ports in the manner described above. However, this is awkward and tedious, so most programs use the second method of performing I/O (see the next paragraph).

The second method of performing I/O is through *interrupts* which are external signals to the microprocessor issued from the device.

A typical example of an interrupt is the pressing of a key on the keyboard. When this action occurs, a signal is sent to the processor, telling it that a key press has occurred. The operating system must then service that interrupt by recognizing which key has been pressed and sending that information to whatever program is running at the time. To be more specific, whenever any interrupt occurs, the interrupt signal will cause the 8086/8088 CPU to stop processing, save its current state of operation, and then service this request. When this servicing is completed, the CPU will return to what it was doing, after restoring its previous state of operation.

In addition to interrupts initiated from external devices, such as a keyboard, interrupts may also occur as a result of *processor faults* (divide by zero, memory parity, etc.). It should also be noted that interrupts may be internally generated. This usually occurs when a program wishes to perform a certain function, such as terminating itself or initiating output to a printer.

In general, most I/O will involve both methods: using instructions to access the I/O ports and using the interrupt mechanism.

Software Interrupts

The same hardware interrupt mechanism may be used in software by programs. Control is passed to software routines by issuing an interrupt *(int)* instruction. Before this instruction can be issued, the address of the routine must be stored in the interrupt vector address.

Each interrupt has an associated vector in the low-order memory of the 8086/8088. This vector is four bytes and contains the offset and segment address of the routine to vector to when the *int* instruction is issued.

Each group of four bytes contains the offset and segment addresses of the routine associated with the specific interrupt number.

Appendix B

BIOS Interrupts

Interrupt Number	Sets Register	Returns Register	Description	
5h			Print screen	
8h			Time of day	
9h			Keyboard service	
10h			Video services	
	ah		0h	Set Video Mode
	al		0h	B/W Text Mode (40*25) CGA
			1h	Color Text Mode (40*25) CGA
			2h	B/W Text Mode (80*25) CGA
			3h	Color Text Mode (80*25) CGA
			4h	Color Graphics Mode (320*200) CGA
			5h	B/W Graphics Mode (320*200) CGA
			6h	B/W Graphics Mode (640*200) CGA
			7h	B/W Text Mode (80*25) MDA
			8h	Color Graphics Mode (160*200) PC Jr
			9h	Color Graphics Mode (320*200) PC Jr
			Ah	Color Graphics Mode (640*200) PC Jr
			Dh	Color Graphics Mode (320*200) EGA
			Eh	Color Graphics Mode (640*200) EGA
			Fh	Color Graphics Mode (640*350) EGA
	ah		1h	Set Cursor Size
	ch			Start row for cursor size (0−7 for CGA) (0−13 for MDA)
	cl			End row for cursor size (0−7 for CGA) (0−13 for MDA)
	ah	2h		Set Cursor Position
	dh			Row (0−24)

Interrupt Number	Sets Register	Returns Register	Description
	dl		Column (0–40 or 0–80)
	bh		Video page (0–7 for 40-column modes) (0–3 for 80-column modes) (0 for graphics modes)
10h	ah	3h	Read Cursor Position
	bh		Video page (0–7 for 40-column modes) (0–3 for 80-column modes) (0 for graphics modes)
		dh	Current row (0–24)
		dl	Current column (0–40 or 0–80)
		ch	Current start row for cursor size (0–7 for CGA) (0–13 for MDA)
		cl	Current end row for cursor size (0–7 for CGA) (0–13 for MDA)
	ah	4h	Read Light Pen Position
		ah	Light Pen State (0 not triggered) (1 triggered)
		dh	Triggered row number in text mode (0–24)
		dl	Triggered column number in text mode (0–39 or 0–79)
		ch	Triggered raster line in graphics mode (0–199)
		bx	Triggered pixel column in graphics mode (0–159 or 0–319 or 0–639)
	ah	5h	Set Display Page
			Display page desired (0–7 for 40-column modes) (0–3 for 80-column modes)
	ah	6h	Scroll Page Up
	al		Number of lines to scroll (0 to blank the screen)
	ch		Row number of upper-left window
	cl		Column number of upper-left window (0–39 for 40-column modes) (0–79 for 80-column modes)
	dh		Row number of lower-right window
	dl		Column number of lower-right window (0–39 for 40-column modes) (0–79 for 80-column modes)

Inter-rupt Number	Sets Regis-ter	Returns Regis-ter	Description
	bh		Display attributes for window
10h	ah	7h	Scroll Page Down
	al		Number of lines to scroll (0 to blank the screen)
	ch		Row number of upper-left window
			Column number of upper-left window (0–39 for 40-column modes) (0–79 for 80-column modes)
	dh		Row number of lower-right window
	dl		Column number of lower-right window (0–39 for 40-column modes) (0–79 for 80-column modes)
	bh		Display attributes for window
	ah	8h	Read Character and Attribute
	bh		Display page desired (0–7 for 40-column modes) (0–3 for 80-column modes)
		al	ASCII code for character read
		ah	Attribute for character read
	ah	9h	Write Character and Attribute
	bh		Display page desired (0–7 for 40-column modes) (0–3 for 80-column modes)
	al		ASCII code of character
	bl		Attribute
	cx		Number of times to write Character and Attribute
	ah	ah	Write Character
	bh		Display page desired (0–7 for 40-column modes) (0–3 for 80-column modes)
	al		ASCII code of character
	bl		Foreground color
	cx		Number of times to write Character
	ah	bh	Set Color Palette
	bh		(0 background color for graphics mode) (0 border color for text mode) (1 palette selection)
	bl		Color or palette (0–1)
	ah	ch	Write Pixel
	al		Palette color

431

Inter- rupt Number	Sets Regis- ter	Returns Regis- ter	Description
	dx		Raster line desired (0–199)
	cx		Pixel column desired (0–159 or 0–319 or 0–639)
10h	ah	dh	Read Pixel
	dx		Raster line desired (0–199)
	cx		Pixel column desired (0–159 or 0–319 or 0–639)
		al	Palette color
	ah	eh	Write Character As TTY
	al		ASCII code of character
	bl		Foreground color in graphics mode
	ah	fh	Get Video Mode
		ah	Characters per line (20 or 40 or 80)
		al	Current video mode (See Set Video Mode)
		bh	Current display page (0–7 for 40-column modes) (0–3 for 80-column modes)
	ah	13h	Write String
	al		Attribute/Color/Cursor Position (0 Attribute/Color in bl cursor position in dh and dl) (1 Attribute/Color in bl cursor position at end of string) (2 Attribute/Color in string cursor position in dh and dl) (3 Attribute/Color in string cursor position at end of string)
	es		Segment address of character string
	bp		Offset address of character string
	cx		Number of characters in string
	bh		Display page desired (0–7 for 40-column modes) (0–3 for 80-column modes)
	bl		Attribute/color
	dh		Start row (0–24)
	dl		Start column (0–39 or 0–79)

Interrupt Number	Sets Register	Returns Register	Description
11h			Equipment Check
		ax	Value as follows:
			Number of printers in bits 15–14
			Game adapter present in bit 12
			Number of serial ports in bits 11–9
			Number of diskette drives in bits 7–6
			(0 = 1 drive)
			(1 = 2 drives)
			(2 = 3 drives)
			(3 = 4 drives)
			Video mode in bits 5–4
			(1 40-column CGA text mode)
			(2 80-column CGA text mode)
			(3 80-column MDA text mode)
			System board memory (original PCs)
			(0 = 16 Kb)
			(1 = 32 Kb)
			(2 = 48 Kb)
			(3 = 64 Kb)
			80287 installed (AT only) in bit 1
			Diskette drives installed in bit 0
12h			Memory Available
		ax	Available memory in Kb units
13h			Disk Services (diskette/fixed disk)
	ah	0h	Reset Disk
	dl		Drive number
			(Add 80h for fixed disk)
		ah	Error number if CF set
			(0h no error)
			(1h invalid function)
			(2h bad address mark)
			(3h write protect violation)
			(4h sector not found)
			(5h reset failed)
			(6h media removed)
			(7h initialization error)
			(8h DMA failure)
			(9h DMA address error)
			(ah bad sector encountered)
13h			(10h parity error)
			(11h corrected parity error)
			(20h controller failure)
			(40h seek failure)
			(80h timeout)
			(aah drive not ready)
			(bbh unknown error)
			(cch write fault)
			(ffh sense failure)

Inter-rupt Number	Sets Regis-ter	Returns Regis-ter	Description
	ah		1h	Get Disk Status
	dl		Drive number (Add 80h for fixed disk)
		al	Status returned (See ah of Reset Disk)
	ah		2h	Read Disk Sectors
	al		Number of sectors to read
	dl		Drive number (Add 80h for fixed disk)
	dh		Head number
	ch		Lower 8 bits of 10-bit cylinder number
	cl		Upper 2 bits of 10-bit cylinder number In bits 6 and 7 Start sector number in bits 0−5
	es		Segment address of data-transfer area
	bx		Offset address of data-transfer area
		ah	Status returned (See Reset Disk)
	ah		3h	Write Disk Sectors
	al		Number of sectors to write
	dl		Drive number (Add 80h for fixed disk)
	dh		Head number
	ch		Lower 8 bits of 10-bit cylinder number
	cl		Upper 2 bits of 10-bit cylinder number In bits 6 and 7 Start sector number in bits 0−5
	es		Segment address of data-transfer area
	bx		Offset address of data-transfer area
		ah	Status returned (See Reset Disk)
13h	ah		4h	Verify Disk Sectors
	al		Number of sectors to verify
	dl		Drive number (Add 80h for fixed disk)
	dh		Head number
	ch		Lower 8 bits of 10-bit cylinder number
	cl		Upper 2 bits of 10-bit cylinder number In bits 6 and 7
			Start sector number in bits 0−5
		ah	Status returned (See Reset Disk)
	ah		5h	Format tracks

Inter-rupt Number	Sets Regis-ter	Returns Regis-ter	Description
	dl		Drive number (Add 80h for fixed disk)
	dh		Head number
	ch		Lower 8 bits of 10-bit cylinder number
	cl		Upper 2 bits of 10-bit cylinder number In bits 6 and 7
	es		Segment address of format table
	bx		Offset address of format table Format table has four fields for each sector on the track: Byte 1 contains the cylinder number Byte 2 contains the head number Byte 3 contains the sector number Byte 4 contains the bytes per sector (0 = 128 bytes) (1 = 256 bytes) (2 = 512 bytes) (3 = 1024 bytes)
		ah	Status returned (See Reset Disk)
	ah	8h	Get Drive Parameters
	dl		Drive number (Add 80h for fixed disk)
		dl	Highest drive number
		dh	Highest head number
		ch	Lower 8 bits of 10-bit cylinder number
		cl	Upper 2 bits of 10-bit cylinder number In bits 6 and 7 Highest sector number in bits 0–5
	ah	9h	Initialize Drive Characteristics
13h	ah	ah	Read (Long) Sectors
	al		Number of sectors to read
	dl		Drive number (Add 80h for fixed disk)
	dh		Head number
	ch		Lower 8 bits of 10-bit cylinder number
	cl		Upper 2 bits of 10-bit cylinder number In bits 6 and 7 Start sector number in bits 0–5
	es		Segment address of data-transfer area
	bx		Offset address of data-transfer area
		ah	Status returned (See Reset Disk)

Interrupt Number	Sets Register	Returns Register	Description
	ah	bh	Write (Long) Sectors
	al		Number of sectors to write
	dl		Drive number (Add 80h for fixed disk)
	dh		Head number
	ch		Lower 8 bits of 10-bit cylinder number
	cl		Upper 2 bits of 10-bit cylinder number In bits 6 and 7 Start sector number in bits 0−5
	es		Segment address of data-transfer area
	bx		Offset address of data-transfer area
		ah	Status returned (See Reset Disk)
	ah	ch	Seek
	dl		Drive number (Add 80h for fixed disk)
	dh		Head number
	ch		Lower 8 bits of 10-bit cylinder number
	cl		Upper 2 bits of 10-bit cylinder number In bits 6 and 7
		ah	Status returned (See Reset Disk)
	ah	dh	Reset Disk (Alternate)
	dl		Drive number (Add 80h for fixed disk)
		ah	Status returned (See Reset Disk)
	ah	10h	Drive Ready Test
	dl		Drive number (Add 80h for fixed disk)
		ah	Status returned (0 = drive ready) (Otherwise, see Reset Disk)
13h	ah	11h	Recalibrate Disk
	dl		Drive number (Add 80h for fixed disk)
		ah	Status returned (See Reset Disk)
	ah	14h	Diagnostics
		ah	Status returned (See Reset Disk)
	ah	15h	Get Disk Type

Interrupt Number	Sets Register	Returns Register	Description
	dl		Drive number (Add 80h for fixed disk)
		ah	Status returned (0 = drive does not exist) (1 = diskette changeline not available) (2 = diskette changeline available) (3 = fixed disk see cx:dx) (Otherwise, see Reset Disk)
		cx	Total sectors in fixed disk
		dx	Total sectors in fixed disk
	ah	16h	Disk Status
	dl		Drive number
		ah	Status returned (0 = diskette has not been changed) (6 = diskette has been changed) (Otherwise, see Reset Disk)
	ah	17h	Set Disk Type
	dl		Drive number
	al		Diskette type (1 = 320/360 Kb disk) (2 = 320/360 Kb disk in 1.2 Mb drive) (3 = 1.2 Mb diskette in 1.2 Mb drive)
		ah	Status Returned (See Reset Disk)
14h			Serial Port Services
	ah	0h	Initialize Serial Port parameters as follows: Baud rate in bits 5−7 (0 = 110 baud) (1 = 150 baud) (2 = 300 baud) (3 = 600 baud) (4 = 1200 baud) (5 = 2400 baud) (6 = 4800 baud) (7 = 9600 baud)
	al		Parity in bits 3−4 (0 = no parity) (1 = odd parity) (2 = no parity) (3 = even parity)
			Number of stop bits in bit 2 (0 = 1 stop bit) (1 = 2 stop bits)
			Bits per character in bits 0−1 (2 = 7-bit ASCII characters) (3 = 8-bit characters)

Interrupt Number	Sets Register	Returns Register		Description
	dx			Serial port desired (0 = first) (1 = second)
		ah		Line status returned (80 = timeout) (40 = shift register is empty) (20 = hold register is empty) (10 = break occurred) (08 = framing error) (04 = parity error) (02 = overrun) (01 = data is ready)
		al		Modem status returned (80 = Carrier detect) (40 = Ring indicator) (20 = DSR) (10 = CTS) (08 = Carrier detect change) (04 = Trailing edge ring detect) (02 = DSR change) (01 = CTS change)
14h	ah		1h	Send One Character
	al			Character to send
	dx			Serial port desired (0 = first) (1 = second)
		ah		Status returned (0 = no error) (Bit 7 set = error See Initialize Serial Port)
	ah		2h	Receive One Character
	dx			Serial port desired (0 = first) (1 = second)
		al		Character received
		ah		Status returned (0 = no error) (Bit 7 set = error See Initialize Serial Port)
	ah		3h	Get Serial Port Status
	dx			Serial port desired (0 = first) (1 = second)
				Status returned
		al		Status returned
		ah		(See Initialize Serial Port)

Inter- rupt Number	Sets Regis- ter	Returns Regis- ter	Description	
15h			Cassette Tape I/O (obsolete)	
16h			Keyboard Services	
	ah		0h	Read Next Character
		al		ASCII character code returned or 0
		ah		Scan code returned
	ah		1h	Check For Next Character
				(ZF set = no character available)
				(ZF not set = character in buffer)
				ASCII character code returned or 0
		al		Scan code returned
		ah		
16h	ah		2h	Get Shift Status
		al		Shift status returned
				(80 = Insert)
				(40 = Caps Lock)
				(20 = Num Lock)
				(10 = Scroll Lock)
				(08 = Alt Key)
				(04 = Ctrl Key)
				(02 = Left Shift Key)
				(01 = Right Shift Key)
17h			Printer Services	
	ah		0h	Print a Character
	al			ASCII character to print
	dx			Printer number
				(0-2)
		ah		Printer status returned
				(80 = not busy)
				(40 = acknowledge)
				(20 = no paper)
				(10 = printer selected)
				(08 = I/O error)
				(01 = timeout)
	ah		1h	Initialize Printer
	dx			Printer number
				(0-2)
		ah		Printer status returned
				(See Print A Character)
	ah		2h	Get Printer Status
	dx			Printer Number
				(0-2)
		ah		Printer status returned
				(See Print A Character)
18h			Activate ROM-based Basic	
19h			Reboot From Disk	

Inter- rupt Number	Sets Regis- ter	Returns Regis- ter	Description	
1ah			Time of Day Services	
	ah		0h	Read System Clock
		al		Newday indicator (0 = not a new day) (not 0 = new day)
		cx		High-order word of clock value
		dx		Low-order word of clock value
	ah		1h	Set System Clock
	cx			High-order word of clock value
	dx			Low-order word of clock value
	ah		2h	Read CMOS Clock (AT only)
		ch		BCD hours
		cl		BCD minutes
		dh		BCD seconds
	ah		3h	Set CMOS Clock (AT only)
	ch			BCD hours
	cl			BCD minutes
	dh			BCD seconds
	dl			Day Light Savings Correction (1 = adjust) (0 = do not adjust)
	ah		4h	Read Calendar (AT only)
		ch		BCD centuries
		cl		BCD years
		dh		BCD month
		dl		BCD day
	ah		5h	Set Calendar (AT only)
	ch			BCD centuries
	cl			BCD years
	dh			BCD month
	dl			BCD day
	ah		6h	Set Alarm Clock (AT only)
	ch			BCD hours elapsed
	cl			BCD minutes elapsed
	dh			BCD seconds elapsed
	ah		7h	Reset Alarm Clock (AT only)
1ch			Timer Tick	

Appendix C

DOS Initialization

DOS initialization is the process that brings DOS into memory from the disk. This is commonly known as a *bootstrap* of the operating system; it is the process by which DOS brings itself and the rest of the operating system into memory. Another term used for this process is the Initial Program Load, or IPL.

DOS System Disks

A DOS system disk must be specially built in order for DOS to be booted from that disk. System disks have the bootstrap routine in the first sector, as well as the special DOS system files. These files are marked with the "hidden" file attribute. The first file contains the BIOS code and the system initialization code (SYSINT) and is generally named IO.SYS for MS-DOS or IBMBIO.COM for PC-DOS. The second file is the DOS kernel and is generally named MSDOS.SYS for MS-DOS systems or IBMDOS.COM for PC-DOS systems.

Building a System Disk

A DOS system disk is built using one of two methods. The first method is to use the FORMAT utility with the /S switch. This formats a disk and places the Boot Record, the two DOS system files, and the COMMAND.COM program on the disk. The second method uses the SYS program to transfer the two DOS system files to the disk. If you use this second method, you will have to format the disk using the /B switch to allocate space for the two DOS system files. In addition, the COMMAND.COM file must be explicitly placed on the disk.

Initializing DOS

When a reset occurs (during power-on), the 8086/8088 starts execution at location ffff:0, which contains ROM code to perform diagnostics on the 8086/8088, memory, and peripherals. The ROM BIOS routines will then try to read the diskette. If the diskette times out (that is, if no diskette is inserted or the drive door is not engaged), an attempt is made to read the hard disk if one is present. If this attempt fails, a *jump* to the BASIC ROM code is performed.

If a read from either disk is successful, the first sector of the disk is brought into memory at location 7c0:0, and control is passed there; the bootstrap loader then takes over.

The bootstrap loader uses the BIOS Parameter Block contained in the first disk sector to determine where the File Directory resides on the disk. The first file in the directory must be the file IBMBIO.COM (PC-DOS) or IO.SYS (MS-DOS). If this file exists, it is read into memory and control is passed to it.

System initialization proceeds with checking for attached peripheral devices and other equipment; standard devices are initialized, the device drivers that are standard for that version of DOS are loaded, and certain interrupt vectors are set.

The file containing the DOS kernel is then brought into memory. It is during this phase that CONFIG.SYS is read for the special commands to tailor DOS. Among the more important commands for the initialization process are DEVICE and SHELL. Each file named in DEVICE statements is opened and read into memory and linked in front of the standard DOS drivers after the NUL: device.

These new *DEVICE*s are linked to the front of the DOS device queue. The associated device headers contain the new device name; DOS will refer to these ahead of the standard driver names. This allows new drivers to use the names of existing device drivers, thus replacing the old drivers. Another function performed at this time is initializing the new drivers to allow them to pass back to DOS certain information concerning the driver. If a certain driver is too large to fit into memory, it is ignored (the DOS error message is "device is bad or missing"). This can occur when RAM disks are used.

If there is a *SHELL* command in CONFIG.SYS, it is loaded into memory, and control is passed to it. If no *SHELL* command has been specified, COMMAND.COM is loaded into memory, and control is passed to it.

Appendix D

Special Features of the Hard Disk

Beginning with version 2.0, DOS provides special features for the hard disk that are not available for floppy disks. These include the ability to partition the hard disk into several drives and to boot from any partition.

Partitions

DOS allows the hard disk to be divided into up to four logical disk drives. These logical drives are also called partitions of the hard disk. Each partition may be formatted to use DOS or a different operating system. Partitioning a hard disk makes it more convenient to manage a large disk for, perhaps, several users.

The FDISK Program

The FDISK program is supplied with DOS and must be used to initialize and set up a hard disk before the disk may be used. There are four functions within the FDISK program: a function to create a partition, one to make a partition active, one to delete a partition, and one to display partition information.

Creating a Partition

This option of the FDISK program is used to set up a hard disk. You need to decide how your hard disk will look: how many partitions of what sizes there should be. For disks larger than the DOS limit of 32 Mb, you need to create partitions that are smaller than this limit. You may also partition the disk into two or more partitions to make it easier to use several operating systems, DOS and others.

Partitions begin on a cylinder boundary. When a partition is defined, its starting and ending positions are specified with cylinder numbers. Thus, the beginning of a partition is surface 0 and sector 1 of the start cylinder. Because tracks are identically numbered for all surfaces, a partition will contain the set of tracks corresponding to all the surfaces. For example, for a disk that has four surfaces with a partition starting at cylinder 200 and ending at cylinder 300, the partition will contain four sets of tracks, numbered 200 through 300.

Each partition of the hard disk is created by using the *create partition* option of the FDISK program. After formatting, the partition will contain the four required sections: the Boot Record, the two FATs, the File Directory, and the user data area.

Deleting a Partition   Displaying Partition Information

The *Delete a Partition* option of the FDISK program removes the partition from use by destroying all the data in it.

The option to *Display Partition Information* displays information about the various partitions of a hard disk. The information returned will tell you the size of each partition, the type of partition (DOS or non-DOS), and whether the partition is active.

Active Partition

Through the *Active Partition* option in the FDISK program, one of the partitions may be selected as the active partition. This allows DOS (or another operating system) to be booted from this partition.

The first sector of the hard disk contains information on the various partitions and is called the *partition sector*.

The Partition Sector

The partition sector is the first sector of the hard disk. Following the partition sector will be one or more partitions. Figure D-1 shows the relationship of the partition sector to the partitions of a hard disk.

The partition sector contains three parts. The first is the partition program code, which is responsible for determining the active partition. The second is the table of partition information. Finally, the last part is a marker for the end of the partition sector. The marker is a hex AA55 that indicates that the partition sector is valid.

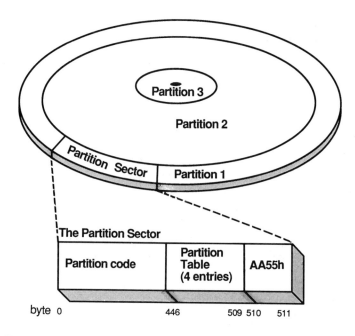

Figure D–1: The three sections of the partition sector

When a PC with a hard disk is booted initially, the partition code is first brought into memory to determine which of the partitions is active. Then the boot code from the active partition is read into memory and control is passed to the bootstrap code. A normal DOS boot of the partition follows.

The Partition Table

The partition table contains four 16-byte entries and is located at offset 446 from the beginning of the partition sector. Each entry describes a particular partition. The format for the partition table entry is described in table D–1.

The active partition indicator is a single byte that describes whether the partition is an active partition or not. A value of 00h indicates that the partition is not active, and a value of 80h indicates that the partition is an active partition. When FDISK sets this value to 80h, all similar fields in other partition table entries are set to 00h; there is only one active partition at any one time.

The beginning head, sector, and cylinder values are those that were specified to FDISK when the partition was defined.

Start	Length	Description
0	1	Active Partition Indicator
1	1	Beginning head number
2	1	Beginning sector number
3	1	Beginning cylinder number
4	1	DOS system indicator
5	1	Ending head number
6	1	Ending sector number
7	1	Ending cylinder number
8	4	Relative sector (from beginning of disk)
12	4	Total size of partition in sectors

Table D–1: The ten fields that comprise the partition table entry. Each entry will describe one partition.

The DOS system indicator contains a value that determines whether the operating system for the partition is DOS or some other operating system. A value of 80h indicates the partition is a DOS partition. A value of 00h indicates the partition is a non-DOS partition.

Ending head, sector, and cylinder numbers are those that were specified to FDISK when the partition was defined.

The relative sector is a double word that contains the number of sectors from the beginning of the disk to the start of the partition. For any partition this is the sum of the total disk space of all preceding partitions plus 1 for the partition sector. This number is also known as the number of hidden sectors for a given partition.

The total size of the partition in sectors is a double word that contains the count of the number of sectors in the partition. This sum includes the four parts of the partition: the boot area, the two FATs, the File Directory, and the user data area. This is numerically equal to all of the sectors between the start cylinder and the end cylinder, inclusive.

Appendix **E**

Answers to Questions

Chapter 1

1. No, it does not matter whether you use MS-DOS or PC-DOS. Although there are minor differences between the two versions, they are essentially equivalent, and for the purposes of this book, they are functionally identical. You may switch from one to the other at any time.

2. Any version of DOS will do, provided it is greater than 2.00. You will see in later chapters that the latest versions of DOS will have more features for device drivers. For the time being, use the DOS version with which you are most comfortable.

3. The examples given in this book will work on both PCs and ATs. The code you will be writing for the 8088-based PC will also work on the 80286-based ATs. There will not be any problems unless the examples are modified to use the special instructions of the 80286, in which case they will not run on the 8088/8086-based machines.

Chapter 2

1. In general, the whole idea of DOS device drivers is that they conform to a standard format and can be interchanged, not only between PC-DOS and MS-DOS but also between different versions of DOS. Not all machines are compatible with the IBM PC, however, and when device drivers take advantage of certain specific features of the IBM machine, they may not work on other PCs. This will depend a lot on whether the machine using MS-DOS is compatible to the IBM PC in the areas in which the device driver has made use of IBM-specific features.

2. Device drivers can use IN and OUT instructions to control devices or they can use BIOS routines. Remember that the purpose of a device driver is to control a device and in many cases there are no BIOS routines to assist in this task. When there are BIOS assist routines, then it would be foolish not to take advantage of them.

3. DOS version 2.00 or later is required to be able to add user-written device drivers.

4. DOS normally supports five printers: up to two that use the serial adapters and up to three that use the parallel adapters.

5. DOS supports up to two serial adapters. This is a limitation imposed by BIOS, because the BIOS supports only two serial adapters and DOS serial device drivers use the BIOS routines.

6. When a new device driver is added to DOS, it is placed right after the nul: device driver.

7. The order will be new2: then new1:. Recall that all user-installable device drivers are added after the nul: device. If new1: is added first, it would be placed right after nul:. Then, when new2: is added, it would appear right after nul:. Thus, the last user-installable device driver added is the first after nul:.

Chapter 3

1. Yes. As shown in the initial procedure, you can use function 9 in a DOS call to print a message to the screen. However, only in processing the Initialization command are DOS functions allowed and these are restricted to 01h through 0Ch and 30h.

2. By inspecting the COMMON EXIT code, you can see that a *ret* instruction is used to return to DOS. The corresponding instruction is the *call* instruction.

3. The STRATEGY procedure has the task of saving the address of the Request Header into the device driver's data storage area.

4. The first entry of the Device Header. The Device Header can specify to DOS that there is more than one device driver program in the file. This allows DOS to be more efficient in processing the several device drivers. By placing a -1 in the double word entry at the beginning of

the Device Header, you indicate that there is no other device driver program in the file.

5. The device driver is initialized just after it is loaded into memory by DOS.

6. The name of a device can be up to eight characters in length.

Chapter 4

1. No. Only DOS services 01h through 0Ch and 30h are allowed in the Initialization command. Caution: DOS service calls cannot be issued when processing any other device driver command.

2. Yes. DOS is often supplied with an ANSI.SYS console driver that allows DOS to interpret escape sequences as screen-control commands. ANSI.SYS is named after the ANSI standard X3.64 for CRTs. Some versions of DOS include the ANSI escape sequences in the standard console device driver.

3. Yes. The Console Device Driver can be customized to display color characters. Note that the display of color is normally the task of the program writing to the screen. It is important to remember that not all monitors are color; many are monochrome.

4. The Console Device Driver uses the ROM BIOS routines because they are easy to use and found on many IBM or IBM-compatible PCs. There is no reason not to use direct I/O instructions. In exchange for speed, however, the job of programming is much harder.

5. The Console Device Driver uses only the Write Character as TTY service (0eh). The reason is that Console Device Drivers do not care about anything other than writing a character to the screen. The use of this particular service allows the ROM BIOS to keep track of the end of lines and scrolling at the bottom of the screen. If we were to use a different video BIOS service, we would have to manage it ourselves.

6. The reason for this is simple. DOS treats all forms of CON as the device. The colon is there to make it easier for you to identify CON as a device; it is not necessary. For example, the following command-level statements are identical in function:

```
copy config.sys con:
copy config.sys con
copy config.sys con.asm
```

7. Yes. The reason for separating each command is that, as part of the skeleton, you may want to reuse it for other device drivers. You could combine the unimplemented commands as follows:

```
Media_Check:
Get_BPB:
Input_Status:
Output_Status:
Output_Flush:
Open:
Close:
            jmp   done        ;set done bit and exit

IOCTL_Input:
IOCTL_Output:
Removable:
Output_Busy:
            jmp   unknown      ;set error bit/code and exit
```

Chapter 5

1. Yes. Because there are three parallel ports and only two serial ports, using the serial port for printers can use up all the serial ports quickly. Mouse devices and modems use serial ports, and they could not both be added to the PC if a printer already used one of the serial ports. In addition printers operate more quickly when using parallel ports, because of the parallel transfer of data.

2. The Printer Device Driver supports only two serial printers because the serial adapter ROM BIOS routines support only two serial ports. Support for additional serial ports can be added to the Printer Device Driver, but then the ROM BIOS routines cannot be used. The solution would be to write direct I/O instructions to these additional serial ports.

3. Yes. Although the PC initializes the serial and parallel adapters during the Power On Self Test (POST) when the PC is turned on, the code to initialize the parallel and serial adapters can be added to the Printer Device Driver. This can be accomplished in two places. During the Initialization command processing, the driver can issue BIOS interrupts to initialize the serial and parallel ports. For the serial port, however, parameters such as baud rate, number of data bits, and type of parity are required. For this reason, it is better to use the I/O Control function to pass these parameters to the driver. Thus, a special I/O Control function with these required parameters specified can be added to the Printer Device Driver.

4. You are correct—DOS can execute only one program at a time. However, there are popular programs called Terminate but Stay Resident programs, which, after being executed, are not removed from memory. These programs are activated periodically to perform some task. Because of the possibility that one of these programs will write to the printer using BIOS interrupts when another program is writing to the printer using the Printer Device Driver, the printer might be busy. Therefore, the Printer Device Driver detects this condition and returns to DOS without wasting time waiting for the printer to become free.

5. Numerous features and functions can be added to the I/O Control processing. For example, I/O Control could be used to print a banner preceding each print job, indicating the job number, time, and date. This would allow easy separation of jobs when the print load is heavy. Another example would be to add code to advance the page, if needed, to provide page printing on even or odd page boundaries. This would allow each print job to start on the same facing page, which would make the jobs easier to find.

I/O Control could also be used to set an indicator within the Printer Device Driver. The Output command-processing code would count the number of pages already printed. At the end of a job, the driver could advance one or two pages to allow the next job to start on the same page boundary.

6. It was easier to write the IOCTL program that way. In addition, it is more economical to set the adapter type rather than determining it and then resetting it.

Chapter 6

1. The Clock Device Driver will not be able to find the clock chip base address, and the driver will abort loading. In short, you need not worry about not having a clock chip present in your PC.

2. The MM58167A clock chip was designed to provide both a clock/calendar function and a timer function. The chip can be used to signal an interrupt when a preset date is reached. The RAM locations are used for this purpose.

3. The reason for the large amount of code for processing and determining leap years is that the MM58167A chip does not do it. If the chip were "smarter," we would not have to write software routines.

4. The easiest way to remove the ability to display the time on the screen is to remove the code starting at label *calc* at the end of the Clock Device Driver. Remove all the instructions beginning with *call display* through *sti*. This eliminates the swapping of the timer interrupt with the one in the Clock Device Driver. Thus, the timer interrupt will no longer pass control to the driver, and the code to display the time will not be executed.

   If you want to make the Clock Device Driver smaller, remove the procedures *clkint, display,* and *cvt2asc.*

Chapter 7

1. The proper order on all disks is: Boot Record, FAT(s), File Directory, and user data area. Every disk must have these four sections, and they must be in this order.

2. The Boot Record is always written to the disk after it has been formatted using the FORMAT.COM program.

3. Because the cluster chain uses each FAT entry to point to the next entry, there is no inherent limit to the length of the cluster chain. However, for any given disk the maximum length is equal to the maximum number of available clusters for that disk. Note that some clusters may not be available because they have been marked as bad during the formatting process.

4. The maximum size of a disk is 32 Mb. This assumes 512-byte sectors.

5. The minimum disk size possible is a 4-sector disk with the Boot Record, one FAT, the File Directory, and the user data area each being allocated one sector.

6. The Get BPB driver command is used to retrieve the BPB from a disk. This is typically done when the Media Check command returns an indication that the disk has changed.

7. An "illegal" file name is one that begins with either an E5 hex or a 00 hex. These are the values that DOS uses in the first byte of the file-name field in the File Directory to indicate that a file has been deleted or that a directory entry has never been used.

Chapter 8

1. The RAM Disk Device Driver simulates a diskette by using memory to store data normally destined for a magnetic disk.

2. All but k, the size of the user data area, which can be calculated from all the other fields.

3. One. Two FATs are not needed.

4. The following commands are implemented in the RAM Disk Device Driver: Initialization (0), Media Check (1), Get BPB (2), Input (3), Output (8), Output With Verify (9), and Removable Media (15).

5. The number of sectors in the user data area is 400 for a 200 Kb RAM disk (see the list of steps for modifying the RAM Disk Device Driver). The sectors per allocation unit do not change. The number of clusters is 400. At 1.5 bytes per cluster, the size of the FAT is 1024, which is rounded up from 600 bytes. Thus, the number of sectors for the FAT is 2; this number is stored in the variable *bpb_fs*. Because the number of files in the File Directory does not change, the variable *bpb_ds* does not change. The number of reserved sectors is 6 (1 for the Boot Record, 2 for the newly enlarged FAT, and 3 for the unchanged File Directory); this number is stored in the variable *res_cnt*. The total number of sectors is 406 (6 reserved and 400 for the new user data area), and this number is stored in the variable *bpb_ts*. Then, the number of paragraphs of memory is 12,992 (406 times 32); this number is stored in the variable *ram_par*. Lastly, the variable *msg1* is changed to display the fact that the RAM disk is now 200Kb.

Chapter 9

1. For DOS version 3.2, this command is requested through the DOS service for I/O Control (44h). Functions provided are read, write, and format a logical drive track. This new feature of DOS allows programs to use DOS services to perform tasks that formerly required BIOS services.

2. No, you do not have to process the argument. In fact, you can use the argument as a comment to document the driver in the CONFIG.SYS file.

3. Yes, it does seem contradictory. Available documentation indicates that the Get/Set Logical Device commands are used for block devices. No mention is made of its use with character device drivers, such as printer drivers. Hopefully, more information will be released on these commands.

4. The Output Til Busy command is used to send a string of characters to a character device driver. Normally, character device drivers are set one character at a time, which is inefficient and slow.

Chapter 10

1. You need only convert the segment address, because the offset address is 0. Device drivers are aligned on paragraph boundaries, which means the offset address is always 0.

2. First, check your device driver against the checklist in figure 10–1. If your driver looks okay, remove code lines in the Initialization command processing until it does work.

   Hint: display a screen message at the beginning and at the end of the Initialization command processing. Then, if the driver fails between the first and the last message, keep moving the first message farther "down" in the code until the driver fails to load. You have just found the problem!

3. No. You will not need this feature in a custom console driver unless you have programs that require "raw-mode" output (recall that this feature is available through the DOS I/O Control service 44h).

4. First use DEBUG to inspect the Device Header. If you have used the code in listing 10–2, the address displayed is the segment address at which your device driver sits in memory. Offset 0 points to the Device Header. Check the Device Header entries to ensure that they have been set correctly.

   Another trick to try is to add the *dump* routine to your driver at the entry point (in the Interrupt routine) and after setting the Status word, just before exiting. This will display the command being sent to the driver as well as some of the Request Header entries. If the *dump* routine displays data on entry but not on exit, you have a bug in that particular command-processing section.

If all else fails, you can try using DEBUG. As we have explained, DEBUG is not the proper tool to use. However, you can set one breakpoint in your device driver before DOS crashes. When a breakpoint is reached, reboot and advance the breakpoint address until the breakpoint display shows you enough information to make an educated guess as to where the problem is: use the listing of your device driver along with the results from the breakpoint output. The process of using DEBUG is long and tedious.

INDEX